Introduction to
SOFTWARE
ENGINEERING

Introduction to
SOFTWARE
ENGINEERING

Ronald J. Leach, Ph.D.

Chair, Department of Systems & Computer Sciences
Howard University, Washington, D.C.

CRC Press
Boca Raton   London   New York   Washington, D.C.

Library of Congress Cataloging-in-Publication Data

Leach, Ronald J.
    Introduction to software engineering / by Ronald J. Leach.
        p. cm.
    Includes bibliographical references and index.
    ISBN 0-8493-1445-3 (alk. paper)
    1. Software engineering. I. Title.
QA76.758.L33 1999
005.1—dc21

99-046521
CIP

© 2000 by CRC Press LLC

No claim to original U.S. Government works
International Standard Book Number 0-8493-1445-3
Library of Congress Card Number 99-046521
Printed in the United States of America   2 3 4 5 6 7 8 9 0
Printed on acid-free paper

Contents

Preface   ix

CHAPTER 1 INTRODUCTION   1
1.1 The Need for Software Engineering   1
1.2 Are Software Teams Really Necessary?   8
1.3 Software Engineering   9
1.4 Typical Software Engineering Tasks   11
1.5 Software Life Cycles   13
    1.5.1 The Classical Waterfall Model   14
    1.5.2 The Rapid Prototyping Model   17
    1.5.3 The Spiral Model   19
    1.5.4 A Market-Driven Model of Software Development   21
    1.5.5 Common Features of All Models of Software Development 22
1.6 Different Views of Software Engineering Activities   23
1.7 Software Engineering as an Engineering Discipline   24
1.8 Some Techniques of Software Engineering   30
    1.8.1 Reuse   31
    1.8.2 Metrics   33
    1.8.3 Computer-Aided Software Engineering (CASE)   36
    1.8.4 Cost Estimation   41
    1.8.5 Reviews and Inspections   42
1.9 Standards Commonly Used for the Software Development   42
    Processes
1.10 The Year 2000 Problem and Similar Problems   46
1.11 Organization of the Book   49
Further Reading   49
Summary   50
Exercises   51

CHAPTER 2 PROJECT MANAGEMENT   53
2.1 Sub-Teams Needed in Software Engineering Projects   54
2.2 The Nature of Project Teams   60
2.3 Project Management   62
2.4 Software Project Estimation   64
2.5 Project Scheduling   75
2.6 Project Measurement   77
2.7 Project Management Tools   78
2.8 The Role of Networks in Project Management   79
2.9 Groupware   81
2.10 An Example: Project Management for a Year 2000 Conversion   82
    Project
Further Reading   85
Summary   85
Exercises   86

CHAPTER 3 REQUIREMENTS   **89**
3.1 Some Problems with Requirements Determination   89
3.2 Requirements Elicitation   92
3.3 Requirements Traceability   98
3.4 Software Architectures and Requirements   100
    3.4.1 Use of data abstraction and information hiding in requirements engineering   102
    3.4.2 Regrouping requirements in requirements engineering   104
    3.4.3 Reuse of requirements in requirements engineering   106
    3.4.4 Automation of the requirements engineering process   107
3.5 Reengineering System Requirements   108
3.6 Assessment of Feasibility of System Requirements   111
3.7 Usability Requirements   112
3.8 Specifying Requirements Using State Diagrams and Decision Tables   119
3.9 Specifying Requirements Using Petri nets   124
3.10 Ethical Issues   125
3.11 Some Metrics for Requirements   130
3.12 The Requirements Review   134
3.13 A Management Viewpoint   141
3.14 The Major Project–Problem Statement   144
3.15 The Major Project–Requirements Elicitation   145
3.16 The Major Software Project–Requirements Analysis   151
Summary   156
Further Reading   157
Exercises   158

CHAPTER 4 SOFTWARE DESIGN   **163**
4.1 Introduction   163
4.2 Software Design Patterns   165
4.3 Introduction to Software Design Representations   168
4.4 Procedurally Oriented Design Representations   176
4.5 Software Architectures   179
4.6 Software Design Principles for Procedurally Oriented Programs   182
4.7 What is an Object?   186
4.8 Object-Oriented Design Representations   191
4.9 Software Design Principles for Object-Oriented Programs   194
4.10 Class Design Issues   197
4.11 An Example of Class Development - The String Class   199
4.12 User Interfaces   207
4.13 Software Interfaces   214
4.14 Some Metrics for Design   216
4.15 Design Reviews   218
4.16 A Manager's Viewpoint of Design   219
4.17 Architecture of the Major Software Engineering Project   220
4.18 Preliminary Design of the Major Software Project   224

4.19 Subsystem Design for the Major Software Project   232
4.20 Detailed Design for the Major Software Project   236
Further Reading   239
Summary   240
Exercises   241

CHAPTER 5 CODING   **245**
5.1 The Choice of Programming Language   245
5.2 Coding Styles   248
5.3 Coding Standards   254
5.4 Coding, Design, Requirements, and Change   257
5.5 Some Coding Metrics   259
5.6 Coding Reviews and Inspections   263
5.7 Configuration Management   263
5.8 A Management Perspective on Coding   266
5.9 Coding of the Major Software Project   267
Summary   283
Further Reading   284
Exercises   284

CHAPTER 6 TESTING AND INTEGRATION   **291**
6.1   Types of Software Testing   293
6.2   Black-box Module Testing   294
6.3   White-box Module Testing   298
6.4   Reducing the Number of Test Cases by Effective Test Strategies 303
6.5   Testing Objects for Encapsulation and Completeness   306
6.6   Testing Objects with Inheritance   310
6.7   General Testing Issues for Object-Oriented Software   311
6.8   Test Plans   313
6.9   Software Integration   315
6.10 Managing Change in the Integration Process   324
6.11 Performance and Stress Testing   326
6.12 Quality Assurance   328
6.13 Software Reliability   328
6.14 A Manager's Viewpoint on Testing and Integration   333
6.15 Testing the Major Software Project   334
6.16 Integrating the Major Software Project   335
Further Reading   338
Summary   339
Exercises   340

CHAPTER 7 DELIVERY, INSTALLATION, AND   **341**
DOCUMENTATION
7.1 Delivery   341
7.2 Installation   347
7.3 Documentation   353

7.4 Internal Documentation   354
7.5 External Documentation   356
7.6 Design Rationales   357
7.7 Installation, User, Training, and Operations Manuals   357
7.8 On-line Documentation   358
7.9 Reading Levels   359
7.10 A Manager's View of Delivery, Installation, and Documentation   360
7.11 Delivery, Installation, and Documentation of the Major Software   360
     Project
Summary   361
Further Reading   362
Exercises   362

CHAPTER 8 MAINTENANCE   **365**
8.1 Introduction   365
8.2 Corrective Software Maintenance   368
8.3 Adaptive Software Maintenance   374
8.4 Preventive Software Maintenance and the Year 2000 Problem   377
8.5 How to Read Requirements, Designs, and Source Code   378
8.6 A Manager's Perspective on Software Maintenance   378
8.7 Maintenance of the Major Software Project   379
Summary   379
Further Reading   380
Exercises   380

CHAPTER 9 RESEARCH ISSUES IN SOFTWARE   **383**
ENGINEERING
9.1 Some Important Research Problems in Software Engineering   384
9.2 How to Read the Software Engineering Research Literature   392
References   395
Exercises   396

APPENDIX 1 COMMAND-LINE ARGUMENTS   **399**

REFERENCES   **403**

INDEX   **423**

Preface

Software engineering lies at the heart of the computer revolution. Software engineering may best be described as the application of engineering techniques to develop and maintain software that runs properly and is constructed in an efficient manner.

Like most areas of computer science, software engineering has been influenced by the Internet and the ready availability of web browsers. You are certainly aware that the Internet has been instrumental in creating new job opportunities in the areas of web page design and server software development using tools such as the Common Gateway Interface (CGI) and Java. Many organizations use both the Internet and networks called "intranets," which are used only within the organization.

However, the Internet is hardly without problems. Poorly designed web pages, links that become outdated because there is no systematic plan for keeping them current, servers that crash under the load from multiple users, applications that use excessive resources, web pages and frame layouts that are unattractive when viewed on 15-inch monitors instead of the developers' 21-inch systems, and computer security failures are familiar issues to any heavy Internet user.

Less evident is the problem of separation of program functionality into servers and client. A changing technology with relatively few standards, many of which are at least slightly inconsistent, causes additional problems. As you will see, these are essentially problems in software engineering, which we will address in this book. Software engineering is necessary for writing programs for single user machines connected to a network, multi-user machines that are either standalone or connected to networks, and to networks themselves.

Software is used in automobiles, airplanes, and many home appliances. As the boundaries between the telecommunications, entertainment, and computer industries continue to blur in multimedia and networking, the need for software will only increase, at least for the foreseeable future. Software engineering is essential if there is to be any hope of meeting the increasing needs for complex, high-quality software at affordable prices.

Almost equally important is the more subtle influence of the Internet on the process of software development. Because of the complexity of modern software systems, nearly all software development is done by teams. As you will see later in this book, networks can be used to aid in the development process.

This book is intended for juniors and seniors majoring in computer science. At some institutions, the book may also be used as a text for a graduate-level course intended for those students who did not take an undergraduate course. A student reading this book will have taken several programming courses, including one that uses a modern programming language such as C, C++, Java, Ada, or Pascal. At a minimum, the student will have had a follow-up course in data structures. Ideally, the student will have some experience with software projects larger than a few hundred lines of code, either as part of an internship or in formal classes.

A book intended for an audience of undergraduates must be short enough for students to read it. It must show the student that there is a major difference between the reality of most industrial software engineering projects and the small, individually written programs that they have written in most of their computer science classes. I believe that projects are an important part of any software engineering course, other than those taught to experienced professionals or advanced graduate students. Therefore, the use of appropriate team projects will be considered as essential to reinforce the material presented in the book.

Like most of us, students learn best by doing. However, their learning is enhanced if a systematic framework is provided, along with many examples of actual software industry practice where appropriate. Examples of this practical approach are present in most chapters of this book. The goal is to take students from an educational situation in which they have written relatively small programs, mostly from scratch and by themselves, and move them toward an understanding of how software systems that are several orders of magnitude more complex are developed.

Whenever it is pedagogically sound, we emphasize some approaches to software development that are used currently in industry and government. Thus. we discuss the Internet as a medium for publishing requirements and design documents, thereby making project coordination easier. This is done because many companies are either currently using, or intend to use, either the Internet or a local "intranet" for communication and coordination of software projects. This trend will certainly continue. The impact of the Java language as a "software backplane" unifying software development across multiple platforms cannot be ignored. Active-X and CORBA (Common Object Request Broker Architecture) are also heavily used in large scale software projects with components written in more than one programming language.

Object-oriented technology (OOT) presents a special problem for the author of any introductory book on software engineering. Certainly the availability of good class libraries is having an impact on the first software engineering projects, as evidenced by the incorporation of a panel on this topic at CSC'96. The Java language is generally considered to be more object oriented than C++ because C++ has support for both procedural and object-oriented programming, and Java enforces the object-oriented paradigm. There are more books on Java programming than on any other programming language. There are four alternative approaches to object-oriented technology in a software engineering book: ignore OOT; use only OOT; use both, thus having two parallel tracks within the same book; or use a hybrid. Each approach has proponents and opponents.

This book uses a hybrid approach, describing object-oriented design and functional decomposition as alternative approaches in a systematic way. The emphasis is on showing that the goals of software engineering; namely, to write programs that are:

- Efficient
- Reliable
- Usable
- Modifiable
- Portable
- Testable
- Reusable
- Maintainable
- Interoperable with other software
- Correct

This book contains a simple but non-trivial running example that is available in electronic form. The software example is composed of components in the C and C++ languages which will be integrated with certain commercial software applications. Multiple languages are used to reflect the reality of modern software development. The example illustrates the need for proper design and implementation of software components as part of the solution to a problem. There is emphasis on all the steps needed in software engineering: requirements; design, including design tradeoffs; testing; installation, and maintenance. Coding, with the exception of coding standards, is touched on only briefly. The book also covers computation and proper use of some software metrics such as lines of code or the McCabe cyclomatic complexity. It stresses the use of software tools whenever possible, and also includes a brief discussion of software reuse. The software associated with the book is available for testing and experimentation. There are several spreadsheets for project schedule and metrics.

The book is organized into nine chapters. Many chapters will include one or more sections that provide typical views of software managers on the relevant technical activities. The purpose of the "managerial view" is to provide you with additional perspective on software engineering, not to prepare you to be a manager in the immediate future. In most organizations, a considerable amount of varied project experience is essential before a person is given a managerial position at any level of responsibility.

Chapter 1 contains a brief introduction to software engineering. The goals of software engineering are discussed, as are the typical responsibilities of team members. Both the classical waterfall and iterative software development models such as rapid prototyping and the spiral approach are discussed.

Chapter 2 contains a brief overview of project management. The intention is to present the minimum amount of information necessary to educate the student about the type of software development environment that is likely to be encountered in the professional work force. An overview of cost and scheduling information is also given here.

We present a unique approach in Chapter 3, which is devoted to the requirements process, with heavy emphasis on the movement from preliminary, informal requirements to more complete ones that describe a system in detail and can be used as the basis for a test plan. We present a hypothetical dialog that illustrates how requirements might be elicited from a potential customer. The large software project that we will discuss in each of the remaining chapters in this book is introduced in this chapter. Issues of interoperability and user interfaces are discussed here as part of the requirements process. The requirements traceability matrix developed here is used throughout the book.

Chapter 4 is devoted to software design. Both object-oriented and procedurally oriented design are discussed and several commonly used design representations are given. We consider matching preexisting software patterns as part of the design process. Software reuse is also emphasized here.

The topic of coding is discussed in Chapter 5, where we examine software implementation techniques. This chapter emphasizes source code file organization, naming conventions, and other coding standards. Since the reader is presumed to have had considerable experience writing source code, this chapter is brief.

In Chapter 6, we discuss testing and integration in detail. Both "white-box" and "black-box" testing are discussed, as are testing methods for object-oriented programs. The "big-bang," "bottom-up," and "top-down" methods of software integration are discussed here.

Chapter 7 is quite short and is devoted primarily to delivery and installation. It also includes a discussion of internal and external documentation and a brief discussion of on-line help systems.

Chapter 8 describes something that is foreign to most beginning software engineering students: software maintenance. It is discussed in detail because maintenance accounts for a large percentage of the funds spent on software projects and because many students will begin their professional careers as software maintainers.

Chapter 9 lists a set of open research problems in software engineering and provides some suggestions to help you read the existing software engineering literature.

Some of the design documents, software and spreadsheets described in this book are available for you to download from the web site http://imappl.org/~rjl/Software-Engineering.

Any book is the result of a team effort. The efforts of the editor, Dawn Mesa at CRC Press, many anonymous reviewers, students who read through the manuscript, and the CRC Press "book team," especially Helena Redshaw and Schuyler Meder, are gratefully acknowledged.

Chapter 1

Introduction

1.1 The Need for Software Engineering

The nature of computer software has changed considerably in the last fifteen to twenty years. In the late 1970s and early 1980s, personal computers were just beginning to be available at reasonable cost. Computer magazines were filled with articles describing how to determine the contents of specific memory locations used by computer operating systems. Other articles described algorithms and their implementation in some dialect of the BASIC programming language. High school students sometimes made more money by programming computers for a few months than their parents made in a year. Media coverage suggested that the possibilities for a talented, solitary programmer were unlimited. It seemed likely that the computerization of society, and the fundamental changes caused by this computerization, were driven by the actions of a large number of independently operating programmers.

However, another trend was occurring, largely hidden from public view. Software was growing greatly in size and becoming extremely complex. The evolution of word processing software is a good illustration.

In the late 1970s, software such as WordStar ran successfully on small personal computers with as little as 64 kilobytes of user memory. The early versions of WordStar allowed the user to insert and delete text at will, to cut and paste blocks of text, use italics and boldface to set off text, change character size, and select from a limited set of fonts. A spelling checker was available. A small number of commands were allowed, and the user was expected to know the options available with each command. Lists of commands were available on plastic or cardboard templates that were placed over the keyboard. The templates generally were sold separately from the software.

WordStar has evolved over time, as has most of its competition. A modern word processing system includes all the functionality of the original word processors. In addition, modern word processing software usually has the following features:

- There is a graphical user interface that uses a mouse or other pointing device.

- There is a set of file formats in which a document can be opened.

- There is a set of file formats in which a document can be saved.

- There is a set of conversion routines to allow files to be transferred to and from different applications.

- There is a large set of allowable fonts.

- The software has the capability to cut and paste graphics.

- The software has the capability to insert, and perhaps edit, tables imported from a spreadsheet.

- The software has the capability to insert, and perhaps edit, other non-textual material.

- There are facilities for producing word counts and other statistics about the document.

- There are optional facilities for checking grammar.

- The software has the capability for automatic creation of tables of contents and indices.

- The software has the capability to format output for different paper sizes.

- The software has the capability to print envelopes.

- The software has the capability to compose and format pages well enough to be considered for "desktop publishing" of material.

Because of the proliferation of printers, a word processing system must contain a large number of printer drivers. Most word processing systems often include an on-line help facility.

The added complexity does not come free, however. One popular word processor requires nine 1.44 MB floppy disks for its installation and the executable file itself is larger than four megabytes. Some are sold both as stand-alone systems and as part of "office suites," that are integrated with other applications, such as spreadsheets and database management software. The need to support many printers and to allow optional features to be loaded if the installer so desires and, assuming there is sufficient disk space, increases the word processing systems' complexity. The preferred delivery medium for many such systems is compact disks, because of their high storage capacity.

The latest version of most word processing systems probably consists of hundreds of files. New releases of the word processing software must occur at frequent intervals. If there are no releases for a year or so, then many users who desire additional features may turn to a competitor's product.

Even if a single individual understood all the source code and related data files needed for a new release of the word processing software, he or she wouldn't have enough time to be able to make the necessary changes in a timely manner. Thus, the competitive nature of the market for word processing software and the complexity of the products themselves essentially force the employment of software development teams. This is typical of modern software development – it is generally done by teams, rather than by individuals. The members of these teams are often referred to as "software engineers." Software engineers may work by themselves on particular projects, but the majority of them are likely to spend most of their careers working as part of software development teams.

The word processing software systems discussed in this section are typical of the problems faced by software engineers. The requirement of being able to cut and paste graphics and tables is essentially forced by the marketplace. This, in turn, requires that the cut-and-paste portion of the word processing software must interface with graphics and spreadsheet applications.

The interface can be created for each pair of possible interoperable applications (word processor and graphics package, word processor and spreadsheet, etc.). Alternately, there can be a single standard interface between each application (word processor, graphics package, spreadsheet, etc.) and the operating system, or some other common software. Figures 1.1 and 1.2 illustrate the two approaches.

The design illustrated in Figure 1.2 is conceptually simpler, with the major complications of device drivers, standards, and interfaces hidden in the interfaces. In either case, the word processing software must adhere to a previously specified interface. This is typical of the software industry; software that does not interface to some existing software is rare.

This simple model illustrates the need for a systematic approach to the issue of system complexity. Clearly, the complexity of a software system is affected by the complexity of its design.

There are also quality issues involved with software. Suppose that, in its rush to release software quickly and beat its competitors to market, a company releases a product that contains serious flaws. As a hypothetical example, suppose that a word processor removes all formatting information from a file, including margins, fonts, and styles, whenever the sequence of commands: save, check spelling, insert page break, and save is entered. It is unlikely that any customers using this inadequately tested version of the word processing software would ever use this product again, even if it were free.

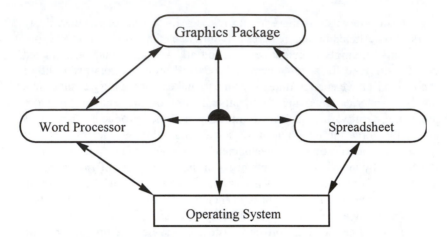

Figure 1.1. A complex interconnection system.

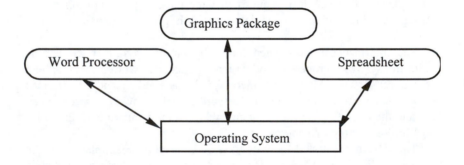

Figure 1.2. A conceptually simpler interconnection system.

You might wonder about the need for any word processor to have all the features listed above. The driving force is often the need to obtain additional market share by selling both upgrades and enticing owners of competing software to switch to your product. Each purchase made by a former owner of a competitor's product both increases one company's profit and reduces its competitor's market share.

Sometimes the decision to add new features to a product may be based on technological factors such as the Internet. At the time that this book is being written, several companies which produce word processing software are considering developing new applications that are network based. Several options are possible, regardless of whether data is stored either locally or remotely:

1. Have all new software reside on the user's local computer, as is presently the case for word processors for personal computers.
2. Have a remote application be invoked over a network whenever the user selects a previously stored document.
3. Have the core of the application reside on the local computer, with specialized features invoked from a remote server only if needed.
4. Have both the document and the remote application reside on the remote server.

The advantage of the first alternative is that there is no change in the company's strategy or basic system design. The risk is a lack of ability to perform advanced operations such as having a document be shared easily by several users who are widely scattered. There is also risk of the popular perception that the software is not up to date in its performance.

Using the second alternative means that the distribution costs essentially are reduced to zero and that there is a steady revenue stream obtained automatically by billing users electronically. The software must become more complex when issues such as security of data, security of billing information, and performance response become very important.

The third alternative has some of the best features of the first two. For example, distribution costs are reduced and the minimal core of the software, which resides on a local computer, can be smaller and simpler. Unfortunately, this alternative also shares the common disadvantages of the first two in terms of technology and complexity.

The fourth alternative is the natural extension of the second and third alternatives. There are some performance drawbacks to this approach, as any user of the Internet is aware.

Regardless of the choice made, it is clear that most word processing software will become more complex in the future. Word processing programs, including the one used to write this book, must interface with multiple applications to share printers and utility functions. They must also share data with other applications.

The problems just described for producers of word processing software are similar to those of software development organizations producing software for a single client, or a small set of potential clients. For example, software used to control the movements of multiple trains sharing the same track system for one geographical area of a country's railway system must be able to interface with software used for similar purposes in another geographical area.

This is not an abstract problem. The coordination of independently developed local systems can be a problem. In Australia, the lack of coordination of even the size of railroad tracks in the different states and territories caused major problems in the development of an Australian national railroad system until national standards were developed and adhered to. There recently have been similar software problems with standardization of railroads in the United States. (Fortunately, in the United States, track sizes have been standardized for many years.)

Similar requirements hold for the computer software used to control aircraft traffic, the software used within the airplanes themselves, the central core of a nuclear power plant, chemical processes in an oil company, or to monitor the dozens of medicines delivered to a patient in a hospital.

Such systems have an even higher degree of testing and analysis than does word processing software, because human life and safety are at stake. The term "safety-critical" is used to describe such systems. Obviously safety-critical systems require more care than, for example, computer games. (However, many computer games are very complex and place many demands on a computer to achieve the level of realism and speed that many users now demand.)

Let's summarize what we have discussed so far. We talked about the explosive growth of personal computers in the 1980s and 1990s. We indicated that many of the initial versions of some of the earlier software products have evolved into very large systems that require more effort than one individual can hope to devote to any project.

A moment's thought might make you think that the advent of the Internet, browsers, standards such as HTML (Hypertext Markup Language), and the Java programming language with its application programming interfaces has changed everything. There are many sixteen year-olds who are making a large amount of money as web page designers. One of the job skills most in demand now is "webmaster," a job title that did not even exist in 1993. A casual reading of the newspaper might lead you to believe that we have gone back to the more freewheeling days of the 1980s.

Certainly, the effects of the Internet and the technologies mentioned in the previous paragraph have been enormous. It is true that the pressure of being first to market a product and the huge, unknown potential of the Internet for electronic commerce have caused, and continue to cause, major changes in the way that software is being developed. It is also true that nearly anyone who is so inclined can learn enough HTML in a few minutes to put together a flashy web page.

However, the problem is not so simple. Even the most casual user of the Internet has noticed major problems in system performance. Delays make waiting for glitzy pictures and on-line animations very unappealing if they slow down access to the information or services that the user desired.

Proper design of web sites is not always a trivial exercise. As part of instruction in user interface design, a student of mine was asked to examine the main web sites of a number of local universities to obtain the answer to a few simple questions. The number of selections (made by clicking a mouse button) ranged from five to eleven for these simple operations. Even more interaction was necessary in some cases because of the need to scroll through on-line documents that were more than one screen long. Efficiency of design is often a virtue.

Several issues may not be transparent to the casual user of the Internet. Perhaps the most troublesome is the lack of systematic configuration management, with servers moving, software and data being reorganized dynamically, and clients not being informed. Who has not been annoyed by the famous message that appears so often when attempting to connect to an interesting web site?

ERROR 404: File not found.

It is obvious what happened to the information that the user wanted, at least if there was no typing error. As we will see later in this book, maintenance of web sites is often a form of "configuration management," which is the systematic treatment of software and related artifacts that change over time as a system evolves.

There are also major issues in assuring the security of data on servers and preventing unwanted server interaction with the user's client computer. Finally, designing the decomposition of large systems into client and server subsystems is not a trivial matter, with considerable consequences if the design is poor.

It is clear that software engineering is necessary to have modern software development done in an efficient manner. These new technologies have refocused software engineering to include the effects of market forces on software development. As we will see, these new technologies are amenable to good software engineering practice.

We will consider project size and its relationship to software teams in more detail in the next section.

1.2 Are Software Teams Really Necessary?

Some anecdotal information appears to suggest that teams of software engineers are not necessary. For example, the initial version of the PC-DOS operating system was largely developed by two people, Bill Gates and Paul Allen of Microsoft. (MS-DOS is the best-known version of PC-DOS.) The AppleDOS disk operating system for the hugely successful Apple II family of computers was developed by two people, Steve Jobs and Steve Wozniak. The UNIX operating system was originally developed by Dennis Ritchie and Kenneth Thompson [RITC78]. The first popular spreadsheet program, VisiCalc, was largely written by one person, Dan Bricklin. The list goes on and on.

However, times have changed. The original PC-DOS operating system ran on a machine with 64K of random access, read-write memory. The AppleDOS operating system used even less memory; it ran on the Apple II machine with as little as 16K memory. UNIX was originally developed for the PDP-11 series of 16-bit minicomputers. Versions of VisiCalc ran on both the Apple II and the 8086-based IBM PC. The executable size of their successor programs is much larger.

Indeed, PC-DOS has been supplanted to a great extent by several variants of Microsoft Windows such as Windows 95. AppleDOS has been supplanted by MacOS. UNIX still exists, but is much larger. On most systems, the UNIX kernel, which is the portion of the operating system that always remains in memory, is far larger than the entire memory space of the PDP-11 series computers for which it was originally written. VisiCalc no longer exists as a commercial product, but its successors, Excel, Lotus 123, and Quattro, are also several orders of magnitude larger, in terms of the size of their executable files. The current version of Excel consists of more than 1.2 million lines of C language source code.

The additional effort to develop systems of this level of complexity does not come cheaply. In his important book, *The Mythical Man-Month*, Fred Brooks gives the rule of thumb that a software project that was created by one or two persons requires an additional eight or nine times the original development effort to change it from something that can be used only by its originators to something useful to others [BROO75]. Brooks' rule of thumb appears to be valid today, as well.

It is important to understand the distinction between initial prototype versions of software, which are often by very small groups of people, and commercial software, which requires much larger organizational structures. Today, any kind of commercial software requires a rock-solid user interface, which is usually graphical. Testing is essential, and a technical support organization to answer customers' questions is necessary. Documentation must be clear, complete, and easy to use for both the first-time user who is learning the software, and the experienced user who wishes to improve his or her productivity by using the advanced features of the package. Thus, the sheer pressure of time and system size requires multiple individuals in a software project. If development of a software product that fills a need requires six months, multiplication by Brooks' conservative factor of eight means that the software will take at least four years to be ready for release. Of course, the product may be irrelevant in four years, because the rest of the software industry is not standing still.

Most successful projects that have given birth to software companies have gotten much larger in terms of the number of people that they employ. Clearly, even software that was originally developed by one or two entrepreneurs is now developed by teams. Even the wildly successful companies that make Internet browsers, the initial versions of which were largely due to the efforts of a small team, are now employers of many software engineers in order to increase the number of available features, to ensure portability to a number of environments, to improve usability by a wide class of users, and even to provide sufficient documentation.

How large should such a software team be? The most important factor seems to be the size of the project. We will discuss estimation of software project size in Chapter 2. For now, just remember one thing – your software is likely to be developed within a team environment.

1.3 Software Engineering

Clearly, organizations involved with producing software have a strong interest in making sure that the software is developed according to accepted industry practice, with good quality control, adherence to standards, and in an efficient and timely manner. For some organizations, it is literally a matter of life and death, both for the organization and for potential users of the software. Software engineering is the term used to describe software development that follows these principles.

Specifically, the term "software engineering" refers to a systematic procedure that is used in the context of a generally accepted set of goals for the analysis, design, implementation, testing, and maintenance of software. The software produced should be efficient, reliable, usable, modifiable, portable, testable, reusable, maintainable, interoperable, and correct. These terms refer both to systems and to their components. Many of the terms are self-explanatory; however, we include their definitions for completeness. You should refer to the IEEE standard glossary of computer terms for related definitions [IEEE95].

- Efficiency: The software is produced in the expected time and within the limits of the available resources. The software that is produced runs within the time expected for various computations to be completed.

- Reliability: The software performs as expected. In multi-user systems, the system performs its functions even with other load on the system.

- Usability: The software can be used properly. This generally refers to the ease of use of the user interface but also concerns the applicability of the software to both the computer's operating system and utility functions and the application environment.

- Modifiability: The software can be easily changed if the requirements of the system change.

- Portability: The software system can be ported to other computers or systems without major rewriting of the software. Software that needs only to be recompiled in order to have a properly working system on the new machine is considered to be very portable.

- Testability: The software can be easily tested. This generally means that the software is written in a modular manner.

- Reusability: Some or all of the software can be used again in other projects. This means that the software is modular, that each individual software module has a well-defined interface, and that each individual module has a clearly defined outcome from its execution. This often means that there is a substantial level of abstraction and generality in the modules that will be reused most often.

- Maintainability: The software can be easily understood and changed over time if problems occur. This term is often used to describe the lifetime of long-lived systems such as the air traffic control system that must operate for decades.

- Interoperability: The software system can interact properly with other systems. This can apply to software on a single, stand-alone computer or to software that is used on a network.

- Correctness: The program produces the correct output.

These goals, while noble, do not help with the development of software that meets these goals. This book will discuss systematic processes and techniques that aid in the efficient development of high-quality software. The software systems that we will use as the basis of our discussion in this book are generally much too large to be developed by a single person. We are much more interested in the process of developing software, such as modern word processors that will be used by many people, than in writing small programs in languages such as BASIC that will be used only by their creators. (These comments do not apply as much to Visual BASIC because of its high-level support for user interface design.)

1.4 Typical Software Engineering Tasks

There are several tasks that are part of every software engineering project:

- Analysis of the problem
- Determination of requirements
- Design of the software
- Coding of the software solution
- Testing and integration of the code
- Installation and delivery of the software
- Documentation
- Maintenance
- Quality assurance
- Training
- Resource estimation
- Project management

We will not describe either the analysis or training activities in this book in any detail. Analysis of a problem is very often undertaken by experts in the particular area of application, although, as we shall see later, the analysis can often benefit from input from software engineers. A discussion of software training is beyond the scope of the book.

We now briefly introduce the other activities necessary in software development. Most of these activities will be described in detail in a separate chapter.

You should note that these tasks are generally not performed in a vacuum. Instead, they are performed as part of an organized sequence of activities that is known as the "software life cycle" of the organization. We will describe several different approaches to the sequencing of software development activities in the next section, when we study software life cycles. For now, just assume that every software development organization has its own individual software life cycle in which the order of these activities is specified.

The requirements phase of an organization's software life cycle involves determining precisely what the functionality of the system will be. If there is a single customer, or set of customers, who are known in advance, then the requirements process will require considerable discussion between the customer and the requirements specialists on the software team. This scenario would apply to the process of developing software to control the flight of an airplane.

If there is no immediately identifiable customer, but a potential set of individual customers, then other methods such as market analysis and preference testing might be used. This approach might be appropriate for the development of software for the Internet.

The process of developing software requirements is so important that we will devote all of Chapter 3 to this subject.

The design phase involves taking the requirements and devising a plan and a representation to allow the requirements to be translated into source code. A software designer must have considerable experience in design methodology and in estimating the trade-offs in the selection of alternative designs. The designer must know the characteristics of available software systems, such as databases, operating systems, graphical user interfaces, or utility programs that can aid in the eventual process of coding. Software design will be discussed in Chapter 4.

The coding activity is most familiar to students and need not be discussed in any detail at this point. We note, however, that many decisions about coding in object-oriented or procedural languages might be deferred until this point in the software life cycle, or they might have been made at the design or even the requirements phase. Since coding standards are often neglected in many first and second-year programming courses, coding standards will be discussed in some detail. Software coding will be discussed in Chapter 5.

A beginning software engineer is very likely to be assigned to either software testing or software maintenance. Software testing is an activity that often begins after the software has been created, but well before it is judged ready to be released to its customer. It is often included with software integration, which is the process of combining separate software modules into larger software systems. Software integration also often requires integration of preexisting software systems in order to make large ones. Software testing and integration will be discussed in Chapter 6.

Documentation includes much more than simply commenting the source code. It involves rationales for requirements and design, help files, user manuals, training manuals, technical guides such as programming reference manuals, and installation manuals. Even internal documentation of source code is much more elaborate than is apparent to a beginning programmer. It is not unusual for a source code file to have twice as many lines of documentation and comments as the number of lines that contain actual code.

After the software is designed, coded, tested, and documented, it must be delivered and installed. Software documentation, delivery, and installation will be discussed in Chapter 7.

The term "software maintenance" is used to describe those activities that are done after the software has been released. Maintenance includes correcting errors found in the software; moving the software to new environments, computers, and operating systems; enhancing the software to increase functionality; and so on. For many software systems, maintenance is the most expensive and time-consuming task in the software development life cycle. Software maintenance will be discussed in Chapter 8.

Of course, all these activities must be coordinated. Project management is perhaps the most critical activity in software engineering. Unfortunately, it is difficult to truly understand the details of project management activities without the experience of actually working on a large-scale software development project. Therefore, we will be content to present an overview of project management activities in Chapter 2. Each of the later chapters will also include a section presenting a typical managerial viewpoint on the technical activities discussed in the chapter.

Quality assurance, or QA, is concerned with making certain that both the software product that is produced and the process by which the software is developed meet the organization's standards for quality. The QA team is often responsible for setting the quality standards. In many organizations, the QA team is separate from the rest of the software development team. QA will be discussed throughout the book, rather than being relegated to a separate chapter. We chose this approach to emphasize that quality cannot be added near the end of a software project's development. Instead, the quality must be a result of the engineering process used to create the software.

1.5 Software Life Cycles

In the previous section, we discussed the different activities that are typically part of systematic process of software engineering. As we saw, there are many such activities.

Knowing that these activities will occur during a software product's lifetime does not tell you anything about the timing in which these activities occur. The activities can occur in a rigid sequence, with each activity completed before the next one begins, or several of the activities can occur simultaneously. In some software development organizations, most of these activities are performed only once. In other organizations, several of the activities may be iterated several times with, for example, the requirements being finalized only after several designs and implementations of source code have been done. The timing of these activities and the choice between iterative and non-iterative methods are often described by what are known as software development models.

We will discuss four basic models of software development life cycles in this section:

- The classical waterfall model
- The rapid prototyping model
- The spiral model
- The market-driven model

Each of these software life cycle models will be discussed in a separate subsection.

1.5.1 The Classical Waterfall Model

The most common model of the software development process is called the classical waterfall model, which is illustrated in Figure 1.3. For simplicity, we will leave documentation out of our models of software development.

In the simplest possible classical waterfall model, the different activities in the software life cycle are considered to occur sequentially. The only exception is that two activities that are adjacent in Figure 1.3 are allowed to communicate via feedback.

A life cycle model such as the one presented in Figure 1.3 illustrates the sequence of many of the major software development activities, at least at a high level. It is clear, for example, that specification of a system's requirements will occur before testing of individual modules. It is also clear from this abstraction of the software development life cycle that there is feedback only between certain pairs of activities: requirements specification and software design; design and implementation of source code; coding and testing; testing and maintenance.

What is not clear from this illustration is the relationship between the different activities and the time when one activity ends and the next one begins. This stylized description of the classical waterfall model is usually

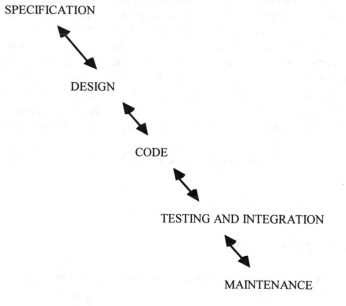

SPECIFICATION

DESIGN

CODE

TESTING AND INTEGRATION

MAINTENANCE

Figure 1.3. A simplified illustration of the classical waterfall life cycle model.

augmented by a sequence of milestones in which each two adjacent phases of the life cycle interface. A simple example of a milestone chart for a software development process that is based on the classical waterfall model is given in Figure 1.4.

Often, there are several opportunities for the software system's designers to interact with the software's requirements specification. The requirements for the system are typically presented in a series of requirements reviews, which might be known by names such as the preliminary requirements review; an intermediate requirements review; and the final, or critical requirements review. In nearly all organizations that use the classical waterfall model of software development, the action of having the requirements presented at the critical requirements review accepted by the designers and customer will mark the "official" end of the requirements phase.

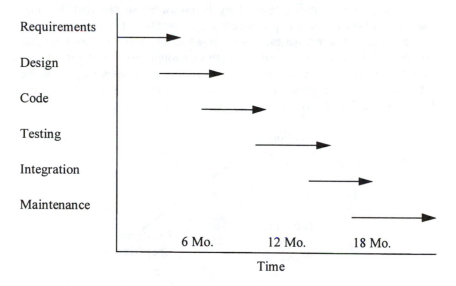

Figure 1.4. An example of a milestone chart for a waterfall software development process.

There is one major consequence of a decision to use the classical waterfall model of software development. Any work by the software's designers during the period between the preliminary and (accepted) final, or critical, requirements reviews may have to be redone if it is no longer consistent with any changes to the requirements. This forces the software development activities to follow essentially the sequence that was illustrated in Figure 1.3.

We note that there is nothing special about the boundary between the requirements specification and design phases of the classical waterfall model. The same holds true for the design and implementation phases, with system design being approved in a preliminary design review; an intermediate design review; and the final, or critical design review. The patterns applies to the other interfaces between life cycle phases, as well.

The classical waterfall model is very appealing for use in those software development projects in which the system requirements can be determined within a reasonable period and, in addition, these requirements do not change very much during the development period. Of course, there are many situations in which this assumption is not valid.

1.5.2 The Rapid Prototyping Model

In many organizations, technology is advancing so fast that the long lead time between setting requirements and delivering a final tested version of a product seems impractical. Such organizations often follow the rapid prototyping or spiral models of software development. These models are iterative and require the creation of one or more prototypes as part of the software development process. The rapid prototyping is illustrated in Figure 1.5. (The spiral model will be discussed in subsection 1.5.3.)

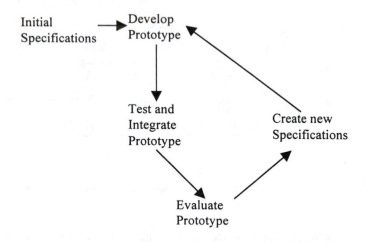

Figure 1.5. The rapid prototyping model of the software development life cycle.

The primary assumption of the rapid prototyping model of software development is that the complete requirements specification of the software is not known before the software is designed and implemented. Instead, the software is developed incrementally, with the specification developing along with the software itself. The central point of the rapid prototyping method is that the final software project produced is considered as the most acceptable of a sequence of software prototypes.

We will now explain the rapid prototyping method in more detail, illustrating the basic principles by the use of a familiar system: a network browser such as Microsoft Internet Explorer. Let's consider the environment in which Microsoft found itself. For strategic reasons, the company decided to enter the field of Internet browsers. The success of Mosaic and Netscape, among others, meant that the development path was constrained to some degree. There had to be support for HTML and most existing web pages had to be readable by the new browser. The user interface had to have many features with the same functionality as those of Netscape and Mosaic. However, the user interfaces had to be substantially different from those systems in order to avoid copyright issues.

Some of the new system could be specified in advance. For example, the new system had to include a parser for HTML documents. In addition, the user interface had to be mouse driven.

However, the system could not be specified fully in advance. The user interface would have to be tested carefully for usability. Several iterations of the software were expected before the user interface could be tested to the satisfaction of Microsoft. The users testing the software would be asked about the collection of features available with each version of Internet Explorer. The user interface not only had to work correctly, but the software had to have a set of features that was of sufficient perceived value to make other potential users change from their existing Internet browsers if they already used one, or purchase Microsoft Internet Explorer if they had never used such a product before.

Thus, the process of development for this software had to be iterative. The software was developed as a series of prototypes, with the specifications of the individual prototypes changing in response to feedback from users.

Several things are necessary for an efficient iterative software development life cycle. There must be an initial step to begin the process. In the rapid prototyping model described in Figure 1.4, an initial set of specifications is needed to start the prototyping process.

There must also be an iterative cycle in order to update and revise prototypes. This is clear from the diagram in Figure 1.5.

Finally, there must be a way to exit from the iteration cycle. This step is indicated in Figure 1.5 by the "evaluate prototype" step. The basis for the evaluation is the perceived completeness, correctness, functionality, and usability of the prototype. This evaluation varies from organization to organization. In many cases, the final prototype is delivered as the final product; in others, the final prototype serves as the basis for the final delivered product.

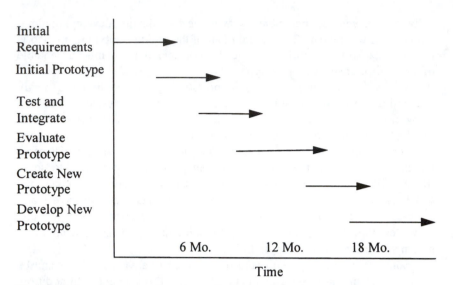

Figure 1.6. An example of a milestone chart for a rapid prototyping software development process.

A milestone chart can also be developed for the rapid prototyping method of software development. A sample milestone chart for the rapid prototyping process model is illustrated in Figure 1.6. Compare this chart to the milestone chart shown in Figure 1.4 for the classical waterfall software development process.

1.5.3 The Spiral Model

Another iterative software development life cycle is the spiral model developed by Barry Boehm [BOEH88]. The spiral model differs from the rapid prototyping model primarily in the explicit emphasis on the assessment of software risk for each prototype during the evaluation period. The term "risk" is used to describe the potential for disaster in the software project.

Clearly there are several levels of disasters and different organizations and projects may view identical situations differently. Examples of commonly occurring disastrous situations in software development projects include the following:

- The software development team is not able to produce the software within the allotted budget and schedule.

- The software development team is able to produce the software and is over either budget or schedule but within an allowable overrun (this may not always be disastrous).

- The software development team is not able to produce the software within anything resembling the allotted budget.

- After considerable expenditure of time and resources, the software development team has determined that the software cannot be built to meet the presumed requirements at any cost.

Planning is also part of the iterative process used in the spiral development model.

The spiral model is illustrated in Figure 1.7.

As we saw before with the classical waterfall and rapid prototyping software development models, a milestone chart can be used for the spiral development process. We illustrate this type of milestone chart in Figure 1.8. Compare the illustration in Figure 1.8 to Figures 1.4 and 1.6. For simplicity, only a small portion of a milestone chart is included.

Both the rapid prototyping and spiral models are classified as iterative because there are several instances of intermediate software that can be evaluated before a final product is produced.

It is easy to see the difference between iterative approaches and the classical waterfall model; the waterfall model has no provision for iteration and interaction with a potential customer after the requirements are complete. Instead, the customer must wait until final product delivery by the development organization.

Many, but not all, organizations that use the classical waterfall model allow the customer to participate in reviews of designs. Even if the customer is involved in evaluation of detailed designs, this is often the last formal interaction between the customer and the developer and the customer is often uneasy until the final delivery (and often even more uneasy after delivery). It is no wonder that iterative software development approaches are popular with customers.

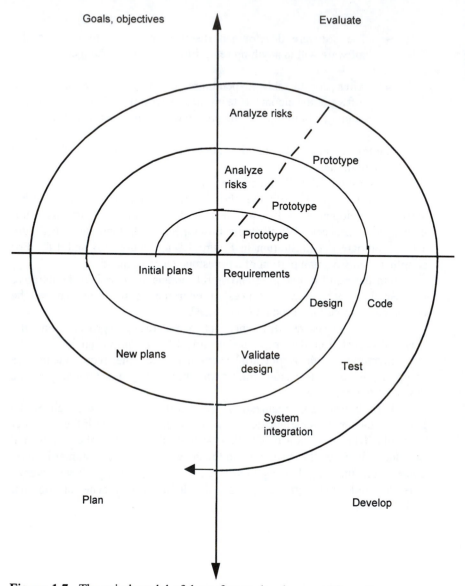

Figure 1.7. The spiral model of the software development life cycle.

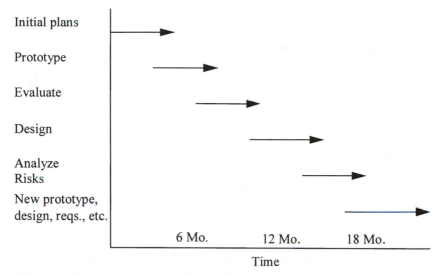

Figure 1.8. An example of a milestone chart for a spiral software development process.

1.5.4 A Market-Driven Model of Software Development

It should be clear that none of the models of the software development life cycle are directly applicable to the modern development of software for the general consumer market. The models discussed previously assumed that there was time for relatively complete initial requirements analysis (as in the classical waterfall model) or for an iterative analysis (as in the rapid prototyping and spiral models with their risk assessment and discarding of unsatisfactory prototypes). These models do not, for example, address the realities of the development of software for personal computers. Here, the primary pressure driving the development process is getting a product to market with sufficient quality to satisfy consumers and enough desirable new features to maintain, and even increase, market share.

This is a relatively new approach to software development and no precise, commonly accepted models of this type of software development process have been advanced as yet, at least not in the general literature. The reality is that the marketing arm of the organization often drives the process by demanding that new features be added, even as the product nears its target release date. Thus there is no concept of a "requirements freeze," which was a common, unwritten assumption of all the previous models.

We indicate the issues with this type of market-driven "concurrent engineering" in the milestone chart illustrated in Figure 1.9. We have reduced the time frame to reflect the reality that many products have several releases each year.

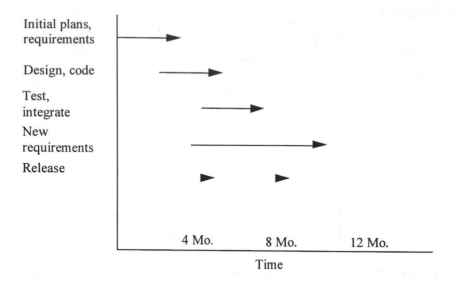

Figure 1.9. An example of a milestone chart for a market-based, concurrently engineered software development process.

1.5.5 Common Features of All Models of Software Development

You should note that many organizations have their own written variants of these software development models, and that any models are stylized approximations to actual software development practice in any case. A more market-driven life cycle might have many more things happening at the same time. We will not pursue these differences in life cycle models any further in this book.

There are many variants of these four life cycle models, but these are the most commonly used. Note that the *activities* in each of these three life cycle models are similar. The primary differences are in the timing of activities and the expectation that some portions of the initial prototypes will be discarded if iterative approaches, such as the rapid prototyping or spiral development models, are used.

The point about timing of life cycle activities cannot be overemphasized. The various life cycle models are, at best, stylized descriptions of a process. Most organizations have their own set of procedures to be followed during software development. Of course, you should follow the guidelines set by your employer. Just be aware that these are the same sets of essential activities that must always occur in software development, regardless of the order in which they occur.

1.6 Different Views of Software Engineering Activities

As we have seen earlier in this chapter, most modern software development projects require teams. There are two obvious ways to organize teams: ensure that each person is a specialist with unique skills, or have each person be a generalist, who is able to perform most, if not all, team responsibilities. Each of the organizational methods has unique advantages and disadvantages.

A team with specialists is likely to have individual tasks done more efficiently than if they were to be done by a generalist. Some technologies are so complex and are changing so rapidly that only a specialist can keep up with them.

On the other hand, a generalist is more able to fill in if there is a short-term emergency such as one of the team members being very sick or having a family emergency. Generalists often see connections between apparently unrelated subjects and can aid in identifying patterns of software development problems that have been solved before.

In any event, different people, both on and off particular software development teams, have different perspectives on the organization's software, the efficiency of the process of developing the software, and the particular project that they are working on.

A software project manager is interested in how the software development process is working, and whether the system will be produced on time and within budget. The manager is especially concerned with the group he or she heads. It also is natural for a lower level manager to be somewhat concerned with the work done by other groups on related projects. After all, an experienced manager is well aware that software projects can be canceled if they are expected to be delivered late or over budget. Higher level management often has to make unpopular decisions based on whatever information is available. Thus, lack of performance of a team working on one subsystem can affect a project adversely, even if the other subsystems are likely to be produced on time by the teams responsible for their development.

Therefore, a manager will often require his or her team to produce measurements on the team's progress. These measurements could include the number of lines of code written, tested, or reused from other projects; the number and types of errors found in systems; the number and size of software modules integrated into larger systems and so on.

Software engineers often hate to fill out forms, because they feel that the time needed to do this takes away from their essential activities. Hopefully, understanding a manager's perspective will make this activity more palatable, even for the most harassed programmer.

1.7 Software Engineering as an Engineering Discipline

The goal of this section is to convince you that software engineering is an engineering discipline. We will do this by presenting a collection of anecdotes relating to current software development practice. We will describe three classes of software application environments: HTML and other programming for the Internet, applications programs for personal computers, and applications that involve health and safety. In each case, we will illustrate the need for a disciplined approach to software engineering.

The current rush to create web sites for the Internet and the shortage of trained personnel means that, as this book is being written, jobs are readily available for people with minimal technical knowledge. However, this unusual situation is unlikely to continue far into the future, for several reasons.

Experimentation with leading edge technology may be appealing to a software engineer, but will be less so to an organization's chief software officer if the future of the organization depends upon this technology working properly. This latter situation is often called "bleeding edge technology." Management is much more likely to support small experimental projects than make major changes to its primary business practice, just to keep up with "leading edge technology."

You should note that, when the rush to create the initial web pages is over, the web pages must be tested for accuracy of content, correctness of links, correctness of other programming using the CGI and related approaches, general usability, and configuration management. (Configuration management is a very general issue in software engineering. For now, think of it as the systematic approach used to make sure that changes in things such as Internet browser software standards do not make the pages unusable, at the same time making sure that the pages are still accessible by older versions of browsers.)

Here is an example of this problem: I recruited a research team to work on web page design. The team consisted of four freshmen majoring in computer science at Howard University. (The students were chosen because of the clever way they tore off portions of a cardboard pizza box when we ran out of paper plates at the departmental student-faculty party at the beginning of the academic year.) The goal of the project was to develop a web site for an on-line archive of examples of source code with known logical software errors to be used by researchers in software testing to validate their theories and testing tools.

After three months of designing web pages, testing alternative designs, and writing HTML and CGI scripts, the web page was essentially produced in its current form. The remainder of the effort was devoted to the students' learning software testing theory, porting examples written in one programming language to other standard languages, database design, and writing driver programs for procedures that were to be included in the software testing archive. You can visit this web site at:

http://www.imappl.org/WASTE/

In short, first-year college students did the web page work in a few months and then turned to standard software engineering activities. Writing web pages is too easy to serve as the basis for a career without considerable design training. The computer science content involved with the use of HTML appears to be very small. The computer science content is involved with the programming of servers, clients, and scripts in Java and other languages. Since HTML is a language (the acronym stands for hypertext markup language), enhancing the language and developing HTML translators is also a computer science effort. It is in this programming portion that the software engineering activity occurs.

The experience of web design is reminiscent of the situation when personal computers became popular. One negative aspect of the tremendous publicity given to the early successful entrepreneurs in the software industry is the common perception among nonprofessionals that software engineering is primarily an art that is best left to a single talented programmer instead of an engineering team. This incorrect perception is much older, going back to the origins of computers. The earliest computer programmers were scientists who wrote their own simple algorithms and implemented them on the computers available to them. The earliest computers were programmed by connecting wires in a wiring frame, although this arduous process was soon replaced by writing programs in the machine language of the computer. Machine language programming was quickly replaced by assembly language programming. All this encouraged the so-called "ace programmer."

Finally, the first attempt at what we now call software engineering emerged in the development of subroutines, or blocks of code that perform one computational task and can be reused again and again. (Admiral Grace Murray Hopper is generally credited with writing the first reusable subroutine.) Higher level languages were then developed, with more and more expressive power and with extensive support for software developments. Indeed, every modern software development environment includes compilers, editors, debuggers, and extensive libraries.

The most modern software development environments include tools to build graphical user interfaces and special software to assist with the software development process itself. The software even has a special name, CASE tools, which stands for Computer Aided Software Engineering.

Even with the improvement in software development environments and the increasing complexity of modern software, the image of the lone programmer persists. Little harm is done if the lone programmer develops software only for his or her use. The lone programmer also is useful when developing small prototype systems.

For larger software projects, an engineering discipline is necessary. This means that the entire software development process is guided by well-understood, agreed-upon principles, and these principles are based on documented experience. The software development process must:

- Allow for accurate estimates of the time and resources needed for completion of the project.

- Have well-understood, quantifiable guidelines for all decisions made.

- Have identifiable milestones.

- Make efficient use of personnel and other resources.

- Be able to deliver the products on time.

- Be amenable to quality control.

The resulting software product must be of high quality and meet the other goals of software engineering. Above all, as an engineering discipline, both the efficiency of the process and the quality of the product must be measurable.

The issue of quality brings us to the discussion of the other two software application environments that we will consider in this chapter: applications programs for personal computers, and applications that involve health and safety.

There is a tremendous amount of competitive pressure in the area of software application development for personal computers. Many software development organizations attempt to release new versions of major applications every six months. For some applications, the interval between releases may be as short as four months. This rapid software development life cycle requires a degree of "concurrent engineering," in which several different life cycle activities are performed simultaneously. The driving factor in this process is the need to provide new features in products.

This efficient production of software comes at a price, however. There is no way that the quality, as measured by such things as ease of installation, interoperability with other applications, or robustness, can be as high as it would be if there were a longer period for testing and design reviews, among other things. Contrary to some views, such software is tested. The decision is release a software product is based on a careful assessment of the number and severity of errors remaining in the software and the relative gain in market share because of new features. Companies such as Microsoft use the technique of software reliability to base decisions on formal data analysis.

It is worthwhile at this point to briefly discuss the software development process used at Microsoft [CUSU97]. Most new software development at Microsoft has three phases:

1. In the planning phase, a vision statement is developed for the software based on customer analysis. The specifications are written, together with a list of features. Finally, a project plan is set.

2. In the development phase, development is performed together with testing and evolution of the specifications. This is an iterative process.

3. In the third and final phase, called "stabilization," comprehensive testing occurs both within Microsoft and with selected "beta sites" for testing by external users.

The later portions of this process are often called "sync and stabilize" to reflect that they allow individual software modules to be placed into the overall product. Most systems under development have a daily "build," in which a clean compilation is done. This allows the synchronization of individual modules.

The stabilization occurs when the number of changes appearing in the software and the number of errors has been reduced below a level that is considered acceptable. The number of detected software errors for the entire software system is computed each day. A typical, but hypothetical, graph of the daily number of software errors for a month is indicated in Figure 1.10.

Since the number of errors remaining in the software illustrated in Figure 1.10 appears to have stabilized below 7, the software development in this hypothetical example would probably be suspended and the software released, at least if the remaining errors were considered to be small and to be of minimal importance. The implicit assumption is that the software will be sufficiently defect-free once the number of remaining known software errors is below a predefined level and the statistical history suggests that this number will remain low. This assumption is based on the subject known as software reliability, which we will discuss when we study testing and quality control.

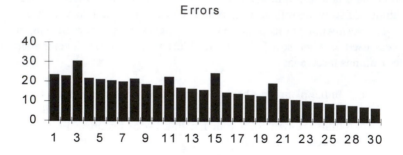

Figure 1.10. A typical graph of the daily number of software errors for a month.

You should be aware that each organization has its own standards for acceptable quality of the products it releases. Note, however, that no company could stay in business if the marketplace generally considered its products to be of extremely low quality.

We emphasize that these systems are developed over a period of time, however short. Software such as Windows NT, which had a much longer development period, had over a thousand separate compilations (builds) before the latest version was released. Also, most Microsoft products now require large development teams. For example, the development team for Windows 95 had over 200 members [CUSU97].

It is clear that Microsoft has a software development process. This process has been tailored to the company's unique corporate culture, understanding of the marketplace, and its financial resources.

Applications that involve health and safety generally have a more rigid software development process and a higher standard for software logical software errors. The reasons are obvious: potential loss of life in a medical monitoring system, considerable hardship if airplanes are grounded because of an error in the air traffic control system, or major disruption to financial markets if database software used for the U.S. Social Security System fails. Considerable financial loss can occur if, for example, a hotel reservation system or a package tracking system have major failures. People could lose jobs. Clearly, there is an even higher need for a formal software development process. Systems in these areas are often much larger than in the areas previously discussed and, thus, in much more need of a careful software engineering process. The process must be carefully documented to meet the approval of agencies such as the U.S. Food and Drug Administration for computer software that controls medical products.

We have illustrated that each type of software development area—Internet, personal computer applications, and safety-critical applications involves some degree of software engineering, although the processes may be different in different areas. There is one other advantage to treating software engineering as an engineering discipline: avoidance of future risk. Risk analysis is a major part of any engineering discipline.

We note that if risk analysis had been applied to software development when programmers were using two digits instead of four to represent dates, the software development industry would not be facing the so-called "Year 2000 problem," with its expected cost of billions of dollars. The problem occurred because programmers were under pressure to save space in their code and data sets and because they did not expect their software to be used twenty or more years after it was developed. The risk analysis would have cost money, but the resources applied to the expected cost of solving the Year 2000 problem could have been used in much more profitable endeavors.

It is appropriate at this point to mention a major controversy in the software engineering community: certification of software professionals. The arguments for certification are that too much software is either produced inefficiently or else is of low quality. The need to ensure the correctness of safety-critical software that affects human life is adding to the pressure in favor of certification. We note that most engineering disciplines require practicing professionals to pass examinations and be licensed, leading to the title "Professional Engineer."

The primary argument against certification of software professionals is the perception of the lack of a common core of engineering knowledge that is relevant to software development. Many opponents of certification of software professionals believe that the field is too new, with few software engineering practices being based on well-defined principles.

We will not take a position on this issue, although we expect a consensus to arise in the next few years. You should note, however, that the number of undergraduate computer science programs accredited by the Computer Sciences Accreditation Commission's Computer Sciences Accreditation Board (CSAB) is increasing rapidly.

1.8 Some Techniques of Software Engineering

Efficiency is one of the goals of software engineering, both in the efficiency of the development process and the run-time efficiency of the resulting software system. We will not discuss run-time efficiency of the software in this book, other than to note that it is often studied under the topics "analysis of algorithms" or "performance evaluation." Developing software efficiently often involves systematic efforts to reuse existing software, as we will see later in this section.

The other goals of software engineering that were presented in Section 1.3 are also important. However, focusing on efficiency of both the software product and the process used to develop the software can clarify the engineering perspective of the discipline known as "software engineering."

We list five major techniques that are typically part of good software engineering practice and which may be familiar to you:

1. There must be a systematic treatment of software reuse.

2. There must be a systematic use of metrics to assess and improve both software quality and process efficiency.

3. There must be a systematic use of CASE tools that are appropriate for the project's development environment.

4. There must be a systematic use of valid software cost estimation models to assess the resources needed for a project and to allocate these resources efficiently.

5. There must be a systematic use of reviews and inspections to ensure that the both the project's software and the process used to develop that software produce a high quality solution to the problem that the software is supposed to solve.

Each of these techniques is discussed briefly in a separate subsection. Note that these techniques are intended to support the efficient performance of the software engineering tasks listed in Section 1.4.

1.8.1 Reuse

Software reuse refers to the development of software systems that use previously written component parts which have been tested and have well-defined, standard interfaces. Software reuse is the key to major improvements in software productivity. The productivity of programmers has remained amazingly constant over the last 30 years, with the average programmer producing somewhere in the range of 8-12 correct, fully documented and tested lines of code per day. At first glance, this number seems appallingly low, but you should realize that this takes into account all meetings, design reviews, documentation checks, code walkthroughs, system tests, training classes, quality control, and so on.

Software reuse has several different meanings in the software engineering community. Different individuals have viewpoints that depend upon their responsibilities.

For example, a high-level software manager might view software reuse as a technique for improving the overall productivity and quality of his or her organization. As such, the focus would be on costs and benefits of organizational reuse plans and on schemes for implementing company-wide schemes.

Software developers who use reusable code written by others probably view software reuse as the efficient use of a collection of available assets. For these developers, who are also consumers of existing software, software reuse is considered a positive goal since it can improve productivity. A project manager for such development would probably view reuse as useful if the appropriate reused software were easy to obtain and were of high quality. The manager would have a different view if he or she were forced to use poorly tested code that caused many problems in system integration and maintenance because of its lack of modularity or adherence to standards.

On the other hand, developers who are producers of reusable code for use for their own projects and for reuse by others might view reuse as a drain on their limited resources. This is especially true if they are required to provide additional quality in their products or to collect and analyze additional metrics.

A reuse librarian, who is responsible for operating and maintaining a library of reusable components, would have a different view. Each new reuse library component would have to be subjected to configuration management. Some degree of cataloging would be necessary for future access. Software reuse makes the job of a reuse librarian necessary.

In general, the term "software reuse" refers to a situation in which some software is used in more than one project. Here "software" is defined loosely as one or more items that are considered part of an organization's standard software engineering process that produces some product. Thus. "software" could refer either to source code or to other products of the software life cycle, such as requirements, designs, test plans, test suites, or documentation. The term "software artifact" is frequently used in this context.

In informal terms, reuse can be defined as using what already exists to achieve what is desired. Reuse can be achieved with no special language, paradigm, library, operating system, or techniques. It has been practiced for many years in many different contexts. In the vast majority of projects, much of the necessary software has been already been developed, even if not in-house.

Reusability is widely believed to be a key to improving software development productivity and quality. By reusing high quality software components, software developers can simplify the product and make it more reliable. Frequently, fewer total subsystems are used and less time is spent on organizing the subsystems.

If a software system is large enough, programmers often work on it during the day and wait until the next day to check the correctness of their code by running it. Many systems are so large that they are compiled only once a day, to reduce computer load and to provide consistency.

The major improvement in computer productivity is due to the improvement in programming languages. A single line of code in a modern programming language - say C++ or Ada - may express the same computational information that requires many lines of assembly language. A spreadsheet language, such as Microsoft Excel or Lotus 123, is even more powerful than most modern, general-purpose programming languages for special applications. Table 1.1 shows the effects of the choice of programming languages on the relative number of statements needed to perform a typical computation. Some of the data can be found in Capers Jones book [JONE83].

In Table 1.2 we present another view of how the expressive power of programming languages can be compared: the cost of a delivered line of code.

We note that there is a much more efficient way to improve software productivity – reuse code. The efficient reuse of source code (and other software engineering items such as requirements, designs, test cases, documentation, and so on) can greatly improve the way in which software is produced.

Table 1.1
Comparison of expressive quality of program languages

Language	Lines of Code
Assembly	320
Ada	71
C	150
Smalltalk	21
COBOL	106
Spreadsheet Languages	6

Source: Donald Reifer, *Crosstalk*, July 1996. [REIF96]. Note the use of the term "spreadsheet language," which refers to commonly available, higher-level programming applications such as spreadsheets or databases.

Table 1.2

Comparison of dollar cost of delivered source line of code for several program languages in several different application domains

Application Domain	Ada83	C	C++	3GL	Domain Norm
Commercial Command and Control	50	40	35	50	45
Military Command and Control	75	75	70	100	80
Commercial Products	35	25	30	40	40
Commercial Telecommunications	55	40	45	50	50
Military Telecommunications	60	50	50	90	75

Source: *Crosstalk*, July 1996.

1.8.2 Metrics

Any engineering discipline has a quantifiable basis. Software engineering is no exception. Here, the relevant measurements include the size of a software system, the quality of a system, the system's performance, and its cost. The most commonly used measurement of the size of a system is the number of lines of source code. We will meet other measurements of software system size in this book, including measurements of the size of a set of requirements.

There are two measurements of software system quality that are in common use. The first is the number of defects, or deviations from the software's specifications. The quality of a system is often measured as the total number of defects, or the "defect ratio," which is the number of defects per thousand lines of code. The terms "fault" and "failure" are sometimes used in the software engineering literature. Unfortunately, the terms "defect," "error," "fault," and "failure," do not always mean the same thing. We will follow the recommendations of the IEEE [IEEE88] and use the following terminology:

A software "fault" is some deviation, however small, from the requirements of a system and a software "failure" is an inability of a system to perform its essential duties.

A second measurement of software system quality is the number of faults per thousand hours of operation. This measurement may be more meaningful than the number of faults per thousand lines of code in practice.

One other much less common measurement is an assessment of the quality of the user interface of a software system. Although the quality of a user interface is hard to measure, good user interfaces are often the keys to the success or failure of a software application in a crowded market. We will discuss user interfaces extensively in Chapter 4 as part of our study of software design.

The term "metrics" is commonly used in the software engineering literature to describe those aspects of software that we wish to measure. There is a huge number of metrics currently in use by software organizations. Many of the metrics are collected, but the resulting values are not frequently used as a guide to improving the organizations' software development process or towards improving the quality of its products. The use of metrics is absolutely essential for a systematic process of software engineering. Without metrics, there is no way to evaluate the status of software development, assess the quality of the result, or track the cost of development.

Our view is that metrics should be collected systematically, but sparingly. Our approach is to use the GQM (Goals, Questions, Metrics) paradigm of Basili and Rombach [BASI88]. The GQM paradigm consists of three things: goals of the process and product, questions we wish to ask about the process and product, and methods of measuring the answers to these questions. The GQM paradigm suggests a systematic answer to the question "which metrics should we collect?"

Typical goals include:

- Quantify software-related costs.

- Characterize software quality.

- Characterize the languages used.

- Characterize software volatility (volatility is the number of changes to the software component per unit time).

There are clearly many questions that can be asked about progress toward these goals. Typical questions include the following (we will only list two questions per goal):

- What are the costs per project? (for costs)

- What are the costs for each life cycle activity? (for costs)

- How many software defects are there? (for quality)

- Is any portion of the software more defect prone than others? (for quality)

- What programming languages are used? (for languages)

- What object-oriented programming language features are used? (for languages)

- How many changes are made to requirements? (for volatility)

- How many changes are made to source code during development? (for volatility)

The clarity of these questions makes the choice of metrics easy in many cases. We note that there are several hidden issues that make metrics data collection complicated.

For example, if there is no tracking mechanism to determine the source of a software error, then it will be difficult to determine if some portion of the software is more defect prone than others. However, if you believe that this question must be answered in order to meet your stated goals, then you must either collect the data (which will certainly cost money, time, and other resources) or else change your goals for information gathering.

There are a few essentials for collection and analysis of metrics data in support of a systematic process of software reuse:

- Metrics should be collected on the same basis as is typical for the organization, with extensions to be able to record and analyze reuse productivity and cost data.

- Predictive models should use the reuse data, and the observed resource and quality metrics must be compared with the ones that were estimated.

- Metrics that measure quality of the product, such as errors per 1000 source lines of code, perceived readability of source code, and simplicity of control flow, should be computed for each module.

Metrics that measure the process, such as resources expended, percentage of cost savings, and customer satisfaction, should be computed for each module and used as part of an assessment of reuse effectiveness.

1.8.3 Computer-Aided Software Engineering (CASE)

There are many vendors of CASE tools, far too many to discuss here in any detail. There are even more prototype CASE tools currently under development by academic and other research institutions. CASE tools can be complex to use and require a considerable amount of effort to develop.

Commercial CASE tools are often expensive and require extensive training. Why are they so popular?

There are several reasons for this popularity. The most important is that software development is extremely expensive for most organizations and anything that improves efficiency and quality of the software process at reasonable cost is welcome. For many organizations, the cost of software development is so high that nearly any tool that improves productivity, however slightly, is worth its price.

Organizations often wish to provide development environments that are considered cutting edge if they are to be competitive in attracting and retaining good personnel. An examination of the larger display ads for organizations hiring software engineers indicates the emphasis on providing good development environments.

Other reasons for the popularity of CASE tools include the need for a common, consistent view of artifacts at several different phases of the organization's software life cycle. Indeed, the requirements, design, and source code implementation of a project can be much more consistent if they are all stored in a common repository, which checks for such consistency. For the most part, this common repository of several different types of software artifacts is present only in expensive, high-end CASE tools.

There is a wide range of CASE tools. Some simple tools merely aid in the production of good quality diagrams to describe the flow of control of a software system or the flow of data through the software during its execution. Examples of control flow diagrams and data flow diagrams are shown in Figures 1.11 and 1.12, respectively.

The earliest popular graphical designs were called "flowcharts" and were control-flow oriented. The term "control flow" is a method of describing a system by means of the major blocks of code that control its operation. Before the advent of CASE tools, a flowchart was generally drawn by hand using a graphical notation in which control of the program was represented as edges in a directed graph that described the program.

The nodes of a control flow graph are represented by boxes whose shape and orientation provide additional information about the program. For example, a rectangular box with horizontal and vertical sides means that a computational process occurs at this step in the program. Such boxes are often called "action boxes." A diamond-shaped box, with its sides at 45-degree angles with respect to the horizontal direction, is known as a "decision box." A decision box represents a branch in the control flow of a program. Other symbols are used to represent commonly occurring situations in program behavior.

Control flow diagrams indicate the structure of a program's control at the expense of ignoring the movement and transformation of data. This is not surprising, since control flow diagrams were developed initially for use in describing scientific programming applications. Programs whose primary function was to manage data, such as payroll applications, were often represented in a different way, using "data flow diagrams."

Data flow representations of systems were developed somewhat later than control flow descriptions. The books by Yourdon and deMarco are probably the most accessible basic sources for information on data flow design. Most software engineering books contain examples of the use of data flow diagrams in the design of software systems.

Since different data can move along different paths in the program, it is traditional for data flow design descriptions to include the name of the data along the arrows indicating the direction of data movement.

Data flow designs also depend on particular notations to represent different aspects of a system. Here, the arrows indicate a data movement. There are different notations used for different types of data treatment. For example, a node of the graph that represents a transformation of input data into output data according to some set of rules might be represented by a rectangular box in a data flow diagram.

A source of an input data stream, such as interactive terminal input, would be represented by another notation, indicating that it is a "data source." On the other hand, a repository from which data can never be recalled, such as a terminal screen, is described by another symbol, indicating that this is a "data sink."

You might ask at this point how these notations are used to describe larger systems. Certainly the systems you will create as practicing software engineers are much too large to be described on a single page. A flowchart will usually connect to another flowchart by having the action or decision box appear both on the initial page where it occurs and on the additional page where the box is needed.

Typical data flow descriptions of systems use several diagrams at different "levels." Each level of a data flow diagram represents a more detailed view of a portion of the system at a previously described, higher level.

Different data flow diagrams are used to reflect different amounts of detail. For example, a "level 0 data flow diagram" provides insight only into the highest level of the system. Each item in a data flow diagram that reflects a transformation of data or a transaction between system components can be expanded into additional data flow diagrams. Each of these data flow diagrams can, in turn, be expanded into data flow diagrams at different levels until the system description is considered sufficiently clear.

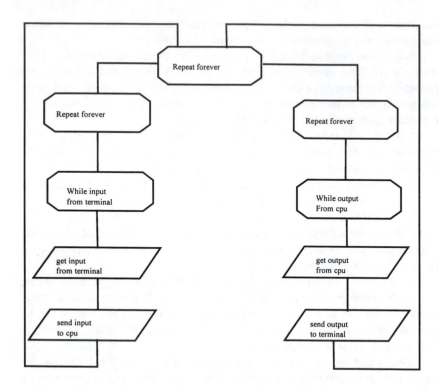

Figure 1.11. An example of a control flow diagram.

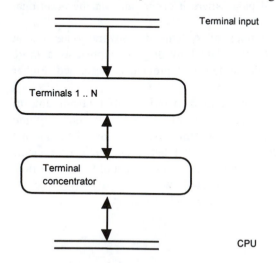

Figure 1.12. An example of a high-level data flow diagram with a data source and a data sink.

Of course, there are other ways to model the behavior of software systems. Many compilers for object-oriented languages such as C++, Eiffel, or Java are part of software development environments that support object modeling. These environments generally allow the user to develop an object model of a system, with the major structure of the objects specified as to the public and private data areas and the operations that can be performed on instances of these objects.

The more elaborate environments include an editor, a drawing tool, and a windowing system that allows the user to view his or her software from many different perspectives. Such advanced environments certainly qualify as CASE tools. An example of a typical advanced software development environment is given in Figure 1.13.

The more advanced software development environments go one step further. An object model created by a user has a description of the public and private data used by an object and the operations that can be performed on the object. The additional step is to allow the generation of frameworks for source code by automatically transferring the information for each object that is stored in the model in a diagram to source code files that describe the object's structure and interfaces. This generated source code can be extended to the creation of complete programs. This code generation is an excellent example of a common CASE tool capability.

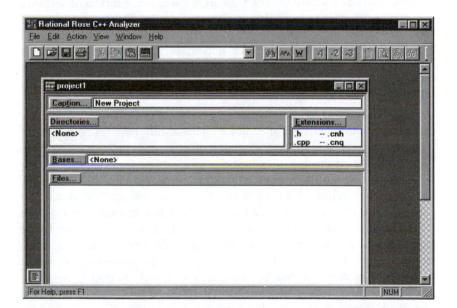

Figure 1.13. An example of a window-based software development environment for an object-oriented system. (From Rational Rose Software opening screen, Rational Software Corporation.)

Many compilation environments include language-sensitive editors that encourage the use of correct language syntax, debuggers to help fix errors in source code, and profilers, which help improve the efficiency of programs by allowing the user to determine the routines that take the largest portion of the program's execution time. These editors, debuggers, and profilers are all CASE tools.

Other tools allow the management of libraries, where several people are working on source code development at the same time. These tools ensure that only one person is working on any particular source code file at the same time. If a source code file is being edited by a software engineer, any request to edit the same document by others is denied access to the file. This technique is called "configuration management." It is an essential part of the software engineering process and is almost always supported by CASE tools.

Clearly CASE tools are pervasive in software engineering. Software development tools have become so popular and inexpensive that many software engineers do not refer to a development tool as a CASE tool unless it is elaborate, expensive, and supports the entire life cycle. We choose to use the term more broadly, in the spirit of the examples described in this subsection.

1.8.4 Cost Estimation

Software cost estimation is both an art and a unique subfield of software engineering. It is far too complex to discuss in detail in any general purpose book on software engineering. We will be content to provide simple rules of thumb and first approximations to determine the cost-benefit ratio of different system design and programming alternatives. The 1981 book by Boehm [BOEH81] is still the best introductory reference to software cost estimation.

The basic idea is to estimate the cost of a software project by comparison with other, similar projects. This in turn requires both a set of "similar" software projects and a method of determining which projects are "similar" to the given one.

In order to determine the cost of projects, a baseline must be established. By the term "baseline," we mean a set of previous projects for which both measurements of size and cost are available. The information obtained from these previously completed projects is stored in a database for future analysis. The baseline information should include the application domain; the size of the project, according to commonly agreed-upon measurements; any special system constraints, such as the system having a real-time response to certain inputs; unusual features of the project, such as being the first time that a new technology, programming language, or software development environment is used; any interoperable software systems that may impact the cost of the software; and, of course, the cost of the software itself. In many organizations, the baseline information may be broken down into the cost of different subsystems.

The determination of "similarity" or "sameness" is made by examining the characteristics of projects in the baseline database and selecting the projects for which information is deemed to be relevant. The effective determination of "similarity" is largely a matter of experience.

Ideally, the cost estimation will be developed in the form of a cost for the system (and each subsystem for which cost estimates are to be made) and an expected range in which the costs are likely to be for the system whose cost is being estimated.

1.8.5 Reviews and Inspections

Different organizations have developed different approaches to ensure that software projects produce useful, correct software. Some techniques appear to work better in certain development environments than others and, thus, there is difficulty in simply adapting one successful approach to a totally different environment.

However, there is one thing that has been shown to be highly successful in every organization in which it is carried out properly – the design review. Reviews should be held at each major milestone of a project, including requirements, design, source code, and test plans. For a software life cycle that uses an iterative process, a review should be held at each iteration of the creation of major items in the life cycle.

The basic idea is simple: each artifact produced for a specific milestone during development must be subjected to a formal review in which all relevant documents are provided; a carefully designed set of questions must be answered; and the results of the review must be written down and disseminated to all concerned parties.

We will describe several kinds of reviews for requirements, design, source code, and test plans. In the sense in which we are using them here, the two terms "review" and "inspection" are synonymous. In the general literature, the term "inspection" may be used in this sense or may instead refer to a procedure for reading the relevant documents.

There is one other point that should be made about reviews and inspections. Throughout this book we will emphasize systematic methods that attempt to determine problems in requirements and design well before the software is reduced to code. This emphasis is consistent with experiences across a wide variety of software projects in nearly every application area.

The "open source" approach of the development of the Linux operating system avoids reviews of requirements and designs and instead relies on the efforts of a large number of programmers who review source code posted on line. Thus, each source code module is reviewed intensively, often by hundreds of programmers. Modifications to the source code are controlled by a much smaller team of experts. Of course, there is also configuration management and testing, just in different order. Consult the article by McConnell [McCO99] for an overview of the open source approach.

1.9 Standards Commonly Used for the Software Development Processes

Many organizations have very specific software development processes in place. These processes are motivated by both organizational experience and the pressures brought on by outside customers from both government and industry. The most common formalized software development processes in the United States are:

- The Capability Maturity Model (CMM) from the Software Engineering Institute (SEI) at Carnegie Mellon University. (Technically, this is not a process, but an evaluation of how systematic an organization's software development process is and a guideline for assessing the possibility of process improvement.)

- The Process Improvement Paradigm (PIP) from the Software Engineering Laboratory (SEL) at NASA's Goddard Space Flight Center. (As with the CMM, technically, this is not a process, but an evaluation of how systematic a software development process is and a guideline for assessing the possibility of process improvement.)

- The Department of Defense standard MIL-STD 2167A

- The Department of Defense standard MIL-STD 1574A

- The Department of Defense standard MIL-STD 882C

- The Electronic Industries Association (EIA) SEB-6-A

Some international standard software development processes include the following:

- The European ESPRIT project

- The International Standards Organization (ISO) standard ISO 9001.

- United Kingdom MOD 0055

Each of these software process models has a heavy emphasis on the collection and use of software metrics to guide the software development process. The models from the SEI and the SEL stress the development of baseline information to measure current software development practice.

These two models can be used with classical waterfall, rapid prototyping, and spiral methodologies of software development. The more rigid standard DOD 2167A is geared primarily towards the waterfall approach, but it, too, is evolving to consider other software development practices.

These are probably the three most common non-proprietary standardized software development processes being used in the United States at the time this book is being written.

We note that all these process models emphasize the importance of software reuse because of its potential for cost savings and quality improvement.

Many private organizations use models based on one of these three. For example, the rating of a software development organization's practice from 1 ("chaotic") to 5 ("optimizing") on the CMM scale is now a factor in the awarding of government contracts in many application domains. The rating is done independently. The reason for rating the development organization's practices is to ensure a high-quality product that is delivered on time and within budget. The details of the CMM scale are given in Table 1.3.

As another example of the importance of software development processes, Bell Communications Research has been using a process assessment tool to evaluate the development procedure of its software subcontractors for many years [BELL89]. An assessment of the subcontractor's software development process is an essential ingredient in the decision to award a contract.

Both Allied Signal Technical Corporation and Computer Sciences Corporation, among others, have an elaborate written manual describing their software development processes. The reference [CSC92] is typical. You should expect that any large software company that you work for will have its own software procedures and will probably have a standards and practices manual.

We note that there are many other software standards that are still being followed to some extent. A recent count of standards activities of the IEEE indicates 35 distinct standards in the area of software engineering at the end of 1995. One of the most important IEEE standards is number P610.12(R), which is entitled "Standard Glossary for Software Engineering."

Any introductory book on the topic of software engineering would be incomplete if it did not mention the cleanroom software development process. This process was developed initially at IBM by Harlan Mills and his colleagues. The cleanroom process is described in detail in the reference [MILL87].

The goal of the cleanroom process is to produce software without errors by never introducing them in the first place. The term "cleanroom" was chosen to evoke images of the clean rooms used for manufacture of silicon wafers or computer chips. The workers in such rooms wear white gowns to reduce the possibility of introducing contaminants into their product. In the cleanroom approach, any errors in software are considered to have arisen from a flawed development process.

Table 1.3
Description of the Levels of the Capability Maturity Model (CMM) Developed by the Software Engineering Institute (SEI).

Level 5 (Optimizing process level)
The major characteristic of this level is continuous improvement. Specifically, the software development organization has quantitative feedback systems in place to identify process weakness and strengthen them proactively. Project teams analyze defects to determine their causes; software processes are evaluated and updated to prevent known types of defects from recurring.

Level 4 (Managed process level)
The major characteristic of this level is predictability. Specifically, detailed software process and product quality metrics are used to establish the quantitative evaluation foundation. Meaningful variations in process performance can be distinguished from random noise, and trends in process and product qualities can be predicted.

Level 3 (Defined process level)
The major characteristic of this level is a standard and consistent process. Specifically, processes for management and engineering are documented, standardized, and integrated into a standard software process for the organization. All projects use an approved, tailored version of the organization's standard software process for developing software.

Level 2 (Repeatable process level)
The major characteristic of this level is that previous experience provides intuition that guides software development. Specifically, basic management processes are established to track cost, schedule, and functionality. Planning and managing new products is based on experience with similar projects.

Level 1 (Initial process level)
The major characteristics of this level are that the software development process is largely ad-hoc. Specifically, few processes are defined, and success depends more on individual heroic efforts than on following a process and using a synergistic team effort. (The term "chaotic" is often used to describe software development processes with these characteristics.)

Source: Software Engineering Institute

The major technique of the cleanroom process is to use mathematical reasoning about correctness of program functions and procedures. The idea is to create the source code with such care that there is no need for testing. Rigorous mathematical reasoning and very formal code reviews are both integral parts of the cleanroom process.

We will indicate in Chapter 6 that the purpose of software testing is to uncover errors in the software, not to show that the software has no errors. The practitioners of the cleanroom approach believe that their approach may be more conducive to the goal of the software development process: producing error-free software.

We will not discuss the cleanroom approach any further in this book. Instead, our limited emphasis on the role of mathematics in software engineering will be restricted largely to reliability theory and a brief mention of some other formal development methods that we will discuss in Chapters 2 and 3.

1.10 The Year 2000 Problem and Similar Problems

We mentioned the Year 2000 Problem in Section 1.7. The situation seems innocuous: many computer programs represented dates using two integers and the year 2000 will require a new interpretation of these existing dates. Why is this problem so important? There are really two parts to the answer: the size of the problem as understood by the organizations that either use software or are responsible for it, and the hidden problems, whose scope can only be guessed at. We will discuss the Y2K problem in more detail before we attempt to answer these questions.

If a database were set up with precise field widths for representation of dates, a movement of all other data fields to make room might cause serious problems in system performance because blocks of data might not be aligned to blocks of memory, causing performance problems. The problem gets worse, because every backup or archive tape must also be changed.

However, the database example described in the previous paragraph is simple compared to other problems that might be hidden. Consider the case of control software for a nuclear reactor. As was pointed out by Richard Lefkon, most recently in the October 1997 issue of *Software* magazine, software that removes a control rod at 10 P.M. on December 31 and is to reinsert this rod three hours later is highly dependent on the correct interpretation of dates and times. Waiting for 100 years to pass is simply not an acceptable solution. This is an example of a hidden instance of the Y2K problem.

How big is the problem? Again we quote from the October 1997 issue of *Software*, which provided three estimates of the size of the problem for the United States (private and government):

Gartner Group	$200 billion
Software Productivity Research	$70 billion
Society for Information Management	$136.4 billion

These estimates are large because the Y2K problem is not confined to databases that are housed on mainframes. Many devices are affected by this problem, not just the types of computer applications that come to mind at first glance. Consider the potential for having problems in the so-called "embedded processors" that are so common in everyday life. What about automatic speed control in your car or in an airplane? Does a problem in a date or time calculation affect the operation of such vehicles?

The popular literature has not provided complete coverage of the Y2K problem. Much of the media coverage has focused on large mainframe systems and has not addressed issues in microprocessors. The problem for embedded microprocessors is related to Moore's Law:

"Computing power doubles approximately every eighteen months."

A related idea is that the amount of code that is placed in an embedded microprocessor doubles in approximately the same time. This means that the same date field size limitations that affect mainframes also affect embedded microprocessors.

As this book is being written, I am the coordinator for a Y2K project team with ten members. Fortunately this team has responsibility for only a small portion of the local effort: a few hundred computers, a reasonable collection of routers and hubs, perhaps fifteen laboratories with embedded microprocessors, a few associated robots, and some process control equipment. We are concerned about our data communications because of some known problems with routers. Our security locks and automated HVAC (heating, ventilation, and air conditioning) systems are also at risk.

Clearly, the problem is huge and hard to estimate. Note that these numbers are only estimates, and that any action taken to solve the Y2K problem will have to be in addition to the other demands for the development of new software. The most important and depressing aspect of the Y2K problem is that the solution will require considerable resources, with no advancement in technology or new functionality of the software affected by the problem.

We will meet the Year 2000 Problem several times throughout this book. Unfortunately, the Y2K problem is only one of many such problems that are guaranteed to occur within the lifetimes of my children and grandchildren (are you listening, John, Anne, and David?). All these problems have at least one thing in common: a design decision to allocate only a limited amount of space for data storage will cause huge problems when this limited amount of space is exceeded.

The most serious of these problems caused by overflowing inadequate resource limitations are listed below in the order of their likely occurrence:

- The Global Positioning System (GPS) is highly dependent on accurate timing information for determining position. Portions of the date calculations are measured in the number of weeks since January 5, 1980, when GPS was first deployed. Arithmetic computations with the weeks in a date are done in modular arithmetic modulo 1024, and there will be a changeover from 1023 to 0 in August 1999.

- The number of telephone numbers that can be stored in ten digits (3 for the area code and 7 for the local number) is likely to be exhausted in the United States in approximately 2015.

- The date and time mechanism in the UNIX operating system is based on the number of seconds that have elapsed since January 1, 1970. The number of seconds is stored in a 32-bit integer, which will overflow on January 19, 2038.

- The number of nine-digit Social Security numbers is likely to be exhausted in the United States in approximately the time period from 2050 to 2075.

Two other problems will occur during the next few years. The European Monetary Union began conversion to the Euro in January 1999. Obviously, this involved transformation of currency representations for new transactions. Unfortunately, this will also involve reevaluating existing data in order to apply long-range financial models for economic projections. There have even been some problems in adding the symbol for this currency to the set of available fonts for many word processors.

The second problem will occur on February 29, 2000. The year 2000 is a leap year for the following reasons:

1. The number 2000 passes the first test of being evenly divisible by 4.
2. The usual proviso that a year divisible by 100 is not a leap year is superceded by the fact that 2000 is also divisible by the number 400.

The second step in determining that 2000 is a leap year may not have been implemented correctly in date calculations.

1.11 Organization of the Book

Each of the major phases of the software development life cycle will be covered in detail in a separate chapter. Beginning with Chapter 3, each of the chapters will consider a relatively large project that will be continued throughout the book.

The purpose of considering the same project throughout the book is to eliminate the effects of different decisions for the requirements, design, and coding of software. Some of the source code and documentation will be given explicitly in the book itself. However, most of the rest will be available only in electronic form.

As you will learn, there are many non-programming activities necessary in software engineering. Some of these activities require cost estimation, or data collection and analyses. Spreadsheet forms have been included to illustrate typical industry practices and to provide you with experience.

Each chapter will include one or more sections that provide typical views of software managers on the relevant technical activities. The purpose of the "managerial view" is to provide you with additional perspective on software engineering, not to prepare you to be a manager. In most organizations, a considerable amount of varied project experience is essential before a person is given a managerial position at any level.

Further Reading

There are many excellent books on software engineering, including ones by Ghezzi, Mandiroli, and Jayazerri [GHEZ91], Jalote [JALO91], Pfleeger [PFLE91], Shooman [SHOO83], Sommerville [SOMM92], and Pressman [PRES92]. The book by Boehm [BOEH81] provides a good overview of software engineering economics. Fenton and Pfleeger [FENT96] provide a detailed, rigorous description of software metrics. Beizer [BEIZ83], [BEIZ90], Howden [HOWD87] and Myers [MYER79] provide excellent introductions to software testing. An excellent introduction to the Cleanroom process can be found in [MILL87].

The 1978 paper by Ritchie and Thompson [RITC78] provides both an overview of the extremely successful UNIX operating system and an insight into the design decisions that were used.

Information on computer languages can be found in many places. The Ada language is described best in [ADA83], [ICHB86], and [ADA95]. The rationale for the original description of C++ is given in [STRO94] and a detailed language manual is described in the book by Ellis and Stroustrup [ELLI90]. The original description of C by Kernighan and Ritchie was given in [KERN82], with the second edition [KERN88] describing the ANSI C features. There are many other excellent books on various computer languages.

Nielsen [NIEL94] and Schneiderman [SCHN80] provide excellent overviews of human computer interaction. A brief introduction to the role of color in user interfaces can be found in the article [WRIG97]. The older paper by Miller [MILL86] provides good empirical justification for limiting the number of choices available to system users. It is especially relevant to a designer of a computer system's menu structure.

An excellent overview of the Year 2000 Problem (and related problems) can be found in an article by Capers Jones in the September 1998 issue of IEEE Spectrum [JONE98].

The article by Cusumano and Selby [CUSU97] provides an excellent overview of some current software development practices at Microsoft.

The paper by Basili and Rombach [BASI88] is a good introduction to the GQM paradigm. Finally, the book by Leach [LEAC96a] is a good introduction to software reuse.

Summary

Software engineering is the application of good engineering practice to produce high-quality software in an efficient manner. Good software engineering practice can reduce the number of problems that occur in software development. The goal of software engineering is to develop software that is efficient, reliable, usable, modifiable, portable, testable, reusable, easy to maintain, and can interact properly with other systems. Most importantly, the software should be correct in the sense of meeting both its specifications and the true wishes of the user.

The goals of software engineering include efficiency, reliability, usability, modifiability, portability, testability, reusability, maintainability, interoperability, and correctness. In support of these goals, software engineering involves many activities:

- Analysis
- Requirements
- Design
- Coding
- Testing and integration
- Installation and delivery
- Documentation
- Maintenance
- Quality assurance
- Training

Project management is essential to coordinate all these activities.

There are several common models of the software development process. In the classical waterfall process model, the requirements; design; coding; testing and integration; delivery and installation; and maintenance steps follow in sequence, with feedback only to the previous step. In the rapid prototyping and spiral development models, the software is developed iteratively, with customer or user feedback given on intermediate systems before a final system is produced.

A disciplined software engineering approach is necessary, regardless of the application domain: development for the Internet, personal computer applications, and health- or safety-critical applications. The risk analysis that is typically part of any engineering activity might have prevented the Year 2000 Problem from occurring.

The use of high-level programming languages can increase programmer productivity. However, reusing high-quality software components can have a greater effect.

Exercises

1. Consider the largest software project you ever completed as part of a class assignment. How large was the project? How long did it take you to develop the system? Did it work perfectly, did it work most of the time, or did it fail the simplest test cases?

2. Repeat question 1 for software that you wrote as part of a job working in industry or government.

3. Examine the classified advertisements of your local newspaper for listings of jobs in the computer field. Classify each of the jobs as being for analysis, requirements, design, coding, testing and integration, installation and delivery, documentation, maintenance, quality assurance, or training.

4. If you have a part-time (or full-time) job in the computer field, ask to see your employer's software development manual. Determine which software development process standard is followed by your employer.

5. We mentioned several software development process standards in this chapter. Find one or more of these in the library or on the Internet. Examine the details of the standard. Can you explain why they are necessary?

6. Examine a relatively large software system that you did not develop yourself and for which source code is available. Can you tell anything about the several software development process standards used in this software from an examination of the source code? Why or why not?

7. We discussed some issues about the role of networking in the future development of word processors. There are other issues, such as the responsibility of system administrators responsible for software updates. Discuss the effect of the four options given in Section 1.1 from the perspective of system administrators.

Chapter 2

Project Management

In this chapter, we will discuss some of the issues involved with project management. As was pointed out in Chapter 1, most of the discussion of this topic will appear quite remote from the experience of a beginning software engineer. It is difficult to communicate the complexity of software project management to a person who has not been part of a multi-person software project in government or industry. Nevertheless, it is useful for every software engineering student to have at least an introduction to those software engineering activities that are typically associated with group projects. Therefore, we will present a high-level view of project management in this chapter. The intention is to introduce the subject, not to create instant experts. Keep in mind the point we have made several times before: most modern software development is done by teams.

Many of the most successful software companies, especially the ones that have achieved almost overnight successes, appear to take considerable risks in the sense that they produce software that performs a task or solves a problem that might not have been considered for a computer solution before the software was created. Software intended for word processing, spreadsheet analysis, or the Internet itself, with its collection of browsers and search engines, were clearly revolutionary breakthroughs. As such, they were considered risky investments until they achieved some success. All so-called "killer apps" have this feature. Risk is inherent in most software engineering endeavors.

Keep in mind, however, that an organization whose existence depends upon the success of its products must take a systematic approach to management of its software projects. This approach must be more systematic than would be necessary for a student who is working on a simple class project that may require only one person or, at most, a small group of classmates. Software project management should attempt to reduce the risk in the way that the software project follows a schedule and is developed efficiently according to reasonable software engineering standards for quality and productivity.

The primary goal of this chapter is to introduce project management issues in sufficient detail so that you can understand the organizational culture when you begin your career as a software engineer. Different organizations will have different software development processes and will structure their software development teams accordingly. However, each project will have a manager who will have to deal with many issues.

There is one final point to be made about project management. Most formal software development processes that are described in the software engineering literature are directly applicable to very large software systems written for a single customer, such as the government.

There are many modifications necessary to apply some of the more formal of these processes in an environment that is highly market driven. Such development environments have a high degree of concurrency, with many activities, such as coding, design, requirements analysis, and testing taking place at the same time in order to meet very tight delivery schedules. In this chapter, we will also discuss some of the issues that affect software development in such market-driven environments.

2.1 Sub-Teams Needed in Software Engineering Projects

It is clear that the systematic development of large, modern software projects requires teams. It is often helpful to think of a software project team as being made up of several "sub-teams." These sub-teams need not be as formally constituted as they are here and, in fact, some of them will consist of a single person in many cases. However, the team's activities still need to be performed, regardless of the overall team organization.

We note that several of these sub-teams are not likely to be in existence during the entire lifetime of the software project. For some software projects, one or more of the teams may consist of a single person whose duties may be split among several projects or activities. In other projects, the teams may be very large and geographically separated. Team members may even report to different companies in some of the larger cooperative software development projects.

Some typical software engineering sub-teams and their duties follow:

- Systems Analysis Team: This team is responsible for determining if the project is feasible. The feasibility study includes cost analysis, estimated revenues, and an estimate of the difficulty of engineering the project. After they produce the feasibility study, this team should interact with the Requirements Team, receiving its feedback. If the software development process is iterative, as in the rapid prototyping and spiral models, then the interaction and feedback should be more frequent and may occur with additional sub-teams.

- Planning Team: This team is responsible for developing the overall management plan for the project and making sure that the project is proceeding within the expected time frame for various activities.

- Requirements Team: The duties of this team are to meet with the customer and determine a complete, precise set of requirements for this project. This will require a set of formal and informal meetings with the customer to finalize the requirements from relatively imprecise and incomplete initial requirements. If no customer is available, then the requirements team is to obtain the same information from one or more potential users. If no potential users are available, then surrogate customers may be used in their place. After they produce the system's requirements, this team should interact with the Design Team, receiving its feedback. If the software development process is iterative, as in the rapid prototyping and spiral models, then the interaction and feedback should be more frequent and may occur with additional sub-teams.

- System Design Team: The duties of this team will be to produce a detailed design of the system after the requirements are set by the Requirements Team. If the software development process uses the classical waterfall model, then they should provide feedback to the Requirements Team about any difficulties encountered. After they produce the design, this team should interact with the Implementation Team, receiving its feedback. If the software development process is iterative, as in the rapid prototyping and spiral models, then the interaction and feedback should be more frequent and may occur with additional sub-teams.

- Implementation Team: The duties of this team will be to implement the software designed by the System Design Team. After they produce the implementation, this team should interact with the Testing and Integration Team, receiving its feedback. If the software development process is iterative, as in the rapid prototyping and spiral models, then the interaction and feedback should be more frequent and may occur with additional sub-teams.

- Testing and Integration Team: The duties of this team are the formulation of test cases for the modules and systems that are created by the implementation team. This team may take some modules from an incomplete system for testing by mutual agreement with the Implementation Team. After they produce the test plan and test the software modules produced, this team will integrate the software modules into a working system. This team should interact with the Implementation Team, receiving its feedback. If the software development process is iterative, as in the rapid prototyping and spiral models, then the interaction and feedback should be more frequent and may also occur with additional sub-teams. The Integration Team is responsible for an Interface Control Document (ICD) that describes precisely the interfaces between major system components.

- Training Team: This team is responsible for the development and production of training materials.

- Delivery and Installation Team: This team is responsible for the delivery and installation of the software.

- Maintenance Team: This team is responsible for the maintenance of the software after it is delivered and installed. After the system is delivered and installed, this team should interact with the Implementation Team, receiving its feedback. If the software development process is iterative, as in the rapid prototyping and spiral models, then the interaction and feedback should be more frequent and may occur with additional sub-teams.

- Quality Assurance Team: This team has two duties. The first is to set standards for the adherence of the project team to a set of agreed-upon processes for the system's creation and set standards for performance of the software produced. The second is to provide an evaluation of how well the project teams meet those standards. Standard industry practice is for the information obtained by this team to be kept internal and not shared with the customer. The information can be released in the event of a legal action and, thus, cannot be destroyed. This information is to be presented to the project manager who will use it to evaluate performance of the QA Team.

- Metrics Team: This team is responsible for keeping statistics on the performance of the teams on the project. Depending on the organization's data collection procedures, some typical statistics kept might be: number of maintenance requests generated, number of maintenance requests serviced, number of lines of code written, number of hours performed on each task, values produced by the tool on each new version of the system. This team will interact with the Requirements, Design, Implementation, Testing and Integration, and Maintenance Teams, providing assessments of quality and efficiency, as well as feedback to these sub-teams.

- Documentation Team: This team is responsible for the project documentation. This includes external documentation of the requirements, design, source code, and other supporting documents.

- System Administration Team: This team is responsible for ensuring that the underlying computer hardware, software, and network support are working as needed by the project team. This team often includes the Network Administration Team.

- Reuse and Reengineering Team: This team is responsible for selection and use of appropriate existing reusable software components. Reengineering may be necessary if the software project depends upon some old code that must be changed because of new advances in technology.

Not surprisingly, there are several managerial tasks involved here, one for each sub-team. Of course, if the teams are small enough, a manager may be one of the technical members of the team (or even the only team member).

The tasks listed above are part of most software projects. Therefore, it is reasonable to ask how they are scheduled. Of course, the scheduling of these tasks is highly dependent on the software life cycle model used by the project.

For example, a software development process based on the waterfall model might have the tasks incorporated into the process as shown in Figure 2.1. You will be asked to produce similar diagrams for the rapid prototyping and spiral software development models in the exercises.

The plan for market-driven software development is interesting. The entire process is compressed, at least in comparison to the classical waterfall process. The steps usually include the following:

- Determination of the market for the product
- Requirements determination
- Combined design and coding
- Testing and integration
- Delivery

At first glance, the process seems similar to others, except for the grouping of the design and implementation phases. The easiest way to see the difference is to consider the milestones that are typical in market-driven software development.

In this model, planning the product's requirements and its marketing are often done in concert. The planning interval rarely exceeds five years and is often much shorter. The goal is to have a project plan that results in a product that the marketing and sales teams can sell. Since technology is changing so fast, longer development periods are not acceptable.

Usability testing is often included in the design and early implementation phase. This is before the detailed testing phase begins.

The delivery process often includes determination of minimal, typical, and maximal installations, together with an installation suite that can select components depending on the user's desires. The software may be packaged in academic, regular, or professional versions, each of which has a different set of incorporated components or system configuration parameters and, therefore, different installation procedures.

In the highly competitive global economy, the product may be shipped to countries where the native language is not English. This means new versions of on-line help and manuals. It may also mean a different configuration of such things as the built-in security, since the United States government does not allow 128-bit encryption to be exported.

You should note that there are several technical tasks that must be performed in addition to the tasks listed above. The persons performing these tasks are often given official or unofficial titles such as the ones given on the next pages. Even without particular titles, software engineers often have to account for the percentage of their time that is spent on particular activities. This time accounting is often necessary to determine the cost of individual projects.

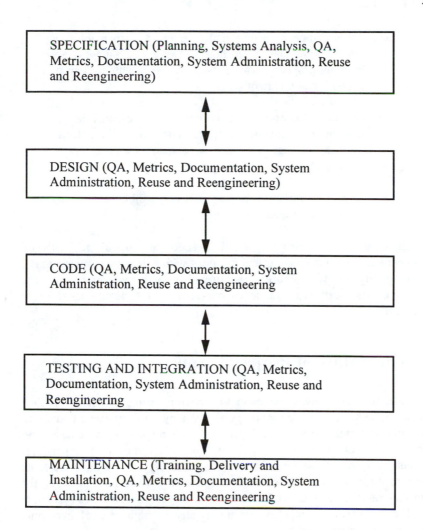

Figure 2.1. Incorporation of basic software engineering tasks into a simplified illustration of the classical waterfall life cycle model.

- Human-Computer Interface Evaluator: This person is responsible for evaluating the type of interaction between the software system and users. At the very least, he or she must have a mental model of the expected skills of both novice and experienced users of the final software product.

- Tools Support Person: This person is responsible for making sure that supporting software environments are working properly. This person will work with system or network administrators.

- Software Economist: This person is responsible for development and use of appropriate models in order to estimate software costs, hardware and software resources, and the time needed for project completion.

- Project Librarian: This person is responsible for keeping track of all project documents.

There may be other personnel needed in specialized software development environments, particularly ones with extensive software reuse. For simplicity, we will ignore these specialists and concentrate on those responsibilities most likely to be encountered by the beginning software engineer.

2.2 The Nature of Project Teams

In typical classroom environments in an academic setting, a software project is done by either one person working alone or by a small team of students. The student teams work together on the same project for a semester or, occasionally, for an entire year. There is little turnover in upper-level computer science courses and, hence, it is relatively easy to have the same teams in class projects. In real-world software development projects, the teams are rarely kept together for the entire life cycle of a software system.

There are several reasons for the relatively high rate of personnel changes in software projects:

- Project staffing needs change. More people may be needed to work during the coding or testing and integration phases than are needed for the initial requirements gathering activity. Often, fewer people are needed for maintenance, especially if the system is expected to have a short life.

- The project may continue for a long period. For example, NASA's International Ultraviolet Explorer satellite was expected to produce scientific data for one year and, thus, the original software maintenance team was expected to work for one year after the satellite was placed into orbit.

Instead, the satellite's scientific life lasted for 19 years, producing as much scientific data and subsequent research in its last year of operation as it did in its first. Clearly, there were many changes in project personnel during this time. Several well-known database systems have been in operation for more than 30 years. Keeping the same level of staffing as in the initial development is extremely wasteful.

- People change jobs. Many software engineers prefer to be associated with new technology and leave projects after the technology used ceases to be cutting edge.

- Contracts are lost by companies. Many organizations merge and business units are refocused. In an extreme case, companies go out of business. If a company was working on a project as a subcontractor which is now defunct, the project team will change.

- People retire or have major illnesses.

- New people are hired to bring fresh ideas and new technology skills into organizations.

It is clear that most real-world projects have numerous changes in their personnel during their lifetimes.

Now that you understand that the composition of project teams often will change considerably over the life of a project, you might consider the ramifications of this relative instability for your own career as a software engineer. Clearly, you will need to be flexible, because different individuals have different learning styles and you will have to interact with many of these different styles over time.

For instance, you might be paired with an individual who always follows the written company policies to the letter, refusing to submit any organization-supplied form unless the sentences are grammatically correct. Another person on the project will use shortcuts, writing phrases and sentence fragments where the other might write formal, proper sentences. Both approaches might be very effective for the person who uses them and you might have to interact with each type of individual. Of course, the final deliverable product will have to be grammatically correct and adhere to the organization's standards.

It is important to accommodate different personality and learning styles within a group and to avoid what James McCarthy of Microsoft called "flipping the bozo bit." [MCC95] This colorful term refers to assessing a person's opinions and suggestions as being irrelevant, because the person is a "bozo," and hence their "bozo bit" is flipped (set to one). Be receptive to all ideas and consider them as being potentially reasonable, regardless of the source of the idea. This will help make you a valuable team member and make your team work better.

It is important to understand the differences between organizational cultures. Some organizations follow a rigid process, demanding that all procedures be carried out and all decisions be documented carefully. An individual who does not follow the organization's procedures precisely often will be ignored or given less-demanding work.

Other organizations have much less formal structure in their process. They often give software development teams only the most general guidelines, with almost complete freedom to perform the essential activities. This freedom occurs most often when the team has a history of completing its projects successfully and within budget. A recent paper by Mandl et al [MAND98] describes an effective software development team that used relatively few formal procedures, but was able to produce actual systems. It should be noted that this team had many years of experience in this application domain.

You should make the distinction yourself in the kind of organization you wish to work for, in order to match your temperament with the organizational development style that is right for you.

2.3 Project Management

The term "project management" refers to the coordination of people, resources, and schedules that are necessary to successfully produce a software product that is of high quality, is delivered within the allotted time period, and is within budget.

Suppose that you were assigned to direct a project whose goal was to develop a particular software system. You would want the project to be a success and so you would try to assemble the best team available. You would want the team to have proper equipment and any software development tools that were appropriate. You would need to know about any other software systems that your software must be interoperable with. You would need to be able to predict when the project would be completed and what the total cost might be.

It is clear that the first task of a project manager is the estimation of the size and complexity of the project. These estimates are necessary in order for the manager to obtain the proper amount of resources for the project. We will discuss software project estimation in Section 2.4.

Once you have determined the resources that are needed for the project, you will develop a schedule. The schedule will contain dates for starting and completing activities that are considered to be essential. These accomplishments are often called "milestones." Since the milestone events might require different levels of effort, different phases of the project might have different demand for resources. Certain project activities might require almost no effort. We will discuss software project scheduling in Section 2.5.

At this point, the project manager has planned the project's resources and schedule. He or she may have had pressure to create the schedule or resource list, but in any event some planning and thoughtful work went into this effort. Unfortunately, many other project activities do not involve the luxury of planning and, instead, can only react to situations that arise.

We illustrate this point below. The rest of the project management activities generally consists of many things, including, but not limited to:

- Managing people
- Allocating resources
- Motivating project personnel
- Dealing with inevitable slippage in the schedule
- Handling changes in the project's requirements
- Reacting to unexpected events such as computer crashes
- Informing upper-level management about problems and successes
- Ensuring that major milestone events have proper reviews
- Interacting with the prospective customer

If a project manager only reacts to crises, as appears to be the case, then there is no time to be "proactive;" that is, to take actions that may head off problems rather than simply react to the "problem du jour."

One of a project manager's major tasks is motivation of the project team. In industry or government, the motivation can be promotions, salary increases, bonuses, or simply praise and recognition. (The absence of such rewards in academic projects is a major reason that such projects are often considered toys. The size of projects and the academic calendar limitations are other contributors to this presumed unreality.)

One thing missing from the above list is any form of continuing education for the managers themselves. Such education involves keeping up with current trends in project management both within the manager's organization and in the outside world. Assuming that the project manager wishes to advance his or her career, he or she may take continuing education or other courses and seminars.

In short, project managers are very busy. You should not expect a great amount of mentoring from a manager with responsibility for multiple projects or a large number of software engineers. There simply is not enough time.

2.4 Software Project Estimation

Software project estimation is part of the general systems engineering process that takes place when a project is planned. It is always a part of major software projects for one basic reason: no reasonable person or organization would begin a large project without some belief that the project can be done with the resources that the person or organization is willing to commit to the project. Clearly, some form of project estimation is necessary. In this section, we will provide some additional details that will extend the discussion begun in section 1.6.4.

Any project will need most of the following resources, with many people, computers, or software performing multiple duties in very small projects or organizations:

- Computers for software development
- Basic software for development such as compilers or linkers
- Methods of communicating between computers such as networks
- CASE tools
- Software packages with which the system must be interoperable
- Computers for testing
- Computers for training
- Documentation tools
- Copying devices
- Programmers
- Testers
- Managers
- Designers
- Requirements engineers

Note that projects of moderate size or larger may require multiple instances of each resource, software tools, such as CASE tools or configuration management systems. In fact, every software team duty mentioned earlier in this chapter would have to be counted as a resource requirement of the project.

We have used the term "size" informally in this section. Determination of the actual size of a project is a non-trivial matter and we will return to it several times. For now, we will simply say that the size of a project is the number of lines of source code created by the organization in order to develop a project. We further simplify the discussion by stating that a line of code is any line in a program that is neither blank nor consists only of comments. (Better definitions of the term "line of code" will be given later in this book.)

Understanding what is meant by the size of an existing system and being able to quantify this size in a consistent manner are absolutely essential if we expect to estimate the size of new systems. Thus, we will turn our attention temporarily to the subject of measuring the size of a software system.

Of course, the measurement of software system size can be very difficult. We can illustrate this difficulty by this example: suppose you write a program 100 lines long that writes its output to a data file. Suppose the data file is then imported into a spreadsheet and that the spreadsheet you created uses the spreadsheet's built-in statistical routines, which are then exported to another file which contains the final result. How big is the system?

Is it the 100 lines of code that you wrote? Is it the 500,000 lines of code that make up the spreadsheet (plus the 100 lines you wrote)? Is it the number of lines you wrote (100) plus the size of the code you entered into your spreadsheet program? The difficulty in measuring software system size requires precise definitions. Is it the number of lines you wrote (100) plus the size of the data output that is written to the spreadsheet?

Unfortunately, there are few standards that are common throughout the software industry. We will return to this point several times in this book when we discuss software metrics. For now, we will just consider the number of lines of code as the measure of the size of a software system and ignore exactly how the number of lines of code was computed.

There is a rule of thumb that says 10,000 is approximately the largest amount of lines of source code that a good software engineer who is experienced in both the application area and the programming language used can understand completely. Let's use this number to estimate the size of a team that would be needed for software development of various sizes. (An assessment of a smaller number as the maximum that anyone can understand would increase the number of software engineers needed, while a larger number would decrease this number.) For simplicity, we will assume that all source code for the project is created by the team. We have summarized the results in Table 2.1.

Note that there are many software projects in each of the larger size ranges. For example, the typical word processor software for a modern personal computer consists of at least 500,000 lines of code. As stated before, Microsoft Excel consists of more than 1.2 million lines of code. The project to revise the United States air traffic control system, which was terminated recently, was expected to consist of well over 10,000,000 lines of code.

Table 2.1
An unrealistically optimistic view of the relationship between the size of a software project in new lines of code vs. the number of programmers on development teams.

Lines of new code	Approximate Number of Software Engineers
5,000	1
10,000	1
20,000	2
50,000	5
100,000	10
200,000	20
500,000	50
1,000,000	100
2,000,000	200
5,000,000	500
10,000,000	1,000
10,000,000	10,000

Unfortunately, the numbers shown in Table 2.1 greatly underestimate the number of people needed for software projects. There are several reasons for this:

- Not all programmers can understand systems at the level of 10,000 lines of code.

- Larger systems mean that the programmers developing the software must be physically separated, on different floors of the same building, in different buildings, different locations, or even in different countries. There is no way for the informal, one-on-one discussions that can solve problems quickly to occur as spontaneously as in a smaller environment.

- Coordination of efforts is essential. This means many meetings, many managers to coordinate meetings, many support personnel to install, maintain, and configure the computers and software needed to support this project. it is extremely rare for a software manager to coordinate more than 20 people, with 8-10 people a much more realistic number.

- The number of middle-level managers increases exponentially with the size of the project. For a small team, one manager might suffice. For a larger team, there may be a first-level software manager for every 8-10 people, a second-level manager for every 8-10 first level managers, and so on. These managers are essential for coordination of efforts and to ensure that one group's changes to a system are localized to their group and don't affect other efforts of the project. Even a flatter organizational structure with more so-called "programmers" and fewer middle-level managers must develop higher levels of administration as the project size gets larger.

- The project team rarely stays together for the duration of a project. Every organization has turnover. There is often an influx of new personnel just out of school ("fresh-outs") who need training in the organization's software standards and practices.

- There are many other activities that are necessary for successful software development. There must be agreement on the requirements in the software being developed. The code must be tested, both at the small module level and at the larger system level. The system must be documented. The system must be maintained.

There are other activities, of course. Higher-level management wants to spend its resources wisely. It wants to know if projects are on schedule and within budget. It does not want to be surprised by last-minute disasters. Ideally, higher-level management wants feedback on process improvement that can make the organization more competitive. Feedback and reporting often require the collection of many measurements, as well as one or more individuals to evaluate the data obtained by these measurements. Project demonstrations must be given and these require careful preparation.

How much of a software engineering project's total effort is devoted to source code? The answer varies slightly from organization to organization and project to project, but most experienced software managers report that development of the source code only takes about fifteen percent of the total effort. This appears to be constant across all sizes of organizations. People who write source code in very small organizations may have to spend much of their time marketing their company's products.

The need for these extra activities suggests a more realistic view of a software team's size, which we present in Table 2.2. We assume that five percent of a programmer's time is spent on measurements, twenty percent of their time is spent on meetings, reporting progress (or explaining the lack of it), and the other activities: requirements, design, testing, documentation, delivery, maintenance, etc. We also assume that programmers have difficulty understanding 5,000 lines of code, much less 10,000.

Table 2.2
A somewhat more realistic view of the relationship between the size of a software project and the number of people employed on the project.

Lines of new code	Approximate Number of Software Engineers
5,000	7
10,000	14
20,000	27
50,000	77
100,000	144
200,000	288
500,000	790
1,000,000	1,480
2,000,000	3,220
5,000,000	8,000
10,000,000	15,960
100,000,000	160,027

It is clear from Table 2.2 that some of the very largest projects require international efforts. The reality is, unless you work for a software organization whose primary activities are training, hardware maintenance, system configuration, or technical support as a part of customer service, most of your work in the software industry will be as a member of a team.

There is one final point to make on this issue. As measured by the number of new lines of code produced, the productivity of the typical programmer has not increased greatly in the last 35 years and is still in the neighborhood of a few documented, tested lines of code written per hour. Yet software systems have increased tremendously in complexity and size, without requiring all an organization's, or even a nation's, resources. How is this possible?

There are two primary reasons for the improvements that have been made in the ability to develop modern complex software systems. The first is the increase in abstraction and expressive power of modern high-level languages over pure assembly language. The second is the leveraging of previous investment by reusing existing software when new software is being developed.

The code of Example 2.1 is a good illustration of of the productivity gained by using high-level languages. It also illustrates how different people view the size of a software system.

Example 2.1
A simple example to illustrate line counting.

```
#include <stdio.h>

main()
{
int i;

for (i = 0; i < 10; i++)
    printf(" %d\n" , i);
}
```

The code source consists of 9 lines, 16 words, and 84 characters according to the UNIX wc utility. The assembly language code generated for the HP-UX operating system consisted of 49 lines, 120 words, and 1659 characters. The true productivity, as measured by the functionality produced, was improved by a factor of 49/9, or 5.44, by using a higher-level language. This number illustrates the effect of the higher-level language. We note that the productivity is even greater than 5.44 when we consider the advantage of reusing the previously written printf() function.

Reuse is even more effective when entire applications can be reused. It is obviously more efficient to use an existing database package than to redevelop the code to insert, delete, and manage the database. An entire application reused without change is called off-the-shelf; the most common occurrence is the use of commercial-off-the-shelf (COTS) software to manage databases, spreadsheets, or similar.

There are several components to a systematic approach to software project estimation:

- Resources must be estimated, preferably with some verifiable measurement.
- An "experience database" describing the histories of the resources used for previous projects should be created.

We address each of these issues in turn.

The first step in resource estimation is predicting the size of the project. The beginning software engineer often wonders how project size is estimated. The most common approach is to reason by analogy. If the system to be developed appears to be similar to other systems with which the project manager is familiar, then the manager can use the previous experiences of the managers for those projects to estimate the resources for the current project. This approach requires that the other "similar" projects are similar enough that their actual resource needs are relevant to the current project. The less familiar a particular project is, the less likely that a manager will be able to estimate its size by reasoning by analogy.

The reasoning-by-analogy approach also involves determining the actual resource needs of the other "similar" projects. This can only be done if the information is readily available in an experience database. An experience database might look something like the one that is illustrated in Table 2.3.

Table 2.3
An example of an experience database for project size estimation. (Only a portion of the database is shown.)

Project Name	Domain	Months	Effort	Size
Application 1	Graphics utility	12	30	5000
Application 2	Graphics utility	10	40	8000
Application 3	Graphics utility	24	30	5000
Application 4	Graphics utility	36	100	20000
Application 5	Graphics utility	12	30	5000
Application 6	Graphics utility	24	30	10000
Application 7	Graphics utility	48	90	25000

Of course, such a table is meaningless unless we have units for the measurements used. In this table, the effort is measured by the number of person-months needed for the project, where the term "person-month" is used to represent the effort of one person working for one month. The size evaluation can be any well-defined measurement. The most commonly used measurement is called "lines of code," or LOC for short. We will discuss the lines of code measurement in several sections later in the book. For now, just use your intuition about what this measurement means.

How can the information in the experience database be used? Let's look at a scatter diagram of the number of months needed for different projects and the size of the projects (which might be measured in lines of code). A typical scatter diagram is shown in Figure 2.2.

This diagram may be uninformative. A model may be created, based on the fitting of a straight line or curve to the data according to some formula. A straight line fitted to the data in Figure 2.2 would slope from lower left to upper right.

The fitting of a straight line to data is often done using the "method of least squares." In this method, the two coefficients m and b of a straight line whose equation is written in the form

$$y = m x + b$$

are determined from the equations

$$m = \left[n \left(\sum x_i y_i \right) - \left(\sum x_i \right) \left(\sum y_i \right) \right] / \left[n \sum x_i^2 - \left(\sum x_i \right)^2 \right]$$

and

$$b = \left[n \sum (y_i) \sum (x_i^2) - \sum (x_i) \sum (x_i y_i) \right] / \left[n \sum (x_i)^2 - \left(\sum x_i \right)^2 \right]$$

In the example illustrated in Figure 2.2, the values of m and b are approximately 0.002 and 1.84, respectively, and the equation of the line is

$$y = 0.002 x + 1.84$$

This formula gives the number of months needed for a project of any particular size. This implies that a project of size 15,000 LOC would take approximately 32 months. (This is clearly an inefficient software development process!)

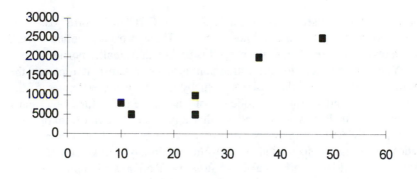

Figure 2.2. A scatter diagram showing the relationship between project size and duration in months for the experience database of Table 2.1.

One commonly used approach to software estimation is based on the COCOMO developed by Boehm [BOEH81] in his important book, *Software Engineering Economics*. Boehm suggests the use of a set of two formulas to compute the amount of effort (measured in person-months) and the time needed for completion of the project (measured in months). Boehm's formulas use data collected from an experience base which is a large collection of software projects in many different application domains.

Boehm developed a hierarchy of three cost models: basic, intermediate, and advanced. We describe the basic and intermediate models briefly in this section, but will ignore the advanced model, referring the reader to Boehm's original book.

Boehm's models are based on an assessment of the size of the system to be produced. In the original COCOMO model, the first step is to estimate the size in lines of code. The assessment of lines of code is often made by using a "work breakdown structure." A work breakdown structure is created as follows.

1. Examine the list of detailed requirements.

2. For each requirement, estimate the number of lines of code needed to implement the requirement.

3. Ignore any requirements for which an existing component can be reused as is.

4. Compute the total of all new lines of code.

This total will be used as the variable K in the COCOMO formulas. It is measured in units of thousand lines of code. The approach is called a work breakdown structure because the project is broken into smaller portions.

You might object to this estimation process, because it replaces the estimate of the size of the entire system by a total of the estimates of the sizes of the individual components of the system. However, many practitioners of this approach believe that any errors in overestimating the size of individual components are likely to be balanced by other errors underestimating the size of other components. In any event, estimating the size of a project by a work breakdown structure is often used in practice.

Once the number of thousands of lines (K) has been estimated, the time and number of personnel can be estimated. We discuss the basic COCOMO model first. The formulas are:

$$E = a_b * K * \exp(b_b)$$

$$D = c_b * E * \exp(d_b)$$

where the coefficients a_b, b_b, c_b, and d_b are based on relatively informal assessments of the relative complexity of the software. The computed quantities E and D are the amount of effort required for the project and D is the time needed for development of the project, but not maintenance.

The values of the constants a_b, b_b, c_b, and d_b should be taken from the appropriate entries in Table 2.4.

Table 2.4
Coefficients for the basic COCOMO model.

Software project type	a_b	b_b	c_b	d_b
Small project, experienced team, flexible requirements ("organic")	2.4	1.05	2.5	0.38
Hard real-time requirements and strict interoperability ("embedded")	3.6	1.2	2.5	0.32
A mixture of the other two type of projects ("intermediate")	3.0	1.12	2.5	0.35

Note that the estimates for the quantities E and D are themselves based on estimates of the quantity K. Thus, it is not reasonable to expect an exact match between estimates and actual values for the size and resources needed for a project. At best, an approximation with an expected range of accuracy can be determined, and this range of allowable error is heavily influenced by both the experience of the estimator and the quality of the information available in the organization for comparison with similar projects.

A typical relationship between the basic COCOMO model and some cost data is shown in Figure 2.3.

The basic COCOMO model can be extended to the so-called "intermediate COCOMO model." The intermediate COCOMO model uses a set of "test driver attributes" which are given in Table 2.5.

The weights of these test driver attributes are to be determined by the person estimating the software's costs, based on his or her experience. The weights are then entered on a scale from 1 to 6 into a spreadsheet based on Table 2.5. The resulting sum is used to create a multiplication factor that is used to modify the results of the basic COCOMO model.

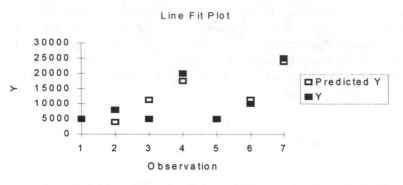

Figure 2.3. An attempt to fit a smooth curve to the data in the scatter diagram of Figure 2.1 using a COCOMO model approach.

Table 2.5
"Test driver attributes" for the intermediate COCOMO model.

Test Driver Attribute	Weight
Product attributes:	
Reliability requirements	
Size of application's database	
Software complexity	
Hardware attributes:	
Run-time performance constraints	
Memory limitations	
Other processes competing for virtual memory	
Personnel attributes:	
Analyst experience	
Software engineer experience	
Application domain experience	
Virtual machine experience	
Programming language experience	
Project attributes:	
Use of software tools	
Use of software engineering methods	
Required development schedule	
TOTAL	

2.5 Project Scheduling

Software project scheduling involves the allocation of resources to a project in a timely manner. It is extremely inefficient to have a project that will take five years to complete and will need one thousand people at its peak and have all one thousand people on the payroll from the first day forward, when only twenty people might be needed for the first year.

The alternative is equally bad, however. If a project is severely understaffed at any critical time, it is likely to be completed much later than desired, if at all. Adding extra people late in the process usually doesn't help because the more experienced project personnel are forced to spend much of their time bringing up the levels of understanding of the new people. In addition, more people always means more meetings to coordinate, as we saw in Chapter 1.

The efficiency of the system's software development is guided by its expected cost. A software economist will often have considerable experience with the pattern of staffing needs for projects of this size. He or she will often expect that the number of people employed on a software project will follow a relationship that might look something like that of Figure 2.4. The different line segments in the graph indicate different life cycle activities, each of which might require different numbers of people. Here the horizontal axis represents time and the vertical axis represents the number of personnel associated with the project between milestones.

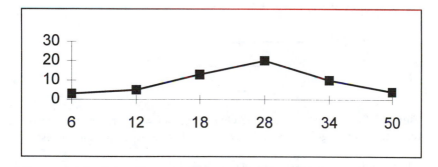

Figure 2.4. A typical pattern of project personnel over time.

The numbers at the beginning of the project represent the requirements team. The project size then increases to its maximum during the coding phase, which is intensive, but limited in time. The number of personnel will decrease as the testing and integration phase comes to an end. The last number represents the people needed for maintenance of the software. If the system has a long operational life, then it is easy to see that the cost of the maintenance phase will be the largest cost in the system, as we stated before.

Several techniques are often used for project scheduling. Two of the most common are:

- Milestone charts
- Critical path methods

A simple example of a milestone chart was shown previously in Figure 1.4. (Other examples of milestone charts were given in Figure 1.6 and Figure 1.8 for the rapid prototyping and spiral models, respectively.) A slightly more elaborate one with milestones for two different releases of the same system displayed is illustrated in Figure 2.5.

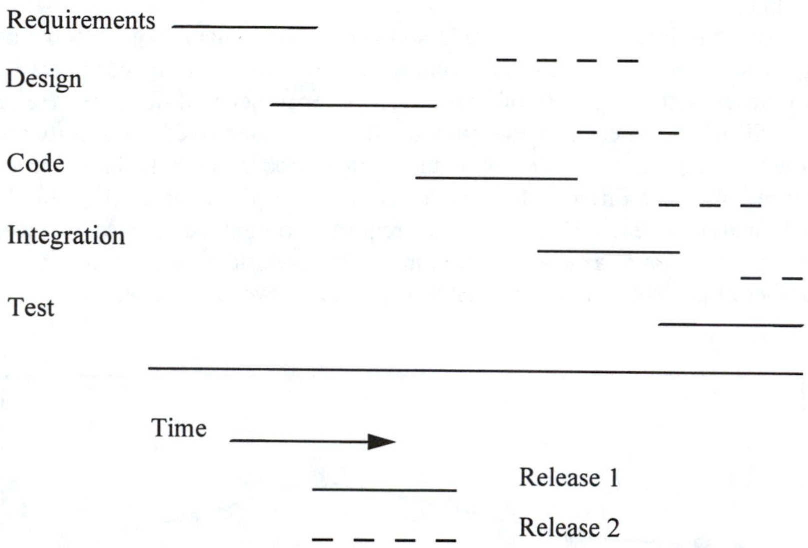

Requirements ─────────

Design   ─────────

Code   ─────────

Integration   ─────────

Test   ─────────

Time ────────▶

──────── Release 1

─ ─ ─ ─ Release 2

Figure 2.5. A typical milestone chart for a software project with multiple releases, following the classical waterfall software development process.

Note the multiple releases of the software. In organizations, such charts will include both the projected and actual dates of the individual milestones. Note also that reviews must be held for each milestone that is a deliverable product.

A less common method of planning and representing schedules is to use so-called "critical path methods." Critical path methods are based on the assessment that certain events are critical in the sense that they fundamentally affect several other decisions. Once these critical decisions have been determined, any events not affected by the critical ones can be scheduled at any time. We will use planning for a Y2K conversion project to illustrate the use of the critical path method in Section 2.10.

For example, an Interface Control Document (ICD) that describes precisely the interfaces between component subsystems must be produced and reviewed before a major effort in subsystem design and implementation begins. (We will describe ICDs in Chapter 4 when we study detailed design.)

You should note how object-oriented design is consistent with the determination of critical paths in software development. If we can describe the methods of an object in terms of an abstract class, then we know the class interface and, hence, anyone developing a class that will interact with this class has enough information to develop code. That is, if we develop a class with complete descriptions of the number and type of arguments to methods of the class, as well as the type of return values of methods in the class, then the design of the implementation of the abstract class's methods can proceed concurrently with the implementation of the details of the methods of the class during coding.

Clearly, the determination of the abstract interface of a class that is to be used by another class is on the critical path, while coding the details of a member function that uses this interface.

A similar situation occurs at many places in every software development life cycle. You will be asked to study this point in the exercises.

2.6 Project Measurement

Systematic project management usually requires measurements of the software development process. Recall that the Capability Maturity Model (CMM) of the Software Engineering Institute specifies that the software development process must be measurable. The higher levels (levels 4 and 5) of the CMM specify that "...the software development organization has quantitative feedback systems in place to identify process weakness and strengthen them proactively..." (level 5) and "... detailed software process and product quality metrics are used to establish the quantitative evaluation foundation. Meaningful variations in process performance can be distinguished from random noise, and trends in process and product qualities can be predicted..." (level 4).

How can a process, as opposed to a tangible product, be measured? As before, using the GQM paradigm of Basili and Rombach is helpful. Some obvious goals are to produce the software to meet the system requirements, on schedule, and within budget.

Related questions for these goals include:

- Have milestones been met?
- Which items are behind schedule?
- When is the project likely to be complete?

A related question is the horrifying one:

- Is the project likely to fail?

Of course, many of these questions require detailed measurements before they can be answered.

It is easy to tell at a glance if a project is behind schedule or not. Unfortunately, this simple piece of information can tell us little without additional information. The additional information might include a graph of how the actual and predicted amounts of time spent on various life cycle phases compares to previous data in the organization's baseline. It may be that the project is actually on schedule for completion, with the only difficulty being the relative amounts of time assigned for the completion of each activity. Alternatively, the project may be in serious trouble. The only way to tell is to develop the proper measurements.

What are the proper measurements? There is no absolute answer, given the wide range of software development environments. However, a manager is expected to have measurements of where the project is according to the schedule, and what costs have been expended so far.

2.7 Project Management Tools

Project management is clearly an essential part of software engineering. As such, it can benefit from the application of high-quality software tools that automate some of the steps needed to coordinate projects. This will be our first discussion of an application of CASE (Computer-Aided Software Engineering) tools.

Modern CASE tools for project management should help with the following tasks:

- Create and modify the project schedule.

- Allow the schedule to be posted so that different project administrative personnel can view it and even make changes as necessary.

- Support efficient resource allocation.

- Identify critical items on the schedule and those items that depend on the critical ones.

- Allow documents to be viewed by all authorized personnel.

- Support different approaches to project management, so that the tool can be tailored to meet the organization's way of doing business, rather than the other way around.

Some typical commercial CASE tools for project management are Microsoft Project 98 from Microsoft, ProjecTrak from Lotus, and SPR KnowledgePLAN from Software Productivity Research. Information on these products can be found at the web sites

```
http://www.microsoft.com/project/
http://www.projectrak.com/screens
and
http://www.spr.com/html/knowledgeplan.htm
```

The tools are flexible and interface with several existing applications for data collection, reporting, and statistical analysis.

What should you expect from software that supports project management? The answer is as varied as there are software development practices. However, you should expect to have support for project scheduling and reporting, resource allocation, management of change, and anything else that is appropriate to the project. In any event, the software should be configurable to the reporting and control processes that are commonly used in your organization.

2.8 The Role of Networks in Project Management

In addition to the project management tools discussed in the previous sections and the CASE tools that will be discussed briefly in future chapters, there are software tools and technologies that help the software development process which are beginning to be put into common use. Since the rate of technology advancement and movement into the marketplace is so rapid, we will be content with a brief overview of some important examples.

The most prominent force in changing the requirements process is, of course, the Internet and its resulting standards, such as HTML (Hypertext Markup Language), various word processors, PostScript and Portable

Display Format (PDF) files, jpeg (Joint Photographic Experts Group), and mpeg (Motion Picture Experts Group). Standard file formats, graphical browsers, and powerful search tools allow relatively easy access to information.

Think of the advantages over the previous methods of project coordination. Project documents filled multiple loose leaf binders, which made some offices impossible to work in because of their sheer size and quantity. There were sets of documents for each release of a software system, often making it impossible to store all of them. If a key member of a team was moved elsewhere within the software development organization, many essential documents were lost. The situation was even worse if the key person left the organization.

One of the most explosive growth areas is in what are commonly called "intranets," which are systems of computers that are networked together using Internet standards, but are effectively cut off from the entire Internet. In this approach, the restricted portions of the Internet can communicate with each other using Internet standards, but with relative confidence that their work is secure from unwanted outside access to sensitive materials. Thus, organizations are able to conduct their business with little worry about the security of commercial application tools.

It has now become commonplace to have requirements documents and project schedules placed on an organization's internal network and occasionally on the Internet itself.

Several persons can work on portions of the same document at the same time, sharing it with all others who need access. The inspections of the requirements and design should be based on written documents and the inspections should be conducted as usual, without regard to the documents being available on the Internet.

Of course, there are some problems associated with the use of electronic files. These problems can be reduced, if not eliminated entirely, by using the following guidelines:

- Determine the standard format to be used for storage of graphical files.

- Make sure that the format is compatible with the browser to be used.

- Determine a mechanism for providing feedback about deficiencies in on-line documents.

- In particular, determine if both paper and electronic versions of documents will be required.

- Make sure that the on-line documents are subject to configuration management and revision control. This could be done by having different directories for each iteration of requirements and design documents.

- Standard text-based configuration management tools should be used for both source code and textual requirements documents.

- Provide easy feedback by means of the `mailto` facility of HTML. This makes communication much easier.

- Use reviews and inspections as they would be used in a software project that was developed without the use of the Internet.

- Use e-mail to coordinate meetings and to notify members of the project team that documents have been changed.

- Determine if "chat rooms" will be employed for project management.

As with many things in software engineering, it is difficult to quantify the effect of certain technologies or techniques. However, preliminary indications are that the improvements in efficiency are enormous. In any event, an organization that is not using networks to assist in project management is generally perceived as being technologically obsolete.

As an indication of the perceived efficiency of Internet and intranet publishing, many new software development projects at NASA's Goddard Space Flight Center post all requirements documents, designs, minutes of project meetings, project schedules, and major action items on the Internet for easy access by project personnel. This reduces the clutter in many offices, where entire shelves of bookcases were used previously for storage of large loose-leaf notebooks that contained project documentation. In addition, few documents are lost. Mandl et al describe some of the positive effects of using the Internet to reduce the number of project meetings [MAND98].

2.9 Groupware

There is one particular tool that is used in some organizations to help coordinate meetings and various project reviews, namely, groupware. The term "groupware" refers to the ability to have a group of people viewing and working on the same document at the same time. There is usually more access control than is available with many network browsers. This can be very useful in certain situations.

For example, the requirements engineers for a project can meet together in a room with a large monitor, with each of the requirements engineers having access to his or her own computer or workstation. Alternatively, the locations can be remote, with network access. All the individual computers are networked and the software that controls the document access is known as groupware.

Perhaps the best-known examples of groupware are Lotus Notes and the products of Ventana Systems. Microsoft also has moved in this direction, with a set of integrated tools.

Groupware goes somewhat farther than Internet access in the sense that it is easy to allow everyone on the project to change a common document, or to restrict the ability to change the document to a single person. This is more transparent than the typical use of operating systems level access permissions for UNIX or Windows NT. This use of groupware is also smoother than the operating system level approach in that there is no need to create new groups of users to allow certain groups of software engineers to change the common document.

We note that use of the Internet or an internal "intranet" for video conferencing has some of the same features as groupware, particularly if there is a mechanism for playback.

2.10 An Example: Project Management for a Year 2000 Conversion Project

What would you do if you were asked to head up a team addressing your organization's readiness for the Y2K problem? Think about this question for a moment, then describe how your answer would change if any of the following were true:

- The organization is responsible for the health and safety of many individuals who use its products or operate its systems.
- The organization is responsible for the salaries and retirement benefits for many individuals who use its services.
- There is clear documentation about the structure of major systems.
- The software is of high quality and rarely fails to operate properly.
- Much of the software used by the organization is run on special-purpose embedded microprocessors.
- The operation is highly centralized.

- The operation is highly decentralized.
- The operation has no single point of failure.
- The operation has many redundant systems to ensure continuous operation.
- It is unclear what the status actually is of ancillary services, such as electric power and heat to the buildings or the electronic locks that control access.
- There are many different types of software applications in use.
- There are only a few different types of software applications in use.
- Many systems are nearing the end of their useful life and can be taken out of operation without affecting the organization's primary business operations.
- There are sufficient resources and software expertise in-house to solve the problem.
- It is 1997 and nothing has been done.
- It is 1998 and nothing has been done.
- It is 1999 and nothing has been done.

Clearly, your answers to these questions will influence the project plan. In an ideal scenario, with all the resources necessary on hand to solve the problem, there might be a detailed inventory, followed by a carefully developed plan, followed by recoding and testing of software developed in house, careful interactions with vendors of externally developed software, followed by a complex set of contingency plans.

The U.S. Social Security System completed its testing of all its software fixes on its mainframe systems in October 1998. There was careful planning, allocation of resources, and plenty of lead time.

In the commercial world, many organizations do not have such luxuries due to competitive pressures. After all, solving the Y2K problem doesn't move a company ahead technologically, it just fixes what is "broken." Therefore, organizations must plan for Y2K problems, taking into account the answers to the questions raised above.

Let's suppose that an organization had ample resources in house, three years lead time, and only a few safety-critical systems. A project plan would have the following items:

1. There would be a complete inventory of all hardware, software, and embedded systems. This would include all interfaces to the outside world and to other units of the organization. It would also include all ancillary systems.
2. There would be a complete assessment of the critical nature of each item found in step 1, primarily focusing on the importance of each to the organization's primary function.

3. There would be an allocation of resources to each item detected in the inventory, according to its importance to the company and the expected remaining service lifetime.
4. There would be software test and integration plans, with ample time and resources allocated for their completion.
5. There would be inspections and walkthroughs, to make sure that no new errors were introduced by the Y2K fixes.
6. There would be contingency plans for those systems that failed unexpectedly, either in their contingency tests or in operation.
7. There would be operational tests of systems many times before the December 31, 1999 deadline.

Now let's suppose that an organization had a more serious problem, with few resources available in house, one year of lead time, and many interactions with other computer systems. A project plan would have the following items:

1. The operations of the organization would be grouped into categories according to their importance to the organization's core function.
2. There would be a limited inventory of hardware, software, and embedded systems that impact the essential systems of the organization. This limited inventory would include all interfaces to the outside world and to other units of the organization. It would also include all ancillary systems.
3. There would be an allocation of resources to each item detected in the inventory, according to its importance to the company and the expected remaining service lifetime.
4. There would be software test and integration plans, with ample time and resources allocated for their completion.
5. There would be inspections and walkthroughs, to make sure that no new errors were introduced by the Y2K fixes.
6. There would be contingency plans for those systems that failed unexpectedly.
7. There would be operational tests of systems many times before the December 31, 1999 deadline.
8. As resources were freed up from the essential systems, they would be deployed on those software systems determined to be valuable, but not essential, in the first step.

Notice the primary difference here. The initial determination of what was critical to the organization affected the order in which the systems determined to be non-essential were to be treated. Such systems are clearly not on the critical path of the organization's Y2K plan.

Further Reading

There are many excellent books on software project management. One of the best is Watts Humphrey's *Managing the Software Process* ([HUMP89]). Tom DeMarco's book on this topic [DeMA82] is also very useful, and is surprisingly up to date for a book written in 1982.

Another book by Humphrey [HUMP95] describes the so-called "personal software process" that can help a programmer determine the software engineering activities (requirements, design, implementation, testing, etc.) that consume most of his or her time. A major feature of this book is a set of graded exercises that are intended to provide a database of quantitative measurements of project experiences.

A somewhat different view of software project management is presented in McCarthy's book [MCCA95] entitled *Dynamics of Software Development*. It describes experiences with some software projects at Microsoft.

The 1981 book by Boehm [BOEH81] is still one of the best references on software project resource estimation. It presents the COCOMO model in detail.

Summary

Software project management is the systematic application of general management tools and techniques in order to improve the efficiency of the software development process. Software team activities include:

- Systems analysis team
- Planning team
- Requirements team
- System design team
- Implementation team
- Testing and integration team
- Training team
- Delivery and installation team
- Maintenance team
- Quality assurance team
- Metrics team
- Documentation team
- System administration team
- Reuse and reengineering team
- Human-computer interface evaluator

- Tools support person
- Software economist
- Project librarian

All these activities have to be coordinated by a project manager. He or she will also be responsible for assuring that the resources available to the project will be used appropriately.

Exercises

1. Examine the Internet web pages of some government organizations that develop software. Choose one project and determine which software requirements or designs are available to you. Then estimate the amount of effort and resources needed to complete the software projects you have found.

2. Examine the Internet web pages of some companies that develop software project management tools. Determine if these tools allow a user to estimate the amount of effort and resources needed to complete the software projects you typically develop.

3. Examine several of the projects you did in your previous computer science courses. Use these projects to determine your productivity by comparing the number of lines of code of each of the projects with the amount of time used for each project, which is the difference between the date the project was assigned and the date you turned it in, multiplied by a factor that represents the average number of hours you spent on the project each day. Did the average amount of time represent an accurate view of how you spent your time, or was most of your work done very close to the project deadline?

4. Draw a diagram showing the major software engineering tasks for the rapid prototyping software development model. Use Figure 2.1 as a model.

5. Draw a diagram showing the major software engineering tasks for the spiral software development model. Use Figure 2.1 as a model.

6. This question concerns the COCOMO model of software cost estimation. Examine a software system for which there have been multiple releases and for which source code is available to you. (The GNU software tools from the Free Software Foundation are an excellent

source for this question.) Describe the system as organic, embedded, or intermediate. Examine the amount of new and reused code in the latest two releases. Does the time estimate predicted by the COCOMO model agree with the time between these releases? Explain.

7. Obtain a copy of an organization's software project management manual. Find out how staffing and resource allocation is determined. Are any CASE tools mentioned in the manual?

8. Examine a project you completed recently. Determine which activities are on the critical path of development and which ones can be done concurrently. Would this knowledge have made the software process more efficient?

9. Develop a Y2K project plan for fixing your own personal computer. There are many websites that can help you with testing your hardware and software. Find them. Also, determine which software requires new service releases or patches to fix the Y2K problem.

10. Develop a project plan for treating the "Year 2038 Problem" where the date fields used in UNIX systems will overflow sometime in the year 2038.

Chapter 3

Requirements

In this chapter, we will discuss what many practitioners believe is the most important part of software engineering: development of a software system's requirements. We will begin by introducing some typical problems of requirements engineering. We will then illustrate how these problems occur regardless of which software development life cycle model is used, whether there is a set of known customers who will provide feedback, or it is hoped that the product will determine its own set of customers after it is delivered. Basic techniques such as information hiding, formal representations, and requirements reviews will be discussed, as will a typical managerial viewpoint of the software requirements engineering process.

After the basic techniques of requirements engineering are presented, we will begin the discussion of the major software project that will be considered throughout the remainder of this book. A set of requirements will be developed, using the problem statement as a basis. We will then evaluate the requirements we develop.

3.1 Some Problems with Requirements Determination

All computer science students get extensive experience in software coding as part of their undergraduate education. Students often have to supply both internal documentation (in the form of comments within their programs) and external documentation (often in the form of project reports). They may also have some experience with software testing within their academic setting. Some students even get experience in software maintenance, although this is relatively rare.

Two topics are often missing from the typical education of computer science students (prior to taking a course emphasizing software engineering principles): detailed, practical instruction in requirements and design.

Unfortunately, most of the other software engineering activities are irrelevant if the requirements are wrong, incomplete, or vague. The term "wrong" here is used in the sense of being inconsistent; one requirement contradicts another. Let's consider what can happen in each of these three cases.

If the requirements for a project are wrong, then the rest of the software engineering activities will have to be redone, assuming that someone recognizes the error or errors in the requirements. This is extremely expensive, and often means that much of the subsequent work is wrong and has to be discarded. In the worst case, all subsequent project effort must be scrapped.

There are two possibilities if the requirements are incomplete. The best-case scenario is that the requirements are so modular that the project's design and code also can be developed in a modular manner. In this case, it is possible that the missing requirement can be fulfilled by additions both to the design and the source code implementation with relatively few changes needed to incorporate the new requirements. This flexibility is one of the main advantages of iterative approaches such as the rapid prototyping or spiral development life cycle models.

If the requirements were complete but not modular, then it is unlikely that the design and the resulting source code will be modular. In this case, major portions of the design and source code will have to be scrapped because they are difficult to create given the lack of consistency with modern programming techniques and the software engineering goal of modularity. The experience of many failed software projects strongly indicates that the lack of modular requirements is very expensive.

The third category of poor requirements occurs when the requirements are vague. In this situation, it is difficult to know if the design is correct, because the software designers do not know precisely what requirements mean. The designers may make some unwarranted assumptions about the intentions of the requirements engineer. These assumptions, if not correct, can be the major source of disaster for projects. The most common problem is that the unwarranted assumptions become part of the "culture" of the project and therefore are never questioned.

The end result of vague requirements are software systems that either do not quite work as the customer wanted, or do not work at all, often because the interfaces with other software were not specified properly. Vague requirements may lead to problems that cannot be solved on technical grounds and, therefore, must be resolved in the legal system. Having software problems resolved in court means that a jury of relatively non-technical people has to determine the precise meaning of requirements that were too vague to be understood by the technical software people involved. This is hardly an appealing scenario.

In fact, the problem is more serious. The cheapest time to correct errors in software is in the requirements development phase, as Table 3.2 illustrates. This is true regardless of the model of development: waterfall, rapid prototyping, spiral, or other. On the other hand, the most expensive time to correct problems in software is during the maintenance phase, because all previous life cycle activities (requirements, design, coding, testing, integration, documentation, delivery, and installation) have been performed. Software maintenance also requires a high level of understanding of the code. We will discuss software maintenance in Chapter 8.

You might think that using an iterative software development approach might eliminate most of these problems. It is true that the iterative models allow incomplete requirements to be discovered earlier than in the classical waterfall model. Inconsistent, or wrong, requirements tend to be discovered earlier with the iterative methods.

However, vague requirements may not be discovered unless the various evaluation reviews are done carefully. Without healthy skepticism at reviews, the vague requirements are still likely to become part of the project's culture, with the vagueness never being resolved.

An ongoing study by Dolores Wallace of the National Institute of Science and Technology (NIST) and Herbert Hecht of SoHar Corporation in California shows that there is a pyramid effect due to the nature of errors in software systems. They are continuing to examine a large number of projects and classify the errors according to the life cycle phase in which the errors occurred. An informal summary of their results is shown in Table 3.1. Clearly, many errors occur during the requirements phase. More up-to-date information can be found at the URL

```
http://hissant.ncsl.nist.gov
```

Table 3.1
Breakdown of sources of errors in software projects

Requirements	Many
Design	Somewhat fewer
Code	Somewhat fewer still
Testing	Somewhat fewer still

How important is it to discover errors or inconsistencies at requirements time? There are many studies that consider the cost of fixing a software problem at different phases of the software life cycle. The results of one (proprietary) study are shown in Table 3.2. Note the huge advantage to finding errors early in the software life cycle, during the requirements phase.

It should be clear that accurate determination of a software system's requirements is essential. Even in an iterative software development process, requirements must be determined eventually and the more accurate and complete the initial requirements are, the fewer and less costly the iterations will be. We will discuss some techniques for the determination of requirements in an efficient manner.

Table 3.2
Cost to fix software errors at different phases of the software life cycle.

Requirements	1.0
Design	5.0
Code	10.0
Testing	30.0

Of course, many projects will have their requirements change over time due to changes in technology and new directions for the organization. This is especially true of larger projects, which might have their development times extend over several years. An initial set of high quality, modular requirements and an effective software development process can support incorporation of changes in a systematic, efficient manner.

3.2 Requirements Elicitation

There are several approaches to requirements engineering. Some of these are classical, such as those described in [DAVI90]. Other are motivated by object-oriented approaches [BERR96]. Still others are motivated by cost issues, such as the reuse-driven requirements approaches described in [KONT95], [LEAC96], or [WAUN95], or the systematic process changes of [MAND98] and others. In this section, we will describe some basic principles that are common to most approaches. The individual differences will be expanded on in the next few sections.

The requirements engineering process should be thought of as beginning with the things that are known about the project's purpose and ending with a set of requirements. These include such things as the environment in which the software system is to operate, the purpose of the system (as perceived by its potential users or customers), and the organization's basic goals.

The output of the requirements process is a complete, detailed, unambiguous description of what the system is supposed to do. The requirements should be so unambiguous that a design may be developed to match their requirements and it should be possible to determine if the design matches the requirements. The basic inputs to the requirements process are illustrated in Figure 3.1.

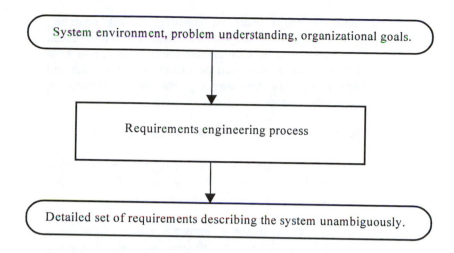

Figure 3.1. A stylized view of the requirements engineering process.

Let us illustrate the basic problem of requirements engineering by a simple example: determination of requirements for a software package that is to be run on a personal computer. We will not discuss the rest of the problem statement, because even this portion of the problem description suffices to illustrate several points. The system requirements must include the following:

- Which hardware platform will be used? (Intel-based microprocessor, Motorola-based, Power-PC-based, or other.)

- Which operating system will be supported? (MS-DOS, Windows, Windows 95, Windows 98, Windows NT, MacOS, UNIX, Linux?) If UNIX or Windows are used, which variant?

- Which operating system versions will be required?

- Will the different versions of software run on different computers and operating systems? If so, which ones?

- Will the file formats be consistent across operating systems? (This is the case for Microsoft Word, Excel, and PowerPoint applications programs, which allow both PC- and Macintosh-based computers to access files and treat them in the same way, regardless of the platform on which the files were originally created.)

- Will the software have a graphical user interface?

- Will the software's graphical user interface be consistent with that of the operating system and with other applications running in the same environment?

- Will there be multiple implementations, such as a minimal size for laptops with small amounts of memory and disk space, and larger implementations with more support files and features, to be used in computers with fewer limitations on memory and size?

- What are the minimal system requirements in terms of memory size and available hard disk space?

- Will the program's existence in memory cause problems for other applications that are also running on the computer?

- Are there any other software packages, such as word processors, spreadsheet programs, database managers, or drawing tools, with which the program must be able to share data?

- Will on-line help be provided within the software?

- How will the software be delivered? Will it use floppy disks or compact disks? What disk format will be used?

- Will the software be provided in compressed or uncompressed form?

- Will installation and setup software be provided?

- Will training be required?

- Are there any time constraints, such as completion of certain operations within specified limits? (These constraints are called "hard" constraints, in contrast to the "soft" constraints described in the next bulleted item. A system with hard timing constraints is called a "hard real-time system.")

- Are there any time constraints, such as completion of a number of certain operations within a single specified limits, so that the constraint is on the average number of operations per unit time? (These constraints are called "soft" constraints, in contrast to the "hard" constraints described in the previous bulleted item. A system with only soft timing constraints is called a "soft real-time system." A system that has either hard or soft real-time constraints is called simply a "real-time system.")

You can see how detailed the software's requirements must be in order to write a complete description of the design. All of this gets much more complicated if the software is supposed to *do* anything! The apparent complexity for any real system seems to be so great that the problem appears to be hopeless. The only way out is to follow an approach that is familiar to computer science students: stepwise refinement.

In this case, the stepwise refinement process involves a systematic process of translation from the initial, very incomplete problem statement, which describes the system at a high level, to a detailed set of requirements that specifies the functionality of the desired system. The result of the translation is simply the restatement of the list of questions into a set of unambiguous statements, with the decisions made as to platform, operating system, etc.

Suppose that these steps have been carried out. At this point, we have a good understanding of the types of requirements that our hypothetical software project must satisfy, at least in the area of the operating systems support and environment. This is the sort of background information and knowledge that a requirements engineer is expected to have *before* the requirements process begins. The common terminology "domain knowledge" is used in the software engineering industry to describe this assumed level of expertise.

What hasn't been done yet is the selection of the specific requirements from the set of all possible options. In our example, it is likely to assume that there will be many customers for our software product, but that none of these customers is known directly by the requirements team. In this case, the requirements team will probably meet with several people, including the marketing and sales teams, in order to make the initial decisions about the requirements for the system.

To fix our ideas for the rest of the section, let us assume that the following decisions have been made:

- The software will be delivered on an Intel-based system.

- The software will run on the Windows 95 operating system.

- Only the current version, called Windows 95, will be supported.

- The software will have a graphical user interface.

- The graphical user interface will be consistent with the interface of the Mystery system, version 3.1, in the menu organization.

- The commands used to create a new file, open an existing file, close a file, save a file in standard format, and save a file in another format are to be chosen from a list that includes pure ASCII text.

- There will be only one version of the system that will be implemented in all installations.

- The system will require less than 4MB memory and 5MB free disk space.

- The software must be able to share data with the Catchall database, version 7.3.

- On-line help will be provided.

- The software is to be delivered on 3.5", 1.44 MB floppy disks, in compressed form.

- The software is to include an installation utility that includes a software decompression utility.

One thing you should note is that requirements statements are part of an agreement between the software developers and the framers of the problem statement. This agreement may in effect be a contract, with the full force of the law behind it in some instances. Software requirements should be precise and complete, for the reasons given earlier in this chapter. Requirements documents are kept on hand long after the initial product has been delivered.

Here is an example of the long life of requirements documents. Several of the computer programs designed to operate spacecraft for NASA were produced by outside commercial organizations, rather than by government employees. Multiple companies often worked on different portions of the same software. Every time an operator of the software found a problem, the occurrence of the problem was verified by comparing the actual operations of the software with the output that was specified by the requirements. When the actual required outputs differed from the output that was specified for this input, then the problem was certified as having happened and it became someone's responsibility to fix.

As was indicated earlier, fixing errors at this late stage was expensive, and none of the companies wanted to incur this expense unless they had to. Therefore, two things had to happen:

1. The problem had to be verified.
2. The company responsible for the software problem had to be determined.

Both required the careful reading of the software's requirements documents. This illustrates that requirements documents have long lives and that precise individual requirements must be met by the software that is to be developed.

By this point in the discussion, you should be aware of the importance of requirements and you should be concerned about ways of dealing with their complexity. You might also wonder just how requirements are developed for actual software systems.

One technique is often described as the process of elicitation. That is, one or more potential customers are interviewed with the intent being to discover precisely what the customer wants. If there is no actual customer known to the requirements team, as would be the case with most personal computer software, a stand-in is used for the customer. In either case, the requirements team will conduct a sequence of meetings with the "customer."

The requirements team must do a considerable amount of work between each pair of these meetings with the "customer." The team must refine the previous set of requirements that was presented to the "customer" and add, delete, or modify any requirements that were objected to by the "customer." Since the "customer" may not have indicated his or her requirements explicitly, there must be an analysis of what the "customer" really wants, not just what he or she has said.

Of course, these requirements-gathering meetings with the "customer" will be more efficient if the "customer" can see an actual system prototype and determine if the system meets his or her needs. If the existing prototype system does not meet the needs of the "customer," the prototype's requirements can be changed and another prototype developed. This flexibility and the reduction of the likelihood of producing an unsatisfactory system are two of the most important reasons for choosing the rapid prototyping, spiral, or other iterative models of software development. Using an object model that automatically generates code for the various actions that can be performed on objects (member functions) can also facilitate the requirements process by giving the "customer" something to see at each iteration of the requirements process.

The requirements-gathering process continues until the "customer" is satisfied with the system's requirements. The end result must be a completely unambiguous description of the system to be designed. In many cases, the requirements process is like the process of writing source code to implement a design: stepwise refinement. After the requirements team is satisfied that it knows the customer's requirements, it then writes a requirements document, which may be given to the customer for review. Unfortunately, the work of the requirements team is not over. We will return to the discussion of the requirements process in Section 3.4.

3.3 Requirements Traceability

One of the most essential portions of a requirements documents is a requirements traceability matrix. Its purpose is to allow easy tracking of requirements throughout a software system's development.

The format of a requirements traceability matrix varies from organization to organization; most organizations have standard forms that they use. They all have several things in common: the individual requirements, places for entries for other life cycle phases, and places to sign off. We illustrate the concept in Table 3.3. An electronic version of this table is available as Spreadsheet 3.3 at the URL

http://imappl.org/~rjl/SoftwareEngineering/

For simplicity, we have numbered the requirements 1, 2, and so on. Unfortunately, this simplistic type of organization of requirements is not typical of industry practice. More realistic software projects will have multiple levels of requirements, generally grouped by functionality. For example, a current software project at NASA has 1156 requirements, which are grouped into four levels of a hierarchy. Thus, the index of the requirement numbered 4.1.3.2 reflects that this is the second requirement in unit 3 of sub-subsystem 1 of subsystem 4.

Table 3.3.
A Requirements Traceability Matrix

Number	Requirement	Design	Code	Test
1	Intel-based			
2	Windows 95			
3	Consistent with User Interface of Windows 95			
4	Graphical User Interface			
5	Consistent With Mystery 3.1			
6	System One Size Only			
7	<4 MB System , <5 MB Disk			
8	Share Data with Catchall 7.3			
9	On-line Help Provided			
10	3.5", 1.44 MB Floppy Disks			
11	Include Installation And Decompression			

The next step in the requirements engineering process is to examine the state of our requirements. (Technically, this should have been done before the requirements traceability matrix was created.) We need to look for any inconsistencies or missing requirements. Of course, we also need to look for any that are vaguely stated, which should show up at this point because vague requirements cannot be tested. Hopefully, most decisions made in the requirements gathering process will be straightforward and can lead to software projects that can be completed.

A moment's reflection should indicate some potential concerns in our requirements. There are difficulties in the area of the user interface. The statement "be consistent with" the user interface of the Windows 95 operating system is entirely too vague. It is simply not testable. There are several potential problems with the meaning of this phrase:

- The software's user interface will not have any conflicts with the user interface of Windows 95.
- The software's user interface will use the same conventions for keystrokes and menu selection that are used in the Windows 95 operating system for identical purposes.
- The software's menu will have the same organization of options as does Windows 95.

- The software will use the same system calls as Windows 95.

It is not clear which of these was meant. The rule of thumb is, "more detail is always appropriate." So is the use of clear verbs, such as "must," "shall," and "will," instead of "might" or "may." Unclear requirements such as these can cause disasters in an actual project. With such variation, it is difficult to trace any decisions about design or implementation back to requirements in order to ensure that the requirements have been met. As you organize requirements into a requirements traceability matrix, watch for statements that cannot be tested.

3.4 Software Architectures and Requirements

It is time to evaluate our understanding of the requirements process. Since we have gotten to this point in the requirements process, we have completed the use of a stepwise refinement process and our knowledge of the application domain to write a set of requirements that are appropriate for our software. In Table 3.3, we showed a set of eleven distinct requirements for our hypothetical system. However long the requirements gathering process took, we did manage to get an initial set of requirements.

Unfortunately, the process is unsatisfactory for more complicated software. A software system with over 1150 requirements will take at least 100 times as much effort as the trivial example we have discussed so far. The larger system is likely to have much more severe requirements for systems that the software will have to interface with. Many of the requirements will affect other requirements, causing some inconsistency. There may even be some real-time requirements. The requirements effort for this system is likely to be closer to 200 times as complex as our example. The resulting effort may be much larger for realistic systems.

How can we handle this increased complexity? Stepwise refinement and abstraction are the obvious approaches, but there is a need for more guidance. There are four general techniques in common use:

1. Use principles of data abstraction and information hiding to produce a complete description of the system's functionality. This approach leads naturally to an object-oriented set of requirements, but can be used with systems that are completely procedurally oriented in nature.

2. Regroup requirements to be consistent with the requirements and design of both existing and planned systems.

3. Reuse requirements in order to be able to reuse existing designs and source code.

4. Automate the requirements engineering process.

For the purpose of consistency of exposition, we will assume that a hypothetical graphical database system has had a set of requirements determined. (A graphical database allows the organization, search, and retrieval of two and three-dimensional objects together with a set of allowable operations. Such databases are often included with solid modeling systems, such as those used in computer-aided design software.)

Table 3.4
Initial requirements for a graphical database system

1. The system must allow up to 100 polyhedra to be represented.
2. The system must allow objects to be either single polyhedra or combinations of up to three polyhedra.
3. The system will allow combinations to be formed by using the standard set operations of union or intersection on one, two, or three polyhedra.
4. The system will keep track of the volume of all objects.
5. The system will keep track of the surface area of all objects.
6. The system will allow the most recent combination of two or three objects into a single larger object to be undone.
7. The system must display objects using a world-to-screen transformation.
8. The system must allow pointers to each face or edge of each polyhedron to be kept.
9. The system must be able to determine the length of each edge of each object.
10. Other requirements related to display of the objects (these will not be mentioned here for simplicity).
11. The system must run on the XYZ computer with 16 MB RAM, 42 MB disk space available, using the operating system version 3.72, DISPLAY Master 3.32, and the WWM database system, version 3.4.

The set of requirements is given in Table 3.4. Different approaches to the refinement of this set of requirements to a complete and unambiguous set will be discussed in a separate subsection.

3.4.1 Use of data abstraction and information hiding in requirements engineering

Data abstraction and information hiding are two of the most important tools of a software engineer. They encourage the reduction of complexity that is necessary for good software engineering. As such, they are present in every successful software project of any size.

Unfortunately, they are also perceived as being impossible to achieve without an object-oriented approach. While object orientation encourages data abstraction and information hiding, it is not necessary in order to achieve them. To emphasize this point, we will develop a completely procedurally oriented set of requirements for the system that has its initial requirements given in Table 3.4, which is on page 101. The discussion in this subsection is influenced heavily by a presentation given by Daniel Berry at Howard University on the topic of "ignorance hiding," and by a recent related paper by Daniel and Orna Berry in the Journal of Systems and Software [BERR96].

The paper is essential reading for requirements engineers. There are two essential participants in the process: a requirements engineer who is extremely knowledgeable about the requirements process, but who is ignorant about the application domain, and a domain expert, who understands the application area, but is not especially knowledgeable about requirements engineering.

The essential message of this paper for the requirements engineering process is clear and may be described by two complementary principles:

1. The requirements for the system must be modified and refined until the system can be developed by software designers and coders who are familiar with the fundamental algorithms of the application domain, but who are ignorant about the requirements engineering process. The eventual requirements will be so complete and unambiguous that the design will be clear and that the coding can be done easily by implementing standard, well-known algorithms.

2. The requirements for the system must be modified and refined until the system requirements can be understood by requirements engineers who are knowledgeable about requirements engineering, but who know nothing about the application domain. The eventual requirements will be so complete and unambiguous that the requirements engineer will understand them completely, even without knowledge of the application domain.

The requirements for the system must be iterated until each of these two principles is true for each of the requirements. The approach is called "ignorance hiding" in [BERR96] because the lack of understanding (ignorance of requirements engineering by the designers and coders; ignorance of the application domain by the requirements engineer) forces both the requirements engineer and the domain expert to communicate precisely, with no preconceived notions. This works only if both sides are persistent in getting unambiguous requirements.

Let's look at the first two requirements listed in Table 3.4. The first requirement is "The system must allow up to 100 polyhedra to be represented." There are two nouns in this requirement: "system" and "polyhedra." The verbs are "allow" and "represent." Other important words are "up to" and "100."

Imagine that you were a requirements engineer with no knowledge of the application domain. The "system" clearly refers to the software to be produced by this project. No confusion there. But what about the term "polyhedra?" Assuming that we recognize this term as a plural, we have to ask the application domain expert what a "polyhedron" is. He or she will reply something like: "A solid figure whose boundary consists of polygons." The discussion would continue, until the requirements engineer is sure about exactly what a "polygon" is. Clearly, the objects indicated in Figures 3.2a and 3.2b are polyhedra, if we assume that we are seeing the visible boundary of some three-dimensional object. However, the degenerate case in Figure 3.2c is more difficult to characterize.

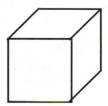 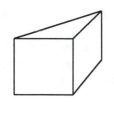 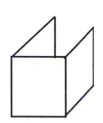

Figure 3.2a. Cube   **Figure 3.2b.** Prism   **Figure 3.2c.** Polyhedron?

Clearly a precise definition of polyhedron must be obtained before any more of the system can be designed. In order to conserve space, we will assume that this term has been defined properly and will turn our attention to the second requirement. The primary difficulty there is with the term "combination."

A three-dimensional geometric figure can be considered as a solid object with a boundary, as a solid object without a boundary, or as a region in space described by its boundary surfaces. The set of operations that eventually will be performed on these polyhedra include construction, destruction, determination of orientation in space, and determination of which faces of the polyhedra are visible to an observer at a certain position and looking in a particular direction.

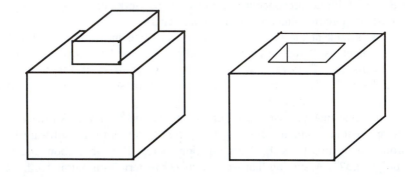

Figure 3.3a. Combination   **Figure 3.3b.** Removal

Thus, the term "combination" can refer to either of the cases illustrated in Figures 3.3a and 3.3b. The requirements need to indicate which, or both, of these combinations will be allowed. Unusual cases, such as removing a rectangular solid from itself, must also be considered. We note in passing that proper treatment of these "unusual cases" can take up most of the programming effort needed by a computer graphics-based solid modeling system.

Several other of the initial requirements of Table 3.4 are lacking in clarity according to the "ignorance hiding" principle. We will leave the discussion of the improvements to the other requirements to the exercises.

3.4.2 Regrouping requirements in requirements engineering

By regrouping requirements we mean that the individual requirements are grouped into sets that can be considered as an entirety. This is a higher-level view than that of individual requirements. Now we are focusing our attention on higher-level components and on a view of the system that is called the system's software architecture. This regrouping process is often considered to be software reengineering when it is applied to existing, complete software systems. (Software reengineering is much broader.)

What would the requirements for such a reengineered system include? Consider the example of an initial set of requirements that was shown in Table 3.4.

The requirements listed in Table 3.4 seem to have been determined in a rather haphazard fashion. This was done deliberately to illustrate the reorganization of the requirements. We now consider a more realistic, efficient organization of the requirements.

There are two other questions to be resolved: how do we use the hypothetical Display Master software for graphics display and the WWM database system for storage? The answer is that we regroup the requirements.

For example, the world-to-screen transformation requirement appears to be redundant, because the Display Master software probably has its own routines for this. (If not, it might be better to use a software utility that is more standardized.)

Use of a hypothetical database package implicitly indicates that several of our requirements can be met by the database package, using standard query facilities. Thus, the requirements for the hypothetical system described in Table 3.4 can be regrouped into those of Table 3.5.

Here we have placed all the database-related requirements at the top of the list in requirements 1 through 5. The display requirements information is kept in items 6 through 8. Notice how much easier it is to determine if a database package has the proper facilities. We could go one step further and design the database itself. For simplicity, we will omit this discussion, since we will return to the point later in a more realistic example.

Note that there is another way to organize the requirements. Most software engineers would agree that in many application domains the requirements for nearly all current software systems are described using hierarchical listings such as those we have used so far. These hierarchical listings are implicitly geared towards eventual implementation of source code in a procedural programming language such as C, Ada, or even FORTRAN.

Therefore, a mapping from the essentially procedural perspective to an objective-oriented one is necessary if the software is to be written in an object-oriented programming language such as Smalltalk or Eiffel, or a hybrid language such as C++. We will not do the mapping at this point, postponing a more complete discussion of object orientation until the design phase. At that time, we will note that the "has-a," "is-a," and "uses-a" relationships will be important in their mapping, regardless of the life cycle phase where it takes place.

Table 3.5

Reorganized requirements for a graphical database system

1.	The system must allow up to 100 polyhedra to be represented in a database using the WWM database software.
2.	The system must allow objects to be either single polyhedra or combinations of up to three polyhedra.
3.	The system will allow combinations to be formed by using the standard set operations of union or intersection on one, two, or three polyhedra.
4.	The system will allow the most recent combination of two or three objects into a single larger object to be undone.
5.	The system must allow pointers to each face or edge of each polyhedron to be kept.
6.	The system must display objects using a world-to-screen transformation.
7.	Other requirements related to display of the objects (these will not be mentioned here for simplicity.)
8.	The system must run on the XYZ computer with 16 MB RAM, 42 MB disk space available, using the operating system version 3.72, DISPLAY Master 3.32, and the WWM database system, version 3.4.

3.4.3 Reuse of requirements in requirements engineering

Reuse of requirements presents one of the greatest opportunities for improving the efficiency of the requirements process. The idea is to carry the process one step further than the regrouping of the requirements. Reusing a set of requirements for a subsystem can ensure that no requirements are missed for this subsystem. In addition, software reuse can reduce further software life cycle costs by allowing an entire subsystem (design, source code, and so on) to be put into place in the final software system.

Reuse of requirements is only possible if there is some sort of repository for requirements that have been used successfully in other systems. One or more persons who are familiar with either the application domain (a so-called domain expert) or the available reusable requirements and other saved software artifacts (a domain engineer) will be necessary.

In this case, we can have the best of both worlds. The system we are trying to set requirements for has already been created. That is, there is another system whose requirements are identical either to the entire system we are trying to create here, or at least to a substantial portion. The existing system has been developed for another project and can, in fact, be found in the source code available with the book *Object-Oriented Design and Programming in C++.* ([LEAC95]) Since I am the author of that book, there is no obstacle (other than obtaining permission from the publisher) to my reusing that code here in its entirety. This code was designed, implemented, and tested, thereby saving considerable development effort.

In more realistic situations, a search of sources of reusable software would be necessary in order to locate the portion of the system that will be reused. In addition, there may be some questions about the ownership of the software that is to be reused.

3.4.4 Automation of the requirements engineering process

Automation of at least a portion of the requirements process is also appealing. The idea is that a single high-level requirement is entered into a so-called "requirements generation system." The requirements generation system then produces a set of additional requirements, which generally will have more detail. The requirements generation system can be applied to all or a portion of the requirements.

The automation can be either complete or partial. In a complete automation process, entering one requirement, such as the target computer environment, will generate all the other relevant requirements that can be determined for this software.

In a partially automated requirements generation process, entering a single requirement will result in a group of questions that must be answered before the complete set of relevant software requirements can be met.

As an example of the operation of a partially automated requirements system, the requirements engineer might enter the phrase "personal computer" and the system would respond with something like:

```
Hardware platform:   Intel, AMD, Motorola,
PowerPC  (select one).
```

If the user enters:

```
Intel
```

then the system might respond with:

```
Operating  System:   MS-DOS,  Windows,
Windows  NT,  Windows  95,  Windows  98,
Linux  (select  one).
```

If the user enters:

```
PowerPC
```

then the system might respond with:

```
MacOS, Windows 95, Linux (select one).
```

After the user has indicated an operating system, he or she might be prompted for a version, such as Windows 95 or Windows 98. The selection of one of these two versions might have an impact on the version of the associated dynamically linked library (DLL). The dialog might continue until the user selects a particular hardware device or network connection, in which case a requirement such as

```
System  must  interface  with  DLL  named
ABC123
```

would be generated by the requirements generation system and so on.

Ideally, a requirements generation system should be organized to make optimal use of both requirements regrouping and reuse.

3.5 Reengineering System Requirements

As we saw earlier in this chapter, determination of a system's requirements is an iterative process. When the requirements are set as to meet the (perceived) needs of clients and potential users, then the requirements gathering process usually terminates. We will call the result of this standard activity the "ideal requirements." In many software development organizations at present, cost pressures require as much use as possible of COTS products and available building blocks. In this section we will show how a systematic reuse program encourages the potential reuser to change "ideal requirements" in order to meet cost pressures.

Suppose that the "ideal requirements" specify that a complex database entry be updated within some specific time requirement. Suppose also that the organization already licenses a commercial database that misses meeting this requirement by 10 %.

The organization now has several options:

- They can reconfigure the database software to obtain better performance.

- They can test other commercial database products to see if any meet the "ideal requirements."

- They can purchase faster hardware.

- They can reduce the computing load on the computer system.

- They can provide a performance analysis of the entire system to locate places where system performance can be improved.

- They can change the requirements from the "ideal requirements" to determine if lesser performance would be acceptable, especially since the existing software is essentially free.

Clearly, some organizations will select the last alternative in many situations. This is an example of how the drive for reuse cost savings, which in this case are due to COTS, can cause changes in requirements.

The high-level description of this "reuse-driven" requirements process is simple:

1. Develop an initial set of requirements. This should be done in concert with the customer. If no customer is known, then the requirements should be chosen according to the perceived needs of the system's end users. For simplicity, we will only describe the interaction of the development team with a known customer. The modification for new systems with no fixed customer but likely end users is similar and will not be discussed.

2. Determine if there is an existing reusable system that meets the set of requirements. If there is such a system, stop the requirements process and return the existing reusable system.

3. Determine if there is an existing reusable system that meets "nearly all" the requirements. If such a system exists, provide the customer with a description of the existing system's requirements, how they differ from the original requirements, and the expected costs of using the existing system to "nearly meet" the customer's requirements. If the customer accepts the modified requirements and is willing to accept the reused existing system at the estimated cost, stop the requirements process and return the existing reusable system.

4. If no existing system meets or "nearly meets" the customer's requirements, then the set of requirements should be separated into sets of requirements for subsystems. The decomposition into subsystems should be guided by the process of domain analysis, since the goal is to determine those subsystems that have the greatest probability for being available as COTS products.

5. Steps 2 through 4 should be carried out for each subsystem. The process will terminate for each subsystem as specified in these steps. The only additional activity is to determine if the reused subsystems meet appropriate interface standards. This should be done during a check of the certification of the reused subsystem. (It is assumed that each reused subsystem was previously certified as to its interface standards.)

6. New software development is limited to subsystems in which no agreement can be made between the customer's fixed requirements and the existing reusable subsystem's requirements.

7. After agreement between customer and the software team on the final set of requirements for the subsystems, the existing subsystem building blocks are integrated together with any new code into the new system, which is then configured, tested, documented, and delivered to the customer.

Incidentally, this is not an unrealistic academic scenario. Several of NASA's software systems for spacecraft control and handling data that is transmitted from satellites are being designed with reuse cost savings factors influencing the requirements process. A paper by Bracken reports on experiences in the innovative IMACCS project with a software development process based heavily on COTS and reuse to drive the requirements [BRAC95]. See also [LEAC96] and [WAUN95].

3.6 Assessment of Feasibility of System Requirements

Engineering is often described as the systematic employment of scientific principles to develop systems in an efficient, cost-effective manner, with proper attention to safety. So far, we have concentrated on describing a systematic employment of scientific or engineering principles. We have not considered efficiency, cost effectiveness, or safety.

It is time for an assessment of the system. Often this assessment is used as part of a proposal to management. Of course, any proposal or feasibility study must address cost. At this point, many requirements documents are given to a "software economist" who will estimate the total cost of producing the system. The software economist is generally experienced in the application domain and can predict the size of the software based on the detailed requirements. He or she is aware of any special features of the application domain such as the need for real-time processing, the complexity of the interface to existing or project applications software or operating systems, and the rate of change of related software and hardware technology and standards.

In short, the software economist performs many of the activities that were described in Chapter 2 when we discussed project estimation.

The safety of software that can affect human lives or have major impact on financial records or people's privacy should also be considered. The requirements may spell out the need for special techniques, including always testing divisors for being non-zero before a division occurs, testing permissions before allowing database access, encrypting certain portions of the software's data, or the use of redundancy techniques to improve software fault tolerance.

There may also be other factors, depending on market pressures. Jim McCarthy of Microsoft described the situation well in a recent book [McCA96]. McCarthy was the project manager for release 1.0 of the Visual C++ product. Because of market competition, it was considered imperative to ship updates, including major system upgrades, at six-month intervals. Keeping these updates on schedule was considered more important than including certain technical improvements, particularly if these improvements were not of highest priority. For example, a decision was made to delay the incorporation of templates into version 1.0 of their product. This decision was made in order to have a more robust (fault-free) implementation of the compilation semantics and an assessment of the importance of including templates. More recent updates of Visual C++ are produced at even shorter intervals.

This is typical of the influence of market factors in much of modern software development. Certain desirable requirements are often postponed until later releases of software. You should note that this assessment may mean that the requirements will have to be rewritten. This is standard practice and is no cause for alarm. As we have seen, it is cheaper to fix problems in the requirements phase than later.

In some cases, the assessment may indicate that the system is too costly to build. At this point, there are two choices: look for cost savings, or scrap the project. The primary sources for cost savings are revision of requirements and the collection of existing, reusable software that can be used in the system.

Requirements can often be contradictory. For example, a system may have a requirement for an elegant user interface and also may have a requirement for real-time performance of certain operations. These may be contradictory and it is the responsibility of the requirements process to determine such conflicts.

The requirements assessment should pay particular attention to any system or subsystem that is safety-critical, in the sense that loss of life or major destruction to property can occur if the software system does not function properly.

3.7 Usability Requirements

One of the goals of software engineering given in Chapter 1 was to produce software that is usable. The beginning software engineer is generally not aware that the usability of software can be measured, at least to a first approximation. Indeed, even experienced software engineers and managers frequently are not aware of the techniques of evaluating user interfaces.

This area is often called human-computer interaction, or HCI. It has been the subject of a considerable amount of research for many years. There is a special interest group, SIGCHI, of the ACM devoted to this issue. (The acronym SIGCHI indicates the Special Interest Group on Computer-Human Interaction.) There are several annual conferences on this topic and a considerable amount of interdisciplinary research, often involving researchers and practitioners from psychology, fine arts, communications (for multimedia applications), and, of course, computer science.

The user interface as an integral part of a computer system and, thus, it must also be subjected to requirements engineering. The requirements for a user interface are often phrased in terminology that is far less precise than the terminology used to describe the actions of software that is used for process control, database management, or even the major software project that we will introduce later in this chapter. The requirements document for a user interface are described as being non-behavioral by Davis in his book on software requirements [DAVI90].

One of the first steps in evaluating a human-computer interface is to model the typical user. Users can range from complete novices unfamiliar with any aspect of computers, to experienced computer users who may be unfamiliar with the particular software, to experienced users of particular software packages. Clearly, the needs and desires of such types of users will be different. The designer of a user interface must have target users in mind when he or she designs the interface.

Ideally, the interface is so simple that a novice user can achieve both reasonable success with little training, but sophisticated enough that an experienced user can accomplish more complex tasks with a minimal amount of effort. Designing user interfaces with this degree of flexibility is not an easy task. Operator error can be dangerous if the software controls an airplane, hospital patient monitor, or power plant. User interface design is serious business.

Many organizations have guidelines for user-interface design. One such set of guidelines can be found at the URL

```
http://www.gsfc.nasa.gov/code522/
```

The relatively high-level guidelines in that document are intended to apply across a wide range of applications. The goal of a style guide is to encourage consistency in the "look and feel" of the application.

The process involved in developing a style guide includes the following steps, as recommended by Bleser [BLES94]:

1. Identify relevant guidelines.
2. From the overall set of guidelines, select those that pertain to the application under development.
3. Narrow down the subset of pertinent guidelines.
4. Develop design rules from the guidelines.
5. Allow for reasonable exceptions.

If a guideline states that displays should be formatted consistently, for example, a set of design rules would be needed to specify the location of such display features as menu titles, icon labels, dialog boxes, and error messages. Design rules take the guidelines down to a concrete, highly specific level.

Because a particular guideline can be translated in numerous ways, translation requires designers to define interface components, application components, and constraints that must be met.

The subset of guidelines selected in the first step may include some that conflict. The choice of which guidelines to retain may be based on relative importance or impact, given constraints of time and budget. Resolve any conflict that arises by considering whether one or the other is more appropriate for their application. When the answer is not clear, however, the team can use a more formal decision-making process, according to the following steps:

1. Identify the attributes of user performance that may be affected by the conflicting guidelines (e.g., color discrimination, target detection, speed of response).

2. Weight the importance of those attributes for overall system performance. These weightings are likely to vary from project to project.

3. Using a numeric scale, rate the conflicting guidelines for their expected effect on each performance outcome.

4. Multiply ratings by weights and sum the products. Select the guideline with the higher total.

Here is an example of the usability guidelines. When the same buttons are used for different windows, consistently place them in the same location and keep related buttons together. Some issues are:

- Which buttons are involved?
- Are there any related buttons?
- Where should these buttons be placed in this application?

Design rules should be specific enough that different developers will produce exactly the same features when applying them. For this reason, they should be pre-tested to ensure that developers will agree in their interpretation. There should be little room for a variety of interpretations.

Consider the two alternative screen designs indicated in Figures 3.4 and 3.5. Note the differences in both placement and the amount of space devoted to textual information. Which screen enables a user to more easily select the proper button in an emergency? We will give a partial answer to this question in the next few paragraphs.

Note that the upper left-hand window in Figure 3.4 contains much more textual information that the corresponding window in Figure 3.5. Note also that there is a button in Figure 3.5 that indicates that all valves are to be closed with a single action from the software user. There is no such facility in Figure 3.4.

Specification of color changes in the graph in the upper right-hand corner can increase the usability of the software, as can having the computer make an audible sound such as an alarm. Such interface specification should be part of the system requirements. Analysis of other issues, such as the amount of text displayed in a window, might be included in the requirements analysis, although it is more likely to be left to system design.

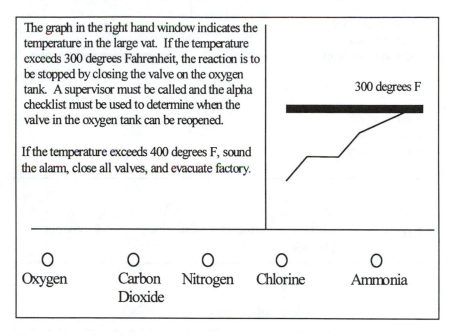

Figure 3.4. A screen design

A more detailed model of a user interface based on an object-entity relationship is given in the remainder of this section. The model incorporates attributes of the user, computer hardware, and I/O devices. It also includes real-time and environmental constraints, as well as the underlying applications software.

The model presents a high level view of the interface and includes formal evaluation of the interface. Both human factors and user interface management systems research ideas are incorporated.

In this model, all the features of a user interface are abstracted as objects with attributes that indicate the properties that the objects may have. Any instance of an object has values for each of its attributes; these values indicate the degree to which the software possesses the attributes. The relationships between the objects making up a user interface are also important and are included in our information model.

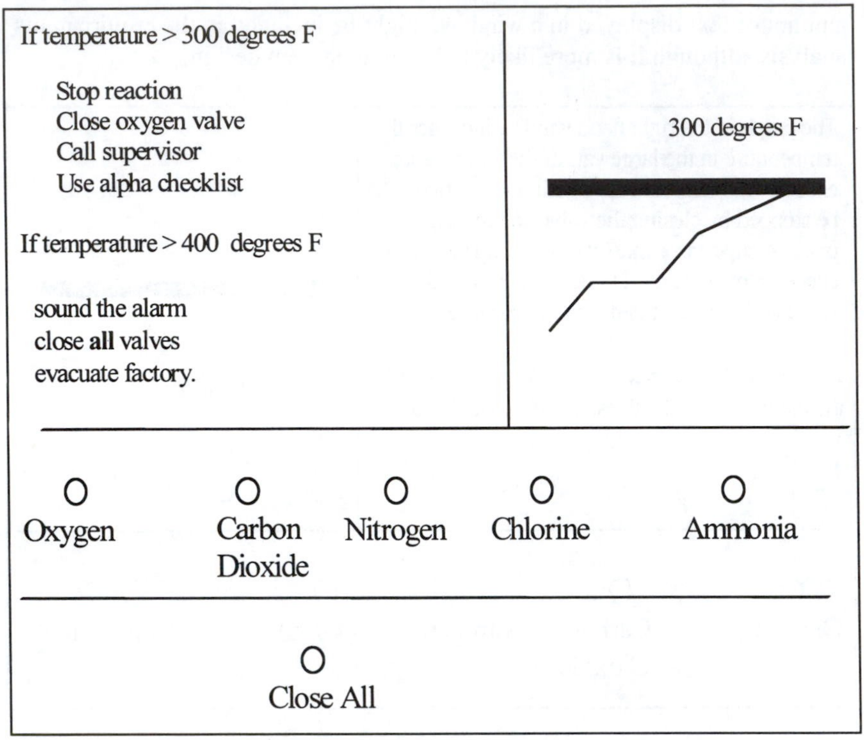

If temperature > 300 degrees F

    Stop reaction
    Close oxygen valve
    Call supervisor
    Use alpha checklist

If temperature > 400 degrees F

    sound the alarm
    close **all** valves
    evacuate factory.

300 degrees F

O	O	O	O	O
Oxygen	Carbon Dioxide	Nitrogen	Chlorine	Ammonia

O
Close All

Figure 3.5. An alternative screen design

The model includes seven objects that make up a user interface:

- Constraint
- Environment
- Hardware
- Input
- Output
- Software
- User

The relationship between these seven basic objects is shown in Figure 3.6.

We provide a brief description of each object in Figure 3.6 together with some of the more important attributes. The sets of attributes of different objects are relatively complex and complete lists of attributes for some of the objects are given in the exercises.

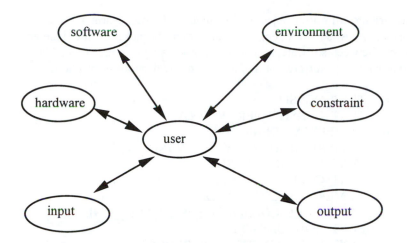

Figure 3.6. The relationship between objects in a User Interface Management System (UIMS).

A constraint object is important for real-time systems in which a user/operator of the system must react to certain situations within prescribed time limits. This is the type of requirement that might apply to a control system for a chemical treatment plant or a medical monitoring device. Constraint objects embody the idea that the user's response is critical and that the timing constraints must be reflected in the model of the user interface. The critical attributes of a constraint object are called TIME_CONSTRAINT, TIME_LIMIT, and CRITICAL; these attributes reflect timing demands that might be present in the interface to a real-time system.

A hardware object involves those portions of the system that are not essentially I/O devices and are primarily hardware oriented. Included here might be portable vs. non-portable computers, presence or absence of networks for remote data access, etc. Typical attributes include OPERATING_SYSTEM, HARDWARE_VERSION, RESPONSE_TIME, HARDWARE_ERRORS, and PORTABLE.

Input and output objects are distinct from one another and from hardware objects. Input objects specifically include keyboards, mice, touch tablets, and light pens; and CRTs, printers, speakers and strip-chart recorders are output objects. Typical attributes of input objects are DEVICE_TYPE and NUM_INPUT_TYPES.

Some typical attributes of output objects are DEVICE_TYPE, NUM_DEVICES, HORIZ_DIMENSION, and VERT_DIMENSION.

Software objects include all of the features of the software being interfaced to while a user object includes all of the features of a user during learning or becoming expert with the software. Of course, the value of certain attributes of a user object will change as the user learns more about the system.   A software object is important because of the inherent differences between software, such as word processing or image processing.

Following are some attributes of alphanumeric portions of displays:

- TEXT_DENSITY
- TEXT_DENSITY_PER_WINDOW
- NUMERICAL_DENSITY
- NUMERICAL_DENSITY_PER_WINDOW
- TEXT_COLUMN_DENSITY
- TEXT_COLUMN_DENSITY_PER_WINDOW
- NUMERICAL_COLUMN_DENSITY
- NUMERICAL_COLUMN_DENSITY_PER_WINDOW
- TEXT_ROW_DENSITY
- TEXT_ROW_DENSITY_PER_WINDOW
- NUMERICAL_ROW_DENSITY
- NUMERICAL_ROW_DENSITY_PER_WINDOW

We now consider how this model can be used in the evaluation of an interface.   Attributes can be classified into three classes:

- Naming attributes give the name of an attribute.
- Descriptive attributes give the description of the attribute.
- Referential attributes refer to an attribute of some other object.

Consider the attributes of a user object, which is an abstraction of the actual human user of a computer system.   Naming, descriptive, and referential attributes are denoted by N, D, and R, respectively.

- NAME : text, the name of the user of the user object. (N)

- EXPERIENCED_WITH_HARDWARE: Boolean, TRUE if the user has experience with the hardware previously, FALSE otherwise.   This attribute indicates the user's experience with this particular computer and may be FALSE if the user has used different models of the same brand and operating system. For example, the computer to be used is a portable one with different key placement from an office system used before. (R)

- EXPERIENCED_WITH_INPUT_DEVICE: Boolean, TRUE if the user has experience with the input device previously, FALSE otherwise. This attribute indicates the user's experience with this particular device and may be FALSE if the user has used similar but different models of the device. For example, the user may have used a three-button mouse previously but now needs to use a one- or two-button device. (R)

- EXPERIENCED_WITH_OUTPUT_DEVICE: Boolean, TRUE if the user has experience with the output device previously, FALSE otherwise. This attribute indicate the user's experience with this particular device and may be FALSE if the user has used similar but different models of the device such as a non-scrollable or a scrollable CRT terminal. (R)

- SOFTWARE_EXPERIENCE: integer valued in the range 1 to 10, with 1 indicating little experience with the particular software and 10 indicating being relatively experienced. (R)

- COMPUTER_EXPERIENCE: Boolean, TRUE if the user is familiar with computers, FALSE otherwise (D)

The numerical values can be used as part of a model of the user interface. It is very clear that detailed evaluation of user interfaces is much more complex than just looking at a site on the World Wide Web and pronouncing it "cool." (Many sites that supposedly have "cool" graphics and animation have poor designs that require users to either wait long periods for desired information to appear on their screens or else not get the desired information at all.) The effective use of computer resources for user interfaces is not trivial.

You might feel that some of the points made in this section appear to be more appropriate for the chapter on software design rather than a chapter devoted to requirements. However, you should recall the goals as stated in the first paragraph of this section: to provide a systematic approach to developing requirements for the non-behavioral portion of the software.

3.8 Specifying Requirements Using State Diagrams and Decision Tables

Until now, we have discussed software requirements using natural language. We have used a relatively structured pseudocode that can serve as the basis for later designs of the software to be developed. This is acceptable for projects that are relatively small. If the requirements are sufficiently small and unambiguous, we can manage with textual descriptions that are augmented by graphics as necessary.

However, in many larger software systems, the inherent ambiguity of natural language descriptions will make the project's requirements unsuitable for textual requirements. Even if the requirements could be written solely in a natural language, the resulting document might be too large to be of any use. Detailed documents that are several thousand pages long are rarely read, much less understood!

In many cases we are lead to the use of more formal and precise methods of specifying system requirements. We will describe two such methods briefly in this section: finite state machines and decision tables. The descriptions are brief and are intended to complement your previous knowledge of these and related concepts in a course in discrete mathematics or automata theory.

A finite state machine is a model of computation in which the behavior of the system is dependent upon which of a finite set of "states" the system is in and which of a set of "events" is observed. One particular state is used to represent the initial state of the system. For a software system that controls a process in a chemical power plant, the states might be those shown in Table 3.6:

Table 3.6
Examples of states in a chemical process

1. Vat empty
2. Base chemical placed in vat
3. Temperature of vat lowered by refrigeration
4. Reagent added
5. Reaction occurs
6. Temperature of vat raised by heating
7. Reaction complete (pressure in vat is normal)
8. Compound in vat poured into molds
9. Failure – chemical plant must be evacuated

The software to control the chemical process would use these ten states to determine which actions would be appropriate at different times. For example, the software should never allow the contents of the vat to be poured into molds until the reaction is complete. The reagent should never be poured into the vat unless the vat's temperature has been reduced by refrigeration.

If the number of states is not too large, then a finite state machine can be described visually as a state diagram according to the following informal conventions:

- Each state is represented as a bubble.

- The flow of control of the software is illustrated by a set of directed arcs between the bubbles.

- Each arc is labeled by the action that occurs.

- Transitions from one bubble to another depend only on the state from which it emanates and the label on the arc.

- The process has one or more preferred states in which it would ideally terminate.

We can use these informal rules to develop a state diagram for the chemical process described in this section. The diagram is given in Figure 3.7.

The movement from state to state is controlled completely by the transition function. Since the transition function is mathematically precise, both the allowable states and the transitions must be specified completely.

The rules describing the creation of state diagrams can be formulated mathematically in a precise definition. Formally, a finite state machine is a quintuple consisting of the following:

- A set of allowable symbols for the inputs
- A non-empty, finite set of " states"
- A single distinguished state called the " start state"
- A (possibly empty) set of states called " final states"
- A transition function that takes as input a state and an allowable symbol and produces as output a single state.

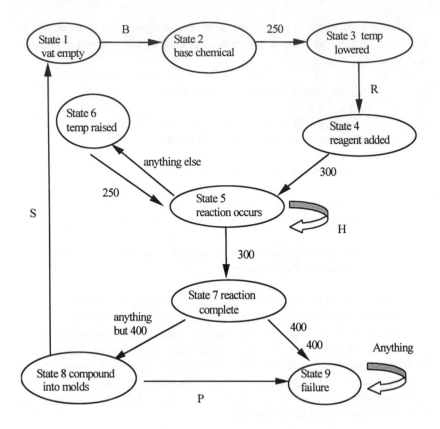

Figure 3.7. A state diagram for a simple chemical reaction.

For our example, the states are those shown in Table 3.6. The allowable inputs and their associated meanings might be the following:

- B (indicating base chemical)
- R (reagent)
- S (solvent)
- 250 (low temperature limit)
- 300 (high temperature limit)
- 400 (temperature failure)
- H (heat)
- C (cool)
- M (ready for molds)

The transition function for the diagram in Figure 3.7 is given in Table 3.8.

Table 3.8
The state transition function for the state diagram shown in Figure 3.7

Current State	Input	New State
1	B	2
2	250	3
3	R	4
4	300	5
5	H	5
5	300	7
5	anything else	6
6	250	5
7	anything but 400	8
7	400	9
8	P	9
8	S	1
9	Anything	9

Table 3.8
The decision table for the state diagram shown in Figure 3.7

Current State	Input	New State
1	B	2
2	if temp <= 250	3
3	R	4
4	if temp >= 300	5
5	H	5
5	if temp >= 300	7
5	if temp >= 400	9
5	anything else	6
6	if temp <= 250	5
7	anything but temp >= 400	8
7	if temp >= 400	9
8	P	9
8·	S	1
9	Anything	9

There is an alternative representation that can be used to describe this system: decision tables. A decision table is essentially a description of the choices made at certain states. A decision table for this system might be something like the illustration given in Table 3.8.

Decision tables have one advantage over the state diagram approach – they can indicate the influence of a range of values, rather than single inputs. Even though we do not illustrate it here in detail, you should be aware that decision tables can allow the associated state changes to reflect several ranges of inputs.

3.9 Specifying Requirements Using Petri Nets

Many software systems must handle concurrent events, with or without synchronization. Several approaches have been developed to specify how concurrency is to be represented, which processes must be synchronized, and which processes may execute concurrently, without synchronization. One such technique is the Petri net [PETR75].

A Petri net is a graph in which the nodes are called "places" and the arcs are called "transitions." Each place in the graph is allowed to contain 0 or more "tokens," which indicate that a computation has reached the place. A transition is said to "be enabled," or "to fire," if there is at least one token in each of its input places. When a transition fires, one token is removed from each of the input places, and new tokens are placed in each of the output places. There is no requirement that the number of input tokens be equal to the number of output tokens.

Examples of Petri nets are given in Figures 3.8 through 3.10. Note that we have used a line between each pair of places to indicate transition. When a transition fires, tokens are put in each of its output places, as illustrated in Figure 3.10.

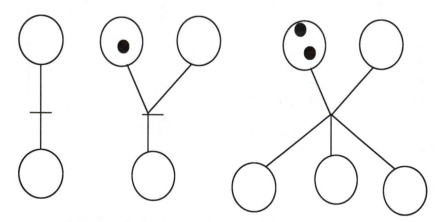

Figure 3.8. Some Petri nets with none of their transitions enabled.

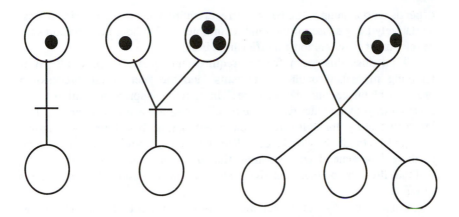

Figure 3.9. Some Petri nets with all their transitions enabled.

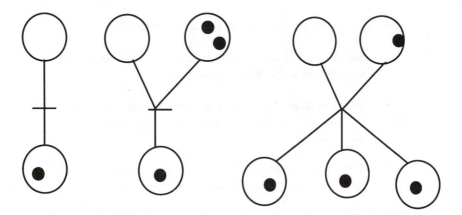

Figure 3.10. The Petri nets in Figure 3.9 after transitions are fired.

A Petri net allows a graphical representation of concurrent software. For non-current software that executes sequentially in a single process, Petri nets have relatively little advantage over flowcharts in their representative power.

3.10 Ethical Issues

There is always a lot of pressure during the requirements portion of the software development process. Every software project manager wants his or her project to produce a high-quality system that is completed on time and within budget. Every commonly used approach to software development depends on obtaining a number of correct requirements that comprise at least a relatively large subset of the final requirements. Without this, the software development is certain to be inefficient at best.

What does this mean for the requirements-gathering process? It is tempting to rush through requirements (and the later design process) in order to begin coding the software. In iterative approaches, this can be acceptable, provided that few of the requirements are actually incorrect. It is less satisfactory for software development that is based on the classical waterfall method. In short, incomplete requirements are acceptable as long as there is a general understanding that the requirements are incomplete, and that they can be made relatively complete with reasonable expenditures of effort.

What is clearly not acceptable is presenting a set of requirements as being correct when they are known to be incorrect. The incorrectness can arise from any of the following:

- Some computations are theoretically impossible.

- Some interactions with different subsystems are inconsistent within the software itself.

- Some interactions are inconsistent with software systems with which the software is intended to be interoperable.

- There may be impossible performance demands on the software's execution time or space requirements.

These types of errors in system requirements are a serious matter. Consider the problem of determining a user's password from its encrypted version. On the UNIX operating system, only an encrypted version of the user's password is stored in a password file. The algorithm for encrypting the password uses what are called "one-way functions." Such functions do not have inverses and, therefore, the password cannot be recovered from the encrypted version. When a user attempts to log on, he or she is prompted for a password. The purported password is run through the one-way function for encryption and the result is matched against the previously encrypted version in the password file. If the two encrypted password versions agree, the user is allowed to log on. Otherwise, the login fails and the potential user is notified of that failure. On modern UNIX systems, the password file is not readable by ordinary users and, thus, the passwords are theoretically completely secure. Clearly, a requirement to recover a user's password from the encrypted version in a UNIX password file is theoretically impossible.

(Technically, the conclusion of the previous paragraph is not correct. A user with essentially unlimited time and unrestricted access could try all one character passwords, then all two character passwords, and so on until he or she either discovered the password or died of old age. A word to the wise: use long passwords with embedded non-alphabetical characters and few recognizable names, dates, or initials as part of your password.)

As another example, consider the problem of developing software for an emergency telephone system that will be used to track the phone numbers and addresses when emergency calls are made. The 911 system in the United States is a typical example. In every area code, there is a maximum of 10^7 possible seven-digit telephone numbers. It is easy to trace the signal of a caller to the emergency telephone service. Indeed, such calls are never terminated even if the calling party hangs up or is disconnected.

Determining the address of the telephone is another matter. Matching an address to a telephone number is effectively a sequential search and this is not feasible if the system is to respond within proper time limits. Thus, the matching of telephone numbers to addresses is generally done one time, before 911 emergency telephone service is installed. In fact, this information has been available for many years in what is known as a "cross directory." The preexistence of such a cross directory, or creation of one if it does not exist already, should be part of the requirements for an emergency telephone system. Otherwise, the requirements are not feasible because of the time needed to search the pairs of telephone numbers and addresses.

Preventing internal software compatibility is the responsibility of the project team and no problems should be set by the requirements team. An example of this problem is requiring two different components of the system to write to memory buffers at the same location. Using the address of the start of a printer's buffer queue for storage of intermediate results in a desktop calculator program on a personal computer is an example of this problem.

External compatibility problems with interoperable software are much harder to detect. The user of COTS software often has to know which ports are being written to or which names are used for binding socket descriptors to locations. A typical example of this unwanted interference between software subsystems might be an existing system that runs on the UNIX and assumed that all relevant files were on the /usr file system. This can cause problems for another software application that used some of the same files and expected that the common files would be on the /var or /usr2 file systems.

A recent examination of the computer listings in the help wanted section of the *Washington Post* showed several jobs in the area of COTS. Industry is beginning to recognize the importance of avoiding such conflicts. Of course, an in-depth knowledge of both the COTS product and the software's application domain are necessary before one can predict with any confidence that no such conflicts occur. Clearly there are ethical considerations in assessing the appropriateness of COTS products as solutions to a system's requirements.

The IEEE Code of Ethics, IEEE Policy Number 7.8, is very informative in this regard. It is posted at the web site

```
http://www.ieee.org/committee/ethics/
```

For completeness, this code is listed here. Note the guidelines for taking responsibility when making technical decisions in item 1 and the need for constant retraining in item 6.

"We, the members of the IEEE, in recognition of the importance of technologies in affecting the quality of life throughout the world, and in accepting a personal obligation to our profession, its members and the communities we serve, do hereby commit ourselves to the highest ethical and professional conduct and agree:

To accept responsibility in making engineering decisions consistent with the safety, health, and welfare of the public, and to disclose promptly factors that might endanger the public or the environment;

To avoid real or perceived conflicts of interest whenever possible, and to disclose them to affected parties when they exist;

To be honest and realistic in stating claims or estimates based on available data;

To reject bribery in all its forms;

To improve the understanding of technology, its appropriate application, and potential consequences;

To maintain and improve our technical competence and to undertake technological tasks for others only if qualified by training or experience, or after full disclosure of pertinent limitations;

To seek, accept, and offer honest criticism of technical work, to acknowledge and correct errors, and to credit promptly the contributions of others;

To treat fairly all persons regardless of such factors as race, religion, gender, disability, age, or national origin;

To avoid injuring others, their property, reputation, or employment by false or malicious action;

To assist colleagues and co-workers in their professional development and to support them in following this code of ethics."

The rest of this section is the author's personal opinion of the ethical issues involved with the software requirements process.

What should you do if you are involved with the requirements gathering team and the requirements include one of the potentially fatal flaws? The first step is to check your analysis and make sure that you have not made a mistake. Don't rely too much on hazy recollections of meetings or on courses dimly recalled from college. Being human, students and professors make mistakes. (So, too, do authors of software engineering books, but at least there is the possibility of errors being caught by one or more technical reviewers, as well as by an editor. Many authors of books are human, as are some editors and reviewers.)

If you haven't made a mistake, consider discussing your concerns informally with a trusted co-worker. Be careful about this, because you don't want your ideas presented to someone else as your own. Keep your own detailed notes about the perceived problem.

Perhaps a more direct approach is to make an appointment with your manager to explain the problem and your analysis. Remember that managers hate unpleasant surprises. Don't spring your objection on him or her in the middle of a meeting or review with the client or your manager's upper level management.

What should you do if your manager doesn't seem to be willing to accept your analysis? Go through the technical reasons with him or her again, allowing for the possibility that you were wrong, or that you didn't explain it well. Pursue the point, perhaps in future public or private meetings, until one of three things happens:

1. The manager does not agree with your analysis.

2. The manager agrees with your analysis and will ask the requirements team to fix the problem.

3. The manager seems to be ignoring the problem, allowing a potentially serious problem to occur.

In the first scenario, you have to consider the possibility that your analysis is wrong, even though you cannot see why. You need to keep a good relationship with this manager, even though he or she probably has some reservations about your judgment. Keep your technical skills up to date and begin to consider the possibility of taking another job.

In the second scenario, continue to be prepared. A bonus or promotion may be in your future.

In the third scenario, there is a serious ethical dilemma. In an operational environment in which human lives are at stake, such as in a computerized monitoring system in a hospital, control of a railroad, or almost anything in a nuclear power plant, there really is no choice: you must take all necessary actions to prevent what could be a disaster.

The choice is almost as clear if a major financial disaster would occur as a result of using software that is implemented to meet these erroneous requirements. You cannot argue that affecting an unknown person or corporation financially is not sufficient grounds for not adhering to the highest level of personal professional conduct.

In essence, the only way to justify taking little or no further action is to claim that the project is a throwaway research prototype with no possibility of becoming operational. If this is not the case, then you must do what Watts Humphrey recommends in his classic book *Managing the Software Process* when an experienced project manager is asked to complete a project with insufficient resources or within too short a time period: resign [HUMP89].

Of course, you must do more. The customer must be made aware of the problem. This is your responsibility. Unfortunately, whistle-blowers rarely have successful, remunerative careers. Be sure that you are right before taking any drastic action.

Ethical problems will be discussed further in the chapter on software testing.

3.11 Some Metrics for Requirements

Many organizations attempt to predict project cost at the requirements phase. This means that they attempt to measure the size of the system that is to be produced. One way to estimate the size (and resources needed to create) of a software system is to determine the size of the system's requirements. There are several commonly used approaches to measuring the size of a set of requirements:

- Count the number of distinct requirements. This method is probably too simplistic, since it does not consider system complexity. In addition, this metric is influenced by the separation of multiple clauses in a single requirements sentence into separate sentences, each representing an individual requirement.

- Compute the sum over all requirements of the "functionality" expressed by each requirement. This approach requires describing the functionality that is associated with each requirement. The functionality is matched to a scale with a set of weighting factors.

- Matching the requirements to those of existing systems that are to be reused. In this method, only new software is counted in any measurement of the size of a system's requirements.

- Compute the "size" of the interfaces to other software systems to which the desired software will be interoperable.

We will now discuss each of these measurement methods in turn.

Computing the number of distinct requirements is the simplest method of estimating the eventual size of the system, since it requires no special analysis of the individual requirements. The number can be computed by examining the number of rows in the requirements traceability matrix.

Unfortunately, simply counting the number of requirements does not take into account the difficulty of implementing different individual requirements. Thus, this approach does not distinguish the complexity of implementing a requirement such as

The software will begin execution when the user enters the single UNIX command "go."

from the complexity of implementing the requirement

The system will be capable of processing 10,000 distinct transactions per minute, with no transaction suspended in a waiting queue for more than one second before it is processed.

In spite of the obvious imprecision, the number of requirements does provide at least a hint as to the amount of difficulty of implementing an entire software system. We can get more accurate information by examining the requirements in detail. The most common technique of estimating the functionality of a set of requirements is called "function point analysis." The term was coined by Albrecht, who first developed the concept at IBM in 1979 [ALBR79]. Capers Jones [JONE93] describes the use of function points in project estimation.

The function point estimation technique is based on an assessment of the functionality needed for each requirement based on the following:

- The number and type of user interactions.
- The number and type of interfaces to internal files
- The number and type of interfaces to external files
- The general perception of the difficulty of programming in the project's application domain.

We will now describe a formal procedure for computing function points. All function point metrics are based on the number and types of interfaces in the program. Interfaces can be either internal or external. The total number and sizes of interfaces are used as the basis for the collection of function points. Once this total is obtained, it is modified by several weighting factors, some of which are subjective and some of which are objective. The subjective factors include an assessment of the complexity of the interfaces and the overall complexity of the system.

More precisely, weights are assigned according to the rules that are given in Table 3.9:

Table 3.9
Use of weights for function point analysis.

	Simple	Average	Complex
External input or files	3	4	6
External outputs or reports	4	5	7
External queries or response	3	4	6
External interfaces to other systems	7	10	15
Internal files	5	7	10

After the weights are assigned, a complexity factor is determined in the range from 0 (representing no influence) to 5 (representing strong influence) for each of the factors given in Table 3.10.

For each software system to be analyzed, the sum of the "complexity adjustment values" f_i is computed using the values determined from Table 3.10. The final result is the total number of function points for the system according to the equation:

```
FP = count_total *(0.65 + sumf_I /100)
```

As you can see, counting the number of function points in a proposed software system is a somewhat subjective in the sense that there is no well-defined definition of terms such as "average," "simple," or "complex." Other terms in the "complexity analysis" list clearly indicate a lack of precision in their definition. Therefore, it is highly probable that different people will produce very different estimates of the number of function points for the same software system. There are two general approaches to the ambiguity that is associated with the function point analysis process.

The first approach is to ignore minor differences, working under the assumption that many software measurements have errors and that minor differences can be ignored because they are not statistically significant. This makes it difficult to determine the cause of any variability between function point data that is gathered from several different software development projects. It might not be clear if any correlation between the number of function points and the amount of effort expended (as measured in person-months) is due to actual relationships or just to differences in counting techniques.

Table 3.10
Use of complexity factors and weights for function point analysis.

Complexity Factor	Weight (0 .. 5)
Reliable system back-up and recovery	
Data communications	
Distributed functions	
Performance	
Heavily-used system	
On-line data entry	
Ease of operation	
On-line updates	
Complex interfaces	
Complex processing	
Reusability	
Ease of installation	
Operation at multiple sites	
Modifiability	

The second approach is to attempt to make the collection of function point data more rigorous. This is the approach taken by the various function point users' groups. There have been several attempts at establishing standards for function point analysis. Rather than describe these standards in detail, we suggest that the reader consult the electronic mailing list for the function point users group at

```
function.point.list-request@crim.ca
```

Regardless of the approach used to standardize the collection of function points, the objectively determined weights are obtained by determining if the program will be interactive or will execute without user interaction. The effect of the program executing concurrently with other applications is also included in these weights.

You should be aware that the function point metric is not directly associated with programming effort or system size. An organization using the function point metrics must define some of the subjective terms carefully, collect data, compare the data with other metrics that are directly computed using correlation and other methods, and then calibrate any models that use this metric. Only then can this metric be used with confidence in a particular environment.

Because of the inherent subjectivity of function point analysis, there are several distinct standards for it. Unfortunately, there is no single international standard that can be used to determine some of the definitions needed for consistent application of the function point method. Thus, there is little reason to expect exact correlations of your organization's experience using function points for cost and schedule estimation with another organization's use of function point data.

3.12 The Requirements Review

Once the requirements team has determined a set of requirements for the system, it is generally necessary to have a requirements review. The purpose of this review is to allow the customer to react to the requirements produced by the requirements team. If no customer is known at the time of the review, then members of the marketing staff and other personnel are often used instead.

A requirements review is the one thing that is common to all software development environments that have more than one software engineer or programmer. A requirements review is a check to ensure that the requirements as set by the requirements team actually meet the needs of the organization for which the software is intended. The basic principle is that it is pointless to proceed if the software to be developed does not meet the needs of its users. As such, a requirements review provides a much-needed "sanity check."

There may be several different requirements reviews, depending on the organization's software development approach. In the classical waterfall software development process, there usually will be at least two scheduled requirements reviews: a preliminary and a functional review. An iterative software development process may use a single requirements review if the resulting requirements are considered to be satisfactory and complete. It is more likely, however, that there will be many reviews in organizations that use an iterative approach. Note that reviews in iterative software development processes often include designs, source code, and requirements.

We will now consider requirements reviews in more detail. Depending on the nature of the organization developing the software, a requirements review can range from a relatively informal presentation where a few people talk while sitting around a table, to a highly scripted, well-rehearsed formal performance with overhead transparencies, slides, multimedia computer-generated presentations, and similar levels of communications aids. In general, the formality and complexity of the requirements review increases as least as fast as the complexity of the software being developed and the size of the organization.

The requirements review can be a fundamental milestone in an organization that uses a process based on the classical waterfall model of software development. As such, its importance is obvious. If the organization uses an iterative software development process, the requirements review might appear to be slightly less important, since a deficiency in the software requirements will be corrected in the next iteration of the software. In fact, one might almost think that requirements reviews are not important at all, since any deficiencies can be repaired in a later iteration.

However, this is not the case. A good requirements review indicates if the requirements are close to being satisfactory, if they are correct but incomplete, or if they are incorrect. (In actuality, all three of these things frequently occur simultaneously in the same software project. However, it is conceptually simpler for our discussion to consider requirements where only one of these things happens at a time.) Even if the software's requirements are expected to undergo one or more additional iterations, the process is certain to be much more efficient if any incorrect requirements are detected early, before too much effort goes into developing software based on these erroneous requirements.

Notice what this view of requirements suggests about software testing. In an academic setting, a student can argue with an instructor that his or her program is correct because it met the requirements as set by the instructor. Often such conversations are exacerbated by an ambiguity in the project specifications as set by the instructor. Only those test cases that are consistent with the instructor's specifications are considered to be fair.

Unfortunately, obtaining good requirements is more essential than this purely academic view of software development would indicate. If the requirements are not satisfactory because of being incomplete or not being what the customer really wanted, then the eventual agreement of the software with the (incorrect) initial requirements does not mean that the software will be correct, or that it will be a success in the marketplace. Think of building a thirty-story building on top of a set of thin wooden boards that rest directly on top of a sandy beach. The rest of the building may match the wooden boards precisely, but the entire structure is inherently unstable.

Clearly, requirements reviews are important, even if they are expected to be repeated as part of an iterative software development process. Even in a relatively non-iterative process such as the classical waterfall process, there may be multiple requirements reviews. The first and last of such reviews are often called preliminary and critical requirements reviews, respectively.

There is another way for you to understand the importance of a professionally run requirements review. Let's begin by estimating the cost of holding the requirements review meeting itself. The typical work year consists of 52 weeks of 40 hours each, or approximately 2000 hours. The typical so-called "loaded cost" of a software engineer includes the following costs:

- His or her yearly salary.
- Fringe benefits (approximately 25 to 30%).
- The average prorated cost of technical writing, secretarial, custodial, and human resources (personnel) support staff.
- The average prorated cost of computer maintenance, network manager, and other technical support staff.
- The prorated cost of equipment, utilities, and other physical costs.

This is frequently considered to be in excess of $100,000 per year, or roughly $50 per hour. Therefore, a four-hour meeting with five people present costs at least a thousand dollars, assuming that there was no preparation time needed for the meeting, no coordination of schedules was necessary in order to schedule the meeting, and that no time was needed to travel to the meeting.

A more realistic estimate for a system of the same size is eight hours of meetings, ten people attending the meeting, with two days of preparation for the meeting. Typically, at least three people are part of the requirements presentation and, thus, they are involved in the rehearsals, with the preparation time including rehearsals, preparation of the documents, slides, transparencies, or computer-generated multimedia presentation, and proofreading the documents to be handed out at the meeting. Another fifteen minutes should be allowed for travel each way, even if the meetings are scheduled in the conference room down the hall. Because of limits to the attention span of human beings, such meetings are often spread out over several days, due to the number of breaks that are usually necessary. This conservative estimate of cost is more than $6500.

The expense is much larger in many environments. Note that there is no special expense listed separately for food, entertainment of customers, or travel to a customer's site. Clearly, reviews must be taken seriously. Wasting the customer's time or that of your upper-level management is not recommended.

Now that we have established the importance of requirements reviews, it is time to describe how they should be conducted. We will describe two types of requirements reviews: a typical relatively formal review process performed in a meeting, and an inspection of the requirements, usually done by one or more individuals, but without formal presentations. Use the discussion here as a guide to how a requirements review should be conducted within the artificial confines of a software engineering class. In an actual software requirements review in industry or government, there may be company policies that supersede the suggestions here. If so, use the company policy.

We first consider a requirements review that is performed during a formal meeting. The most effective reviews have a person responsible for taking notes and providing a transcript of the meeting. The purpose of the note taker is to provide a written document that indicates any changes made to the requirements as part of the meeting. Such written documentation is provided to all meeting participants after the meeting is over. This allows the organization to have a complete record of all major actions on the project. Reviews are often recorded using audio tape, with some organizations also using videotape or electronic storage of data passed by means of conferencing systems.

Generally, one person is responsible for the organization of the presentation. The person may be called the requirements team manager. In some organizations, he or she may also be the project manager. In other organizations, he or she may have no other project administrative responsibility. In any case, the person will introduce the members of the requirements presentation team and coordinate the rest of the discussion.

A checklist for a requirements review meeting is given in Table 3.10.

The details given at the requirements review will depend on the nature of the review. At a preliminary requirements review, the requirements may be given at a very high level. This is especially true for software development that follows the classical waterfall model. Most other requirements reviews are much more detailed.

The organization of a requirements review presentation is generally guided by the organization of the software. A typical review presentation has the following topics:

- Introduction
- System Overview
- Subsystem Requirements
- Subsystem 1 Requirements
- Subsystem 2 Requirements
- Subsystem 3 Requirements
- Subsystem 4 Requirements
- Subsystem 1 Interfaces
- Subsystem 2 Interfaces
- Subsystem 3 Interfaces
- Subsystem 4 Interfaces
- Proposed Resources
- Proposed Schedule
- Potential Problems
- Summary

Table 3.11
Checklist for a Requirements Review Meeting

Presentation rehearsed.
Time of presentation within allotted limits.
Sufficient time is available for questions.
People who can answer technical questions are in attendance.
Slides, transparencies, and multimedia materials checked for accuracy.
Slides, transparencies, and multimedia materials checked for spelling.
Paper copies of slides, transparencies, and multimedia materials are available to all participants.
Meeting room has all necessary equipment: microphones, overhead projector, slide projector, videotape player and monitor, computer-monitor hookup, etc.
An attendance list with names, addresses, phone numbers, and affiliations is passed around, and all attendees sign it.

Sufficient time should be allotted for questions during each major subsection of the requirements review. The goal is to have a clear, comprehensive document.

The next type of requirements review we consider may be characterized as an inspection. We describe a typical set of (oversimplified) inspection guidelines below.

The system requirements must include the following:

- Which hardware platform will be used? (Intel-based microprocessor, Motorola-based, Power-PC-based, or other.)
- Which operating system will be supported? (DOS, Windows, Windows 95, Windows NT, MacOS, UNIX, Linux, XENIX?) If UNIX or Windows are used, which variant?
- Which operating system versions will be required?
- Will the different versions of software run on different computers and operating systems? If so, which ones?
- Will the file formats be consistent across operating systems? (This is the case for Microsoft Word, Excel, and PowerPoint applications programs which allow both PC- and Macintosh-based computers to access files and treat them in the same way, regardless of the platform on which the files were originally created. The same is true for HTML and, to a lesser degree, Java.)
- Will the software have a graphical user interface?

- Will the software's graphical user interface be consistent with that of the operating system and with other applications running in the same environment?
- Will there be multiple implementations, such as a minimal size for laptops with small amounts of memory and disk space, and larger implementations with more support files and features, to be used in computers with fewer limitations on memory and size?
- What are the minimal system requirements, in terms of memory size and available hard disk space?
- Will the program's existence in memory cause problems for other applications that are also running on the computer?
- Are there any other software packages, such as word processors, spreadsheet programs, database managers, or drawing tools, with which the program must be able to share data?
- Will on-line help be provided within the software?
- How will the software be delivered? Will it use floppy disks or compact disks? What disk format will be used?
- Will the software be provided in compressed or uncompressed form?
- Will installation and setup software be provided?
- Will training be required?
- Are there any time constraints, such as completion of certain operations within specified limits? (These constraints are called "hard" constraints, in contrast to the "soft" constraints described in the next bulleted item. A system with hard timing constraints is called a "hard real-time system.")
- Are there any time constraints, such as completion of a number of certain operations within a single specified limits, so that the constraint is on the average number of operations per unit time? (These constraints are called "soft" constraints, in contrast to the "hard" constraints described in the previous bulleted item. A system with only soft timing constraints is called a "soft real-time system." A system that has either hard or soft real-time constraints is called simply a "real-time system.")

The requirements gathering process has two complementary principles:

1. The requirements for the system must be modified and refined until the system can be developed by software designers and coders who are familiar with the fundamental algorithms of

the application domain, but who are ignorant about the requirements engineering process. The eventual requirements will be so complete and unambiguous that the design will be clear and the coding can be done easily by implementing standard, well-known algorithms.

2. The requirements for the system must be modified and refined until the system requirements can be understood by requirements engineers who are knowledgeable about requirements engineering, but who know nothing about the application domain. The eventual requirements will be so complete and unambiguous that the requirements engineer will understand them completely, even without knowledge of the application domain.

The requirements for the system must be iterated until each of these two principles is true for each of the requirements.

The following tasks must be completed in order to develop specific verifiable requirements:

1. Number each of the requirements.
2. For each requirement, develop a specific, unambiguous test case that will determine if the requirement is met.
3. If you are unable to develop a specific, unambiguous test case that will determine if the requirement is met, either rewrite the requirement, or break it down into smaller requirements until you can develop a specific, unambiguous test case that will determine if the new requirement is met. If new requirements are created as a result of breaking down existing requirements, number them using dotted notations showing the origin of the requirements. (Thus, new requirements obtained by breaking down requirement 3 will be numbered 3.1, 3.2, and so on.)
4. Repeat the process in steps 1 through 3 until you can develop a specific, unambiguous test case that will determine if the requirement is met.

Once you have developed a specific, unambiguous test case that will determine if each system requirement is met, it is time to determine the feasibility of implementing the requirements.

For each requirement developed for the system, perform the following tasks:

1. Develop a high-level design that will be used to implement the specific requirement.

2. Iterate that design until the design is sufficiently detailed to bring to a programmer.

3. If any requirement cannot be designed so that it can be implemented as code, mark the requirement as ambiguous or unimplementable and then review the requirements. (Some of the requirements, although individually testable, may be inconsistent with other requirements).

4. If any of the requirements are inconsistent, revise the set of requirements to remove the inconsistency.

Once requirements have been developed, the customer must be given an opportunity to interact with them. Determine if you will present the system to the customer as a series of prototypes or as a single delivered system.

If the customer will be given a series of prototypes, begin development of the initial prototype. In this case, the customer is allowed to interact with the development process and to make changes up to the last possible minute.

If the customer will only be given a single-system delivery, iterate with the customer to determine if the project team is "building the right system."

You can see from the above guidelines that requirements reviews are serious affairs and demand considerable resources from an organization. Experience indicates that they are worth it.

It is clear that development of requirements is a major part of software engineering. An assessment by the quality assurance (QA) team is definitely appropriate for any requirements document produced. The QA assessment can take place before, during, or after a requirements review, depending on the organizational structure.

3.13 A Management Viewpoint

In many very large software projects, the project manager may have a separate manager for the requirements, design coding, and testing teams. It is perhaps more common for the project manager to provide guidance to each of these teams, while remaining in overall control. For simplicity, we will have to ignore the extra level of management and assume that one manager is responsible for the entire project. In this section, we will describe what this manager expects from the requirements phase. We describe both the product that he or she expects to be delivered and the process by which it is created.

The goal of the requirements process is to obtain a clear, unambiguous, consistent, and complete set of requirements. The manager wants these in a timely manner because he or she has deadlines that are usually imposed by higher authorities within the organization. He or she will expect frequent updates as to the requirements gathering process. These updates may be informal.   More likely, there will be weekly or monthly written status reports, perhaps with requirements reviews.

At most meetings, a manager wishes to show off the progress of his or her project. Often the most important thing is to avoid giving the manager an unpleasant surprise. Generally, a manager prefers to receive a report that is incomplete (and which he or she knows is incomplete before the meeting begins) than one which is inconsistent. The manager expects to see a lot of "action items" to perform specific tasks with roughly accurate estimates of when the tasks will be completed.

The manager will expect his or her people to attend briefings and reviews in a manner that is consistent with the organization's "culture" and the people present. In an internal meeting of a casual organization, there may not be any special dress code. In a meeting with customers, or in a more formal environment, coats and ties may be expected of men, with equivalently formal work clothes for women. The rule of thumb is, don't embarrass the manager, the customer, or the organization. When in doubt, ask.

There will always be a final presentation of the requirements. The manager expects the presentation to be carefully rehearsed, with media aids that include overhead transparencies, slides, videotapes, or computer-generated slide shows, as appropriate. Sufficient copies of all relevant documentation should be handed out to all participants. Copies of slides and overhead transparencies for all attendees are a must.

The manager also expects that all documents intended for internal use be given to him or her at the appropriate time and place. Generally, the customer does not need to see the requirements traceability matrix document. (This is not correct if the process must be certified by QA, as might be the case for medical software products needing approval by the Food and Drug Administration.) Therefore, this document should not be given to the customer. Internal memorandums should also be kept private.

The manager expects to have cost and staffing estimates for the system. If such estimates already exist, then the manager needs to understand any changes in the estimates so that he or she can make a case for more resources for the proposal.

The manager also wants to be knowledgeable about any unanticipated problems and how they were resolved. The basic reason for this information is that the manager wants to be prepared for similar situations in the future. Managers hate unpleasant surprises, especially at the end of a software life cycle phase activity.

The manager also must be certain that all essential project documents are shared in an appropriate project archive. Hopefully the organization has prepared against computer crashes and other disasters by having multiple copies of all essential documents stored in separate locations safe from fire, flood, and theft.

Essentially, the manager wants one of two states to occur, depending on the organization's software development practices:

- If the organization uses the standard waterfall approach, then the requirements should be complete, consistent, and free of any ambiguities. The software design process should be ready to begin.

- If the organization uses an iterative approach to software development, then the next iteration should be able to continue without delay. This means that the requirements should be consistent and free of any ambiguities. Any incompleteness in the requirements should be resolvable in the next iteration of the software's development. The requirements should be more complete than they were at the end of the previous iteration of development, if there was one.

A software project manager wants his or her project to produce software to be developed efficiently and the final product to be of high quality. Some inefficiency or detours during the setting of requirements and the system's design are probably unavoidable. What a manager hates is unexpected surprises.

Some typical unpleasant surprises include:

- Incoherent requirements review presentations.
- Missing documentation.
- Obvious omissions.
- Anger on the part of the customer because technical and other issues raised at an earlier meeting were ignored.
- Missing logistical infrastructure, such as proper audio-visual equipment or a room that is much too small.

The old adage is still valid: "you only get one chance to make a first impression." Keep this in mind when planning a requirements review. Act as if both your future and your company's are at stake. They are.

Keep in mind, however, that requirements are likely to change, even in the classical waterfall process. A software manager expects changes in the system requirements and will have a systematic plan for determining which to treat first and which to defer for future action. Change management is a vital part of the software process.

The project management plans will have been developed earlier and will have included development of requirements and planning for the requirements review. Once the requirements have been relatively set, the project plan can be described in more detail. In general, a project manager will expect to have a relatively detailed project management plan in place after the requirements review is complete.

3.14 The Major Project–Problem Statement

So far, we have discussed the requirements process at a relatively abstract level. It is now time to illustrate the process by considering a concrete example of moderate size. As was indicated in both the Preface and Chapter 1, this example will be discussed throughout the remaining chapters of this book. The only thing unrealistic about the running example is that it is necessarily small enough in order to be discussed completely within the context of this book.

We now describe the setting of the problem to be solved. A major difficulty faced by software managers is the lack of good tools for measurement of software and for determining if an implementation of source code for a project is consistent with the original software design.

Imagine two software professionals meeting over an informal meal at a local restaurant. The two of them are old friends, with one of them being a high level employee whose many responsibilities include managing the other. We will call them Manager and Software Engineer, respectively. The Software Engineer is also a manager, but only manages a small team. Being ambitious, the Software Engineer wishes to change this. Career advancement is a major goal of the Software Engineer.

The Manager is complaining about the difficulty in obtaining good information about the size of the projects that are under her direct or indirect control. The Manager also complains about having to monitor the organization's software development in three different languages: C, C++, and Java. The Manager also complains about the lack of software tools that enable maintainers of code to examine the program's control flow structure. In addition, she doesn't have any good way of tracking the software problems reported against systems at a lower level to the particular functions or source code files involved. There is a lot of data that has been collected about software errors, but the Manager just can't use it efficiently.

The Software Engineer hears the problems of an old friend and would like to help. In addition, providing a set of high-quality software tools quickly can provide enormous visibility, aiding in career enhancement. The

Software Engineer makes a mental note to consider this problem more fully. The conversation then turns to office gossip and politics.

While driving back to the office, the Software Engineer decides to work with a colleague to develop a set of requirements for what the Manager needs. The two of them will work together as a requirements team. They will produce a proposal to develop the software to meet the Manager's needs. If the proposal is accepted, resources will be allocated.

This scenario is not as far-fetched as it might appear. Many of the best software products had their inception at informal meetings such as the one described in this section. Many other excellent ideas never became products because there was no follow-through. The Software Engineer is aware of this and is also aware of the many current demands on the time of the Manager, who will have the final say about the approval of the proposed project. The Software Engineer thus resolves to do the best job possible in developing the requirements, while making as few demands as possible on the time of the Manager.

3.15 The Major Project–Requirements Elicitation

The next step in our discussion of requirements development for this example will take the form of an imaginary dialogue between the customer and the requirements team. The purpose of the dialogue is to illustrate the way that experienced requirements teams discern any omissions or hidden biases from the customer so that they can be used in the requirements as appropriate. Since not all of the dialogue will take place in the presence of the customer, we will use interludes to indicate these internal discussions that should be hidden away from the customer. We follow the approach of "ignorance hiding" discussed earlier in Section 3.4.1.

In our case, the requirements team is the Software Engineer and the unspecified colleague. To make the dialog easier to understand, we will not distinguish which of them is speaking at any time. They meet in a small conference room with a large whiteboard, but no phones.

"I think we can produce something for the customer that can also help us move up within the company."

"What does the customer want?"

"I think there are real problems to solve. There is no way to figure out the size of software at present."

"What about our current techniques for counting code? We've been doing this for years. What's new?"

"Well, we now develop code in C, C++, and Java. Three different languages, three different approaches, three different counting standards."

"OK, let's write a new standard for code counting."

"We'd have to write lots of new utilities. If we have to do that, why not do it right?"

"OK, I'm convinced. But what about the other stuff? What should we do there?"

"Well, I think she wants some kind of graphical tool that shows the program's structure. Maybe the call graph."

"Remind me. The call graph is the listing of which function call other functions, right?"

"That's right. And if a function isn't in the call graph, then it's dead code and we can ignore it when we try to understand the code."

"Should we actually draw a graph, or just determine the functions that call other functions?"

"I don't know."

"What about different tools for different programming languages?"

"That might be a problem. I don't know about command-line arguments. Maybe a GUI should be used to avoid the command line problem."

"I don't know. It might be easier to use the tool if there were no GUI, if the tool could be used in batch mode."

"What about our existing data on software errors? Can we interface to them?"

"Who knows? They may not be in electronic form."

"We have a lot of questions to be answered. Let's meet Tuesday at 10."

"OK."

After thinking about the problem for a few days, they meet again. They have prepared for the meeting and have brought in both a statement of the problem and lists of potential requirements for the software solution to the problem. Because each of them is familiar with the company's business strategy, they have already made the decision to include the requirements that were given previously in Table 3.1.

The requirements team members provide each other with copies of their prepared materials and resume their dialog.

"OK, we agree on the problem statement."

"Yes."

"What do we do about the multiple languages? Are there separate tools?"

"We want a common output so that only a small amount of new training is necessary for users."

"What about a common input?"

"Yes, as much as possible. Let's keep a GUI out of it until the last possible moment. Perhaps we should delay GUI introduction to the second generation of the tool."

"I agree. Keep the user interface simple."

"Let's do a demo of the simplest prototype."

"We'll handle one source code input file at a time."

"What about multiple languages used for source? That's the way we develop source code now, multiple languages for software systems. We use Motif and Builder Xcessory for UNIX software development, spreadsheet software for PC applications, and SQL everywhere. Many of our systems get ported to other environments as part of the company's reuse program. We often have to interface software components written in different languages."

"Let's simplify. We'll only consider software subsystems written in a single language."

"Huh?"

"OK, that was vague. Just restrict the requirements to have only one source code language treated at a time. That is the system must be invoked one time to handle C source code files, a second time for C++, and a third time for Java."

"Do we prompt the user, or allow the type of input files to be specified as a command-line argument?"

"Command-line arguments force coding in C or C++. Do we want to make this decision yet?"

"Probably not. Let's defer action on this item until the customer decides."

"OK."

"What about displaying the call graph?"

"That's a more fundamental problem. If we only analyze portions of a program at a time, say the portion written in C, then how do we treat calls to functions not included in the source code files we analyze?"

"It's the same problem if the entire program being analyzed was written in C, but we only analyzed some of the source files in the program at a time. We would simply flag any functions that were called, but for which the source code was not provided to be analyzed."

"I see. It's the same way we would treat any library functions."

"Right. Anything else?"

"No. Let's write these up. I think we are ready to talk to management. Let me set up a meeting next week."

"OK. Let me know a few days early so that we can prepare. Don't want to look bad in front of management. See you next week."

Before meeting with the Manager, who will act as the customer in this example, the requirements team will prepare for a formal presentation. There will be overhead transparencies and paper documents that will be made available to the "Customer." The documents comprise a formal proposal to develop the software. It includes an assessment of cost.

We now turn to the hypothetical meeting between the requirements team and the customer. Because the two members of the requirements team should speak as a unit, we will identify the participants in the dialog as Requirements Team and Customer, abbreviated R and C, respectively.

R: "Thank you for meeting with us today."

C: "You're welcome. What's on your mind."

R: "Two weeks ago you talked about a problem in software tools. You mentioned a need for a good tool to measure software size."

C: "Sure. But that's not my only problem in the software tools arena. I need some other things, too."

R: "We think we know some of your needs. We've developed a set of requirements for a simple software system to meet these needs."

C: "Go ahead."

R: "The first thing is a consistent way to measure the size of software. Since the maintenance and testing groups provide their test data according to functions in which the problems occur, you need to compute the size of each function included in the source code. The size of individual functions must then be totaled into the size of each source code file. This must be repeated to compute the total size of a software system by adding the sizes of each of the component source code files. Of course, these totals should be computed automatically."

C: "Sounds good. Please go on."

R: "We want a standard way of doing this computation, since the company develops software in three different languages: C, C++, and Java."

C: "Yes. It's a terrible problem for us. We can't get good numbers."

R: "We want to have a simple, batch-oriented system with as simple a user interface as possible. We don't want the software to be too complicated."

C: "I want a standard definition of a line of code. I've heard too many horror stories about how programmers organize their code to look more productive. They bump up the lines of code measurements artificially to make themselves look better."

R: "We've thought about that. Here's an example."

The Requirements Team then shows the Customer the well-known C program that is listed below. (This example was discussed previously in Chapter 1.) The Requirements Team and the Customer then discuss the size of this C program.

```
1. #include <stdio.h>

2. main(int argc, char * argv[])
3. {
4.    int i;

5.    for (i = 1; i < 10; i++)
6.       {
7.       printf(" %d\n" , i);
8.       }
9. }
```

R: "How many lines of code are there in this program?"
C: "Looks like nine to me."
R: "Look at lines 6 and 8. They really aren't necessary. The program would have the same meaning and be shorter if we remove those two lines."

C: "I agree. There's also a difference if we join all the statements together on the same line, or if we count all the function prototypes in the header file. What does this have to do with your tool?"

R: "Just that we will develop a precise measurement that is consistent with different language standard practices, such as the Ada style guide. Our requirements will specify standards for code counting measurements."

C: "Sounds good. I need this tool right away. When can I get it and how much will it cost?"

R: "We have some cost numbers and a tentative schedule for you. It might be better to wait until we discuss all the tools we have developed requirements for."

C: "OK."

R: "We also want to develop a tool that will provide a description of the program's call graph."

C: "What's that?"

R: "The call graph tells which functions call which functions. It provides a view of the program's structure and organization. The maintenance people really want this."

C: "I can see how it is important. You said 'graph.' Do you actually have a graphical output?"

R: "Not in the first prototype. However, we do have it in our requirements for the second iteration of our tools."

C: "Is there a single tool or a set of programs forming a software tool kit?"

R: "There is a single system. It may be made up of several software tools that can be used either as stand-alone utilities or as part of an integrated system."

C: "I like this. It seems like a flexible system."

R: "It should be. At least, we hope so."

C: "This means that I can get something useful out of this effort, even if it doesn't produce all that I want."

R: "That's right. We can do prototyping and show you interim progress frequently."

C: "OK. How are you going to handle multiple languages? Many of the company's systems use a combination of programming languages."

R: "We are going to measure the C, C++, and Java codes separately. We'll make the user responsible for determining the input files and making sure that they are all the same type of source code language."

C: "I'd really prefer to see a system that took all kinds of source code as input, regardless of the language."

R: "We've thought about that. There are too many options with this, too much error checking. We'll try this in a later prototype."

C: "I hope there's a good reason for this."

R: "It's easier this way. We're going to specify a software interface that will allow some flexibility."

C: "Anything else I should know?"

R: "Yes. We've decided to write the front end of the tool in either C or C++ in order to be able to use command-line arguments."

C: "What's the point?"

R: "We can use the tool for batch processing. It can work overnight if it has a lot of files to analyze."

C: "Will your tool work on our systems? I don't want to buy any more equipment or software that we can't charge to a project."

R: "Yes. We'll use the minimal interface and make as little use of platform-specific software as we can."

C: "What about file names? Can wild cards be used?"

R: "We don't know. We'll get back to you on that."

C: "It seems to be well thought out. The tool fits our needs. When can I get it and how much will it cost?"

At this point in an actual project, the Requirements Team would defer to a person who had produced an initial cost estimate for the project. The schedule would also be developed by a person who was likely to be the project manager. Often, the detailed cost estimate is not presented to the customer at this point because charging the correct amount for software may be the difference between a company thriving or going bankrupt. Cost estimates should be done with extreme care, as should project schedules.

In our example, this was not necessary, because the project was to be done internally, a preliminary cost estimate and schedule had been produced already, and the requirements were not changed appreciably during the meetings with the potential customer.

This hypothetical discussion illustrates some of the ways that a dialog takes place between members of a requirements gathering team and potential customers or their surrogates. In the next section, we will provide a complete set of requirements for the system. The rest of the discussion will follow a more formal approach. Always keep in mind, however, that some sort of informal elicitation of the initial system requirements is almost always necessary.

3.16 The Major Software Project–Requirements Analysis

We will now consider the requirements for the software development project that we will discuss throughout the remainder of this book. Our starting point will be the set of requirements that was elicited by the requirements team. The goal is to take these informally obtained initial requirements and transform them into requirements that are precise enough for us to tell if the software system that we eventually develop will have actually met the desired requirements.

We will assume that the initial attempts at a requirements document would look something like the following:

Problem statement for the major software project :

- Determine the size of software source code written in any one of three languages: C, C++, and Java.
- Develop a common standard for code counting for programs written in C, C++, or Java.
- Develop a tool that shows the program's call graph.
- Integrate the code counting and the call graph display into a single software system.

Let's go through the list, applying the "ignorance hiding" technique of Daniel and Orna Berry as was presented in section 3.4.1. Which of these words and phrases are vague and untestable?

"standard"
"As simple a user interface as possible"
"flexible enough"
"should have a common output interface"
"treated as library functions"

The list could certainly go on. The term "front end" almost certainly means "user interface" to a user of the system, but might mean the initial component of the software; the one that interfaces with the operating system and software such as spreadsheets and databases. We will not belabor the point, but will simply indicate a revision of the initial requirements list.

The requirements traceability matrix is given in Table 3.12. We have included some of our generic requirements into this matrix.

You may have some objections to the list of requirements (and the associated requirements traceability matrix) given above. We have not attempted to improve the software architecture to make it more modular. Certainly we have not considered the possibility of reusing any existing software at this time.

Initial requirements list for the major software project:

- The project must develop a standard way of computing lines of code for C, C++, and Java.
- The system is to be batch-oriented.
- The system is to have as simple a user interface as possible, since we have it in our requirements for the second iteration of our tools."
- All input is assumed to be syntactically and semantically valid. No error checking will be provided.
- No special compilers or application programs will be needed.
- The system will determine the functions that call other functions. It will be flexible enough to be extended to the drawing of a graph in a future release.
- The system will be flexible enough to be extended to interfacing with existing maintenance and testing data on software errors in a future release.
- Dead code can be ignored.
- The system should have a common output interface for multiple languages.
- The system should have a common input for multiple languages.
- It will be assumed that each input software subsystem is written in a single language.
- The front end is to be coded in C or C++ to use command-line arguments.
- Calls to functions not included in the source code files being analyzed are to be flagged and treated as library functions.
- The software must compute the size of each function included in the source code.
- The software must compute the size of each source code file from the sizes of individual functions.
- The software must compute the total size of a software system by adding the sizes of each of the component source code files.

However, we have some flexibility. The back end of the system appears to be interfaced to the Microsoft Excel spreadsheet. So we are at least using a COTS product for any additional analysis of the data that our new software tools will collect. This approach to software development emphasizes reuse at the highest levels and is becoming very common in industry.

As we indicated earlier in this chapter, when the essential requirements have been determined, the project manager must complete the details of a project plan for developing a system that meets these requirements. (We did not create a preliminary project plan until now because we had not introduced the problem statement previously.)

Table 3.12

Requirements Traceability Matrix for the Major Software Project

#	Requirement	Design	Code	Test
1.	Intel-based			
2.	Windows 95			
3.	Windows 95 UI			
4.	Consistent With Excel 4.0			
5.	System One Size Only			
6.	One MB System			
7.	One MB Disk Space			
8.	One 1.44 MB Floppy Disk			
9.	Includes Installation			
10.	No Decompression Utility			
11.	One input file at a time			
12.	Develop standard for C, C++, Java			
13.	Size of each function			
14.	Size of each file			
15.	Size of system			
16.	Compute totals			
17.	Front end in C or C++			
18.	Batch-oriented system			
19.	Precisely define LOC			
20.	Measure separately			
21.	No error checking of input			
22.	File names limited to 8.3			
23.	Wild cards can be used			
24.	Dead code ignored			
25.	No special compilers needed			
26.	Microsoft Excel 4.0 needed			

This section will close with the following change to the requirements for the major project. Can you guess what it is? The hypothetical discussion we presented earlier is based on command lines and batch processing, not a modern networked-based environment. The customer now wants a web-based user interface, with opening and closing screens such as the ones shown in figure 3.11 and figure 3.12, respectively.

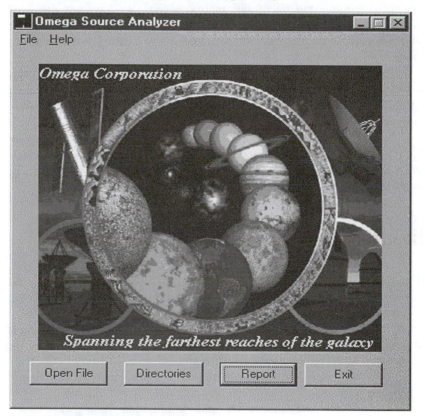

Figure 3.11. A sample opening screen. (Source: software system prepared by Sean Armstrong, Aaron Rogers, and Melvin Henry.

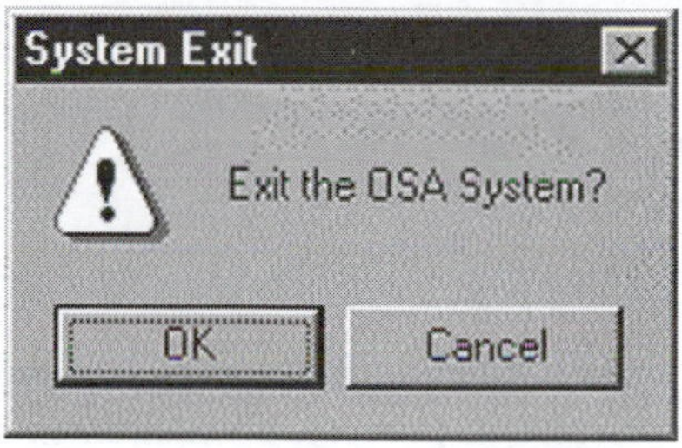

Figure 3.12. A sample closing screen. (Source: software system prepared by Sean Armstrong, Aaron Rogers, and Melvin Henry.)

Obviously, some changes need to be made to the requirements. You will be asked to modify the requirements in the exercises.

You may have some objections to the list of requirements (and the associated requirements traceability matrix) given. We have not attempted to improve the software architecture to make it more modular. Certainly we have not considered the possibility of reusing any existing software at this time.

However, we have some flexibility. The back end of the system appears to be interfaced to the Microsoft Excel spreadsheet. So, we are at least using a COTS product for any additional analysis of the data that our new software tools will collect. This approach is very common in industry.

This section will close with the following change to the requirements for the major project. The customer now wants a web-based user interface. What changes need to be made to the requirements process? You will be asked to modify the requirements in the exercises.

Summary

The development of a proper set of requirements for a software system is the key to the success of the project. Without complete, consistent, and clear requirements, the project is doomed to failure. This is true regardless of whether the software is developed according to the classical waterfall, rapid prototyping, or spiral model. Eventually, the requirements must be determined correctly, even in an iterative process.

There are several techniques that can aid in requirements organization:

1. Use data abstraction and information hiding to produce a complete description of the system's functionality.
2. Regroup requirements to be consistent with the requirements and design of both existing and planned systems.
3. Reuse requirements in order to be able to reuse existing designs and source code.
4. Automate the requirements engineering process.

The requirements must be clear and unambiguous. In order to trace the requirements throughout the software development process, a requirements traceability matrix must be created. This matrix lists the requirements number, each of the requirements, and entries for checking off that the requirement was met in the design, code, and testing phases.

Once developed, requirements should be assessed for their efficiency, potential cost, and attention to safety-critical issues. A study of current technology to determine feasibility might be appropriate at this point. Ideally, the organization's software development process includes metrics to estimate project size and cost.

Requirements represent a major portion of software development effort. As such, they will be emphasized in project schedules and will be subjected to one or more requirements reviews. The purpose of a review is to ensure that the product being evaluated (in this case requirements) is of sufficiently high quality. A quality assurance evaluation is often used with requirements reviews.

Software requirements often change, even if the development process was not explicitly iterative. Management of change includes prioritizing tasks, reallocating resources, and making sure that the effects of the change make the most efficient use of existing requirements.

Further Reading

There are few books devoted exclusively to the requirements generation process. Perhaps the books *Software Requirements: Analysis and Specification* by Alan Davis [DAVI90] and the second edition of *Software Requirements* by Richard Thayer and Merlin Dorfman [THAY97] are the most accessible. One of the major advantages of the book by Davis is that it includes an annotated bibliography of 598 references in software requirements and related research. The book by Thayer and Dorfman includes many of the most important papers on software requirements and provides an excellent overview of the state of the art in this active area of research.

The recent paper by Daniel and Orna Berry in the *Journal of Systems and Software* [BERR96] is essential reading in requirements engineering.

Albrecht introduced the notion of function points as a measurement of program size in [ALBR79]. He noted that function points could be applied at many places in the software life cycle, including requirements engineering. The book by T. Capers Jones [JONE89] describes the use of function points in project size estimation.

User interface research has been concentrated in two major areas: psychological experiment to determine efficiency and usability of I/O devices or screen organizations and development of software models and associated tools to assist an interface designer. See [CARD82] and [MILL68] for examples of some psychologically based work. The two references [GREE85] and [OLSE86] describe some projects in user interface management systems (UIMS) that are tools for the rapid development of user interfaces. An article by Hartson and Hix in *ACM Computing Surveys* [HART89] has a large bibliography. Schneiderman [SCHN80] and Nielsen [NIEL94] have excellent introductory texts on this subject. The work of Bleser [BLES94] and Campbell [CAMP94] provide more recent information on guidelines.

Exercises

1. In our initial discussion of software engineering, we presented in Table 3.3 a simple example of the decisions that had to be made before marketing software for personal computers. This is an ideal opportunity for automation. Write a set of requirements for a software system, called RGS, that will interact with a user to determine the eleven requirements with minimal input from a requirements engineer. (The acronym RGS stands for requirements generation system.)

2. Complete the analysis of the remaining requirements in Table 3.4 using the "ignorance hiding" approach of Daniel and Orna Berry that was discussed in Section 3.4.

3. Provide a state diagram for the requirements given in Table 3.4.

4. Provide a decision table for the requirements given in Table 3.4.

5. Provide a Petri net for the requirements given in Table 3.4.

6. Estimate the size of the requirements given in Table 3.4, using the function point approach.

7. This exercise concerns the model of a user interface that was discussed in this chapter. Use the detailed descriptions of object to develop a quantifiable evaluation of the displays shown in Figures 3.4 and 3.5. Apply the model to your favorite word processing software.

8. A system will have two concurrently executing processes, A and B. Consider the requirements:

    a. Processes A and B will execute on different machines on a network.

    b. Processes A and B will communicate as little as possible.

Which of these two requirements is most consistent with the system having no single point of failure? Which is most consistent with a real-time performance requirement? Explain your answers.

9. Develop a Petri net for synchronization of the following tasks, which may occur concurrently:

   Task 1: Put on sock
   Task 2: Put on sock
   Task 3: Put on right shoe
   Task 4: Put on left shoe

   The synchronization requirement is that at least one of tasks one and two must be complete before either task three or four can happen.

10. Same as question 9, except that both tasks one and two must be complete before either task three or four can happen.

11. Select a software package with which you are familiar. Use the software package to perform some operation that you have done many times before. While you are doing this, note the changes in the user interface, including any new screens or messages that might appear. Now write down a list of requirements that this software must have had. (Determination of a system's requirements from its performance without any existing requirements documents is part of a process called "reverse engineering."

12. Consider the state diagram given on the next page. It is related, but not identical to, the diagram given in Example 3.7. How can you determine if these requirements are inconsistent?

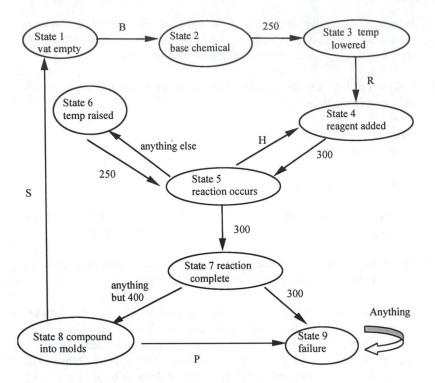

Exercises for the major software project

1. Write a state diagram for the requirements of our continuing software project as they were developed in Section 3.17.

2. Write a decision table for the requirements of our continuing software project as they were developed in Section 3.17.

3. Write a Petri net for the requirements of our continuing software project as they were developed in Section 3.17.

4. Estimate the size of the requirements of our continuing software project as they were developed in Section 3.17, using the function point approach.

5. Consider the requirements for our continuing software project as they were developed in Section 3.17. Apply the suggestions in this chapter to reorganize the requirements to make the software architecture simpler.

6. Write a state diagram for the requirements of our continuing software project as they were developed in Section 3.17 and as they were modified in question 6.

7. Write a decision table for the requirements of our continuing software project as they were developed in Section 3.17 and as they were modified in question 6.

8. Write a Petri net for the requirements of our continuing software project as they were developed in Section 3.17 and as they were modified in question 6.

9. Change the requirements to allow the software to have a web-based interface. Apply the ignorance hiding technique of Section 3.4.1 to analyze these new requirements. What sort of technology assessment must take place? Which existing requirements must be changed?

10. Develop a detailed project plan for the major software project we introduced in this chapter.

Chapter 4

Software Design

4.1 Introduction

It is essential to develop a model of a system before writing any software that will be used to control the system or to interact with it. Modeling the software is probably the hardest part of software design. Producing good software designs requires a considerable amount of practice, with a great deal of feedback on the quality of the designs with the resulting software products influencing the design of the next software system.

We view software design as an iterative process, with the goal being design improvement at each iteration. The purpose of this chapter is to discuss some basic principles that can guide the software design process. These principles will be illustrated by several examples.

You are undoubtedly aware that a fundamental change is taking place in the software industry. There is heavy emphasis on object-oriented technology and on software reuse. Some aspects of the object-oriented methodology are so different from corresponding issues in the standard, procedural approach to software design that they should be discussed separately. This is especially true in software design.

However, a considerable amount of current software engineering effort is still far more focused on requirements analysis, design, implementation, testing, and maintenance of programs that have been developed under the more familiar procedural approach rather than object-oriented techniques. Therefore, a software engineer must be familiar with designing both types of software systems. This presents a problem for the writer of a book on software engineering.

Our solution, and the one most appropriate for both the current software engineering world and that in the foreseeable future, is to use a hybrid approach that combines components that are written in either procedural or object-oriented languages. After all, an existing software module that performs a specific requirement well should not be rejected for potential reuse just because a new application is object oriented.

This hybrid approach is common in the software engineering community and has been formalized by several organizations. Consider the experience of the U.S. Department of Defense, which spends an enormous amount of money on software development and maintenance. A survey in the late 1970s showed that software was being developed or maintained in more than 1600 different computer languages and dialects. This was the impetus for the development of the Ada programming language, which was designed to make use of the lessons learned in many years of software development ([Ada83], [ICHB86]).

The Ada language incorporated many of these lessons, including information hiding, separate compilation of software interfaces and software internals using package specifications and bodies, support for polymorphism and abstraction through "generics," and strong typing. The modern reader will note the appearance of many object-oriented features in the 1983 version of the Ada language, which is now called Ada83.

Equally important was the standardization of the language and the validation of Ada compilers as meeting the language standards. An "Ada mandate" required that all new Department of Defense software development was to be developed in Ada unless there were substantial, well-documented reasons given for an exception to the mandate. (The complexity of the Ada language made it difficult for the first generation of Ada compilers to produce executable code that ran quickly and, thus, most exceptions were based on the need for run-time efficiency.)

Almost simultaneously with the updating of the Ada language in 1995 to address efficiency issues and increase the support for object-oriented software development, the Ada mandate was changed to reflect the explosion in high-quality software products and the enormous quantities of software that had already been developed in object-oriented and other commercial programming languages. The increased importance of COTS products and reuse is clear from the new mandate, which is described in Table 4.1.

The rest of this chapter will be organized as follows: first, we will present some basic, general-purpose design principles. Some of the design principles will be based on the basic technique of software pattern matching. The goal is to reuse software components at as high a level as possible.

This discussion will be followed by some representations that are commonly used for the design of procedurally oriented systems, with examples of each representation. After completing our initial discussion of the design of procedurally oriented systems, we will discuss some design representations for them, again with examples. The same steps will be followed for object-oriented software. This will complete our initial discussion of software design techniques.

The last three sections of this chapter will be devoted primarily to the design of the example begun earlier in this book. This example will be discussed in detail. Special emphasis will be placed on those issues that arise because of the necessary combination of both procedurally and object-oriented designs.

Table 4.1

A synopsis of the most recent version of the Ada mandate for software systems in the Department of Defense, with the preferred software solutions given in the order of preference.
Source: DoD 5000.2-R, item 4.3.5 Software Engineering (Change Three, 23 March 1998) , information from the web site http://sw-eng.falls-church.va.us/dod5000-2.html.

Software shall be managed and engineered using best processes that are known to reduce cost, schedule and performance risks. It is DoD policy to design and develop software systems based on systems engineering principles (CCA) to include:
1. Developing software system architectures that support open system concepts; exploit commercial off-the-shelf (COTS) computer systems products; and provide for incremental improvements based on modular, reusable, extensible software;
2. Identifying and exploiting software reuse opportunities, government and commercial, before beginning new software development;
3. Selection of programming language in the context of the systems and software engineering factors that influence overall life-cycle costs, risks, and potential for interoperability. Additional guidance is contained in ASD(C3I) memorandum, "Use of the Ada Programming Language," April 29, 1997;
4. Use of DoD standard data. Additional guidance is contained in DoDD 8320.1;
5. Selecting contractors with the domain experience in developing comparable software systems, a successful past performance record, and a demonstrable mature software development capability and process;
6. Use of a software measurement process in planning and tracking the software program, and to assess and improve the software development process and associated software product;
7. Ensuring that information operations risks have been assessed (DoDD S-3600.1); and
8. Ensuring software is Year 2000 compliant.

4.2 Software Design Patterns

One possible way of designing software is to attempt to match the problem to be solved with a preexisting software system that solves the same type of problem. This approach reduces at least a portion of the software design to pattern matching. The effectiveness depends upon a set of previously developed software modules and some way of recognizing different patterns.

Following are some types of patterns that seem to occur over and over in software development. Our patterns are relatively high level, as opposed to the patterns described in [GAMM95]. These high-level patterns are:

1. A menu-driven system, where the user must pass through several steps in a hierarchy in order to perform the work he or she wants to perform. The menus may be of the "pull-down" type such as is common on personal computers, or may be entirely text based.

2. An event-driven system, where the user must select steps in order to perform the work he or she wants to perform. The steps need not be taken in a hierarchical order. This pattern is most commonly with control of concurrent processes where actions may be repeated indefinitely, in contrast to pattern number three. It is also typical of a user interface that is guided by selection of options from both menus and combinations of keystrokes, such as in menus that may "pop-up" in response to user requests. In any case, there is less of a hierarchy than in the previous pattern.

3. A system in which the actions taken depend on one of a small number of "states" and a small set of optional actions that can be taken for each state. The optional action taken depends on both the state and the value of an input "token." In this pattern, the tokens are usually presented as a stream. Once a token is processed, it is removed from the input stream.

4. A system in which a sequence of input tokens (usually in text format) is processed, one token at a time. This pattern differs from the previous pattern in that the decision about which action to take may depend on more information than is available from just the pair consisting of the state and the input token. In this pattern, the tokens may still remain in the input stream after being processed.

5. A system in which a large amount of information is searched for one or more specific pieces of information. The searches may occur once or many times.

6. A system that can be used in a variety of applications, but which needs adjustments to work properly in new settings.

7. A system in which everything is primarily guided by an algorithm, rather than depending primarily on data.

8. A system that is distributed, with many relatively independent computational actions taking place. Some of the computational actions may communicate with other computational actions.

How many of these patterns are familiar to you? The first two describe human-computer interfaces, with the first one being a rigid, menu-driven system, and the other being controlled by actions such as moving a mouse or other pointer and pressing a button.

Software pattern number three describes what is often known as a "finite state machine" or "deterministic finite automaton." This pattern is especially useful in controlling some processes in a manufacturing plant.

Pattern number four occurs often in utility software. It is the basis for lexical analyzers and the parsing actions of compilers. Many software systems have some sort of parser to process input commands.

Obviously, software pattern number five refers to a database searching problem.

Pattern number six is quite general, but suggests that there is a general-purpose system that must be specially configured for each application setting. The installation of a printer for a personal computer (or a network of computers) follows this model.

Software patterns seven and eight are also very general in nature. However, pattern number seven appears to suggest that the solution will be procedural in nature, while pattern number eight might be better suited to a solution using object-oriented methods.

These software patterns are not absolute rules. Neither are they intended as a complete classification of software. Nonetheless, they can guide us in the design and implementation portions of the software development process.

We note explicitly that is not necessary to have the entire software system under consideration match one of the above patterns. It is perfectly reasonable to have different portions of the same software system match several different patterns. This will be the case when we discuss our large software engineering example later in this chapter.

Separation of a software system into several subsystems is common during software design. Indeed, some sort of stepwise refinement of designs is essential for an efficient software design process. Decomposition of system designs will be a recurring theme during this chapter. For now, we will ignore system decomposition and concentrate on software patterns.

Let us consider how these patterns can be used as part of a design process. Suppose that we recognize that a particular pattern is applicable to a software system that we are to design. Where do we go from there?

The first step is to see if we can make our work simpler. Specifically, we should search through any software available to see if, in fact, we already have a full or partial solution to our problem. This situation is an example of software reuse, which is the most efficient way to produce software. If the pre-existing software solves the problem exactly, then we are done. The needed modifications should be compared with the estimated cost of entirely new software to see if we should attempt to reuse a partial match. We will illustrate the application of software reuse to our continuing discussion of our major software engineering example in Section 4.16 of this chapter.

4.3 Introduction to Software Design Representations

Any notations, techniques, or tools that can help to understand systems or describe them should receive serious consideration from the person modeling the system. We will focus our attention in this section on techniques for modeling and will briefly discuss design notations.

Suppose that we cannot find any existing software that either solves our problem directly, or else is a candidate solution after it is modified. In this case, we are forced to design new software to solve the problem. How do we do this?

There are several ways to describe a software system:

- The software can be described by the flow of control through the system.
- The software can be described by the flow of data through the system.
- The software can be described by the actions performed by the system.
- The software can be described by the objects that are acted on by the system.

The first description of software leads us to the concept of a flow graph or flowchart. The earliest popular graphical design representations were called "flowcharts" which were control flow-oriented. The term "control flow" is a method of describing a system by means of the major blocks of code that control its operation. In the 1950s and 1960s, a flowchart was generally drawn by hand using a graphical notation in which control of the program was represented as edges in a directed graph that described the program. Plastic templates were used for consistency of notation.

The nodes of a control flow graph are boxes whose shape and orientation provided additional information about the program. For example, a rectangular box with sides either horizontal or vertical means that a computational process occurs at this step in the program. A diamond-shaped box, with its sides at a 45-degree angle with respect to the horizontal direction, is known as a "decision box." A decision box represents a branch in the control flow of a program. Other symbols are used to represent commonly occurring situations in program behavior. An example of a flow chart for a hypothetical program is given in Figure 4.1.

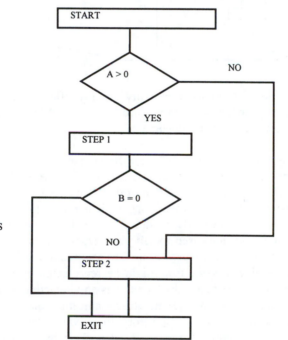

Figure 4.1. A flowchart description of a hypothetical program.

As we indicated, there are many symbols that can be used in flowcharts. The drawing feature of Microsoft Word has twenty-eight predefined icons that represent the different symbols most commonly used within flowcharts. Five of these common symbols are shown in Figure 4.2.

The second method of describing designs is appropriate for a data flow representation of the software. As was mentioned in Chapter 1, data flow representations of systems were developed somewhat later than control flow descriptions. The books by Yourdon, one by him and the other coauthored with Constantine, are probably the most accessible basic sources for information on data flow design ([YOUR79], [YOUR89]). Most software engineering books contain examples of the use of data flow diagrams in the design of software systems.

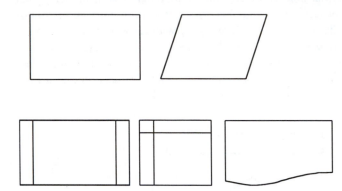

Figure 4.2. Some symbols commonly used in flowcharts. Reading clockwise from upper left, the symbols are "process," "data," "predefined process," "internal data," and "document."

Since different data can move along different paths in the program, it is traditional for data flow design descriptions to include the name of the data along the arrows indicating the direction of data movement.

Data flow designs also depend on particular notations to represent different aspects of a system. Here, the arrows indicate a data movement. There are different notations used for different types of data treatment. For example, a node of the graph representing a transformation of input data into output data according to some rule might be represented by a rectangular box. A source of an input data stream such as an interactive terminal input would be represented by another notation, indicating that it is a "data source." On the other hand, a repository from which data can never be recalled, such as a terminal screen, is described by another symbol, indicating that this is a "data sink."

Since different data can move along different paths in the program, it is traditional for data flow design descriptions to include the name of the data along the arrows indicating the direction of data movement.

Typical data flow descriptions of systems use several diagrams at different "levels." Each level of a data flow diagram represents a more detailed view of a portion of the system at a previously described, higher level. A very high-level view of the preliminary analysis of the data flow for a hypothetical program is shown in Figure 4.3. This simple diagram would probably be called a level 1 data flow diagram, with level 0 data flow diagrams simply representing input and output.

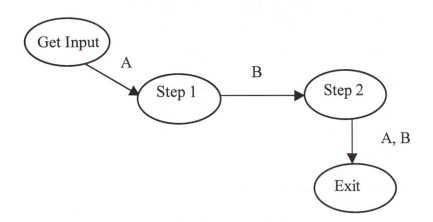

Figure 4.3. A level 1 data flow diagram DFD description of a hypothetical computer system.

The third method of representing a software system's design is clearly most appropriate for a procedurally oriented view of the system. It may include either control flow or data flow, or even combined descriptions of the software. The notations used for this hybrid approach are not standard. Such a design may be as simple as having a link from, for example, the box labeled "Step 1" in Figure 4.1 to the flow chart described in Figure 4.3.

Finally, the fourth method is clearly most appropriate for an object-oriented view of the system. This is obviously a different paradigm from the previous ones. We have chosen to use a modeling representation known as Unified Modeling Language, or UML. UML is an attempt to describe the relationships between objects within a system, but does not describe the flow of control or the transformation of data directly.

Note that each of the boxes shown in Figure 4.4 represents an object for which the inheritance structure is clearly indicated by the direction of the arrow: the object of type class 1 is a superclass of the object of type class 3. In an actual design using the unified object model, the horizontal line would contain information about the type of relationship (one-to-one, many-to-one, one-to-many) and about the aggregation of multiple objects into a single object. We omit those details here.

It is often very difficult for a beginning software engineer to determine the objects that are appropriate for a software system's design. Although there is little comparative research to support the hypothesis that good object-oriented design is harder to create than design using traditional procedurally oriented approaches, we do believe that considerable training is necessary to appreciate the subtleties of the object-oriented approach. The student unfamiliar with the object-oriented approach is encouraged to read this and related discussions throughout this book several times after he or she has become more familiar with software development in order to understand why certain design decisions were made.

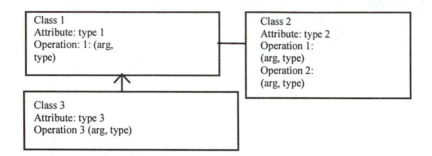

Figure 4.4. An oversimplified object-oriented description of a hypothetical computer system using an object model in UML notation.

A helpful approach is to think of a description of the system's functionality in complete sentences. The verbs in the sentences are the actions in the system; the nouns represent the objects. We will use this simple approach when developing that portion of the design of our major software engineering project example for which the object-oriented approach makes sense.

It is natural for the beginning student of software engineering to ask why multiple design representation approaches are necessary. Of course some techniques evolved for historical reasons. However, many techniques and representations have survived because they provide useful, alternative views of software design.

The familiar problem of sorting an array of data provides a good illustration of the distinction among the four approaches. Consider the well-known quicksort algorithm developed by C.A.R. Hoare.

The quicksort algorithm partitions an array into two subarrays of (perhaps) unequal size. The two subarrays are separated by a "pivot element," which is at least as large as all elements in one subarray, and is also no larger than the elements in the other subarray. Each of the subarrays is then subjected to the same process. The process terminates with a completely sorted array. Note that this algorithm description is recursive in nature. Think of the quicksort algorithm as being used in a design to meet some requirements for an efficient sort of a data set of unknown size. (Students wishing a more detailed description of the quicksort algorithm are advised to consult a reference on data structures, such as one of the books listed in the section on further reading near the end of this chapter.)

A control flow description of the algorithm would lead to a design that would be heavily dependent on the logical decomposition of the program's logic. Think of implementing the recursive quicksort algorithm in a language such as FORTRAN or BASIC that does not support recursion. The logic of the design would be all important. On the other hand, too large a data set might mean too many levels of recursive function calls if a purely recursive algorithm is used. This control flow view might point out some limitations of the design of a simple quicksort algorithm.

A data flow description of the algorithm would emphasize the data movement between arrays and the two smaller subarrays that are created at each iteration of the quicksort algorithm. Attention to the details of setting aside storage locations for these subarrays might lead to a consideration of what to do if there is no room in memory. Most courses in data structures ignore the effects of data sets that are too large to fit into memory. However, such sets exist often in applications and efficient sorting programs must treat them carefully.

A third view can be obtained by considering a purely procedural solution. In this case, a standard library function can be used. For example, the standard C library has a function called qsort(), which takes an array argument and produces a sorted array in the same location. That is, the input array is overwritten by the output array.

A user of the qsort() function in the standard C library must provide a comparison function to do comparisons between array elements. The function prototype for this comparison function is illustrated below:

```
int *compare(*element1, *element2);
```

This user-defined comparison function takes two arguments (which represent arbitrary array elements) and returns 0 if the two arguments are the same. The comparison function must return −1 if the first argument is "less than" the second, and returns 1 otherwise. The number of elements in the array and the size of an array element must also be provided.

The qsort() function in the standard C library is accessed by including the header file stdlib.h within a C program. This function has the syntax

```
void qsort(
  const void *base,
  size_t num_elts,
  size_t elt_size,
  int (*compare(const void *, const void *)
  );
```

and the typical usage is

```
ptr=qsort(arr,num_elts,elt_size, compare);
```

Finally, an object-oriented approach would most likely use a general class for the array of elements, and invoke a standard member function for sorting. Such a function typically would be found in a class library for some abstract class. An example of this can be found in the class libraries that are provided with most C++ software development systems.

A general class in an object-oriented system will contain the methods that can be applied to the object represented by the class. In C++, the methods that are associated with an object are called the "member functions" of the class. In the case of C++, a class description is likely to contain what are called "templates," or general classes in which the specific type of a member of the class is only relevant when the class is used. Thus a template class can refer to an abstract array of integers, character strings, or any other relevant type for which the class operations can make sense.

Provided that the methods of the template class can be implemented for the particular type of object in the class, the general method known as a sorting method can be invoked by simply calling a member function as in

```
A.sort();
```

Here, the type of the object A is compatible with the template type and the sort() member function for that object is used.

Even for the simple case of a sorting algorithm, we have seen several different approaches that can be used for software system design. Each has advantages and disadvantages. We have not examined any of the disadvantages in detail. In particular, we have never considered the question of the efficiency of software written according to any of the designs given previously. For example, a slow sorting algorithm, or one that uses recursion, would be completely inadequate for many software applications.

There is one other commonly used method for describing a system. This involves pseudocode which provides an English-like (at least in English-speaking software development environments) description of the system. The pseudocode is successively refined until the implementation of the source code is straightforward, at least in theory. Note that pseudocode is a non-graphical notation. An example of pseudocode is shown in Example 4.1. The pseudocode describes a portion of an authentication system for password protection in a hypothetical computer system.

Pseudocode representations have two major advantages over the graphical ones: they can be presented as textual information in ASCII files, and pseudocode descriptions of large systems are no more complicated to represent than those of small systems. Of course, pseudocode representations may be so long and have so many levels of nesting in their statement outline that they are extremely difficult to understand.

```
GET login_id as input from keyboard
Compare Input to entries in login_id database
IF not a match THEN
   WAIT 10 seconds
   SET error_count to 1
   REPEAT
             PROMPT user for new login_id
             IF login_id matches database
                   THEN PROMPT for password
             ELSE increment error_count
                WAIT 10 seconds
             END IF
   IF error_count > 3 EXIT password PROMPT
   END REPEAT
ELSE
   GET password as input from keyboard
   Compare password entries in password database
   IF error THEN
      EXIT
   ELSE
      BEGIN login process
END IF
```

Example 4.1. A pseudocode description of a hypothetical computer system.

You should note one other advantage of pseudocode representations when used for designs: they can produce instant internal documentation of source code files. We will address this point in the exercises.

The design representations described in this section by no means exhaust the number of representations available. Other commonly used design representations include Buhr diagrams, Booch diagrams, HIPO charts, and Nassi-Schneiderman charts. Booch diagrams can be used easily with object-oriented systems, while most of the other representations cannot. Descriptions of each of these can be found in several software engineering books and in some of the original writings of the inventors of the notations. Consult the references for more information.

4.4 Procedurally Oriented Design Representations

In this section, we will provide some examples of the use of different procedurally oriented design representations for a single-system example. We will consider object-oriented design representations for the same system in Section 4.9.

Consider a familiar situation – software that controls a terminal concentrator. A terminal concentrator is a hardware device that allows many different terminal lines to access the same CPU. Input from any of the terminal lines is associated with the terminal to which the line is attached at one end. Corresponding output for a program running on one of the terminals is sent from the CPU to the appropriate terminal screen.

In order to keep the data being sent to and from different terminals from going to the wrong place, the signals are "multiplexed" by the terminal concentrator. Multiplexing hardware and software allow the attachment of many terminals to the same port of the computer, thereby allowing for more simultaneous users (at a potential cost of reduced processing speed). All terminals on the same terminal concentrator share the same connection to the computer, as is shown in Figure 4.5.

Multiplexing means that a single set of wires is used for the connection from the terminal concentrator to the CPU. The decision about which terminal to communicate with along these wires can be made by using different frequencies for the signals or by attaching routing information to each packet of information sent.

The essential data structure in a multiplexed system is a queue. A user's data is sent from his or her terminal to the CPU in a stream in a first-in, first-out manner. The data passes through the multiplexing operation of the terminal concentrator and is sent to the CPU when the process is scheduled for execution. All other processes (and the I/O from their terminals) wait for the process to relinquish control of the CPU. Output is then sent from the CPU to the appropriate terminal, also by means of the multiplexing operation of the terminal concentrator.

Thus, there are queues for input, queues for output, and mechanisms for determining which data is attached to which terminal (for either input or output).

A flowchart for the software that controls a terminal concentrator is shown in Figure 4.6. You should compare this with the example of pseudocode for the terminal concentrator system, which is shown in Example 4.2 on page 179.

terminals

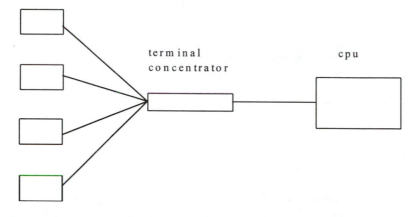

Figure 4.5. A terminal concentrator. Source: Leach, *Object-Oriented Design and Programming with C++*, Academic Press, 1995.

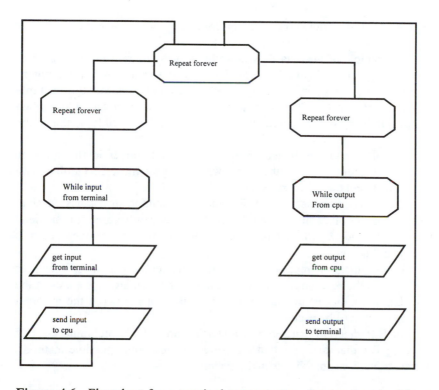

Figure 4.6. Flowchart for a terminal concentrator. Source: Leach, *Object-Oriented Design and Programming with C++*, Academic Press, 1995.

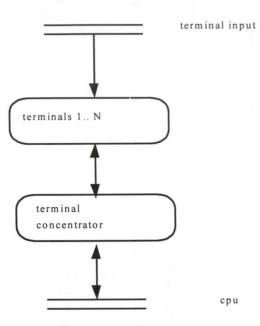
terminal input

cpu

Figure 4.7. A data flow representation for a terminal concentrator.

An example of the data flow description of a program in one graphical notation is given in Figure 4.7. The data flow diagram shown in this figure describes one direction of flow for the terminal concentrator example described previously. The terminator concentrator system can be described completely by a more elaborate diagram. You will be asked to do this in the exercises.

In reality, changes in technology and rapid turnover in the software engineering industry mean that a software designer must be familiar with several different design representations.

The entity-relationship, or E-R, model is common in database design. Another is the information model that is frequently used in artificial intelligence and expert systems. We will discuss each of these models briefly in this section.

An E-R diagram represents a set of fundamental quantities, known as entities, and the relationships between them. The labeling of the arcs in the E-R diagram indicates the nature of the relationships between the different entities connected by each arc.

An E-R diagram can serve as a starting point for a preliminary set of objects. The diagrams' relationships often suggest some possible methods, or transformations, on objects in the system.

```
For each terminal
 {
 Repeat forever
  {
   When time for input to CPU
   {
   get input from terminal's input queue
   place on concentrator input queue to CPU
   include information to identify terminal
   send input data from concentrator to CPU
   remove data from concentrator queue
   }
   When time for output from CPU
   {
   receive output data from CPU
   place on concentrator's output queue
   include information to identify terminal
   send output data to terminal queue
   remove data from concentrator queue
   }
  }
 }
```

Example 4.2. A pseudocode representation for a terminal concentrator.

This method is only a first step in the development of a complete description of the objects and methods in a system because the E-R diagram generally lacks any self transformations of an object. Thus, constructors, destructors, and initializers are not generally evident from E-R diagrams. Tests for equality are typically not clear. Many other common methods are not easily represented in E-R diagrams.

The observations of the utility of E-R diagrams in objects can be summarized as follows:

- If an E-R diagram already exists, use the entities as initial choices of objects and methods. Pay particular attention to the need for self-transforming methods such as constructors, destructors, and initializers.

- If no E-R diagram exists, do not bother writing one. Instead, proceed to the description of objects using the process in Table 4.2 directly.

4.5 Software Architectures

The term "software architecture" has been used in many different, often conflicting ways in the software engineering community. Regardless of the specific context, the term is commonly used to describe the organization of software systems.

We define it as follows: an "architecture" is the definition of the key elements that constitute a system, their relationships, and any constraints. We will view architectures as being composed of several types, each of which is also an architecture. We use the approach of Ezran, Morisio, and Tully in our description and classification of architecture types [EZRA99].

Generally speaking, architectures of software-based systems can be classified into several categories:

- A business architecture describes the structure of the business tasks performed by the organization and the mechanisms by which the system supports these business tasks. The description of the business architecture is often created by a business analyst who is an expert in this particular business.

- A physical architecture describes the structure of the hardware platform(s) or network(s) on which the system will operate.

- A logical architecture describes the structure of the business and application objects. This architecture is often part of an object-oriented view of a system. Accordingly, the description of the logical architecture is often created by an object analyst who is well versed in object technology.

- A functional architecture describes the structure of the potential use cases and the requirements from a user's point of view. Again, this architecture is often part of an object-oriented view of a system.

- A software architecture describes the structure of the system into layers, such as the OSI seven-layer model of data communications or the layered architecture of the UNIX operating system. (See figure 4.8 for a view of the layered architecture of UNIX.) A decision to decompose a system into a client and a server would be part of a software architecture.

- A technical architecture describes the structure of the major interfaces in the software architecture. Elements of a technical architecture include the application programming interfaces (APIs), middleware, database management systems, graphical user interfaces, and other glueware or bridgeware needed to interface components at various layers in the software architecture. Decisions to use CORBA, DCOM, Java RMI, or RPC would be reflected in this type of system architecture.

- A system architecture describes the structure of the business, application, and technical objects and their relationships. The description of the system architecture is often created by a systems analyst.

- A deployment architecture describes the structure of the mapping of the system and technical architectures onto the physical architecture. The deployment architecture includes a static view of the basic files that will be necessary and a dynamic view of the concurrent processes and threads and the mechanisms for their synchronization and communication. Decisions to place a thread on a particular computer, or to have an autonomous agent performing computation on a processor that is idle, would be reflected in this type of architecture.

Why are architectures considered important? The success of the OSI model and the UNIX operating system show the power of the layered approach to software architecture. The other types of architectures are attempts to increase the level of reuse in systems by encouraging the description of systems at different levels of detail and abstraction.

The layered architecture of the UNIX operating system is shown in figure 4.8. The architecture makes it clear that, for example, system calls interact with the UNIX kernel by means of the "syscall vector," that the UNIX kernel interacts with the hardware by means of device drivers, and so on.

It should be noted that the use of a notation such as UML (Unified Modeling Language) can promote a consistency between different architectural views. Whether such consistency can be incorporated into CASE tools and development processes in such a way as to improve efficiency remains to be seen, although preliminary efforts are promising.

At this point, we will be content with this high-level description of different architectural types. We will return to their descriptions when we illustrate the design of our major software project in section 4.17.

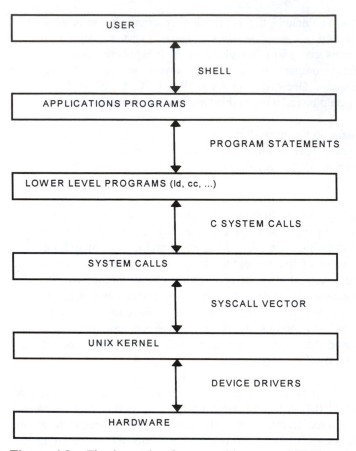

Figure 4.8. The layered software architecture of UNIX. Source: Leach, *Advanced Topics in UNIX*, John Wiley, 1994.

4.6 Software Design Principles for Procedurally Oriented Programs

Before we begin the study of software design representations in depth, we will introduce an element of reality into the discussion. Consider the case of a program of approximately 500 lines of code, with perhaps seven or eight functions. A high-level view of the program's design is likely to be relatively small, regardless of the design technique or representation used. It is likely that a reasonably complete view of the design can fit on one page. Clearly any of the design representations described earlier in this chapter could be used if the systems were not too complicated.

We should not expect this to be the case for realistic programs that are used in industry or government. Clearly, the design of a program of 500,000 lines of code with over 2000 functions and complex control and data flow cannot be represented accurately on a single sheet of paper. Thus, every design representation technique will include some method of decomposing design representations into smaller units that are linked together.

Here is an example of this decomposition approach: the diagram on the next page has been taken from a CASE tool called Technology for the Automatic Generation of Systems (TAGS) which is available from Teledyne Brown Engineering. The version presented here is a public domain version of the "front end" of the tool that was implemented for the Macintosh. This "front end" contained only the design representation portion of the full software. It used a special system description language called IORL (Input Output Requirements Language). Features of the complete CASE tool included a consistency check for the designs that were graphically represented and a code generation feature that allowed source code to be generated from the system's graphical description.

We will only present an example of the decomposition representation here in Figure 4.9. This figure describes the interaction of the Macintosh version of TAGS, called MacTAGS, with the Macintosh MacOS operating system and the Macintosh toolbox, which contains some of the routines for access to the Macintosh graphical utilities. (The diagram has been compressed in order to fit within standard page margins.)

It is not appropriate for us to discuss Figure 4.10 in detail. However, there are several things to note. The boxes are connected by well-drawn arrows. It is clear that this was done automatically, rather than by a simple drawing package. The arrows are labeled, providing more information about the interfaces of the boxes linked by the arrows. The labels on the arrows indicate the number of an interface.

The boxes in Figure 4.9 are also labeled, but for a different purpose. The numbers in the top left-hand corner of the boxes indicate other subsystems, which are also represented by similar diagrams. This is the mechanism for linking different graphical pages to the same system.

MacTAGS used the approach of having software made up of "systems," which in turn are composed of one or more sections. Sections are represented by "system block diagrams." The diagram in Figure 4.9 is system block diagram 0 and is denoted as section "SBD-0" of the system named "MacTAGS."

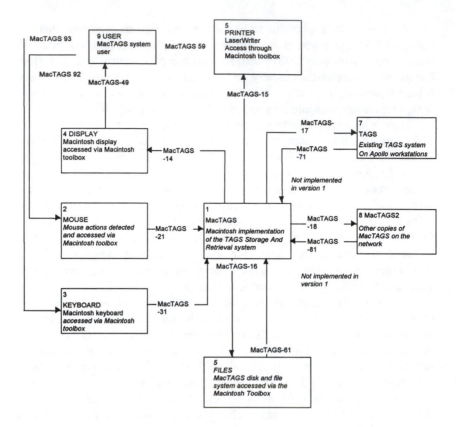

Figure 4.9. An example of a design representation using a CASE tool.

We note that this CASE tool is more than a drawing aid for providing a graphical representation of software. It also includes a "context editor" in the sense that double clicking on any interface arrow or labeled block provides access to additional detailed information such as the creator of the box or interface, the data flowing along the interface between different boxes, and so on. This very useful technique is similar to clicking on a Uniform Resource Locator (URL) in a mail document where the Eudora™ mailer software will automatically open a copy of an associated network browser. The same approach also works for other applications that have been associated with a particular type of file name, such as:

```
http://       WWW document
.doc          Microsoft Word document
.xls          Microsoft Excel document
.ppt          Microsoft PowerPoint document
.wp           WordPerfect document
.exe          MS-DOS executable file
```

The tool is even more advanced, as may be seen from the software's interconnection with other versions on a network. The advanced versions of the software for networks include an optional code generator so that a correct graphical design representation can also used to generate source code for the system being designed. Even if the source code that is generated by this tool is not complete or does not meet proper performance requirements, the source code produced can save considerable development time.

We now return to the study of design decomposition. The goal of design decomposition is to produce a detailed design from a very high-level one. How detailed should a detailed design document be? It should be sufficiently detailed to be able to have one or more software engineers implement source code on the basis of just this document. The source code should be implemented unambiguously, in the sense that minor variations in the implementation details should still be consistent with the design.

Unfortunately, it is not well understood how the choice of design representation leads to any particular decomposition of a high-level design into a more detailed design. For example, a decomposition of a system based on an analysis of the control flow would naturally lead to a detailed description of the actions taken by the system.

On the other hand, a decomposition technique based on a data flow representation would lead to a detailed description of the movement of data that are made by the system. Transformations of data are easy to detect in a detailed, data flow-based design representation.

Other design representations have different influences on the design decomposition approach. The effect of pseudocode, state diagrams, and Petri nets on designs will be discussed in the exercises.

Clearly, different design representations and decomposition strategies have a major influence on the eventual detailed design. Of course, there is considerable variation between individual designers; designers working independently will also produce different detailed designs for the same system. Thus, it is often important for management to perform comparative analyses of designs.

We view the design decomposition step as one that must be examined to make certain that the resulting design is modular, efficient and, above all, meets the requirements of the system. It goes without saying that the detailed design should be checked against the requirements traceability matrix to ensure that the requirements can be met by an implementation that is based on this design.

4.7 What is an Object?

In this section, we will give some guidelines for determining the objects that are present in a system we wish to design. The basic idea is that an object has attributes and that in any instance of an object, these attributes will have values.

Suppose that you have chosen a candidate to be an object in your system, and that you have determined a set of attributes and their possible sets of values. What informal tests can you apply to be sure that your objects are the most appropriate abstractions for your system?

The first test is the "multiple examples test." Simply stated, if there is only one example of an instance of an object, then the concept is not sufficiently general to have object-oriented techniques used to implement it.

The multiple-examples test is consistent with the procedural programming dictum: "If you use it once, just write the code. If you use it twice, write a procedure or function." It is also consistent with the advice commonly given to young mathematicians: "If a concept or theory does not have at least three different hard examples, it is not worth studying."

Once our candidate for an object passes the multiple examples test, it is placed in a set of potential objects. The attributes of the objects are now tested using the "has-a" relationship, which can help to formalize the set of attributes of the objects. We should write an initial set of member functions for this potential object based on reasonable transformations of the values of some of the attributes of the proposed object.

The next informal rule used for checking the appropriateness of objects concerns the class hierarchy in which new classes are designed from old ones. This relationship between the base class and the derived class is best described as the "is-a" relationship. If the sentence:

```
object 1 is a object 2
```

does not seem to make sense (ignoring the grammar), then the relationship is not of the form

```
(base class, derived class)
```

and, hence, we do not have an inheritance relationship.

On the other hand, if the sentence does seem to make sense, then we have a candidate for such a relationship. This is called the "is-a relation test." In this case, we should draw a diagram of the object and any relationship between the object and other objects.

We should list the potential member functions and be alert for any examples of polymorphism. The appearance of polymorphism suggests that we have chosen our inheritance relationships properly. If there is no polymorphism, then we should be suspicious that we have not described the member functions correctly, or at least not in sufficient detail.

The set of potential objects and the descriptions of their member functions should be refined at each step.

There is one final relationship test that should be performed in order to incorporate the objects into a preliminary object-oriented design of a software system. The concern here is that the objects listed should form a complete set of the objects needed for the software system being designed. The relationship we are looking for is the "uses-a relation."

We use this relationship by asking if the sentence

```
object 1 uses object 2
```

makes sense for the pairs of objects considered. Every meaningful sentence suggests either a client-server or agent-based relationship and is to be considered as part of the program's design. If we cannot find any instances of this sentence making sense, then there are two possibilities: either the objects are insufficiently specified for us to be able to describe the entire system, or the natural description of the system is as a procedural program controlling objects.

Note that objects can be related to many other objects. Multiple inheritance is possible and so are multiple objects. Thus the previous steps should be repeated for groups of three objects, four objects, and so on, until the designer feels that the system's essential object-oriented features have been described.

We summarize the recommended steps for determining objects in Table 4.2 below.

Table 4.2
A methodology for determination of objects

1. Choose a candidate to be an object.

2. Determine a set of attributes and their possible sets of values. Use the has-a relation. List all relevant transformations on the object.

3. Develop an initial set of transformations on the object to serve as member functions. The list of attributes and their values provide an initial set of transformations by determining the value of, and assigning a value to, each attribute of an object. Constructor, destructor, and I/O functions should also be included.

4. Determine if there is more than one example of the object. If so, then place the proposed object in a set of potential objects. If not, discard it because it fails the multiple-examples test.

5. Apply the is-a relation by considering all sentences of the form

```
object 1 is a object 2
```

Objects considered for this relation should include the object under development and any other objects believed to be related. (The class library may be consulted during this step of the process.) Each valid sentence should lead to an inheritance relationship. Each inheritance relationship should be illustrated graphically.

6. Use polymorphism and overloading of operators (and functions) to check if we have described the objects in sufficient detail. Check the object description if no polymorphism or overloading is found.

7. Use the `uses-a` relation

```
object 1 uses object 2
```

to determine all instances of client-server or agent-based relationships. Use these relationships to determine issues of program design.

8. Review the object, its attributes, member functions, inheritance properties, polymorphism, overloading, and relationships to other objects to determine if the object is complete in the sense that no other functions, attributes, or relationships are necessary.

9. Repeat steps two through eight for all combinations of relevant objects (triples, quadruples, and so on) until the object's role in any proposed system has been described adequately.

Make sure you understand the steps used in this process of determining objects.

The importance of data abstraction and information hiding in objects should be clear to you. In addition, you should have some appreciation for the power of the concepts of operator overloading and inheritance. We now consider the development of larger object-oriented programs.

In the next few sections of this chapter, we will discuss some issues in object-oriented design and indicate how the object-oriented paradigm for software design differs from the procedurally oriented one. We will also indicate a methodology for the development of object-oriented systems which determines the fundamental objects (and appropriate methods) in these systems. This will be done in the context of the development of a class that describes strings.

We now return to the topic of object-oriented modeling of systems. The first fundamental question that we must address is: what are the objects in the system?

Once we have determined the objects, we must answer the second fundamental question: what is the set of transformations that can be applied to these objects?

A few definitions may be helpful. An abstract object is said to have *attributes*, which describe some property or aspect of the abstract object. For any instance of an abstract object, each attribute may have values.

The listing of attributes is helpful in assessing our candidate for an object. The attributes must be independent in the sense that a change in the value of one attribute should not affect the value of another attribute.

There is one other judgment that should be made from the attribute list. If there is a single attribute, then it is likely that the object is at a low level of abstraction. This should generally be avoided and, hence, we want to have at least two attributes per object.

We will illustrate these concepts by several examples in this and some of the following sections.

Consider the development of a class to describe the abstract concept of a string. Some typical attributes of a string might include its length, its contents, its creation or destruction, and its display. These lead us to some potential values for these attributes: its length might be 42, its contents might be "I like this Software Engineering book" (not counting the delimiting quotes), it might be in a state called "created" and it might be displayed on the standard output stream cout. Alternate values of some attributes for a string object might be 80 for the length, "I like this Software Engineering book and wish to buy many copies," and a file named "outfile" for the "display" of the string.

The determination of the attributes of an object and the set of possible values for each attribute then suggests the functions and data types necessary to implement methods to be used with the class. For example, we must have a member function for the String class that is able to compute the length of the string. This length must be an int (since this is the appropriate elementary predefined data type in C). We must have a constructor function to initialize the contents of the string and we must have a function to display the contents on the appropriate output stream.

Note what we haven't determined yet. There has been no mention of the null byte \0 to be used as a termination byte to indicate the end of the string; then, another question arises as to whether or not their termination byte is to be counted as part of the string, thereby increasing its length by one.

Indeed, there is no requirement that the string should be implemented as a set of contiguous bytes. We could choose to follow the lead of many word processing programs (including the one in which this book is written) and use linked lists to chain together contiguous arrays of characters (and other objects, such as graphs, in the case of the word processor). Linked lists are especially suited to insertions and deletions of text within a word processing document. Other data organizations are possible.

The important point is to note that none of the decisions about the implementation organization or details is relevant to the string object. What we need now is a determination of the attributes of the object and a set of possible values for each attribute. With such a determination, we can write the first attempt of a description of the class. Thus, the first attempt at the definition of a string object will probably have a definition something like the class string defined below. We won't worry about syntax at this point.

```
class String

Member functions:
   int length;
   int strlen( String s);
   void display( String s);
```

Some problems arise here because we haven't determined the interface precisely. The constructor member function needs to have a size specified for the length of the string. Other member functions will have to have their interfaces determined, also. Thus, we will have to make a second iteration of the design of the class representing strings.

```
class String

Member functions:
  int length;
  String (char *arr); //terminated by \0
  int strlen();
  operator << ;
```

There are more iterations that need to be performed in order to have a complete definition of the interfaces of this class. Of course, we still have to develop an implementation of the methods. We omit the details of the iteration for the class description at this point since we will describe them in detail in Section 4.10 after we have discussed some methodologies for developing classes. Implementation of the code for the member functions is left as an exercise.

4.8 Object-Oriented Design Representations

In this section, we will present a simple object model for the terminal concentrator software system described in Section 4.4. We will make no attempt to refine the object model and will keep it at the same high level that we used for the previous models using different design representations.

The representation is simple (at least at this point). We will use a rectangular box to describe an object, with diamond-shaped boxes and line segments used to indicate relationships between objects. The name of the class is given above a horizontal line inside the box. We will follow the convention of having class names begin with an upper-case letter.

The relationship between the objects is given a name in this representation. The relationship is called " is connected to" and behaves in a similar manner to the "uses" relationship that we will discuss later in this chapter.

Some of the attributes of an arbitrary object in the class are included in the box. We would have included all attributes, but there were too many of them.

At the bottom of the diagram, we again list the classes that are in the upper part of the diagram, again using a graphical representation. The classes in this list have typical values for each of the attributes of an object in each class.

Note that this model makes no mention of the queue data structure that will probably be used to keep information going to and from the terminal concentrator in buffers.

We can have two different views of an object-oriented system: the object model and the interface model. We will discuss these two views in order.

In the object model representation, we will use an extended entity-relationship (E-R) notation. We will use the convention that the name of a class will be given in upper case and the instances of a class will be given in lower case.

Our starting point for this discussion is the diagrams given in section 4.4. Such diagrams provide a good high-level view of a system.

The object diagrams can be refined further by incorporating the cardinality of each relationship into the diagram. Figure 4.10 illustrates this. The numbers on the side or top of a relation indicate the number of items on each side having the relationship. The cardinality can be one of the following: a precise value, a range of values, the symbol '*' denoting 0 or more, or the symbol '+' denoting 1 or more. We have used the '+' and a range in Figure 4.10.

An object model should be expanded until it describes the essential abstractions of objects in the system. Unfortunately, the object model as indicated so far in this section is inadequate to fully describe the relationship between different objects. In view of this limitation, we will attempt to incorporate the interfaces between objects into our model. There are several methods of doing this.

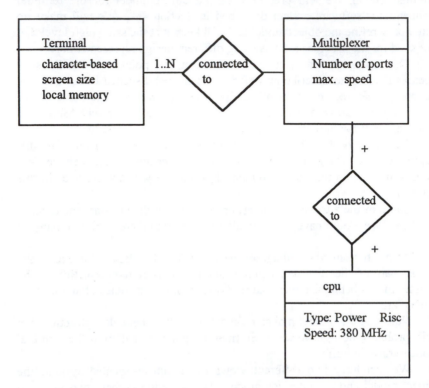

Figure 4.10. Addition of cardinality information to an object model notation. Source: Leach, *Object-Oriented Design and Programming with C++*, Academic Press, 1995.

One method is the use of state tables. The terms "state diagram," "state machine," and "finite state machine" are often used instead of "state table." This is one of the oldest methods for describing systems. It certainly predates any of the current efforts in object-oriented design.

A state table for the terminal concentrator system might have six states, which we will call TIR, CIR, CPUIR, CPUOR, COR, and TOR. The acronyms stand for Terminal Input Ready, Concentrator Input Ready, CPU Input Ready, CPU Output Ready, Concentrator Output Ready, and Terminal Output Ready, respectively.

We illustrate the states for the terminal concentrator system in Figure 4.11. The notation is slightly different from the most common one in that we have not specified the initial state where the inputs to the system arrive (from the keyboard) and the final state where the outputs leave the system for good (when they get displayed on the terminal screen).

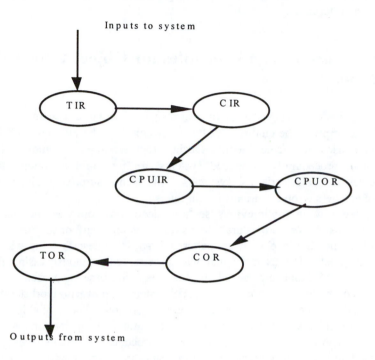

Figure 4.11. A state diagram for the terminal concentrator system. Source: Leach, *Object-Oriented Design and Programming with C++*, Academic Press, 1995.

It is useful to know how to use existing representations for systems when attempting to describe them in object-oriented terms. We often have an object model for a system. Our suggestions for the use of existing information models and diagrams in object modeling can be summarized as follows:

- If an information model diagram exists, use it to determine initial relationships, especially those of aggregation.

- Examine attribute lists, for indication of data structures and a preliminary set of transformations to operate on the values of these attributes.

- If no information model is available, then proceed directly to a description of objects in the system.

For additional information on E-R diagrams and information modeling, consult the references.

4.9 Software Design Principles for Object-Oriented Programs

All the methods of design representation discussed previously were created in order to improve the quality of software designs and the efficiency of the processes used to create them.   Design representation techniques for traditional, procedurally organized systems are far more common than techniques for object-oriented systems.   This is not surprising given the relative newness of object-oriented techniques.

As we saw in the previous section, decomposition was the major technique used for procedural software development once we had determined the high-level software patterns, if any, that described the system to be designed.   The example that was constructed previously using the MacTAGS CASE tool emphasized this decomposition-based approach.

The complete installation of the TAGS system on powerful workstations also included a facility for automatic code generation.   The availability of CASE tool enhancements that provide automatic code generators is not restricted to those CASE tools that support procedurally oriented designs. We note that some related features can be found in several readily available software packages used for object-oriented development.   For example, versions 5.0 and higher of the Borland C++™ Development System include the facility to generate code frameworks with header files and class descriptions from graphical models of the objects that comprise a system. The ROSE™ system from Rational Corporation is another popular system that supports object-oriented analysis with code frameworks.

However, object-oriented design often focuses on the development of complete classes to describe objects.   The idea is that all the necessary methods or member functions will be provided in the class description. Thus, the primary issue is the design of the class for completeness, so that the possible interactions are treated by having proper interfaces.   Objects then interact by sending messages from one class to another and the individual classes react only to the messages that they receive.   The objects are viewed as autonomous, with no interactions other than those specified in the object's interface.

The use of abstract classes can be especially useful if the software's requirements are not identified completely before design begins, as is certainly the case for the concurrently engineered, market driven software development process so common in the personal computer world.

In this approach, the interfaces for an object in the system are specified at an early stage. The implementation details for the methods can be developed later. If new functionality is required, it is provided in the methods associated with an object, not in the object's interface. A pure virtual function (one which has no implementation details and is used as a base class with interfaces to be used by the classes that inherit from it) is often used for this purpose in C++.

Even in a worst case scenario, development of an object's member functions can proceed concurrently with the object's design. If a new interaction is added to an object's interface, most of the existing methods do not have to be changed. Only new methods have to be added to implement the additional interface.

Here is an illustration of the effect of different design approaches to object-oriented systems. We consider the simple situation of describing a class to represent quadrilaterals, which are four-sided geometrical objects. We wish to develop a class structure to describe quadrilaterals, with squares and rectangles as special types of geometrical shapes.

There are several choices available to us. We can create a hierarchy with a primitive class called `vertex`. We can build a class called `edge` using the `vertex` class, and then use the `vertex` class to build a new class called `figure`. The `figure` class can be used to construct quadrilaterals as a subset.

This construction is illustrated in Figure 4.12. We present some C++ source code to implement this organization in Example 4.3.

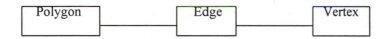

Figure 4.12. An illustration of a design organization of some geometric figures based on the vertex primitive.

Unfortunately, there is no obvious way to capture the notion of a geometric figure being a square or a rectangle. We could modify the class given in the file `figure.cpp`, but this seems awkward. Another potential design uses a hierarchy of objects based on the is-a relation, since a square is a rectangle and a rectangle is a quadrilateral. We invite the reader to examine any standard class library that has graphical objects to see that neither of these approaches is used in practice. Instead, the hierarchy is often reversed to have a rectangle inherit from a square. We note that the flexibility of the object-oriented paradigm allows us to choose from these alternate designs.

```
// FILE: vertex.cpp
class Vertex
{
public:
  double x, y;   // coordinates
  Vertex(double x1 = 0, double y1 = 0);
};


// FILE: edge.cpp
#include "vertex.cpp"
class Edge : public Vertex
{
public:
  Vertex first, second;
  Edge();
  void init( Vertex, Vertex);
  boolean is_adjacent_to(Edge E);
  double length;
 };


// FILE: figure.cpp
#include "edge.cpp"
class Figure : public Edge
{
public:
  List<Edge> set_of_edges;
  List<Vertex> set_of_vertices;
  void init(List<Edge> &,  List<Vertex> &);
  boolean is_adjacent_to(Figure F);
  int number_of_edges;
  int number_of_vertices;
};
```

Example 4.3. Some C++ source code for an organization of figures based on the vertex primitive.

There is one disadvantage to allowing this flexibility of concurrent requirements, design, and coding. Any method added to a class at the last minute before release will have minimal testing due to time pressures. It is highly unlikely that an object will be tested for all possible types of responses to methods, particularly if the interfaces are polymorphic or if any operators are overloaded. Thus, a user of the software may observe many system malfunctions, especially if the user operates the software in ways that were not expected by its designers.

In many software development organizations, treatment of such potential problems is postponed until the next release. Thus, corrective testing of software components of a previously released version may occur during development (requirements, design, coding, testing) of the next release. Determining when to release software, when to demand additional testing, and determining which features to incorporate in new releases are clearly essential to success in the market-driven software environment. We will return to this point in Chapter 6 when we study testing and again in Chapter 8 (and elsewhere) when we study configuration management.

The models we present in this chapter are intended for illustration only. Any realistic model of a complete system would be much more detailed than what we will present in the next few sections. The models given here only describe the system at its highest level. After reading this chapter, you should appreciate the expressive power of several different design representations for both object-oriented and procedurally oriented software systems.

4.10 Class Design Issues

It is necessary to discuss some of the difficulties associated with the development of programs that use the class definition methods described in the previous section. The methodology described in the previous section assumes that the software system has been developed in a vacuum. That is, we have described some of the attributes that we believe are associated with a type of object and have described some potentially useful interfaces between this object and others (such as character arrays and I/O streams). We have not paid attention to any of the previously developed classes that might be related to our class and would encourage the use of similar interfaces.

If there is a set of related classes with similar standards for their interfaces, then we must at least consider these interfaces before we set in stone the interfaces that are part of the current description of the object.

This point cannot be emphasized enough. Development of an object must take place along the lines of defining its attributes and typical values for these attributes. This can be done by the usual method of stepwise refinement so familiar to software engineers. Development of a *useful* object (one that can be used in a variety of important situations) requires that one consider the interfaces to existing objects in the development stage. Otherwise, the objects that we develop will have very limited utility.

We illustrate the point by this analogy: consider the current state of development of computer hardware. Unless a hardware designer is designing a special-purpose, high-performance supercomputer or a custom microprocessor for control of an embedded system, he or she will use previously developed components with well-defined and well-documented interfaces. These existing well-designed hardware components have predictable levels of performance in terms of clock speed, data transfer rate, reaction to specified interrupts, power usage, etc. A new piece of hardware that does not adhere to these standard interfaces is unlikely to be very useful outside a narrow range of applications. Only a revolutionary design with tremendous applicability or performance is likely to be useful; an unusual interface with only mundane applications or average performance is not likely to be very successful.

This is exactly the same situation that applies to developing classes that can be used as reusable software components. The development of a class cannot be done in a vacuum. It must take into account the other classes in the class library in order to make efficient use of previously developed classes. The library catalog and any software tools for examining the different libraries are extremely important when developing classes to interact with real systems.

Note that we must do one other thing to ensure that the classes we develop make efficient use of resources, especially programmer time. If there is a relationship between our class and one or more pre-existing classes, it is possible that we can then make use of previously developed functions that were members of a pre-existing class. This is easy to do if we can use inheritance.

We can also use functions associated with an object if the functions were originally declared as being `friend` functions. (Recall that `friend` functions are allowed in C++, but not in pure object-oriented languages such as Java.) Even if the functions were not declared originally as `friend` functions, we might be able to change the definition of the pre-existing class to make the required functions member functions and recompile the system.

In any event, an efficient software design process requires a check of available software resources.

Grady Booch is one of the most highly regarded experts in the object-oriented programming community. He observes that in most high-quality, object-oriented programs, many essential objects are clustered into several related classes, rather than being grouped solely by inheritance. He states that the only programs that have all objects related are relatively trivial ones.

Clearly, the determination of available classes in class libraries is only a starting point when designing object-oriented programs. However, it is essential step in designing an object-oriented system.

4.11 An Example of Class Development - The String Class

In this section, we will return to the discussion of the class `String` that we began briefly in Section 4.7. We will apply the rules listed in Table 4.2 to this class and obtain what we hope is a satisfactory abstraction of the properties we want in an abstract `String` class. The `String` class presented in this chapter was originally developed by Eric Charles for a project under the direction of Bernard Woolfolk at Howard University.

Initially, we noted that this class had two member functions: a constructor function `String()` and a function `strlen()` to compute the length of an object of the class. We are at step one of the process described in Table 4.2: we have selected a candidate for an object.

Step two in the process requires us to list the attributes of this object. The list of attributes indicated previously was:

```
length
```

There was no explicit mention of the data to be stored in the `String` in our previous discussion. We clearly expected to use the data in the String in the function `strlen()`. Let's fix the oversight now by including the data. The next list of attributes for the `String` object is:

```
length
```
data in the `String`

These attributes make sense as potential attributes for `String` objects, because the sentences

```
A String has a length.
```

and

```
A String has data.
```

both make sense. The second sentence could probably be phrased better as

```
A String has contents.
```

and, hence, we will use the term `contents` instead of `data` in our initial list of attributes.

To make sure that these are reasonable attributes, we list some typical values in a table:

Attribute	Typical value
length	19
contents	Please buy this book.

In step three, we consider possible transformations of the object. Relevant member functions include:

- Constructor
- Destructor
- Initialization of a string
- Assignment of contents to another string (copy constructor)
- Input of a string
- Output of a string

It is essential that we begin to consider what the interfaces of these member functions should look like. The C++ default constructor and destructor functions take no arguments and return no values. If we wish to initialize a `String` object, then we should specify this here. It is likely that we will wish to have a constructor of the form

```
String(char * init);
```

or perhaps

```
String(const char * init);
```

Here, `init` represents a null-terminated array of characters.

The I/O member functions will almost certainly overload the << and >> operators. It will probably be useful to allow writing of strings to streams other than `cin`, `cout`, and `cerr`, so that our I/O functions will be overloaded again.

Note that we have not addressed issues such as whether or not the null byte is included as part of the length of the object. These are details that are relevant to either the interface to other objects or the specifics of an implementation.

There are many examples of strings, so our proposed `String` object clearly passes the "many examples test" of step four.

We now apply step five of the process to determine if there are any inheritance relationships. In order to do this, we must determine a set of objects that we believe have an inheritance relationship with our proposed new object. With the possible exceptions of lists and arrays, there are no objects that seem likely at this time, so we proceed to step six of the process. If we felt that there was a strong `is-a` relationship between the `String` class and an (abstract) array class, then we would have inheritance relationships between these classes. A similar statement holds for the `String` class and an (abstract) linked list class.

In example 4.4, we illustrate the state of our `String` class after using steps one through five of the process that we stated previously in Table 4.2. The header file `String.h` includes the basic definitions needed for the `String` class described so far.

```
// Initial attempt at a class definition
// of the String class using steps 1
// through 5 of the object development
// process.

class String
{
private:
  char *d_string_p;
public:
  // Constructors
  String();
  String(const char *str);
  // Destructor
  ~String();
  // Assignment
  String &operator = (const char* str);
  int length() const;
  // overloaded conversion operator
  // converts String to char*
  operator char*(); // converts to std type
};
```

Example 4.4. A user-defined string class – first iteration using steps one through five of our class development process.

As we will see, the code of Example 4.4 is not very complete as a description of the String class. We will now continue the process of class development.

In step six of our process, we ask if any polymorphism or overloading is found. If not, we have probably not described all transformations (member functions) for the object. In this case we have overloading of (at least) the constructor and I/O functions, so that it is likely that we have made at least some use of object-oriented features of the class.

In step seven, we ask if there is any instance of the uses-a relationship between our object and other objects. Here, we are looking for client-server or agent-based relations. Because of the simplicity of our String object, such a relationship is unlikely, so we proceed to step eight.

Step eight of the process involves reviewing the current state of development of the class and checking for any missing relationships or transformations. This is an ideal time for a structured walkthrough of the object, preferably with the walkthrough and review being done by someone other than the designer. The purpose of the review is to check for inconsistencies in the design, for missing or misapplied relationships, and for any unnecessary complications.

In our example, we have provided very few of the functions available in the standard collection of C functions for string manipulation. Some typical functions accessed in the standard C language header file `string.h` are `strcmp()`, `strcat()`, and `strcpy()`. It would be appropriate to add many of these to our `String` class at this time.

Step nine allows us to extend the `is-a` relationship to several classes at once, thereby adding the possibility of multiple inheritance to our class description. More complex instances of the `uses-a` relationship will also appear at this time.

It is probably sensible to repeat steps two through eight only up to triples of classes in most beginning designs, unless we expect a more complex relationship to surface.

After completing this process, we will have obtained a description of the internal data and interfaces of the `String` object. The only things we must do to actually create such a class are to present the definition of the data and member functions in syntactically correct form, and encode the details of the member functions.

We present a more complete description of the `String` class in example 4.5. Note that there are many more member functions than before. Some of the new member functions are included because we wish to have interfaces to other objects of class `String`, not just to data of the type `char*`.

We have included the possibility of modifying values of arguments by using the `&` operator in several places within our member function declarations. The declarations were declared `const`, as in the argument signature

```
const String& string;
```

because we wish to avoid the overhead of copying the entire contents of the `String` object, but leave the value of the argument unchanged. Recall that this is called passing parameters by constant reference.

You should also note the wide range of operators in example 4.5 for such actions as lexical comparison. Many of these operators are overloaded.

We have also included a `friend` operator for interaction with the `ostream` class in the declaration in example 4.5.

```
friend ostream& operator << (ostream& s, String
&str);

// Contains the class definition of String,
// using the nine steps of the object
// development process.
```

Example 4.5. A more complete version of the string class (continued).

```
class String
{
private:
  char *d_string_p;
public:
  // Constructors
  String();
  String(const String& string);
  String(const char *str);
  // Destructor
  ~String();
  // Assignment
  String &operator =(const String &string);
  String &operator =(const char* str);
  // Manipulators
  String &operator +=(const String&string);
  String &operator += (const char* str);
  // Concatenation (to this string)

  // Accessors
  int length() const;
  String operator + (const String& str)
      const;
  String operator + (const char* string)
      const;
      // Concatenation (to a new string)

  // Lexical Comparison Operators
  int operator == (const String& string)  const;
  int operator == (const char* str) const;
  int operator != (const String& string)  const;
  int operator != (const char* str) const;
  int operator < (const String& string)  const;
  int operator < (const char* str) const;
  int operator <= (const String& string)  const;
  int operator <= (const char* str) const;
  int operator > (const String& string)  const;
  int operator > (const char* str) const;
  int operator >= (const String& string)  const;
  int operator >= (const char* str) const;

  // overloaded conversion operator
  operator char*(); // converts to std type
  // friend for overloaded I/O operator of
  // ostream class
  friend ostream& operator << (ostream& s,
      String &str);
};
```

Example 4.5 (continued). A more complete version of the string class.

There are many ways to describe the abstract object represented by the String class. You should compare the description of the two class descriptions given so far in this section with the equivalent String class available with your C++ compiler. You should also consult the C++ standard library when it becomes available, or Plauger's book on the draft ANSI standard for a C++ library that is listed in the references.

Additional steps are appropriate if the goal is to develop classes that encourage the use of reusable software components. The suggestions of Johnson and Foote are typical of methods for development of reusable classes of objects. The goal is to create classes that not only represent relevant data abstractions, but that are also easily tested. Their suggestions are presented in Table 4.3.

Table 4.3
Some methods for encouraging reusable classes.

Introduce recursion into the class to aid in abstraction.
Eliminate case analysis in the development of member functions.
Reduce the number of arguments.
Reduce the size of methods.
Class hierarchies should be deep and narrow.
The top of the hierarchy should be abstract.
Minimize access to variables.
Subclasses should be specializations of larger classes.
Split large classes into several smaller classes.
Factor implementation differences.
Separate methods that do not communicate.
Send messages to components instead of the object itself.
Reduce implicit parameter passing.

These rules are helpful when designing large systems with complex classes. They are probably too much for the simple examples that are presented in this chapter.

We will now present the final description of our String class. It is illustrated in example 4.6. The new features include a set of non-member (free) functions to perform other actions. As before, you should compare this class with the String class available with your system.

The class description is complete and shows the effects of the different iterations of the object development process. The methods (member functions) are small, each performing specific actions on selected types of operands.

There are many instances of overloading operators such as <= and += in order to have simple programs to compare and concatenate strings. You should note the proper use of constant pointers within the member functions implementing these operations for concatenation to new strings and to existing ones.

Note also the presence of free functions to perform compare and concatenation. These free functions are used when the first argument is a null-terminated character array, rather than an object of class String. This is an indication of the completeness of our String class.

As indicated above, the class is described in Example 4.6 below, which continues on the next page.

```
// Contains class definitions of String,
// and non-member overloaded operator
// functions.
class String
{
private:
  char *d_string_p; //character pointer

public:
  // Constructors
  String();
  String(const String& string);
  String(const char *str);

// Destructor
  ~String();

  // Assignment
  String &operator =(const String& string);
  String &operator =(const char* str);


  // Manipulators for concatenation to this string
  String &operator +=(const String&string);
  String &operator += (const char* str);

  int length() const;

  // Concatenation (to a new string)
  String operator +(const String& str) const;
  String operator + (const char* string) const;

  // Comparison Operators (lexical)
  int operator == (const String& string) const;
  int operator == (const char* str) const;
  int operator != (const String& string) const;
  int operator != (const char* str) const;
```

Example 4.6. Our final attempt at a user-defined string class.

```
int operator < (const String& string) const;
int operator < (const char* str) const;
int operator <= (const String& string) const;
int operator <= (const char* str) const;
int operator > (const String& string) const;
int operator > (const char* str) const;
int operator >= (const String& string) const;
int operator >= (const char* str) const;


// overloaded conversion operator converts
// String to char*
operator char*() // convert to standard
{ return d_string_p; }


// friend -- overloaded I/O operator of
// ostream class
    friend ostream& operator << (ostream& s, String
&str);
};

// Non-Member (Free) Operators
String operator + (const char* str, const String&
string);
int operator == (const char* str, const String&
string);
int operator != (const char* str, const String&
string);
int operator > (const char* str, const String&
string);
int operator >= (const char* str, const String&
string);
int operator < (const char* str, const String&
string);
int operator <= (const char* str, const String&
string);
```

Example 4.6 (continued). Our final attempt at a user-defined string class.

Of course, we would need implementations of each of the member functions for this class. For reasons of space, we have not included the source code in this book. Most of the details of implementation of the methods are straightforward. You should compare the design of our class with the equivalent one in the ANSI standard class library. You should note the heavy use of passing arguments by reference, using the ampersand symbol (&) after the name of the argument.

There are many member functions because there are many opportunities for operator overloading. This leads to a large number of potential test cases. We will discuss testing of object-oriented programs in Chapter 6.

4.12 User Interfaces

The marketplace success of many software products depends much more on the software's user interface or the set of visible features than on hidden features such as robustness. This is especially true in crowded markets such as applications software for personal computers in which there are many competing products.

In this section, we will present a brief overview of this essential topic. The intention is to convince you that there is more to user interface design than the use of multiple colors, flashing messages, clever icons, sound, or computer animation.

There is both an art and a science to user interface design. More detailed information on user interfaces can be found in the books by Jakob Nielsen [NIEL94] and Ben Schneiderman [SCHN80], publications such as that of the Special Interest Group in Human-Computer Interaction (SIGCHI) of the ACM, many conferences devoted to human-computer interaction, as well as some of the publications listed in the references.

Most current software systems have user interfaces based on the WIMP (Window, Interaction, Mouse, Pointer) paradigm. The Macintosh operating system and the Microsoft Windows variants, Windows 97, Windows 95, Windows, Windows NT and Windows for Workgroups, follow this paradigm, as does software written to use the X Windows utilities for UNIX and other environments.

The graphical user interfaces of high-quality software packages and web pages all have a consistency that is reflected in the simplicity of their menu design. For example, most graphical user interfaces for personal computer software have pull-down menus with file operations at the top of the screen on the left-hand side.

We will now distinguish between a pull-down and a pop-up menu. A "pull-down" menu is one in which the user selects an option from a set of options by moving a pointing device such as a mouse to a fixed position and selecting that position by pressing a mouse button or some other selection device. This sequence of operations makes a menu appear below the place where the pointing device was placed. The user then moves the pointing device down the list of menu options until he or she selects one of the options. (The user has the option of terminating this process by releasing the mouse button or moving the mouse to another position.) The initial set of options listed in a pull-down menu are always available to the user.

In contrast to the information in a pull-down menu, none of the information in a "pop-up" menu is visible to a user unless the user takes a specific action, such as pressing a mouse button or the equivalent combination of keystrokes.

The action of a typical pull-down menu before and after a mouse button is pressed is illustrated in Figures 4.13 and 4.14. Compare these menus to Figures 4.15 and 4.16, which illustrate the action of pop-up menus.

Note that the pull-down menus appear at the top of the screen illustrated in Figure 4.13 as long as this application (Microsoft Word) is running and the window is displayed on the screen. Contrast this to the situation in Figure 4.14 in which the same pull-down menu is shown together with a new menu that is obtained by the selection of an option from this menu.

Figure 4.13 An example of a pull-down menu before a selection is made.

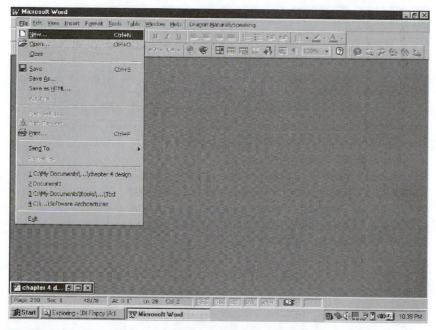

Figure 4.14 An example of a pull-down menu after a selection is made.

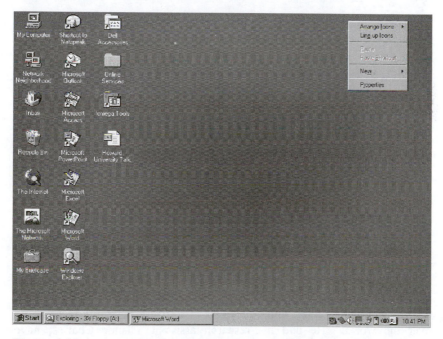

Figure 4.15 An example of a pop-up menu before an initial selection.

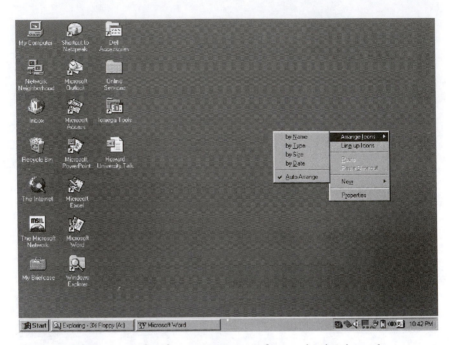

Figure 4.16 An example of a pop-up menu after a selection is made.

The wide range of options caused by the availability of pull-down and pop-up menus causes great problems for an interface designer. He or she has to be careful to not use these tempting features just because they are available. The following guidelines are helpful:

- Use a pull-down menu when the options should always be visible.
- Use a pull-down menu to supply a set of options for a novice user.
- Use a pop-up menu when the options need not always be visible.
- Use a pop-up menu to provide shortcuts for an experienced user.

The guidelines are necessarily incomplete because of space limitations and because of the wide range of applications and potential users. Nonetheless, they illustrate some of the major problems for an interface designer: needing a consistent approach to the interface's design, while simultaneously providing the necessary help for a novice user and powerful time-saving shortcuts to make an experienced user more productive.

We note that in many situations, a graphical user interface is not appropriate. Consider the case of my colleague at Howard University, Peter Keiller, who collaborates with colleagues in software reliability research all over the world. He and his research assistant, Claude Charles, have developed a set of tools to analyze data files to assess the rate of growth in the reliability of software systems. The data files contain the times that software faults occurred during the testing process.

Because many of the systems Dr. Keiller considers are not connected to the Internet for security reasons, he often has to do this research without access to workstations and servers available at his home environment at Howard University. He thus developed a smaller version for his software tool set for a personal computer. The tool set must work in all environments and, thus, the graphical user interface appropriate for Windows 95, or any other version of Microsoft Windows could not be used.

Instead, the software works perfectly in a MS-DOS environment. The simplest interface is best in this case. (Of course, he also carries a windows-based version of his software.)

Here is another example of a menu-driven, non-graphical user interface for a system used to select a series of files to be analyzed by a software system. It was developed on a system with character-based terminals and considerable effort went into the development of text files that were printed to simulate graphical terminal screens. Several menus, compressed to save space, are shown in Figures 4.17 through 4.22.

```
SANAC System for ANalyzing Ada Coupling
1989   B&S Enterprises, Inc.
```

Figure 4.17 An example of an opening screen from a text-based, menu-driven system.

```
S    A    N    A    C    Main Menu
1. Coupling Measures
2. Coupling Description
3. Help
4. Exit
```

Figure 4.18. An example of a main menu from a text-based, menu-driven system.

```
S    A    N    A    C    Secondary Menu
1. Main Menu
2. Coupling Description
3. Help
4. Exit
```

Figure 4.19. An example of a second menu from a text-based, menu-driven system.

```
Coupling Output Specification
You may have output sent to a file
or to the screen.
The default output file is
   " Coupling.Out" .
The default option is the screen.

1 = Screen
2 = File
```

Figure 4.20. An example of a menu of output choices from a text-based, menu-driven system.

Now imagine that the executable version of the software is called "sanac." (As the opening screen suggests, the software is named sanac to reflect that it is intended as a system to analyze coupling of software written in the Ada programming language.) By setting up a simple command line argument such as in C or C++, we can reduce the six menu selections in Figures 4.17 through 4.22 to the single command line

sanac file.a

which is much simpler and has far fewer keystrokes than the menu-driven system. The simplicity is appreciated most by an experienced user.

```
                    H E L P

The System for ANalyzing Ada Coupling
(SANAC) measures the level of
interconnections (coupling) between
Ada modules contained in user-
specified Ada source files.  The code
must be syntactically correct for
accurate results.

Select options from the Main Menu:

   1. Perform Coupling Analysis on the
      Ada Source files you specify.
   2. Get a Description of Coupling
      types.
   3. Get Help (* Presently Invoked *)
   4. Exit from SANAC.
```

Figure 4.21. An example of a help screen from a text-based, menu-driven system.

```
COME BACK TO SANAC
1989 B&S Enterprises, Inc.
RELEASE 2.0
```

Figure 4.22. An example of a closing screen from a text-based, menu-driven system.

Menu items can be grouped in several ways; the most common organizations are by functionality or alphabetically. It is generally preferable to order different options by the ones most likely to be used. It is generally agreed that the exit option should be the last one available in each menu in which it appears.

Of course, the worst possible mistake in user interface design is to expect the user to provide input without a prompt and a description of the input. What do you do in response to a user interface prompt such as that shown in Figure 4.23?

```
c:\
```

Figure 4.23. The worst possible user interface?

There is one final note about user interfaces. Use a spell checker in all text files, menu screens, or menu options. Follow this by proofreading carefully. If no spell checker is available, use a dictionary and proofread carefully. The point cannot be stressed enough. A sloppy user interface is a red flag to anyone evaluating the software. If the public face of the software is not correct, why should anyone have confidence in the software's internal correctness?

4.13 Software Interfaces

Some of the most interesting types of new sofware utilities for personal computers are known as "conflict resolvers." A conflict resolver examines software configuration files for possible inconsistencies among different applications, or even among different versions of the same application. These utilities attempt to solve the problems that can occur when software is interfaced to an environment with different versions of operating systems, compilers, utilities, or application programs. Conflict resolution detection programs are often run by users who are frustrated by apparently correct software that does not run correctly, crashes their computers, or even destroys data created by other application programs.

Of course, the same problems can occur when a software system is created from individual software components. The market-driven need to release software updates every few months places heavy emphasis on software reuse and higher-level software components, including complete subsystems. This, in turn, can lead to significant problems with interfaces between subsystems. Since these interfaces often are not seen by users of the software, the results of conflicts or inconsistencies are not obviously clear, especially to the casual or inexperienced user.

Many software development organizations create a formal document, usually known as an "interface control document," or ICD, to help manage the interfaces between software components or subsystems. A typical ICD for a very small project will include the names of each of the major subsystems, together with a formal description of the interfaces between them. The interfaces can be as simple as the number, type, and usage for each argument to a function. the type and usage of any values returned, and any side effects of a function's operation, especially in the case of error conditions.

In more realistic applications, the ICD will be more elaborate. Frequently, the ICD is given as a matrix, where the rows and columns are labeled with the names of the major subsystems or components. The entries in the matrix are often names of documents that describe the actual interfaces in more detail than can be given in a small space.

For example, an ICD for a project with three subsystems named A, B, and C, might look something like this:

	System A	System B	System C
System A		Doc 2.0	Doc 2.3
System B			Doc 1.1
System C			

There is one point that needs to be mentioned. One of the purported benefits of object-oriented analysis and design is the separation of the interfaces of objects from their implementation. A software development project that determines the public interface of the major objects in a system at an early stage in the process will allow implementation of both the object whose interface is published and all objects that use that interface to proceed with little need for additional coordination. The disadvantage is that, while it is easy to determine the interfaces between small objects, it is hard to describe the interfaces between major subsystem components.

We note that software interfaces are easiest to manage when all software components are in the same application domain so there is control over component or subsystem interfaces. Established standards in the particular application domain contribute to reusability success. When there are enforced standards, the following good things can happen:

- The problem of reusing source code within a domain becomes more manageable, since the domain is more likely to be narrow.

- Components in the library have a higher probability of being reused than if no standards are used.

- There are few data types and the reusable parts are small and, therefore, more likely to be reused in multiple applications.

- The cost of development and maintenance is reduced because there is less need to write filters or glueware to interface between different components.

The use of standard interfaces means that decisions made for one module or subsystem should not cause conflicts with other modules or subsystems.

Some standards are easier to determine than others. For example, storage of fundamental data types such as characters, integers, and floating point numbers might be different in different computer languages or even in different compilers for the same language. The movement toward internationalization of character sets can cause great difficulty for the interaction of software intended for the wide character set (the type w_char) of newer versions of C with the older versions in which the simple declaration (the type char) are sufficient. These differences can be found by searching the source code files for the presence of such words as w_char.

On the other hand, determining whether two software components handle dates properly might be harder. For example, one component might store the date as a set of three integers, for month, day, and year. Another might conserve space by using only six characters with the form MMDDYY. The conversion routines, together with the limitations caused by the implicit assumption that two characters would always be sufficient to represent a year are not trivial, especially if the date is used in many different ways in the software components. Of course, this is the major difficulty with the Y2K problem.

The basic questions to ask about interfaces between software components are:

- Have the software components been developed according to coding standards?
- Have the necessary configuration and header files been documented?
- Are the software components of high quality?
- How much effort must be expended to incorporate the components into a system?

In the next section, we will address these points in the context of our large continuing software engineering project example.

4.14 Some Metrics for Design

The purpose of this section is to introduce you to the idea of measuring designs of software systems. Unfortunately, very few approaches are standard in this area and there is little definitive research as to the most effective metrics. Nonetheless, it seems clear that there will be increased emphasis on metrics that can provide some guidance to managers evaluating designs. Accordingly, we will provide a few suggestions for managers on this topic.

A major concern of many software managers at this point in the software development process is the modularity of their designs. Therefore, we suggest the following metrics for measuring the size of the interfaces between subsystems at the design stage:

- One possible measure is a count of the number of functions, modules, subsystems, or components in the system.

- Another possible measure is a count of the number of objects, functions, modules, subsystems, or components with which each component must interface.

- Another possible measure is a description of the size of the interfaces between distinct functions, modules, subsystems, or components. This measurement may include a count of the number of shared variables, or may be enhanced to include an assessment of the complexity of the shared variables.

- Still another possible measure is a count of the number of loops in a control flow graph used to describe a system's design.

- There are some obvious metrics that a project manager may apply to the design produced by the design team. The function point metrics that we discussed in Chapter 3 can be used at this stage to provide an assessment of the difficulty in implementing the design.

- A design that encourages high productivity by means of reuse should make certain that the different software components have standard interfaces. The degree of adherence to standards is also important and is measurable to some extent.

Here the goal of the metrics is to produce as simple a design as possible, with the coupling between subsystems minimized. Metrics that compute the degree of interconnection among different subsystems or modules should be collected. System designs with broad interfaces should be reviewed to reduce integration and testing costs.

- Cost metrics can be very important at the design phase. The cost estimates for the previous systems built using the design that is to be reused should be compared to the actual costs for implementation of the design, and any unusual deviations should be noted and explained.

You may be able to suggest some other metrics. Suggesting metrics for designs is easy; the hard task is collecting the metrics and analyzing the data collected to determine whether the metrics actually describe some aspect of a system. We discuss this issue briefly in Chapter 9.

Your software development project may develop other design metrics depending on the organization's experience and the preferred development environment.

4.15 Design Reviews

Recall that a major goal of a software manager is to predict risk in a software development project. He or she would like to minimize risks entirely. Thus, there is heavy emphasis on those activities that the manager believes will reduce risk and allow the current software to be created to meet the customer's specifications and will ensure that the entire project will be completed on time and within budget.

Thus, the manager is likely to expect two things: a detailed design review and some sort of inspection. In many organizations there will be several design reviews, often with increasingly detailed views of the design being presented.

Design reviews have much in common with requirements reviews. They are extremely important to the success of a project. They require considerable planning, and a large expenditure of time and resources.

There is at least one fundamental difference between requirements and design reviews, however. In a properly conducted review of a detailed design, the design will often be examined in order to be certain of what could happen if the system was used in an unexpected way. That is, the design may be checked to make sure that the system keeps errors that occur in one particular module of a subsystem from propagating into other modules of other subsystem.

A checklist for a design review is given in Table 4.4.

Table 4.4
Checklist for a design review

- The presentation should be rehearsed.
- The time of the presentation should fall within allotted limits.
- Sufficient time should be available for questions.
- People who can answer technical questions should be in attendance.
- All slides, transparencies, and multimedia materials must be checked for accuracy.
- All slides, transparencies, and multimedia materials must be checked for spelling.
- Paper copies of slides, transparencies, and multimedia materials are available to all participants.
- Someone must verify that the meeting room has all necessary equipment: microphones, overhead projector, slide projector, videotape player and monitor, computer-monitor hookup, etc.
- An attendance list with names, addresses, phone numbers, and affiliations must be passed around, and all attendees must sign it.

One last step that is becoming more common in software engineering practice is putting each approved design document (preliminary, intermediate, or final) on either a local organizational network or the Internet. The design documents may be as simple as a set of attachments of files created by a word processor. They may include the project's design diagrams in some drawing tool's format. They may also be digital photographic images of other documents stored in a format such as a .gif file. In an extreme case, some of the documents may be stored in animated formats such as .jpg or .mpg files.

Why are design documents posted electronically in many organizations? The reason is simple: people lose paper documents with personnel moves, office relocation, and they generally wish to reduce the amount of clutter in offices. In addition, documents that are available on networks can be used by any personnel who have security access to the files.

On a personal note, I recently worked on a reengineering project where all the original requirements and design documents were lost and the source code had to be ported to a new machine because the existing hardware was no longer manufactured. A considerable amount of the reengineering effort was spent obtaining the system's design by analyzing the source code's organization. The project would have been much smoother if *any* written documentation for the system had been available. This loss of all paper documents associated with a project is not an unknown phenomenon. You should expect to use networks for document storage in many projects.

The availability of networks for designs suggests the possibility of designing systems using some form of groupware such as those we discussed in Chapter 3. Several organizations are experimenting with the use of groupware as part of their design process.

4.16 A Manager's Viewpoint of Design

As we indicated in the previous section, a project manager is likely to expect two things: a detailed design review and some sort of inspection. In many organizations, there will be several design reviews, often with increasingly detailed views of the design being presented. The manager will usually consider these reviews to be extremely important.

The project manager will want to have every item in the requirements traceability matrix checked against the detailed design to make certain that the written system requirements will be met by every possible software system that can be implemented according to this detailed design.

Because the manager's job-performance evaluation by his or her supervisors often depends upon successful completion of a project, the prudent manager will attempt to use some quantitative methods to determine the status of his or her project. Metrics may be characterized as being used to measure a product such as a design, or the process by which the product is created. We discussed metrics to describe design artifacts in section 4.14.

A manager may apply some metrics to evaluate the efficiency of the process of creating a successful design. He or she may compare the number of people working on the design team for this project with the design of other, similar projects to get an informal evaluation of the efficiency of the design team. The number of design reviews can be a negative factor if the design team does not seem to be making progress in successive design iterations.

The manager will require that the design team work with the organization's technical publications staff to ensure that the design adheres to standard formats for the company and the client.

4.17 Architecture of the Major Software Engineering Project

We are now ready to describe the architecture of the major software engineering project that we will study throughout the remainder of this book. To refresh your memory, you should look at the requirements traceability matrix requirements for this system that we developed in chapter 3 (and at the detailed requirements, if you have time). To make the architecture easier to understand, we will concentrate on the most relevant architecture types.

Also, we will be content with combinations of textual and graphical representations rather than being confined to UML, because we want to make the process as general as possible.

Recall that there are several different architecture types:

- Physical architecture
- Logical architecture
- Functional architecture
- Software architecture
- Technical architecture
- System architecture
- Deployment architecture

We will begin with the simplest ideas first. The software is to run on some version of the Windows operating system. Therefore we can make use of the facilities that are available in Windows to interface to the operating system. Also, if the computer is on a network, we can make use of the network to separate the computation between a client and a server, or between multiple clients and servers. Some of the options are shown in figures 4.24 and 4.25.

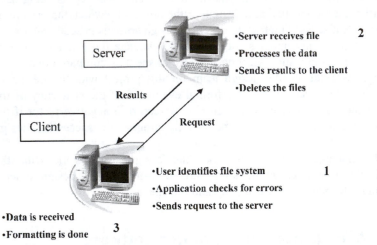

Figure 4.24 One possible organization, with heavy computation on client. (Source: M. Armstrong, C. Barnes, B. Fough, senior project design, Howard University.)

One advantage of the close integration of Windows Explorer with the operating system is that several of the user interfaces are the same for networked systems as for stand-alone ones. (This close integration was a major part of the basis for the antitrust suit filed against Microsoft by the U.S. government.) The commonality of the user interface makes both the user interface and the back end computational subsystem highly portable within the Windows environment and relatively easy to be interoperable with other (Microsoft-based) systems.

Server contains source analyzer
Clients contain source files

TCP/IP Network
Connection

Figure 4.25 An alternative design with computation done on the server. (Source: S. Armstrong, M. Henry, A. Rogers, Senior project, Howard University.)

Thus, we can use existing dialog boxes for file input with very few modifications, as shown in figures 4.26 and 4.27. The presence of the dialog box labeled "drive" makes it clear that we can access files on local hard drives, on local floppy drives, and on drives of other computers on the same network.

Recall that the technical architecture of a system involves mapping of software to the physical architecture. The decision should be made at this time. The interfaces shown in figures 4.26 and 4.27 illustrate the feasibility of nearly any mapping to the physical architecture. In an ideal world, with considerable time, many alternative architectures would be considered. In reality, the choice might be limited to a smaller set based on the decision to have everything done on one system or on a small number of clients and servers.

We will be content to indicate the system architecture in Figure 4.28. We note that the architectural design should indicate the interactions with the operating system; in this case, whether to use Java or existing Microsoft DLLs. (We have chosen DLLs.) The rest of the architecture should be clear from reading the next two sections.

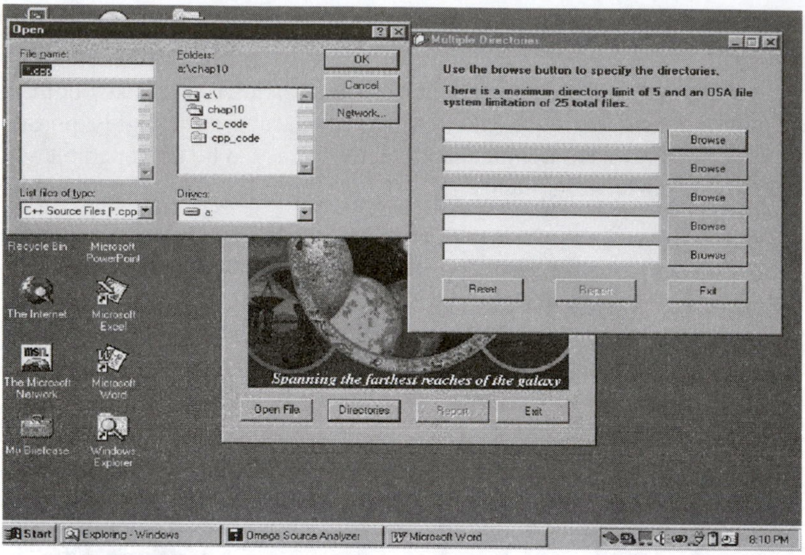

Figure 4.26 An illustration of how a software system can interface with an operating system.

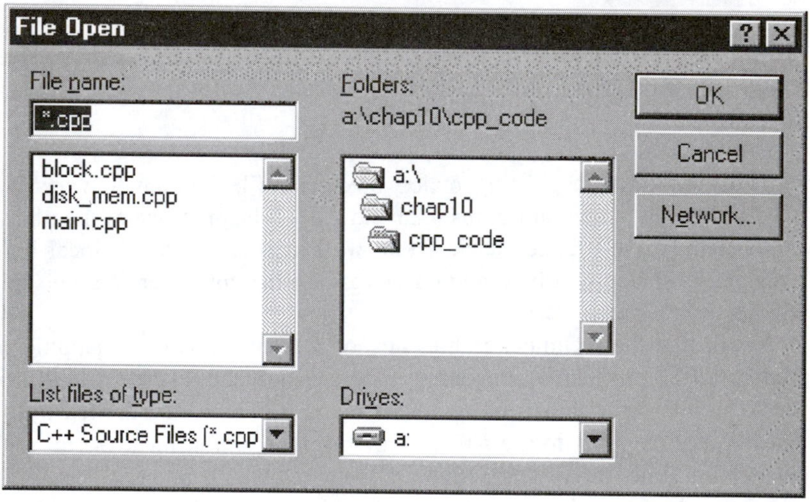

Figure 4.27 A more detailed illustration of how a software system can interface with an operating system.

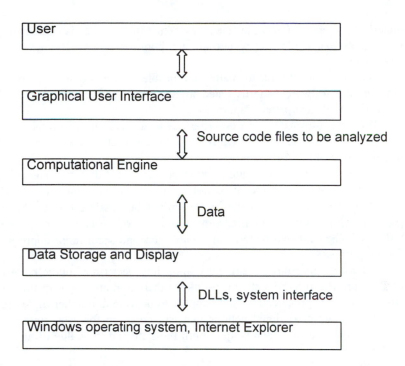

Figure 4.28. A high-level view of the architecture of the major software design project.

4.18 Preliminary Design of the Major Software Project

We will now turn to an application of our design approach: our continuing software project for which we developed requirements in Chapter 3. You should review the design information and the requirements traceability matrix in Table 3.6 before continuing with the discussion. In this section, we will develop both the preliminary and detailed designs of our continuing example of a software system. There are several questions that must be answered if we are to have a proper design that will lead to an eventual software system that adheres to the software engineering goals given in Chapter 1.

We wish to develop a design that is easy to implement in an efficient manner, keeping in mind the goals of software engineering that were listed in Chapter 1. At the same time, we want our design to map to the requirements in the sense that we can determine if each requirement is met. We have seen a large amount of information on software patterns, design representations, and a large number of techniques. The sheer volume of material presented (and the clear evidence that there is much more information than could ever be put into any book) makes it difficult to know where to start.

Let's begin by trying to match our problem's requirements to one or more of the software patterns listed in Section 4.2. We will discuss the applicability of each pattern in turn.

The first software pattern describes a menu-driven user interface. It is clearly not applicable because we wish to have a batch driven system in the initial version of the software.

The second software pattern describes an event-driven system. An event-driven user interface is clearly not appropriate for our system. Modeling the system as a set of states might be possible due to the text processing necessary to compute our lines of code. However, it seems unlikely. The next two patterns also use states and seem more appropriate for our purposes.

Pattern number three seems very appealing because a source code file can be considered to be a stream of tokens that are removed from the input stream once it is processed. There appear to be a small number of "states" and a small set of optional actions that can be taken for each state. The optional action taken depends upon both the state and the value of an input "token."

Pattern number four seems less promising than number three in that the decision about which action to take may depend on more information than is available from just the pair consisting of the state and the input token. In this pattern, the tokens may still remain in the input stream after being processed.

Pattern number five suggests a database system. This might be appropriate for the back end of the software. A spreadsheet also fits this pattern.

Pattern number six, a general, flexible, configurable system, seems to be inappropriate.

Pattern numbers seven and eight present several reasonable possibilities. If the system has everything primarily guided by an algorithm, rather than depending primarily on data, then a procedural system is appropriate. This is the case with pattern seven.

On the other hand, a system with many relatively independent computational actions taking place might be more appropriate as an object-oriented system, which is the case with pattern number eight.

There seem to be some clear conclusions and some issues left to be decided. Treating the inputs to our software system as a stream of tokens seems appropriate, as does thinking of the back end of the software as a database, or at least interfacing to one.

Unfortunately, there is no obvious choice between writing a procedurally oriented or an object-oriented system, at least in our first attempt at system design.

The place to start is with the highest-level view of the system: the system's software architecture. Let's examine the basic functionality of the system. The software appears to have the basic architectural building blocks that are described in Table 4.5.

Table 4.5
A first list of large components and software architecture of the major software project.

1. A front end that will interact with the user and manage the input files that will be analyzed by our system.
2. A user interface that will include the front end described above.
3. A set of analysis routines to evaluate the input files provided in step one. The analysis routines will compute the lines of code for each function and the other necessary information.
4. Output routines to interface to a database or spreadsheet for later analysis.
5. A database or spreadsheet program to perform additional statistical analyses and data storage for the output obtained in step four.

These activities seem to exhaust the basic functionality of the system. We now turn to the problem of representing these high-level activities in order to develop an initial design and to allow us to improve the initial design through iteration. A preliminary, procedurally oriented design is given in Figure 4.29.

This flow chart represents the intent of the requirements of our continuing software project. There is a common interface, a determination of the type of the source code files used as input, a separation of functionality into three different analysis subsystems, a common data collection routine, and an interface to a database or spreadsheet program.

Of course, we should not be content with this preliminary design, since we have flexibility. No particular design methodology is being enforced by our employer. Let's consider what a data flow-oriented design might look like for the same system. A level 0 data flow diagram is shown in Figure 4.30.

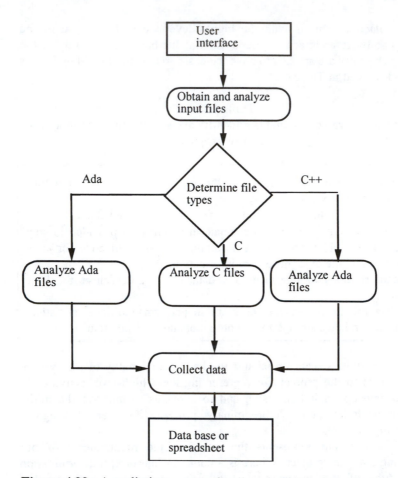

Figure 4.29. A preliminary, procedurally oriented design of our continuing software project.

It appears as if the control flow-based design representation provides more information than the representation using the data flow approach. Of course, we might reach a different conclusion if we used these two design representations to develop more detailed designs. The control flow representation of Figure 4.29 also appears to lead more easily to a decomposition into subsystems.

We reject an object-oriented design (not shown here) of the complete system for the same reason. Thus, we will use Figure 4.30 as the basis for our high-level system design, which will be procedurally based. There will be some object-oriented components, as we will see. Note that this design does not conflict with the requirements traceability matrix given in Example 3.6.

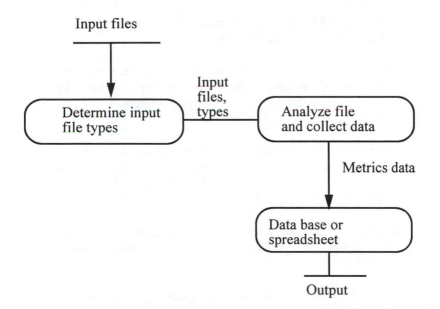

Figure 4.30. A preliminary data flow design (DFD level 0) of our continuing software project.

It is now reasonable to examine any software utilities, complete programs, integrated tools, or other resources that can be used as part of our system. If we can find such utilities, programs, or tools, then we can make our future development easier by reusing them. Recall from Chapter 1 that reusability is one of the goals of software engineering. Any satisfactory, reusable software utilities can simplify the design process by eliminating the need for detailed design functionality provided by the tool or utility. (In addition, the need for coding the functionality provided by the tool or utility is also avoided through such reuse.)

An examination of Internet resources on January 30, 1997 suggests examining the following web site maintained by Christopher Lott:

```
http://www.qucis.queensu.ca/Software-
Engineering/Cmetrics.html
```

This site includes entries for several different programs. We quote Lott:

"`csize:` A tool to measure the size of C programs, written by Christopher Lott in 1994.

`cyclo:` A tool to analyze cyclomatic complexity of a piece of ANSI C or C++ code, written by Roger Binns in 1993. Can generate a postscript flowgraph of the functions.

lc: A tool to count lines of code in C files, written by Brian Marick in 1983 and updated 1992.

hp_mas: Mas is a maintainability assessment tool for analyzing C programs that was developed under the sponsorship of Hewlett-Packard Corporate Engineering at the University of Idaho in 1992.

metre: A software-metrics tool (McCabe, Halstead, backfired function points, and various statement and lines-of-code metrics) and a call-graph tool for ANSI/ISO Standard C, written by Paul Long in 1994 and updated in 1995.

metrics: A collection of tools (control, Halstead, KDSI, McCabe) which was put together by Brian Renau around 1989.

spr: A tool to measure NCSS for C source programs, written by Ted Shapin in 1989.

I successfully built all of them using gcc on a Sun using SunOS 4.1.3. For packages 'csize' and 'metre', the authors went to considerable trouble to write portable code and flexible Makefiles. For cyclo and c-metr-pkg, no such effort was made, and consequently I had to monkey with some makefiles. Packages lc and spr are relatively simple and should not present any problems.

However, I have not used all of the tools extensively, so unfortunately I can't make any helpful statements about reliability or ease of use."

This quote emphasizes what should be clear to anyone who has used freeware: there are no guarantees. In the language of software reuse, the software packages from this site have not been certified except for the ability to compile them on a Sun computer running SunOS 4.1.3. (This operating system version is also known as Solaris 1.1, which is very different from later versions of Solaris.)

Another search was conducted. This time, we examined the WSRD catalog of the reuse library maintained by SAIC (Scientific Applications International Corporation). This library can be found at the URL

http://source.asset.com

The WSRD catalog listed 171 hits under the search query "software metrics." Of these, many were documentary material, educational material, links to commercial tools such as the Grace components from EVB Software, or similar. A few free software tools were available via the anonymous ftp from the STARS (Software Technology for Adaptable, Reliable Software) program.

Our assessment of the Ada software packages available suggested that some of them could be used for some of the analysis portion of the software system to be developed. Specifically, it could be used in the analysis of the Ada software source code files. However, they would have to be extended to produce the analysis of the Ada source code files that we need to meet the project's specifications. These software tools would also produce too much extraneous information to be used as is.

Some of the same issues that we observed in our examination of publicly available analysis tools for measuring C or Ada source code files also would have occurred with analysis tools for C++ source code files. The problem would occur when attempting to reuse publicly available software for larger systems other than the one that we discuss in this text.

While we have not examined the existing software tools mentioned above in detail, there is sufficient information to believe that several of them provide sufficient functionality to satisfy our project. Even if the preliminary assessment of the reusable tools' quality is incorrect, we can use the existence of the tools as a guide in our design. In other words, the question of the quality of the existing reusable software tools can be deferred until the coding phase of the project. We don't need to certify the quality of the tools at this point because they do not affect the design (at this point).

We now turn to the problem of transforming the high-level design represented in Figure 4.30 into a more detailed design that is complete in the sense that the interfaces between system components are well understood and the functionality of each system component is spelled out in sufficient detail. The final design should be sufficiently detailed so that it can be implemented without excessive difficulty.

The first step is to consider the interfaces between different subsystems. There appear to be six subsystems in the complete system; they are listed in Table 4.6.

Recall that before we changed the requirements to use a GUI, the requirements specified that the user interface be by means of command-line arguments. We will return to this simpler case in the exercises. Since we have illustrated the feasibility of using existing dialog boxes for file input, getting the files seems to be no problem.

However, there is one issue that may occur if the system is to be used in practice. The system requirements specifically noted that input need not be checked. Thus, we don't have to worry about someone using the system with an executable file as input in this release of the project. The difficulty is that realistic software systems are usually spread out over several different directories, so our software system might be given an input which is a directory. How can we incorporate the processing of directories into the design of this software?

Table 4.6
The set of subsystems in the initial design of our continuing software project.

1. Subsystem for the user interface.
2. Subsystem for obtaining files and analyzing file types.
3. Subsystem for passing input files to data collection subsystem.
4. Subsystem for collecting data for each input file.
5. Subsystem for sending data to spreadsheet or database.
6. Spreadsheet or database program.

There are several issues, depending on our knowledge of the operating system on which the software system will be used and the naming standards that we can assume have been followed for the input files. (Naming standards will be discussed in detail in Chapter 5, when we discuss coding issues.)

We will make the following assumptions about naming conventions for our input files:

- All input files written in C have names that end in either the .c or .C extensions.
- All input files written in C++ have names that end in either the .cpp or .C extensions.
- All input files written in Ada have names that end in either the .a, .A, or .ada extensions.
- All C or C++ header files have names that end in .h and are not to be processed further.
- Any files named Makefile or makefile are compilation instructions and and are not to be processed further.
- Any files named readme, read.me, README, READ.ME, or ending in .doc or .txt are documentation and are not to be processed further.
- Any files with names that end in either .exe or .obj can be ignored.
- All other files are directories and may contain source code as well as other files. (This means, for example, that any so-

called "special files" such as device drivers in UNIX will be ignored.)

The assumption that the input source code was developed using a naming convention makes designing this portion of the subsystem easy. We just get the input files and pass them to the next subsystem. In the case of a directory, which can be determined by its name not matching one of the other possibilities, the contents of the directory must be searched also. The search of each directory should be recursive, so that source code files located in directories that are included in other directories will be analyzed.

A moment's look at our basic set of subsystems suggests that the first two subsystems for user interface and for obtaining files and analyzing file types should be combined. This is a natural result of our assumption that the naming conventions listed above were followed in the creation of the input files to our system. The subsystem for passing input files to data collection subsystem also seems redundant. Hence, it too can be combined with the initial subsystems. Thus, the six subsystems listed in Table 4.5 can be combined into the four subsystems listed in Table 4.7.

Table 4.7

Final set of four subsystems in the design of our continuing software project.

1. Subsystem for the user interface, obtaining files and analyzing types
2. Subsystem for collecting data for each input file
3. Subsystem for sending data to spreadsheet or database
4. Spreadsheet or database program

4.19 Subsystem Design for the Major Software Project

Let's attempt to design the first subsystem. As a basis, we will use the control flow-oriented diagram given in Figure 4.31. The upper portions of the design are adequate for our purposes, except that they do not indicate the actions that will be taken in response to specific types of inputs. That is, the diagram in Figure 4.31 does not indicate any mechanism for checking on the types of input files, for determining if there are directory files to be examined further, which files can be ignored, and whether there are any input files at all.

Recall that the requirements document for our software project specified that wild cards could be used as names of input source code files. This will create some problems in implementation because it will imply interaction with the operating system's command processor to parse command lines to translate wild cards into names of actual files. However, we can design this portion of the software carefully as long as we know how the operating system actually stores command-line arguments and makes them available to C or C++ programs. Thus, determining this information is an essential part of the design process at this point. The design must take into account whether performing any proposed interaction with the operating system is possible.

The subsystem for collecting data for each input file will be based on the existing software tools located on the Internet that we discussed earlier in this section. Specifically, we will examine each of these tools for its functionality and determine the interface. If the tool's functionality is sufficient for our project's requirements, we will then provide an interface to the tool. If none of the tools has appropriate functionality, then at least some portion of the software to provide the necessary functionality will be written from scratch. This means that the new software tool must be designed.

We would like to put off the decision to write new software tools as long as possible, emphasizing an efficient software development process based on software reuse. However, this means that the software tools must be evaluated for three things: functionality, quality, and interface to the rest of the system. An interface control document (ICD) must be used here. Also, if the software tools are likely to change, we must institute some form of configuration management.

The third subsystem to be considered will provide the connection and aggregation of the data from the various reused software tools that form the major part of subsystem two. It is clear that the individual tools count the data differently. Thus, we need some consistency in the data definition and in the way that the data will be sent to the final subsystem, which is the database or spreadsheet.

There is one other point that needs to be made before we design the third subsystem. Several of the tools may not provide the desired information. Thus, there may be several pieces of information that are either not available, or else have to be replaced by a default value. This seems to suggest the presence of polymorphism, which in turn suggests an object-oriented approach.

With an object-oriented approach, the most important step is determining the objects. Recall the steps suggested in Table 4.2 for determination of objects:

1. Choose a candidate to be an object.
2. Determine a set of attributes and their possible sets of values. Use the has-a relation. List all relevant transformations on the object.

3. Develop an initial set of transformations on the object to serve as member functions.
4. Determine if there is more than one example of the object.
5. Apply the is-a relation.
6. Use polymorphism and overloading of operators (and functions) to check if we have described the objects in sufficient detail.
7. Use the uses-a relation to determine all instances of client-server or agent-based relationships.
8. Review the object for completeness.
9. Repeat steps two through eight for all combinations of relevant objects (triples, quadruples, and so on) until the object's role has been described adequately.

There are a few candidate objects to be considered for the fundamental object: individual functions, source code files, or collections of source code files into subsystems. As before, we use the term "function" to include "function" or "procedure." We examine each of these choices for the basic objects in turn.

If the object is "function," then the most obvious attributes and some potential values are:

Attribute	Typical Value
Name	Character string
Size	Integer
Module in which located	Character string

If the object is "source code file," then the most obvious attributes and some potential values are:

Attribute	Typical Value
Name	Character string
Size	Integer
Number of functions	Integer
List of functions	Linked list of character strings
Subsystem in which located	Character string

If the object is "subsystem," the most obvious attributes and values are:

Attribute	Typical Value
Name	Character string
Size	Integer
Number of source code files	Integer
List of source code files	Linked list of character strings

We have to know the spreadsheet or database input format. For the Microsoft Excel spreadsheet software, input to a spreadsheet can be in several forms, including, but not limited to, the following:

- An existing spreadsheet created in Excel
- An existing spreadsheet created in another spreadsheet program for which translators are available
- A text file with commas used as delimiters
- A text file with tabs used as delimiters

We choose to use the comma-delimited form, because file names are unlikely to consist of commas. This will work for spreadsheet input. (Note: This means that the requirements must be changed to handle source code files with names that include commas.)

There are similar issues for interfacing with a database management program. Unfortunately, the use of commas as delimiters here may cause more problems, because commas are perfectly valid as punctuation marks. Most databases use a non-printable ASCII character such as Control-R as a delimiter to separate different fields. We leave the details of the design of the interface to a database to the exercises.

The design should now be checked for internal consistency according to the principles discussed in Section 4.12. As was indicated there, any interface standards should be consistent with the software requirements of all modules or subsystems affected by the interface.

Now that we have a design, it is necessary to check the design against the requirements traceability matrix for the project. Item nine in the requirements traceability matrix calls for an installation routine. Since we have not discussed this previously, we must now include it in our set of subsystems to be designed. The installation subsystem should be relatively independent of the other subsystems of the complete software product, since the requirements specify that only a single size of the system will be produced and, thus, little configuration is necessary. Note that the software pattern of a general, flexible, highly configurable system might be used to characterize the installation subsystem. The newest version of the requirements traceability matrix is given in table 4.8.

You might wonder if we need to make an explicit link to a spreadsheet program such as Microsoft Excel, or if the output can be obtained by using various DLLs from the Microsoft library. Of course, the requirements say one thing, and changing them might cause difficulty.

However, if we illustrate the feasibility of using these DLL components in a design review, it is possible that a potential client may allow the requirements to be changed. Changing of system requirements is common in the market-driven software world.

Table 4.8
Requirements traceability matrix for the major continuing software engineering project.

#	Requirement	Design	Code	Test
1.	Intel-based	Y		
2.	Windows 95	Y		
3.	Windows 95 UI	Y		
4.	Consistent With Excel 4.0	Y		
5.	System One Size Only	Y		
6.	One MB System			
7.	One MB Disk Space			
8.	One 1.44 MB Floppy Disk			
9.	Includes Installation	Y		
10.	No Decompression Utility	Y		
11.	One input file at a time	Y		
12.	Size of each function	Y		
13.	Size of each file	Y		
14.	Size of system	Y		
15.	Compute totals	Y		
16.	Develop std for C,C++,Ada	Y		
17.	Batch-oriented system	Y		
18.	Precisely define LOC	Y		
19.	Measure separately	Y		
20.	No error checking of input	Y		
21.	Front end in C or C++	Y		
22.	Batch processing	Y		
23.	File names limited to 8.3	Y		
24.	Wild cards can be used	Y		
25.	Dead code ignored	N		
26.	No special compilers needed	Y		
27.	Microsoft Excel 4.0 used	Y		

You should also note that some of the issues involve setting standards and, as such, have not been considered at this point in the design process. Other requirements cannot be addressed fully in the design at this time. We leave the design of the installation subsystem to the exercises.

For example, we cannot precisely determine the size of the complete system at this time. The size of the software tools that we intend to use can be determined accurately, because these software tools already exist.

We will consider the detailed design of our software system in the next section.

4.20 Detailed Design for the Major Software Project

The next activity for our major software engineering project is to "flesh out" the previous designs in order to describe the system in detail. How much detail is needed? The answer is essentially the same as the one we gave when discussing the approach of Daniel and Orna Berry to the problem of determining software requirements: the requirements are considered to be complete and specified in sufficient detail when a programmer has enough information to be able to tell if he or she can develop a system to meet these requirements.

The major distinction between this degree of detail in the requirements and a similar level of detail in the design is that the use of higher-level languages may make some of the implementation details of the system unnecessary. Allocation of resources for the detailed implementation may be unnecessary because some of the design prototypes and GUI diagrams will be sufficiently developed to make further implementation effort redundant.

The diagram shown in figure 4.31 illustrates the point. This diagram shows the interface to the operating system and makes it clear that the output can be displayed in a simple pop-up window. Other aspects of the GUI are shown in figures 4.32 through 4.34.

What else must be specified in a detailed design? We need to see the descriptions of the interfaces, the functionality of software we write as "bridgeware" between the components we are obtaining from the Internet and other sources. We leave this to the exercises.

It seems likely that this project is well suited to concurrent development. Thus, we need an interface control document (ICD) to make sure that all developers use the same common interfaces. We leave this to the exercises, too.

From a project management perspective, we should also do a status check. Are we ahead of schedule (unlikely), behind schedule (likely), or approximately on target? Have there been any unpleasant surprises, any portions of the system that were more difficult than we had expected? Does any portion of the system require extra attention, perhaps additional resources? Have technology or market pressures rendered any portion of the system obsolete? Are there any changes that could affect our ability to complete this project?

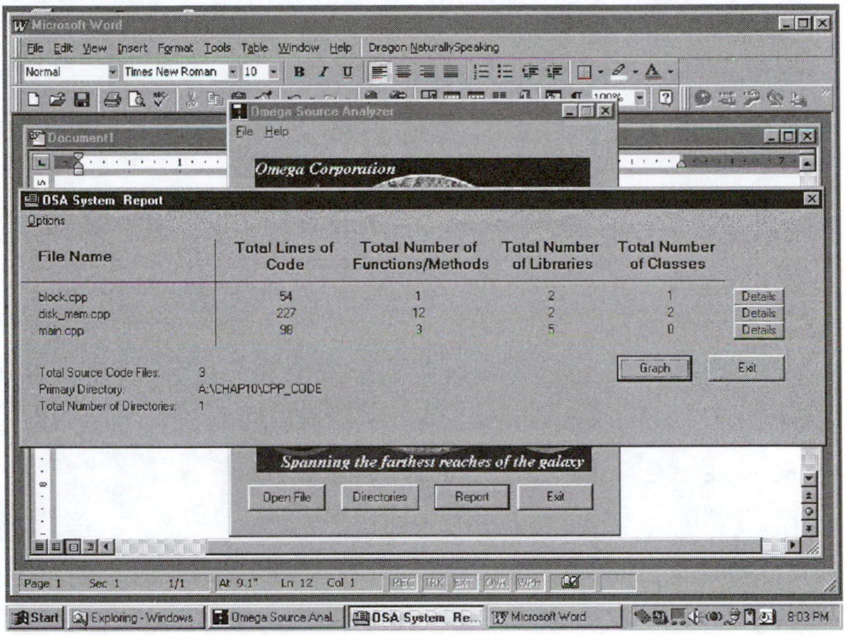

Figure 4.31. An illustration of system output. The output is shown in a window with dialog boxes overlayed on top of another application. (Source: S. Armstrong, M. Henry, and A. Rogers, proprietary software system.)

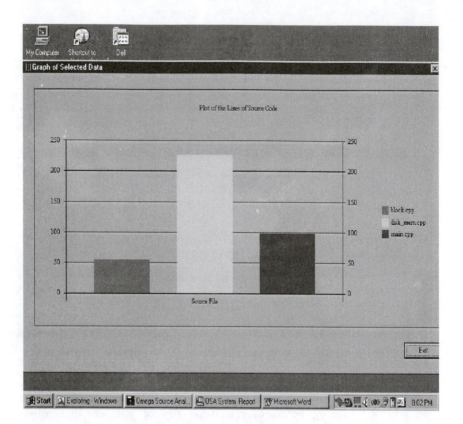

Figure 4.32. An illustration of the graphical output of our system. The output is shown in a window with a single dialog box. (Source: S. Armstrong, M. Henry, and A. Rogers, proprietary software system.)

Figure 4.33. A dialog box to control the type of output of our system. (Source: S. Armstrong, M. Henry, and A. Rogers, proprietary software system.)

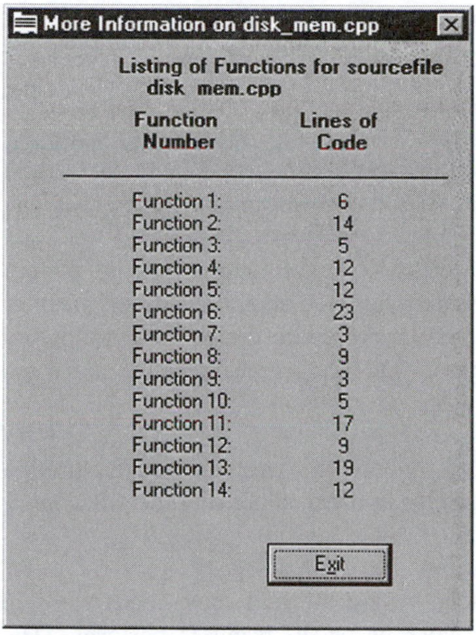

```
More Information on disk_mem.cpp        [X]

        Listing of Functions for sourcefile
                    disk_mem.cpp

        Function              Lines of
        Number                 Code
        ─────────────────────────────────
        Function 1:              6
        Function 2:             14
        Function 3:              5
        Function 4:             12
        Function 5:             12
        Function 6:             23
        Function 7:              3
        Function 8:              9
        Function 9:              3
        Function 10:             5
        Function 11:            17
        Function 12:             9
        Function 13:            19
        Function 14:            12


                    [    Exit    ]
```

Figure 4.34. Detailed output of our system. (Source: S. Armstrong, M. Henry, and A. Rogers, proprietary software system.)

Further Reading

There are many excellent books on software design. Jackson [JACK83] describes a method that is commonly known as "Jackson Structured Design," or JSD. Yourdon [YOUR89], Yourdon and Constantine [YOUR79], Coad and Yourdon [COAD90], and Booch [BOOC93] also have excellent books on the subject.

The paper by David Parnas [PARN72] on design decomposition issues is still worth reading. This paper provides an assessment of the effect of several alternative design decisions that can be made even in a relatively simple situation.

A recent paper by Binder [BIND94] discusses the effect that design choices can have on testing object-oriented programs.

Nielsen [NEIL94] and Schneiderman [SCHN80] provide excellent overviews of human-computer interaction and their roles in good software design.

Summary

Design is a major part of the software engineering process. The goals of software engineering include efficiency, reliability, modularity, usability, modifiability, portability, testability, reusability, maintainability, and interoperability with other systems. Good software design techniques can support these goals.

One of the most powerful software design approaches is pattern matching. Determining that a subsystem, or even an entire system, matches a pattern can encourage reuse and make both design and follow-up implementation much more efficient and can produce better software. Common software patterns include:

1. A menu-driven system, where the user must pass through several steps in a hierarchy in order to perform the work he or she wants to perform.

2. An event-driven system, where the user must select steps in order to perform the work he or she wants to perform. The steps need not be taken in a hierarchical order.

3. A system in which the actions taken depend on one of a small number of "states" and a small set of optional actions that can be taken for each state depending on both the state and the value of an input "token."

4. A system in which a sequence of input tokens (usually in text format) is processed, one token at a time.

5. A system in which a large amount of information is searched for one or more specific pieces of information.

6. A system which can be used in a variety of applications, but which needs adjustments to work properly in new settings.

7. A system in which everything is primarily guided by an algorithm, rather than depending primarily on data.

8. A system that is distributed, with many relatively independent computational actions taking place.

Design representations can make a system easier to understand by using a graphical representation to provide a high-level view, hiding relatively unimportant details. Common design representations for procedurally based designs include flow charts and data flow diagrams. Pseudocode is also frequently used.

The most important design technique for procedurally developed software systems is decomposition of existing high-level designs. For object-oriented systems, the emphasis is on developing high-quality, reusable classes that can act autonomously.

The first step in designing an object-oriented system is to determine the relevant objects. Objects have attributes, and for each instance of an object, the attributes can take on a set of possible values. Determination of the attributes of an object and the set of possible values helps in the development of the function prototypes for the class.

Objects should not be defined in a vacuum for realistic descriptions of systems. The interfaces for a particular class may make it difficult to use other classes already present in the class library. Thus, the class library must be examined, either by a catalog (listing) of the classes, or by using a software tool called a browser.

The interface of the class should be consistent with that of related classes performing similar services.

Preexisting classes in the class library should be examined for the possible availability of usable friend functions.

The development of a set of objects for a system should be an iterative process. Candidates for objects should be able to pass the "multiple example" and other tests. Attributes of objects can be found by the "has-a relationship." A derived class must be related to a base class by the is-a relationship. Other relationships between classes can be found using the "uses-a relationship."

Design representations for object-oriented systems can be either graphical or text based. Graphical ones are often based on information models or entity-relationship (E-R) graphs.

A major goal of software design is to promote reuse. Designs should be reviewed to make certain that existing reusable software components are reused whenever possible.

Exercises

1. Take any non-object-oriented program that you have written with approximately 50-300 lines of code. Write a flow chart for this program.

2. Repeat Exercise 1, writing a data flow diagram.

3. What are the objects in the system that you chose for Exercises 1 and 2? List the attributes and the set of possible attribute values for each.

4. Take any object-oriented program that you have written with approximately 50-300 lines of code. Write a flow chart for this program.

5. Repeat Exercise 4, writing a data flow diagram.

6. Consider the development of an external computer system to evaluate how well a human subject is learning the use of a computer. The user is to interact with the I/O devices of monitor, keyboard, trackball, and mouse. The "user object" has an attribute called "experience level," which has the possible values "novice computer user," "frequent computer user," and "experienced computer user." List other possible attributes that might be appropriate for describing the user. (For simplicity, assume that there is a single software application running and that the user is not familiar with it.) Refer to the model of a user interface that was given in Figure 3.6.

7. Rewrite the String class of examples 8.3 and 8.4 to avoid the use of free (non-member) functions.

8. Write a description of the String class discussed in Section 8.5 using an Array class as a base class.

9. Write a description of the String class discussed in Section 8.5 using a List class as a base class.

10. Describe how does the String class given in examples 8.3 and 8.4 compare with the String class available in your class library.

11. Describe how you would test the member functions in the String class given in examples 8.3 and 8.4. How would you test the free (non-member) functions?

12. Write a control flow diagram for the MacTAGS example given in Figure 4.5.

13. Examine four or five books on data structures and determine how they implement the quicksort algorithm. Classify their presentations as being control flow oriented, data flow oriented, procedurally oriented, or object-oriented. Compare these approaches with the algorithm in Hoare's original paper [HOARE85].

14. Consider the system requirements for a simple chemical reaction process control system that were written in the form of a finite state machine

with an associated state diagram. These requirements were described in Section 3.8. Use this formal design representation to develop a detailed design.

15. Consider the system requirements for a simple chemical reaction process control system that were written in the form of a decision table. These requirements were described in Section 3.8. Use this formal design representation to develop a detailed design.

16. Consider the system requirements for a simple chemical reaction process control system that were written in the form of Petri net. These requirements were described in Section 3.8. Use this formal design representation to develop a detailed design.

Questions on the major software project.

1. Suppose that we wished to add a graphical user interface to the major software engineering project. An electronic list of such tools can be found at the URL

   ```
   http://www.cs.cmu.edu/afs/cs.cmu.edu/user/bam/www
   /toolnames.html
   ```

   This web site is managed by Brad Myers, who is a well-known researcher in the area of user interface design. Indicate how the incorporation of GUI tools would affect the design.

2. In Chapter 3, we presented a hypothetical dialog during our requirements elicitation. The initial requirements were later changed to allow for the web-based interface whose architecture was described in this chapter. Modify the architectures we presented here to reflect the high-level design of this (simpler) system. What changes did you make? Do you think it is easy to modify the design of a complex system to create a simpler one, or to design the simpler system from scratch?

3. Expand the design of the major software engineering project to include analysis of source code files written in Java.

4. What is the effect of moving the project to a different operating system, such as one running UNIX or MacOS, on the assumptions made in the design of the first subsystem for the user interface?

5. How does the design change if the data is to be collected in a database program instead of a spreadsheet?

6. Design the installation subsystem for the major software engineering project.

7. The user interface was to be written in either C or C++ to allow command-line arguments. Thus, this subsystem is very easy to design. It has two major features: interfacing with the operating system to obtain the command-line arguments and determining which arguments are to be passed on to the next subsystem. (The reader unfamiliar with the usage of command-line arguments should read Appendix 1.) We note that the system's software requirements did not specify the development of a GUI for the project. Therefore, we did not consider any GUI tools. The incorporation of a GUI into the design is discussed in section 17 of this chapter. The command-line argument interface is so simple that it does not appear to require any special design; at first glance, using the code in Appendix 1 as a template appears to be sufficient for our purposes.

8. Give the details of the design of the interface to a database for our major software project. Be sure that you specify the fields in the database.

Chapter 5

Coding

You are probably surprised to see an entire chapter of a software engineering book devoted to coding. After all, you have been writing code during much of your computer science education. You may even have had some work experience or an internship in which you wrote source code. You probably think that you are a good programmer. (You probably are.) Why, then, is there a chapter on coding?

In this chapter, we will describe some typical industry practices that go far beyond what is normally required to complete typical classroom programming projects. This chapter will include a discussion of coding styles, coding standards, naming conventions, code organization, and code reviews that both promote reuse and encourage efficient program execution. Each of these topics will be discussed in a separate section.

In addition, we will talk about coding the major software project.

5.1 The Choice of Programming Language

It is important to understand that the choice of a programming language for implementation of a system is often made on non-technical grounds. For example, market pressures, the availability of particular compilers, existence of software tools and development environments, or the experience of the software engineering staff may be more important than the perceived technical advantages of any particular language. Technical issues in programming-language selection include such things as ease of integration with existing software components, adherence to technical mandates, real-time or other performance requirements, and the need to keep the staff happy by giving them access to new technologies.

You probably feel confident with your ability to program in at least one high-level language. You may feel that you have mastered all of one particular programming language's idiosyncrasies. You may have even mastered the idiosyncrasies of several languages. However, there are many subtle language features that even an expert may not have mastered. The primary reason for this is the increasing complexity of programming languages.

Table 5.1 emphasizes this viewpoint. The information in this table was pointed out by Dr. Les Hatton in his keynote lecture at the 1997 Conference on Computer Assurance, ComPASS'97, in Washington, D.C. ([HATT97]).

Table 5.1

Size of several computer language manuals.

Language	Approximate number of pages in language manual
FORTRAN 77	150
Ada83	280
C (1990)	190
FORTRAN 90	400
Ada95	600
C++ (1998?)	800 (and growing)

It is clear that programming languages are complex and that some of the more obscure features will be difficult to understand if used in programs. Some of the more obscure language features may not be implemented correctly by your compiler. The following statement from the *Annotated C++ Reference Manual* by Margaret Ellis and Bjarne Stroustrup ([ELLI90]) indicates the level of language complexity of C++:

> If a class base contains a `virtual` function `vf`, and a class `derived` from it also contains a function `vf` of the same type, then a call of `vf` for an object of class `derived` invokes `derived::vf` (even if the access is through a pointer or reference to `base`). The derived class function is said to *override* the base class function. If the function types are different, however, the functions are considered different and the virtual mechanism is not invoked. It is an error for a derived class function to differ from a base class's virtual function in the return type only. ... The interpretation of the virtual function depends on the type of the object for which it is called, whereas the interpretation of a call of a nonvirtual member function depends only on the type of the pointer or reference denoting that object.

There is no reason to single out the C++ language on this list as being overly complex. The basic issue applies to nearly all programming languages. The potential obfuscation in C language statements such as

```
*(--a[i++])  += - *(--a[i++]);
```

is obvious.

Similar complexities occur with Ada packages that have multiple combinations of `with` and `use` clauses, as in

```
with package1; use package1;
```

```
with package2; use package2;
with package3;

package confusing is
 begin
 . . .
 package3.doit(); -- the one from package 3
 doit(); -- this the one from package 1 ?
 doit(); -- this the one from package 2 ?
end package confusing;
```

You can figure out what this software is supposed to do if you understand the naming and scoping rules of the with and use clauses in the Ada language. Still, the source code is hard to read. A similar example can be constructed in Java.

Java presents a special problem for software developers. The Java language itself is relatively small. Java is a purely object-oriented language. A software developer confining his or her Java classes to those provided in a standard such as the Java Development Kit (JDK), version 1.1, is likely to create software that is relatively easy to port.

Major factors in the success of Java are the well-defined interfaces known as application programming interfaces, or APIs. A software system that must interface to one or more existing programs may be written easily in Java if there is a smooth API. Writing the same software system may be much harder, or even impossible, to create in a reasonable time if there are no APIs available to interface to the pre-existing programs.

Visual BASIC (and the other languages that are part of the Microsoft Visual Studio) provides an easy interface to many operating system services by means of library components. For example, the user interfaces illustrated in figures 3.5 and 3.6 use linkages to Microsoft's library components to provide the familiar look and feel of these windows and the associated selections to be made by the mouse, which is the preferred input device for most Windows applications.

From the perspective of providing high-quality, maintainable components, esoteric language features should be avoided as much as possible. If such features must be used, they should be avoided as much as possible and their use should be confined to a few, well-documented and tested components.

In any event, the choice of programming language may be severely restricted by the system requirements. A software system with many components, most of which are loaded or removed during system operation is very likely to be written in Java. On the other hand, a software system that makes extensive use of UNIX system calls will probably be written in C or C++.

5.2 Coding Styles

Consider the following three fragments of C source code. These three fragments are all intended to be equivalent when executed. (Recall that in the C programming language, the statement "i++" means that the variable "i" is to be incremented by 1; this is equivalent to the longer statement i = i + 1.)

```
while (i>0)
  {
  mystery (i);
  i++;
  }

while (i>0) {
  mystery (i);
  i++;
}

while (i>0)
    {mystery (i);
     i++; }
```

The three code fragments illustrate distinct approaches to formatting source code so that the body of the while-loop can be recognized easily. In the first approach, the curly braces are lined up vertically, and are indented the same number of spaces or tabs. The braces appear with no other characters on the same line.

In the second approach, the initial left curly brace appears immediately after the Boolean expression in the while-loop. The terminating right curly base is aligned with the "while" statement. The closing brace appears on a line by itself.

Finally, the third code fragment illustrates a compromise. The initial left brace appears on the line after the "while" condition, but the terminating right brace is no longer aligned with it.

The three distinct styles here should not be mixed. This means that you should pick one style and stay with it. We emphasize stylistic issues not for the difficulty in reading these simple examples, but for having to understand large amounts of source code when debugging or maintaining a realistic software system.

Which coding style should you use? The simple answer is: use whatever style is specified by your organization's coding style manual.

There are many different coding standards that have been published. A readily available coding standard for the C++ language has been developed by the Flight Dynamics Division of NASA's Goddard Space Flight Center. This is the parent organization of the Software Engineering Laboratory. The document can be found on the Internet by starting at the location indicated in the URL and following the appropriate links (the site is being reorganized as this book is being written)

```
http://gsfc.nasa.gov
```

(There is another style guide at the Goddard site, prepared by the Software and Automation Systems Branch.)

Henricson and Nyquist [HENR96] developed a different coding standard for C++, which can be found on the Internet at the URL

```
http://sunsite.icm.edu.pl/oo/cpprules.txt
```

Coding standards for C can be fund in similar places.

Coding standards for Ada are more formal. The most readily available coding standards for Ada can be found in the Public Ada Catalog portion of the ASSET library at the URL

```
http://source.asset.com
```

If no coding standards exist, then follow the lead of a senior person in the organization. Above all, be consistent.

Our examples might lead you to believe that coding standards are merely a matter of formatting and indentation. There is more to style than just indentation, however. Most organizations' coding standards require a large amount of internal documentation; that is, documentation which is included within the actual source code. We list some of the basic elements of a coding standard below and on the next page.

Standards for Coding
1. White space
   - Blank lines
   - Spacing
   - Indentation
   - Continuation lines
   - Braces and parentheses
2. Comments

3. Standard naming conventions
   - Name formats
   - General guidelines for variable names

Standards for Program Organization
1. Program files
2. Encapsulation and information hiding
3. Readme file
4. Header files
5. Source files
6. Makefiles

Standards for File Organization
1. File prolog
2. Header file (class definition) (*.h)
   - Order of contents
   - Format of class declarations
   - Method (function) documentation in header file
3. Method function implementation and documentation in source file

The amount of internal documentation required is often surprising to the student beginning a career in software engineering. The reason for this emphasis is the need to keep the documentation within the source code. This ensures that documentation will be available, regardless of any external documents that may be lost or any changes in project personnel.

Let me give a personal example. I recently worked on a project that involved moving a combination of old FORTRAN code (most of which did not even adhere to the standards of FORTRAN 66, let alone FORTRAN 77, or the modern FORTRAN 90) and the assembly language used for Unisys mainframes. The goal of the project was to have equivalent software run on modern UNIX workstations. The project had to determine which source code modules could be moved as is, which could be moved with few changes, and which software modules had to be redesigned and rewritten for the new host computer environment.

The code was well documented in terms of having extensive internal documentation, with nearly two-thirds of each source code file consisting of comments. This was a life-saver, because all external design and requirements documents had been lost during the software's 25 years of operation. Recall that in Chapter 2, we discussed the potential for storage of design and requirements documents on a computer network. If these documents had been available electronically, the process would have been much easier.

Documentation and code formatting obviously are important parts of coding style. There are also coding issues that affect code quality in the sense of making the code inefficient. One such factor is how many unnecessary assignments are made.

The trivial example

```
x = 1;
y = x - z;
x = y + 1;
temp = x;
x = y + temp;
```

shows the effect of an unnecessary assignment statement to an equally unnecessary variable. Compare this code fragment to the equivalent

```
x = 1;
y = x - z;
x = y + x;
```

Of course, the selection of an optimizing option of a computer can remove the effect of such unnecessary assignments on the program's execution time. However, the use of optimization cannot change the increased difficulties that such unnecessary assignments will cause a software engineer trying to maintain this code.

The problems caused by poor programming style become worse if an unusual style causes a major problem in the performance because of typical virtual memory implementation. Consider the initialization of a matrix of size 1024 by 1024 in which the entries have the value 0. The double loop to perform the initialization can be written as either

```
#define MAX_SIZE 1024

for (i = 0; i < MAX_SIZE; i++)
   for (j = 0; j< MAX_SIZE; j++)
      a[i][j] = 0;
```

or

```
for (j= 0; j < MAX_SIZE; j++)
   for (i = 0; i < MAX_SIZE; i++)
      a[i][j] = 0;
```

Here, the coding examples are given in C, which stores two-dimensional arrays in what is called row-major form, with the array entries
a[0][0] , a[0][1], ... a[0][MAX_SIZE]

stored together, followed by the entries

```
a[1][0], a[1][1], ... a[1][MAX_SIZE]
```

and so on. (Technically, C does not allow two-dimensional arrays; it only allows one-dimensional arrays whose entries are also one dimensional.) The same storage pattern holds for programs written in Pascal, although the notation and the index of the starting array elements may be different from that of C. (FORTRAN uses a different arrangement for storage of two-dimensional arrays and so FORTRAN programs would have the loop variables reversed.)

The problem with the improper organization of the logic is that the underlying operating system must map the program's statement about the addresses of array elements in the program's logical memory space onto a set of pages that are mapped into physical memory when needed. The second nested loop has many more changes in the pages being accessed than does the first related loop. Therefore the second nested loop will probably run much slower than the first. (A good optimizing routine in a compiler may improve the run-time performance, but this cannot be counted on.)

Coding styles can affect performance in other ways, as a more complicated situation shows. Here the matrix entries are either +1 or -1, with the successive entries alternating as in

```
 1      -1     1      -1     .      .      .
-1       1    -1       1     .      .      .
 1      -1     1      -1     .      .      .
-1       1    -1       1     .      .      .
 .       .     .       .     .      .      .
 .       .     .       .     .      .      .
```

The entry in the ith row and j^{th} columns is simply -1 raised to the power of $i+j$.

There are several options for implementation. We discuss the major ones below.

> **Option 1.** We could use the built-in power pow() function to compute the powers of -1 as in
>
> ```
> a[i][j] = pow(-1, i+j);
> ```
>
> in C. Unfortunately, this would involve the overhead of a function call. We might be able to use a macro on C or an inline function in C++ to perform the action performed by the function pow(). This point is discussed in the exercises.

Option 2. We could use a Boolean selection and the modulus operator % in statements such as the C code

```
if (((i+j) % 2) == 0)
        a[i][j] = 1;
else
        a[i][j] = -1;
```

or the Ada equivalent

```
if ((i+j) mod j) = 0)
        a(i,j) := 1;
else
        a(i,j) := -1;
end if;
```

The idea in each code fragment is to determine if the index is an even integer or an odd integer.

Option 3. We could use the single C statement using the special, but hard to read, conditional operator in the C language

```
a[i][j] = ((i+j) %2) ? 1 : -1;
```

In many situations, none of these approaches is satisfactory because they introduce extra logical decisions, in addition to an addition of the two indices i and j and a division by 2. Each of these additional operations is repeated 1024 * 1024 times, which means that there are more than one million of these unnecessary operations.

It is easier to note that the entries in each row alternate in signs with the first entry in the two-dimensional array being a 1. Thus, a more efficient solution to our problem is illustrated by the nested loop

```
a[0][0] = 1;
for (i = 0; i < MAX_SIZE; i++)
  {
  if (i > 0)
      a[i][0] = a[i-1][0] * (-1);
      for (j = 1; j < MAX_SIZE; j++)
        a[i][j] = a[i][j-1] * (-1);
  }
```

Further improvements are possible, as you will see in the exercises.

Obviously there are many ways to solve this problem. Your coding style should encourage both program reliability and program efficiency. Recall that efficiency was one of the software engineering goals discussed in Chapter 1.

You should be aware that some commonly available utilities can help you improve the performance of your software. One of the most useful of these performance-improving utilities is known as a profiler. Most modern programming environments include profilers, which are typically invoked as an option when the source code is compiled.

The purpose of a profiler is to provide a software engineer with a detailed analysis of how the execution time of a running program is spent executing individual functions or program subunits. This analysis can be used to determine bottlenecks in program execution. Such bottlenecks are candidates for recoding to improve system performance.

Profilers are available on most UNIX C compilers, among others. To use a profiler on a C program running on a UNIX system, simply compile the program with the -p option:

```
cc -p file.c
```

and run the program. Each time the program completes successfully, a file named mon.out is created. This file contains the various functions called (both user-defined and low-level system functions), as well as the time that is spent executing each function.

The file mon.out is read automatically when a profiler is used. Either the prof or gprof utilities are readily available as part of the standard software distribution on UNIX systems. They are also available on the GNU compilers from the Free Software Foundation.

Details of other profiling techniques can be found in most compiler manuals.

5.3 Coding Standards

In the previous section, we discussed ways that you could organize your code to make it easier to read or more efficient. Now, we will turn to the reality of modern software development, with its need for coding standards.

It is very difficult for the beginning computer science student to understand the need for such standards. Generally, he or she is able to do the assignments given by the instructor. The student is usually able to read his or her source code, even if it was written months before.

The situation is much more difficult in typical software development environments. The fundamental problem is that it is extremely hard to understand more than 10,000 lines of source code-this seems to be the limit of human comprehension. Software development organizations are doing everything they can to reduce costs and simplify their systems. At the same time, software is becoming more complex, thus forcing development organizations to produce more elaborate systems with fewer resources. The motto of many organizations seems to be "More! Better! Cheaper! Faster!"

In the 1990s the myth of the lone wolf programmer who develops large systems on a diet of caffeinated colas and junk food has been exposed as just that, a myth. The myth was promulgated by the personal computer magazines of the early 1980s, and was associated with the undeniable initial success of microcomputer operating systems developed by Steven Jobs and Steven Wozniak for the Apple II and Bill Gates and Paul Allen for the IBM PC.

The nature of software for personal computers has changed greatly since its early days. Almost all software has a graphical user interface and a large number of features. This is well beyond the capacity of a single programmer at this time.

The book by Jim McCarthy of Microsoft describes the development environment for the successful C++ project [MCCA95]. It makes clear the need for team activities.

On a personal note, I had firsthand knowledge of this point in the 1980s at NASA while working with private contractors providing government service. An employee of a well-known computer software company was notorious for producing source code that was correct, but poorly documented and inconsistently formatted. The company fired this programmer after it became clear that the lack of adherence to the company's coding standards was costing the company much more in software maintenance costs than the individual's productivity could ever justify.

Incidentally, some engineering students from Howard University who were working as summer interns were able to speed up the performance of one of his implementations of an important algorithm. The improved efficiency made it feasible to consider using relatively low-cost personal computers for certain graphical displays instead of what, at the time, were extremely expensive graphics terminals.

It is likely that the professional programmer overlooked the potential for improving program performance simply because this code was so poorly presented and documented that even he didn't understand it. Don't let this happen to you. Follow your organization's coding standards.

A coding standard is usually developed by an organization to meet its needs and different organizations usually have different standards.

A coding standard will include the following:

- Conventions for naming variables

- Conventions for naming files
- Conventions for organizing source code files into directories
- Conventions for the size or complexity of source code
- Requirements for documentation of source code
- Elaborate style guides
- Restrictions in the use of certain functions

We will now discuss each of these issues in turn.

A convention for naming variables is a natural extension of what you probably already do when choosing variable's names. A coding standard for naming variables will require meaningful names. The coding standard may require that all non-local variable names be in several distinct parts which are separated by symbols such as underscores, periods, or the judicious use of upper-case letters.

Different portions of a name have different meanings. The intention is to allow a person reading the code to determine at a glance that the two names db_index and DbIndex refer to an index with a database. In a similar manner, the rather long variable names input_channel_index and Input_Channel_Index refer to an index of input channels. The naming convention for variables will include the appropriate style, generally allowing the use of (one group of) underscores or upper-case letters.

Another issue may be addressed by the variable naming portion of a coding standard: the need to be compatible with compilers with severe limits to the length of variable names. In any event, the coding standard should address this.

File-naming standards have all the features of variable naming standards and also should reflect the contents of the file. Many standards require a single function, procedure, or object per file, others simply place a limit on the total size of a file that contains multiple functions, procedures, or objects. The need for compatibility with older operating systems, such as MS-DOS systems with a limit of eight characters per name followed by an optional extension of up to three characters, must be addressed in coding standards.

Ideally, the names of source code files should indicate the files' contents so well that it is easy to determine the appropriateness for future potential reuse of the source code file.

The issues with file naming standards also apply to organization of files into directories. Each directory represents a subsystem. Here, the most important issue is developing high-level directories whose names are related to the functionality of the subsystem whose code is included in the directory and its subdirectories.

Of course, this is precisely the way that operating systems are organized. The 3784 distinct files on my PC are organized into directories with meaningful names that represent the relevant subsystems. Most applications follow the same organizational approach

There are several other issues related to file organization. It is easiest to have separate directories for development of the source code and for the final source code. It may even be easier to separate the object code and source code into separate directories. This means that for most realistic software systems, makefiles (or other instructions about which source code, object code, libraries, or data files are used for installation) will use relative file names.

The use of relative, as opposed to absolute, file names, allows a directory and its contents to be used whenever it is most appropriate, as opposed to being restricted to a specific location. Appropriate use of relative file names also allows the final executable code to be placed wherever the installer wishes, instead of being limited to the current directory. We will discuss installation details in Chapter 7 when we describe the installation and delivery process.

5.4 Coding, Design, Requirements, and Change

Many software projects are so large that the entire source code is compiled relatively infrequently. For example, in many of its software systems, Microsoft creates a "build," or clean compilation and linkage of all source code only once a day. This is done because too much time would be spent compiling source code, and not enough time spent thinking about it. This approach is common in large software systems, especially those that develop software in several geographically separate locations.

This approach requires a new way of thinking that is very different from the typical edit-compile-execute-debug cycle that is so common among computer science students. In most organizations, the software development process must be much more systematic than this hit-or-miss approach.

It is often surprising to beginning software engineers how little time is actually spent writing code and how much time is spent on other software life cycle activities. Typically, only 15% of the time allotted for a project's completion is devoted to coding. Of course, there are many reasons for this distribution of effort.

One problem that occurs frequently during the implementation process involves the requirements traceability matrix. The problem is that often the requirements were not sufficiently detailed to make certain that the software's implementation matched the precise requirements. In short, each requirement must be traceable to an implementation action. If not, the requirements have not been met.

What about changes in design? The major deficiency of the waterfall software life cycle approach is the assumption that the requirements are so well understood that they can be set well in advance of the actual implementation or deployment of the software. The strictest interpretation of the waterfall life cycle model allows just the requirements to be changed only when major issues arise during the design process. Similarly, the strictest interpretation of the waterfall life cycle model allows the design to be modified only when major changes have to be made during the coding process. Of course, the more flexible iterative software development approaches of the spiral and prototyping models involve changing design consistently.

Changes in software design can occur during coding for several reasons:

- Changes in technology have made portions of the design obsolete or irrelevant.

- Software libraries have been changed or reorganized.

- The reusable software components do not work as promised. (This is especially true of special commercial software packages with heavy marketing.)

- The reusable software components are not of high quality. (This is especially true of public domain software or software written by companies under great pressure to maintain market share. Many such companies follow the " good enough" approach when releasing new versions of their software.)

- The compiler did not generate sufficiently fast executable code to meet the real-time requirements of the system on its target operating system environment.

Many other problems can occur during software implementation. As a member of a software team, be prepared for change; your manager should be.

Each change will create pressure on a project's schedule and you may be tempted to skip some documentation and ignore coding standards when under pressure. Don't do it. Your work won't really go any faster; you will only create more work for testing and quality assurance and your work won't be good enough to be included in a reuse library.

5.5 Some Coding Metrics

Since software engineering is, after all, an engineering discipline, measurement is an important activity. In this section, we will describe several issues associated with measurement of source code.

Since our major software project develops a tool to measure the size of software source code, we will not consider size metrics in this section. Instead, we will consider two commonly used types of metrics: control flow metrics, which attempt to describe the possible execution paths of a program, and coupling metrics, which treat the interfaces between program subunits. We will describe control-flow metrics first.

The McCabe cyclomatic complexity metric [McCA76] measures the complexity of the flow of control within source code. The metrics process creates a representation of the control flow graph of a program based on Euler's formula for the number of components in a graph. All statements in a program are considered vertices of a graph. Edges are drawn between vertices if there is direct connection between two statements by a loop, conditional branch, call to a subprogram, or if the statements are in sequential order. McCabe's metric is $E - V + 2P$, where E is the number of edges, V is the number of vertices, and P is the number of separate parts (the number of subprograms called), including the main program.

The cyclomatic complexity metric essentially reduces to the total number of logical predicates plus 1. As such, it is invariant under changes of names of variables and under changes of the ordering of arguments in expressions. This metric is also invariant under any changes in the format of the control structure. Thus, changing a while-loop from the form

```
while (!found)
      {...
      }
```

to one of the form

```
while (found != 0)
      {...
      }
```

leaves the McCabe cyclomatic complexity unchanged.

Each of these program fragments has a graph similar to the one shown in Figure 5.1.

Each of these graphs has three relevant vertices (nodes), corresponding to the three identified lines in the program. There are also three edges in each graph. Therefore, both of these two loops have a McCabe cyclomatic complexity of $3 - 3 + 2$, or 2. Adding non-branching statements between the braces adds one to both the count of vertices and the count of edges, leaving the value of this metric unchanged. Note that changing a while-loop to an equivalent do-while-loop also leaves this metric invariant.

while (!found)

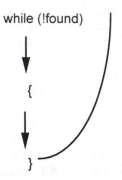
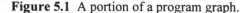

Figure 5.1 A portion of a program graph.

The cyclomatic complexity metric considers only control flow, ignoring the complexity of the number and occurrence of operators and operands, or the general program structure and, thus, cannot be a complete measure of program complexity. However, the cyclomatic complexity can be applied to an entire program, to a single file, or to a single module. It can also be applied to detailed designs and to PDL (program design language) before a module is coded.   It is one of the few metrics that can be applied at several places in the life cycle.

We now consider coupling metrics. In the simplest case considered here, coupling metrics are based on a count of the number of arguments and global variables that can be accessed by a function. A more refined analysis distinguishes between arguments and global variables that can be modified within a module, control the flow of a module, or are merely used as data sources.

The BVA metric [LEAC97] is based on an assessment of the number of cases required for testing of a module based on its interface and results from testing theory that indicate that logical errors in software are most likely to occur at certain boundary values in the domain of the software. It is a measurement of modularity and testability. The BVA values associated with a function's arguments are defined as follows:

- Arguments of type Boolean are given a weight of 2 (true, false)
- Arguments of type int are given a weight of 5 (MININT, -1, 0, 1, MAXINT)

- Arguments of type `float` are given a weight of 5 (MINFLOAT, -1.0, 0.0, 1.0, MAXFLOAT)
- Arguments of type `struct` are given a weight that is the product of the weights of the components
- Arguments of type pointer are given a weight of one plus the type of the object pointed to
- Arguments of type array are given a weight of two plus the type of the element in the array. (The difference in treatment of arrays and pointers is a reflection of common usage, not syntax, since arrays and pointers are the same idea in C.)
- Global variables that are visible to a function are treated the same way as function arguments.
- For a function with multiple arguments, the BVA value is the product of the BVA values associated with the individual arguments.
- For a file, the BVA value is the sum of the BVA values of the individual functions.

We chose to omit qualifiers such as `long`, `short`, or `unsigned` since the first two do not change the BVA value. The qualifier `unsigned` restricts the integer to be non-negative. This is a small decrease in the BVA value; we chose to ignore it because the qualifier is rarely used, and is often used incorrectly. We would use a weight of three (0, 1, MAXINT) for function arguments with the type classification NATURAL in the Ada programming language, since the proper use of this type is more likely to be enforced by an Ada compiler.

The storage class qualifiers `static`, `register`, and `extern` were also ignored in our BVA computations since they specify where and how the data type is stored, not what the set of possible values is.

As an example of the calculation of this metric, consider the C code implementation of a stack given below.

```
struct stack
    {
    int    ITEM[MAXSTACK];
    int top;
    };
```

There are two fields in this structured data type: an array of fixed size whose name is ITEM and whose entries are integers, and an integer variable named `top`. Any function that uses a parameter of this stack data type has to consider the two fields. The second field, `top`, has an infinite range (if we ignore the construction of a stack) and has several likely candidates to select for black-box testing. The five cases that we use are: -1, 0, 1, MAXSTACK , MAXSTACK + 1, assuming that top takes only values either inside or near the range of index values.

The array indices are tested at the upper and lower bounds plus or minus 1; the test cases are 0, 1, 2, MAXSTACK -1, MAXSTACK, MAXSTACK + 1. Thus the total number of test cases to be added to the value of the BVA metric is 5 * 6, or 30.

The count of the number of cases for the BVA metric will be different in programming languages that support strong typing and run-time checking. For example, a definition of a stack in Ada might look like

```
record STACK is
   ITEM: array(1 .. MAXSTACK) of integer;
   TOP: integer range 0 .. MAXSTACK;
end STACK;
```

There are still two fields in this structured data type that must be considered by any function that uses a parameter of this stack data type. The second field, TOP, has a finite range and has several obvious values to select for black-box testing. The four cases that we use are: 0, 1, MAXSTACK - 1, and MAXSTACK. This implementation of a stack in Ada has a BVA metric value of 4 * 4, or 16.

Note that neither count makes use of the typical way in which a stack is used (access to the stack is usually limited to the top element of the stack, which should be done only by using functions to push and pop the stack). Therefore, the BVA metric may overstate the effect of the complexity of the data, particularly in an object-oriented environment in which access to internal data of an object is restricted to specially written member functions of that object. Thus, the BVA metric is only a first approximation to a data structure-based metric. We view the lack of a consistent industry standard for a data structure-based metric that is validated as a measure of software structure is a severe deficiency of research in this area.

5.6 Coding Reviews and Inspections

There is a growing body of software engineering research literature that suggests that careful inspection of source code has a greater chance of detecting faults (at least in small programs) than does software testing. While this hypothesis has not been proved conclusively and has not been examined in detail for larger programs, it is worthwhile to describe the review and inspection process in more detail at this point.

Fagan [FAGA76] was the first to write extensively about inspections in the open literature and, thus, inspections are often called "Fagan inspections." Results of [BARN94] and [BASI85] have shown that the following types of approaches can be very helpful, whether the inspection is performed by a team or by an individual.

As with the requirements and design of software systems, source code can also be reviewed. In tables 3.10 and 4.3 we gave checklists for requirements and design reviews, respectively. You should review those checklists now.

As with requirements and design reviews, we may also perform an inspection of source code. The inspection may take the following forms:

- The source code may be examined for adherence to coding standards.
- The directory structure may be examined for adherence to naming conventions.
- The inputs or outputs from each function may be checked by hand for correctness.
- The invariants of each loop may be checked to make sure that the loop exit conditions are met.
- Objects may be checked for completeness of coverage of all conditions if some of the object's methods are overloaded.

Note that there are several different ways in which the code may be examined for correctness. You should read the current literature to determine the most recent thinking on this complex subject.

5.7 Configuration Management

One of the most troublesome problems in coding occurs when there is more than one programmer working on the same part of the system. Even if the programmers adhere rigidly to the standards set in the interface control document, the changes made by one programmer may affect the code written by another. Often, even a single programmer wishes to go back to code written the day before. This is not always easy, due to the likelihood that many changes were made during the elapsed time period.

The situation is much worse if there are many developers working in different locations. Since this is becoming common in larger, distributed software development projects, there is a critical need for a smooth mechanism to allow changes to be made systematically, and to allow the changes to be undone if necessary.

The general problem of controlling changes systematically during software is called "configuration management," or "CM." It is pervasive in the software industry. Simply put, if you haven't used configuration management, you haven't worked on large software projects. You may hear the term "version control" used instead of configuration management; the terms are synonymous.

There are many commercial systems and free utilities that perform CM. They all keep a master set of each document under the control of the CM system. Changes are entered with a version number and a date and it is easy to go back to any previous version.

In most CM systems, once a file is "checked out" (being worked on by a developer) the file is logged into the CM system as being read-only for others. This blocking of edits by developers other than the one who has the file "checked out" helps ensure system consistency. (A few powerful CM systems relax this rule because the organizations need to have simultaneous access from locations that are widely separated, but this approach is hardly the norm.)

We illustrate the behavior of a CM system by using the powerful sccs utility developed for UNIX systems by Marc Rochkind. The acronym stands for Source Code Control System. It is available free of charge on most UNIX systems. Instead of forcing you to keep copies of your entire document every time you want to make a backup, the sccs utility only keeps copies of the changes that you have made, along with a copy of the most recent version of the document.

At the most elementary level, the sccs utility is used as follows: a programmer wishing to use this tool creates a directory named SCCS. The files that are to be under CM are placed in this directory. We illustrate this with the directory whose contents are shown in example 5.2.

```
s.makefile              s.file1.c
s.file2.c               s.file1.h
```

Example 5.2. Contents of a directory named SCCS that is used for a project under configuration management by the sccs utility.

You may be wondering how the files are placed into this directory and how they get such strange names. They are put there by the command

```
sccs create file1.c
```

that looks for the proper directory and places a copy of the file file1.c in this directory.

Suppose that a programmer wishes to edit the file file1.c which is under the control of sccs . (The file is named s.file1.c in the SCCS directory.) From the parent directory, the programmer types the command

```
sccs edit file1.c
```

The `sccs` utility responds by opening the file for editing. The file will be visible to you as a collection of bytes and some indication of the version number, as is shown in example 5.3. (The version number will change as the file goes through successive edits.)

```
/*  Version 1.1 */
main()
{int i;
for (i = 1;  i <= 10;  i++)
    {printf("%d\n",  I);
}
```

Example 5.3 A file under `sccs` control.

The `sccs` paradigm is that you will leave your files as "read-only" except when you are explicitly editing them. When one user wishes to edit a file, it is checked out of the SCCS directory by the `sccs` utility and no one else can edit it.

When the file is made ready for use in a system (as would be the case if the make command were typed at the appropriate directory level), the file might appear to a user as in example 5.4.

```
main()
{int i;
for (i = 1;  i <= 10;  i++)
    {printf("%d\n",  I);
}
```

Example 5.4 .

When you are done editing a file, you can enter the command

```
sccs delta myfile.c
```

You will be asked for a comment about what changes you have made. Documenting the reason for the changes can make program maintenance much easier.

5.8 A Management Perspective on Coding

As we have discussed several times previously, once an organization is committed to a project, the project's manager wants to minimize risk and to make the consequences of any necessary risk predictable. Unfortunately, the coding phase is where any problems that have been glossed over during the requirements or design phases cannot be avoided.

In many projects, the manager is in this position because of the nature of the programming process. The difficulty is of course that the manager has to trust the promises of his or her programming team that the software will be created on time and will work. The manager often has no way to know whether these promises will be ever be kept.

Let us expand on this statement. If the software development follows the classical waterfall approach, then the manager will not have seen any software until very close to the date scheduled for its completion. He or she cannot anticipate disaster.

The iterative software development methods may offer more comfort to a manager. Obvious disasters can be seen more quickly. Many new software development environments for object-oriented designs can show object models, with prototypes of programs readily available to the potential users very early in the software's development. Unfortunately, the hard problems rarely surface so quickly, unless the software's design is poor or incomplete.

Software implementation is always the most tense portion of the life cycle for managers. In many cases, managers depend on a carefully defined process, such as the higher levels of the Software Engineering Institute's Capability Maturity Model (CMM). This can help, because monitoring activities are built into the process model. Clearly, the manager's goal is to prevent disaster if the project is to be delivered very late or cannot be delivered at all.

Metrics are extremely important in providing a snapshot of the state of the software and the progress toward the goal of releasing a high-quality product within budget and on schedule.

The requirements traceability matrix is used to make sure that each feature that was specified in the system requirements and promised in the design has been implemented in the actual source code and tested before the final product is released.

5.9 Coding of the Major Software Project

In this section, we will begin the process of implementing the design of the major project that we have been considering in the last few chapters. The most important things for us to keep in mind are that that we must adhere to the design as much as is reasonable, and that any changes must be carefully documented. After all, the goal is to provide our customer with the system that he or she wants. You should begin by reviewing the design documents and the project's requirements as necessary.

We will not present the complete source code, since it is available to you electronically. Instead, we will focus our attention on a few essential implementation details.

For example, the user interface of the system is coded in C. In Example 5.5, we show a portion of this code, in order to illustrate the coding standard we are using for the C code:

```java
import java.awt.*;
import java.net.URL;

import symantec.itools.multimedia.ImageViewer;
import symantec.itools.awt.util.dialog.ModalDialog;
import com.sun.java.swing.JLabel;

public class AttentionDialog extends ModalDialog
{
     public AttentionDialog(Frame parent, String
title, String message, URL iconURL)
     {
          super(parent, title);

          if (iconURL != null)
          {
               ImageViewer img = new
ImageViewer(iconURL);
               add(img);
          }


          // This code is automatically generated
by Visual Cafe when you add
          // components to the visual
environment. It instantiates and initializes
          // the components. To modify the code,
only use code syntax that matches
          // what Visual Cafe can generate, or
Visual Cafe may be unable to back
          // parse your Java file into its visual
environment.
          //{{INIT_CONTROLS
          setLayout(new
FlowLayout(FlowLayout.LEFT,5,5));
```

Example 5.5. A portion of the Java code (the front-end interface to the operating system) in our project showing the coding standards (continued).

```
            setSize(305,114);
            setVisible(false);
            add(label1);
            label1.setBounds(5,5,14,23);
            okButton1.setLabel("OK");
            add(okButton1);
            okButton1.setBackground(java.awt.Color.
lightGray);
            okButton1.setFont(new Font("Dialog",
Font.BOLD, 12));
            okButton1.setBounds(24,5,31,23);

            if(InputFrame.showMessage == 1)

ErrorLabel.setText(InputFrame.msg1);
            else if (InputFrame.showMessage == 2)

ErrorLabel.setText(InputFrame.msg2);
            else if (InputFrame.showMessage == 3)

ErrorLabel.setText(InputFrame.msg3);
            else if (InputFrame.showMessage == 4)

ErrorLabel.setText(InputFrame.msg4);
        add(ErrorLabel);
        ErrorLabel.setForeground(java.awt.Color.red);
        ErrorLabel.setBounds(5,33,413,15);
        //}}

        label1.setText(message);

        //{{REGISTER_LISTENERS
        SymAction lSymAction = new SymAction();
        okButton1.addActionListener(lSymAction);
        //}}
        }

        public AttentionDialog(Frame parent)
        {
        this(parent, "Attention", "Event", null);
        }
```

Example 5.5. A portion of the Java code (the front-end interface to the operating system) in our project showing the coding standards (continued).

```
      // Add a constructor for Interactions
(ignoring modal)
      public AttentionDialog(Frame parent, boolean
modal)
      {
      this(parent);
      }

      // Add a constructor for Interactions
(ignoring modal)
      public AttentionDialog(Frame parent, String
message, boolean modal)
      {
      this(parent, "Attention", message, null);
      }

      public void addNotify()
      {
      // Record the size of the window prior to
calling parents addNotify.
      Dimension d = getSize();

      super.addNotify();

      if (fComponentsAdjusted)
            return;

      // Adjust components according to the insets
      Insets insets = getInsets();
      setSize(insets.left + insets.right + d.width,
insets.top + insets.bottom + d.height);
      Component components[] = getComponents();
      for (int i = 0; i < components.length; i++)
            {
            Point p = components[i].getLocation();
            p.translate(insets.left, insets.top);
                  components[i].setLocation(p);
            }
            fComponentsAdjusted = true;
      }
```

Example 5.5. A portion of the Java code (the front-end interface to the operating system) in our project showing the coding standards (continued).

```
    // Used for addNotify check.
      boolean fComponentsAdjusted = false;
      //{{DECLARE_CONTROLS
      java.awt.Label label1 = new java.awt.Label();
      java.awt.Button okButton1 = new
java.awt.Button();
      com.sun.java.swing.JLabel ErrorLabel = new
com.sun.java.swing.JLabel();
      //}}


    class SymAction implements
java.awt.event.ActionListener
      {
      public void
actionPerformed(java.awt.event.ActionEvent event)
      {
      Object object = event.getSource();
      if (object == okButton1)
                okButton1_ActionPerformed(event);
      }
      }


    void
okButton1_ActionPerformed(java.awt.event.ActionEven
t event)
      {
      // to do: code goes here.
      okButton1_ActionPerformed_Interaction1(event);
      }


    void
okButton1_ActionPerformed_Interaction1(java.awt.eve
nt.ActionEvent event)
      {
      try {
            this.dispose();
            } catch (Exception e) {
            }
      }
}
```

Example 5.5 (continued). A portion of the Java code (the front-end interface to the operating system) in our project showing the coding standards.

As another example, the back end of the system, which must interface to standard spreadsheets, is coded in Java. In Example 5.6, we show a portion of this code, in order to illustrate the coding standard we would use for the Java code:

```java
import java.rmi.*;
import java.rmi.server.*;
import COM.stevesoft.pat.*;
import java.util.*;
import java.io.*;
import java.lang.*;

public class SoftwareEval
{

    public sMetrics [] m1;

    public sMetrics[] compute(sFile[] s) //throws
RemoteException
        {
        total_files = s.length;

        for(int i=0; i<total_files; i++) // do the
following for each file
            {
            try{
                BufferedReader r = new
BufferedReader(new FileReader(s[i].filename));

                FileInputStream fin = new
FileInputStream(s[i].filename);
                fin.read(s[i].fc);

                while((line = r.readLine()) !=null){
//read each line of current file

if(nonwhitespace.search(line) &&
!lineCom.search(line) &&
                            !comOpen.search(line) &&
!commentFlag)
                        s[i].total_loc++;
```

Example 5.6. A portion of the Java in our project showing the coding standards (continued).

```
    // check for imported packages/libraries

if((line.startsWith("#include <") ||
(line.startsWith("import ")))))

s[i].total_lib_pkg++;

    // check for comment line
                        if(lineCom.search(line))
    {
if(!nonwhitespace.search(lineCom.left()))
   {
   tcl++; //true comment
   s[i].total_comments++;
   }
else{

   s[i].total_comments++;
   if(isFxn)

s[i].xlpf[s[i].total_fxns-1]++;
      else if (isClass && !isFxn)

s[i].xlpc[s[i].total_classes-1]++;

s[i].xtra++;
      }
}
  //advanced comment check
if( comOpen.search(line) && comClose.search(line))
      {
      cl++; // comment line

    if(nonwhitespace.search((comOpen.left())) ||
          nonwhitespace.search(comClose.right()))
      {
      ncl++; //non-comment line
      }
    else
        tcl++;
    }
```

Example 5.6. A portion of the Java in our project showing the coding standards (continued).

```
                //check for opening comment blocks

if(comOpen.search(line))
        {
        commentFlag = true;
        s[i].total_comments++;
if(nonwhitespace.search(comOpen.left()))
        {
        if(isFxn)
s[i].xlpf[s[i].total_fxns-1]++;

else if (isClass && !isFxn)

s[i].xlpc[s[i].total_classes-1]++;

s[i].xtra++;
        }
        }
        //check for closing comment blocks

if(comClose.search(line))
        {
        commentFlag = false;
if(nonwhitespace.search(comClose.right()))
        {
        if(isFxn)
s[i].xlpf[s[i].total_fxns-1]++;
        else if (isClass && !isFxn)

s[i].xlpc[s[i].total_classes-1]++;
s[i].xtra++;
}
}

// start class actions----------------------
// check for class definition
lineCom.search(line);

if(classDec.search(line) && !commentFlag &&
        !classDec.search(lineCom.right())) {
```

Example 5.6. A portion of the Java in our project showing the coding standards (continued).

```
s[i].total_classes++;
    isClass  = true;

if((s[i].filetype).equals("C"))

s[i].filetype = "C++";
}
if(isClass && nonwhitespace.search(line) &&
!lineCom.search(line) &&

!comOpen.search(line) && !commentFlag)

s[i].lpc[s[i].total_classes-1]++; //loc for current
class

if((openBrace.search(line)))
    cStack.push("{");
if((closeBrace.search(line)))
    cStack.pop();
if(cStack.empty()) //check for end of class
    isClass = false;

// end class actions--------------------------
// start function actions--------------------
lineCom.search(line);

if(fxnDec.search(line) && !semi.search(line) &&
!commentFlag  { // check for function definition

s[i].total_fxns++;
isFxn = true;
}
//lines of code per function
if(isFxn && nonwhitespace.search(line) &&
!lineCom.search(line) &&
!comOpen.search(line) && !commentFlag)

s[i].lpf[s[i].total_fxns-1]++;
//handle opening & closing braces
if((openBrace.search(line)) &&  isFxn)
    fbraces++;
```

Example 5.6. A portion of the Java in our project showing the coding standards (continued).

```
if((closeBrace.search(line)) && isFxn)
      fbraces--;
if( isFxn && (fbraces == 0) &&
      closeBrace.search(line)))
isFxn = false;
// end function actions-----------------------
}//end of while loop to read file

}//end of try

catch (IOException e){}
} // end of for loop


for(int r=0; r<total_files; r++)
 {
 m1[r].filename = s[r].filename;
 m1[r].filetype = s[r].filetype;
 m1[r].lpc = s[r].lpc;
 m1[r].lpf = s[r].lpf;
 m1[r].total_classes = s[r].total_classes;
 m1[r].total_loc = s[r].total_loc;
 m1[r].total_lib_pkg = s[r].total_lib_pkg;
 m1[r].total_fxns = s[r].total_fxns;
 m1[r].total_comments = s[r].total_comments;
 m1[r].xtra = s[r].xtra;
 m1[r].xlpc = s[r].xlpc;
 m1[r].xlpf = s[r].xlpf;
 }


return m1;

} //end of compute fxn


//init constructor
public SoftwareEval(){
```

Example 5.6. A portion of the Java in our project showing the coding standards (continued).

```
m1 = new sMetrics[15];
for (int j=0; j<15; j++)
m1[j] = new sMetrics();
}

    //declare regular expressions
    Regex visibility = new Regex ("(public |private
|protected )"); // accessor types list
    Regex identifier = new Regex ("[^A-Za-z0-
9_]"); // shorthand for a proper variable name
    Regex cls = new Regex("class "); // the class
keyword

    Regex retType = new Regex("([^A-Za-z0-
9_]|abstract |boolean |byte |char |const |double
|float |final |int |long |short |static |transient
|void )");
    Regex comOpen = new Regex("/\\*");
//traditional or documentation comment open
    Regex comClose = new Regex("\\*/"); //
tradiitonal or documentation comment close
    Regex lineCom = new Regex("//"); // line
comment
    Regex paramList = new Regex("(?@())"); //
parameter list
    Regex fxnDec = new Regex("(?Q)(public
|private |protected
)*(?Q)(abstract|boolean|byte|char|const|double|floa
t|final|int|long|short|static|transient|void)+(?Q)[
^A-Za-z0-9_(?@())]");
    Regex classDec = new Regex("(?Q)(public
|private |protected )*(?Q)class[^A-Za-z0-9_]");
    Regex openBrace = new Regex("{");
    Regex closeBrace = new Regex("}");
    Regex semi = new Regex(";");
    Regex nonwhitespace=new Regex("[^
\b\r\t\n]"); //line is NOT empty
    //end of regular expression declarations

    int fbraces = 0;
    int total_files = 0;
```

Example 5.6. A portion of the Java in our project showing the coding standards (continued).

```
      Stack cStack = new Stack();
      // holds open and close braces for classes,
when empty the end of a class is found
      String line; // a line of code
      int cl = 0; // comment line
      int ncl = 0; //non comment line
      int tcl = 0; // true comment line
      //flags
      boolean commentFlag = false;
      boolean isClass = false;
      boolean isFxn = false;
}
```

Example 5.6 (continued). A portion of the Java in our project showing the coding standards.

One other example is of sufficient importance for us to devote space to it in this book: the interface between two high-level software components. We illustrate the interface between two such subsystems in Example 5.7. (This interface uses the Java language):

```
/* A basic implementation of the JDialog class. */
import java.awt.*;
import com.sun.java.swing.*;
public class JAboutDialog extends
com.sun.java.swing.JDialog
{
      public JAboutDialog(Frame parentFrame)
      {
      super(parentFrame);
      // This code is automatically generated by
Visual Cafe when you add
      // components to the visual environment. It
instantiates and initializes
      // the components. To modify the code, only
use code syntax that matches
      // what Visual Cafe can generate, or Visual
Cafe may be unable to back
      // parse your Java file into its visual
environment.
```

Example 5.7. A portion of the Java code (interface between the computational subsystem and the operating subsystem) in our project showing the coding standards (continued).

```
      //{{INIT_CONTROLS
      setTitle("JFC Application - About");
      setModal(true);
      getContentPane().setLayout(new
GridBagLayout());
      setSize(248,94);
      setVisible(false);
      okButton.setText("OK");
      okButton.setActionCommand("OK");
      okButton.setOpaque(false);
      okButton.setMnemonic((int)'O');
      getContentPane().add(okButton, new
com.symantec.itools.awt.GridBagConstraintsD(2,1,1,1
,0.0,0.0,java.awt.GridBagConstraints.CENTER,java.aw
t.GridBagConstraints.NONE,new
Insets(0,0,10,0),0,0));

okButton.setBounds(98,59,51,25);
      aboutLabel.setHorizontalAlignment(com.sun.jav
a.swing.SwingConstants.CENTER);
      aboutLabel.setText("A JFC Application");
      getContentPane().add(aboutLabel, new
com.symantec.itools.awt.GridBagConstraintsD(0,0,3,1
,1.0,1.0,java.awt.GridBagConstraints.CENTER,java.aw
t.GridBagConstraints.BOTH,new
Insets(0,0,0,0),0,0));
      aboutLabel.setBounds(0,0,248,59);
      //}}

      //{{REGISTER_LISTENERS
      SymWindow aSymWindow = new SymWindow();
      this.addWindowListener(aSymWindow);
      SymAction lSymAction = new SymAction();
      okButton.addActionListener(lSymAction);
      //}}
      }
```

Example 5.7. A portion of the Java code (interface between the computational subsystem and the operating subsystem) in our project showing the coding standards (continued).

```
public void setVisible(boolean b)
{
if (b)
{
Rectangle bounds = (getParent()).getBounds();
Dimension size = getSize();
setLocation(bounds.x + (bounds.width -
size.width)/2,
bounds.y + (bounds.height - size.height)/2);
}
super.setVisible(b);
}

public void addNotify()
{
// Record the size of the window prior to
calling parent's addNotify.
Dimension d = getSize();
super.addNotify();

if (fComponentsAdjusted)
        return;

// Adjust components according to the insets
Insets insets = getInsets();
setSize(insets.left + insets.right + d.width,
insets.top + insets.bottom + d.height);
Component components[] =
getContentPane().getComponents();
for (int i = 0; i < components.length; i++)
{
Point p = components[i].getLocation();
p.translate(insets.left, insets.top);
components[i].setLocation(p);
}
fComponentsAdjusted = true;
}

// Used for addNotify check.
boolean fComponentsAdjusted = false;
```

Example 5.7. A portion of the Java code (interface between the computational subsystem and the operating subsystem) in our project showing the coding standards (continued).

```
//{{DECLARE_CONTROLS
com.sun.java.swing.JButton okButton = new
com.sun.java.swing.JButton();
com.sun.java.swing.JLabel aboutLabel = new
com.sun.java.swing.JLabel();
//}}


class SymWindow extends
java.awt.event.WindowAdapter
{
public void
windowClosing(java.awt.event.WindowEvent event)
{
Object object = event.getSource();
if (object == JAboutDialog.this)
    jAboutDialog_windowClosing(event);
}
}

void
jAboutDialog_windowClosing(java.awt.event.WindowEve
nt event)
{
// to do: code goes here.

jAboutDialog_windowClosing_Interaction1(event);
}

void
jAboutDialog_windowClosing_Interaction1(java.awt.ev
ent.WindowEvent event) {
try {
    // JAboutDialog Hide the JAboutDialog
    this.setVisible(false);
} catch (Exception e) {
}
}
```

Example 5.7. A portion of the Java code (interface between the computational subsystem and the operating subsystem) in our project showing the coding standards (continued).

```
      class SymAction implements
java.awt.event.ActionListener
      {
      public void
actionPerformed(java.awt.event.ActionEvent event)
      {
      Object object = event.getSource();
            if (object == okButton)
                  okButton_actionPerformed(event);
            }
      }

      void
okButton_actionPerformed(java.awt.event.ActionEvent
event)
      {
      // to do: code goes here.

      okButton_actionPerformed_Interaction1(event);
      }

      void
okButton_actionPerformed_Interaction1(java.awt.even
t.ActionEvent event) {
      try {
            // JAboutDialog Hide the JAboutDialog
            this.setVisible(false);
      } catch (Exception e) {
      }
      }
}
```

Example 5.7 (continued). A portion of the Java code (interface between the computational subsystem and the operating subsystem) in our project showing the coding standards.

These three code samples are indicative of the coding standards used in our project.

The code given in examples 5.5, 5.6, and 5.7 also illustrates the naming conventions used in our software system. It should be pointed out, however, that the software tools used as part of our system probably used different coding and naming standards. Assuming that they work properly, it doesn't make sense to recode these existing software utilities just to meet our coding or naming standards. We are trying to make the software development process more efficient by emphasizing software reuse. Hence, we should treat these software tools as black boxes. The only things to worry about are the degree to which these software tools meet the project requirements and the quality of the tools themselves, including their correctness and robustness.

You should note that the approach of the previous paragraph is not satisfactory if safety-critical software is being developed. For such software applications, every component used in the system must have been certified as to both its correctness and its adherence to appropriate standards.

Let us assume that the software development has been completed, with testing and integration to follow. Of course, we must relate our design to the requirements traceability matrix for the project. The changed matrix is given in Table 5.2. Note that the requirements for a small system (1 MB disk space, 1.44 MB floppy) have been deleted because of the change to a graphical, web-based user interface.

You might also note that we have changed a requirement for a C or C++ based user interface. It is clear from some of the code samples that we can implement the project in either Java or one of the "visual" family of languages such as Visual C, Visual C++, or Visual BASIC. It is probably the case that our requirements were too confining and that we should have left the functionality of the requirements to the requirements documents and kept decisions about implementation details to the design process.

On the other hand, we may have violated the requirements of our customer and made all our efforts useful. In a real-world situation, the customer would be consulted before such a change is made. Just keep in mind the possible tradeoffs.

What do we need to focus our attention on at this point? We must know that the individual software components have been linked together, that the filters or "glueware" have been created and that the software works well enough (or at least the individual modules do) for us to show it to another person: a software tester. The testing and integration process is the next step in the development of this software system.

From a project management perspective, we should also do a status check. Are we ahead of schedule (unlikely), behind schedule (likely), or approximately on target? Have there been any unpleasant surprises, any portions of the system that were more difficult than we expected? Does any portion of the system require extra attention, perhaps additional resources? Have technology or market pressures rendered any portion of the system obsolete? (Recall that we did this status check earlier.)

Table 5.2
Requirements traceability matrix for the major continuing software engineering project.

#	Requirement	Design	Code	Test
1.	Intel-based	Y	Y	
2.	Windows 95	Y	Y	
3.	Windows 95 UI	Y	Y	
4.	Consistent With Excel 4.0	Y	Y	
5.	System One Size Only	Y	Y	
6.	One MB System	*	*	*
7.	One MB Disk Space	*	*	*
8.	One 1.44 MB Floppy Disk	*	*	*
9.	Includes Installation	Y	Y	
10.	No Decompression Utility	Y	Y	
11.	One input file at a time	Y	Y	
12.	Size of each function	Y	Y	
13.	Size of each file	Y	Y	
14.	Size of system	Y	Y	
15.	Compute totals	Y	Y	
16.	Develop std for C,C++,Ada	Y	Y	
17.	Batch-oriented system	Y	Y	
18.	Precisely define LOC	Y	Y	
19.	Measure separately	Y	Y	
20.	No error checking of input	Y	Y	
21.	Front end in C or C++	Y	N	
22.	Batch processing	Y	Y	
23.	File names limited to 8.3	Y	Y	
24.	Wild cards can be used	Y	Y	
25.	Dead code ignored			
26.	No special compilers needed	Y	Y	
27.	Microsoft Excel 4.0 needed	Y	Y	

Summary

This chapter has considered some of the issues that can affect the maintainability, readability, and performance of source code. These issues include coding style, coding standards, and file organization.

Some commonly used software metrics for source code were also considered. The intention of these metrics is to provide some assessment of the size and complexity of the source code. The metrics discussed were:

- Lines of code
- Halstead Software Science Metrics
- McCabe cyclomatic complexity
- Module interconnection metrics

In many organizations, the implementation team is responsible for providing the testing team with a system that compiles cleanly and has many obvious bugs or faults removed. In others, the implementation team is responsible for providing a software system to the testing team that the implementation team believes is free of major faults or bugs.

A software manager expects the implementation team to follow the organization's established coding process whenever possible. He or she may require the collection of several different types of metrics data for both the software source code and the process of developing it.

Further Reading

There are few references on coding standards. The Public Ada Catalog available at the URL `source.asset.com` provides some information for Ada programmers in both programming style and language philosophy. A sample C++ coding guide is available from the Internet source

`http://sunsite.icm.edu.pl/oo/cpprules.txt`

and is described in the book [HENR96]. The book [McCA95] by Jim McCarthy of Microsoft illustrates the team-building activities and corporate culture that apply in many software development organizations.

There are several excellent sources for information on software metrics. The original paper by McCabe [MCCAB76] and the recent book by Fenton and Pfleeger [FENT96] are perhaps the most accessible.

Many books on particular programming languages include discussions of style issues and programming standards. The list of references includes: [ADA83], [ADA95], the classic C programming language books by Kernighan and Ritchie ([KERN82], [KERN88]), several general C++ books such as [LEAC93], [LEAC95A], [SORD78], two classic books by Stroustrup (STRO91], [STRO94]), the annotated reference manual for C++ by Ellis and Stroustrup ([ELLI90]), three or four Java books, as well as nearly any related books on the shelves of your local library.

Exercises

1. Examine some software you have written previously from the perspective of coding style. Are there any improvements you would make? Why?

2. Same as question 1, but now consider coding standards.

3. Examine a reasonable amount of the source code available to you in a relatively large project that you did not write yourself. (You might look at software available from the Internet if you cannot find any locally.) List some of the coding standards that must have been in place during the project's software development.

4. There are several differences between the coding standards listed in this chapter. Give an explanation for these differences.

5. Determine if your software development environment has a "pretty printer" available. If so, determine if it is flexible enough to meet multiple coding standards.

6. Develop a C macro or a C++ inline function to compute the `pow()` function. Compare the efficiency of your iteration with that of the built-in `pow()` function.

7. Consider the simple C or C++ language statements:

    ```
    a ++;
    ```

    and

    ```
    a = a + 1;
    ```

    For integer variables they are completely equivalent. For pointers in C and C++, the assignment `a = a+ 1` indicates pointer arithmetic – the pointer a (which represents a location) is set to the location computed by the expression

    ```
    a + sizeof(type of expression pointed to by a)
    ```

    This equality is the basis for the equivalence of `a[1]` and `*(a + 1)` in C.

Unfortunately, there are problems with the use of these notations interchangeably in C++, due to the design of the standard C++ library. List the problems than can occur when mixing the expressions a++ and a = a+ 1 in C++ programs. Do the same for a-- and a = a - 1; (Recall that the standard C++ library offers five kinds of iterators: input, output, forward, bi-directional, and random access.)

8. Devise an experiment to determine which of two distinct implementations of the algorithm presented in Section 5.1 is fastest. Recall that the purpose of these algorithms was to initialize a square matrix to alternating ones and negative ones. Implement the algorithm so that the code runs as fast as you think is possible. Then analyze the code to determine if there are any additional improvements that you might have missed.

9. Use the profiler option on your compiler to examine the code fragment at the end of Section 5.1. (As stated in Section 5.2, the purpose of a profiler is to create executable code that includes timing information on the functions and operating system-level operations that the program spends most of its running time executing.) The profiler output should include sufficient information to determine the parts of the program that take the longest. Rewrite these parts and run the new program through the profiler again. Compare the two outputs.

10. Write a program that will solve a system of linear equations of the form

    A X = B

    where A is an n by n array of floating point numbers that has all entries other than those on the main diagonal equal to 0, X is an n by 1 array of floating point numbers that represents the array of unknowns to be solved for, and B is an n by 1 array of floating point numbers.

11. The next program is an example of poor programming practice. It is based on an actual program that was used to control the display of a moving object. The main consideration at that time was speeding up the program as much as possible. That is your objective here. Some of the code was the actual code used in the first attempt to perform the desired action. I added a few nasty features to slow the program down. Try to find as many ways as possible to speed up the code. You should concentrate on minimizing the number of floating point operations. There are at least nine separate improvements that can be made.

NOTE: The functions move_to( ) and draw_to( ) were actual graphics functions; use the ones given here to simulate the time that such functions take.

```
#include <stdio.h>
#include <math.h>

#define PI 3.14159

static double old[3][3] =
   {
   {0.0, 0.0, 0.0},
   {0.0, 0.0, 0.0},
   {0.0, 0.0, 0.0}
   };
static double new[3][3] =
   {
   {1.0, 0.0, 0.0},
   {0.0, 1.0, 0.0 },
   {0.0, 0.0, 1.0}
   };
static double trans[3][3]=
   {
   {0.0, 0.0, 0.0},
   {0.0, 0.0, 0.0},
   {0.0, 0.0, 0.0}
   };

static double x,y,z,theta = PI, phi = PI, psi =
2* PI ;

/* function prototypes */
void get_angles(void)
void move_to(double x,double y,double z);


main(void)
{
int i,j,k,
count,p,q,r,s,t,u,v,w,a,b,c,d,e,f,g,h,l,m,n,o;

for (count =1; count <= 500; count ++)
   {
```

```
   get_angles();

get_transformation_matrix(theta,phi,psi);
  for(i=0 ; i <= 3-1; i ++)
     {
    for (j = 0; j <= 3-1;   j++)
       {
       new[i][j] = 0.0;
       for(k =0; k <=3-1; k++)
          new[i][j] = new[i][j] +
     new[i][k]* trans[k][j];
       new[i][j] = (new[i][0]*0.9
       +new[i][1]*0.9 +
    new[i][2]*1.2) / 4.60;

       x = new[0][0];
       y = new[0][1];
       z = new[0][2];
       }
     }
    if (count %2 == 0)
      move_to(x,y,z);
    else
      draw_to(x,y,z);
}                    /* end of count loop */
}                          /* end of main */


/*-------------------------------------
This is a poor simulation of a random number
generator - note the range of
values of theta, psi, and phi.
------------------------------------*/

void get_angles(void)
{
static int i;
float result = PI;

if ( i == -1)
   i =1;
theta = result /(i+6);
phi = (theta)/( i +2);
psi = (((psi))/(i + 4));
```

```
i = i + 1.000;
}

/*----------------------------------------*/

get_transformation_matrix(double
        theta,double phi,double psi)
{
int i,j,k ;
/* a lot of matrix multiplication */

trans[0][0] = cos(theta);
trans[0][1] = sin(theta);

trans[1][0] = - sin(theta);
trans[1][1] = cos(theta);
trans[2][2] = 1.0 ;
trans[0][1] = trans[0][1] * cos_phi;
trans[0][2] = trans[0][1] * sin_phi +
    trans[0][2] * cos_phi;
trans[1][1] = trans[1][1] * -sin_phi;
trans[1][2] = trans[1][1] * sin_phi;
trans[2][1] = trans[2][2] * -sin_phi;
trans[2][1] = trans[2][2] * cos_phi;
trans[0][0] = trans[0][0] * cos_psi +
    trans[0][2] * sin_psi ;
trans[1][0] = trans[1][0] * cos_psi +
        trans[1][2] * sin_psi ;
trans[2][0] = trans[2][0] * cos_psi +
    trans[2][2] * sin_psi ;
trans[0][2] = trans[0][0] * -sin_psi +
    trans[0][2] * cos_psi;
trans[1][2] = trans[1][0] * -sin_psi +
      trans[1][2] *cos_psi;
trans[2][2] = trans[2][0] * -sin_psi +
      trans[2][2] *cos_psi;
}

/*----------------------------------------
Don't change this function - it does nothing but
simulate the cursor moving time
----------------------------------------*/
void move_to(double x,double y,double z)
{
```

```
int i;
for (i=1;i <= 1000000;i++)
        ;
}


/*-------------------------------------
Don't change this function - it does nothing but
simulate the cursor moving time ----------------
--------------------*/
draw_to(double x,double y,double z)
{
int i ;
for (i=1;i <= 1000000;i++)
        ;
}
```

Chapter 6

Testing and Integration

At this point, you have developed your software in the sense that the individual modules compile and seem to be correct. The system may itself compile successfully, link with all necessary libraries to produce an executable file, and even may have produced some correct output. These questions should be asked about the software's condition at this point in its development:

- Would you be willing to release the software now, knowing that the software performing its functions correctly will determine your or your organization's economic future based on the correctness of the software?

- What is the justification for your answer to the previous question?

- If you are not willing to release the software as it currently stands, what procedures would you take to improve the software's correctness?

- How much would the procedures cost to improve the software's quality?

- How long should the additional testing take?

- When should testing stop? In particular, is there a point beyond which further testing will not improve the software's quality enough to make it economically feasible?

- What can be done to ensure that changes made to parts of the software during its testing do not cause problems in other portions that have already been tested?

- How would your answers to any of the above questions change if you knew that the software was to be used in some safety-critical application where human life was at stake?

The purpose of these questions is to illustrate the importance of one of the two major subjects of this chapter: software testing. It is clear from even this brief introduction that a systematic approach to software testing is required.

The goal of software testing is to discover defects in software, not to show that none are present. That is, software testing cannot prove that software is correct (meets its specifications) for any realistic system. This is due to the large number of possible execution paths, possible combinations of function arguments, and the general complexity of various program statements. All that software testing can be expected to do is detect existing defects. There is a corollary to this: if software testing doesn't find many errors, then the testing process is likely to be at fault, at least for many software systems.

The statements in the previous paragraph suggest that the best we can hope for is some disciplined procedure that can detect the most likely sources of errors in software. It is becoming clear that the best defense against residual software errors (those that remain after a completion of phase of the software life cycle or release of a system) is proper design and coding practice.

Occasionally, the relationship between testers and developers is tense. There are good reasons for this. The goal of the testing process is to uncover faults left by the developers. The goal of the development process is to enable the developers to produce a satisfactory version of the software within budget and on schedule. Thus, the two goals are somewhat in opposition. Balancing them is one of the goals of the project manager.

Software testing occurs at several stages in the life of a system; these stages are frequently called the module level, unit level, and system level, depending on the size of the item being tested.

The second major topic covered in this chapter is software integration. Integration is the process of combining individual software modules and subsystems into a single working product. Software integration is not a trivial task, especially if the individual software units were developed in different locations or even by different companies separated geographically. This coordinated situation is typical in modern software development.

6.1 Types of Software Testing

There are several ways of viewing software from the perspective of testing. For software that is written in procedural languages such as C, Ada, Modula2, Pascal, or FORTRAN, the fundamental unit is the function. Some languages such as Pascal and Ada distinguish between a function, which may perform a computation and return a value, and a procedure, which performs a computation without returning a value. (FORTRAN uses the term "subroutine" instead of "procedure"). Languages such as these are often called "procedural" or "imperative" languages. We will use the term procedural in this book. We will also use the term "module" to refer to a function, procedure, or subroutine as necessary.

For procedural languages, there is a natural hierarchy of items to be tested:

- Module
- Unit
- Subsystem
- System

The preferred testing approach is to develop a systematic way of testing an individual source code module. The tested modules are then combined into larger testable groupings that are called units, subsystems, or systems, depending on how large they are or how much of the eventual complete software system is being combined. The process of combining tested modules into larger ones is called integration.

Once a software system has been through the gamut of tests, it may be subjected to additional testing to determine how the software functions with heavy load on the computer (in the case of a multi-processing system). Another test of the software may be to examine system behavior if the essential tables and other data structures of the software are close to being filled up. This additional testing is called "stress testing" or "performance testing."

The situation is quite different for object-oriented software, such as those typically developed in the C++, Java, Smalltalk, or Eiffel languages. The object-oriented programming paradigm is that a program consists of a set of independent objects that communicate and cooperate by sending messages to one another.

For object-oriented languages, there is a natural hierarchy of items to be tested:

- Class
- Class interaction with other classes that are either directly accessed by, or directly accessing, the class
- Subsystem
- System

The theoretical testing basis for object-oriented programming is in its infancy relative to the theory of testing procedural programs and, thus, we will be content to discuss only the most general integration issues in this circumstance.

Of course, a major factor in the popularity of several modern programming languages is the collection of powerful libraries available in some environments. The use of Microsoft Foundation classes or the X-Window toolkit, for example, provides a rich collection of utilities. Often, unless the application is safety-critical, such readily available facilities may be assumed to be correct during testing. Testing is hard enough without trying to test everything.

Unfortunately, there are even fewer theoretical discussions or published practical guidelines for testing functional programs written in languages such as Lisp, or for testing logic programs written in languages such as Prolog. We will not discuss testing issues for programs written in functional or logical languages any further in this book.

We note that most testing techniques are often described as using either a black-box or a white-box approach. The term black-box testing refers to the concept that a module is to be tested as to how well it meets its specifications, without any attention being paid to the structure of the actual source code within the module. In white-box testing, the structure of the module's source code is used together with the module's specifications to guide the test cases used to test the module. We will illustrate both white-box and black-box testing methods in this chapter.

6.2 Black-Box Module Testing

We will first consider the topic of black-box module testing. This testing method is based on a comparison of the software's performance on a test. Black-box testing requires several things which are listed in Table 6.1.

Table 6.1
Inputs to a black-box test plan of a module.

1. A module to be tested.
2. A set of specifications for the module's output on particular inputs.
3. A set of test cases to indicate that the module is correct. This set of test cases is usually created by the tester.
4. A method of comparing actual results with results expected from the module's specifications.
5. A method of storing test case results for further analysis.
6. A set of software tools to aid in automation of the testing process.

The first two items are generally available during the testing process. However, if they are not available, then there is no point in continuing to test, since we cannot tell if our results mean anything. We thus turn to the essential issue of selection of a set of test cases: a so-called test suite.

The first thing to note about black-box testing is that, in general, exhaustive testing is impossible due to the complexity of arguments to software modules. It follows that most non-trivial software cannot be tested completely. Therefore, a compromise must be reached between the impossible goal of exhaustive testing and the desire to release an acceptable version of the software product within a reasonable time. This compromise is often considered to be an art, not a science.

We now illustrate the issue that was raised in the previous paragraph. Consider for a moment the problem of testing a function that has a single Boolean argument. Clearly, there are only two possible test cases and, thus, exhaustive testing is possible for this function.

On the other hand, consider a function with a single integer argument. Because of the nature of computer arithmetic, there is a finite number of potential values for the integer argument. However, it is not reasonable to test the function for all possible arguments.

The situation is more complicated for functions with arguments whose type is one of the following: floating point, arrays, pointers, or some structured data type. The correctness of a software module may depend upon the architecture of the underlying machine, especially the hardware representation for floating point numbers and the arithmetic algorithms encoded in the computer's microcode.

It is clear that exhaustive testing is generally not appropriate for most software. In general, exhaustive black-box testing of software modules is impossible because of the large, even infinite set of possible test cases. Thus, test cases must be reduced in realistic software projects.

Since we have shown that exhaustive testing is not realistic, it is reasonable to ask what sort of test cases might be used. There is no absolute answer that will apply to every testing situation in every possible environment or application domain. Perhaps the best we can do is apply a reasonable set of guidelines. A set of guidelines for a minimum amount of testing is given in Table 6.2.

The motivation for our choices for testing numerical types and array indices is the commonly held belief that most software errors occur at the boundaries and are of the off-by-one type.

Note that this guideline yields a small number of test cases only if the number of arguments to a function is small. A function with three floating point arguments will give rise to 5*5*5, or 125 possible test cases. This is a very large number and, in reality, a much smaller number will be used in most software organizations. Reducing the guidelines for a floating point variable to 4 or even 3 reduces the number to 64 or 27, respectively. This still may be too many for a number of environments.

If the function has multiple arguments which are of different types, the total number of test cases is the product of the number of test cases for each argument, which is exactly the same approach we used for multiple arguments of the same type.

We note that production quality software development environments usually include a test driver utility to compute the results of running these test cases. Thus, the number of test cases is not completely unreasonable. However, if the number of test cases is too large for the test utility, it may be necessary to substitute some paper-and-pencil-tests.

Table 6.2
Some guidelines for test-case selection in black-box module testing.

Argument Type	Test Cases
Boolean	True, False
Integer	MIN_INT,-1,0, 1, MAX_INT
Positive integer	1, MAX_INT
Non-negative integer	0,1, MAX_INT
Float	MIN_FLOAT,-1.0, 0.0, 1.0, MAX_FLOAT
Double precision	MIN_DOUBLE,-1.0,0.0, 1.0, MAX_DOUBLE
Character	Printable, "escape sequence," null-byte
Array index	Min index, max index
Array	Test arbitrary array index
Pointer	NULL, normal
Structured type	One or more test cases for each field of the structure, depending on the type of the field
String	NULL, length 2, MAX_STRING_ LENGTH

Here is a simple example of how black-box testing works. The code in Example 6.1 on the next page is intended to compute the factorial of an non-negative integer whose value is given as its only input argument.

The problem with this source code is a common one in C: the test for equality in the if-else statement (line 8) has as its argument the assignment statement n = 0 instead of the expected Boolean comparison n == 0. (This unfortunate notation has been the source of many unexpected errors in C programs. Many, but not all, C compilers produce a warning when they encounter this pattern.)

We can see this logical error easily, particularly if we have had it pointed out to us. However, our problem is different with black-box testing. The real question to be considered is: how do we detect this logical software fault without being able to see any of the source code for this module? That is, how do we determine the appropriate test cases using only information in the interfaces of the function and the function's specifications? We note that this function will fail nearly every type of testing. In particular, it will fail the simple test case n = 2.

```
1.  int fact(int n)
2.  {
3.    if (n < 0)
4.       {
5.       printf(" Error-negative int\n" );
6.       return (-1);
7.       }
8.    else if (n = 0)
9.       return 1;   /* 0! is defined as 1 */
10.   else
11.      return (n * fact (n-1))
12. }
```

Example 6.1 An incorrect function intended to compute factorials

Another more complex example is due to Pleszkoch, Linger, and Hevner [PLES92]. They examined several different implementations of the specifications given in Example 6.2 as part of their research on the use of a formal program transformation scheme during software reengineering. The specification of the function they considered is:

```
For each i in 1..N, search A(i,1), A(i,2), A(i,3),
..., for the first non-zero entry.  Place the
position of the first non-zero entry in W(i), and
the type (+1 for positive, -1 for negative) in
T(i).  Assume that there will always be a non-zero
entry.
```

Example 6.2 Specifications for a sample function

What test cases should we develop for this function, knowing only the function's specifications? Some cases come to mind:

- All entries in the matrix A have the value zero.
- All entries in the matrix A have positive values.
- All entries in the matrix A have negative values.
- Each row in the matrix A has entries that are positive and entries that are negative.
- Each row in the matrix A has entries that are nonzero and entries that have the value zero.

- Problems can occur because of special positions in the first and last rows.
- Problems can occur because of special positions in the first and last columns.
- There may be system limitations on the number N.

You may be able to think of some others.

We will defer presentation of the source code for one implementation of this function until we discuss white-box testing in the next section. (The code will be given in Example 6.3.)

6.3 White-Box Module Testing

White-box testing differs from black-box testing in that the suite of test cases is chosen using additional information obtained from the internal structure of the source code. This type of testing requires the items listed in the set of testing guidelines provided in Table 6.1, especially a set of specifications for output of the module based on certain inputs. Additional guidelines for white-box testing are almost always based on the information in Table 6.3.

Table 6.3
Inputs to a white-box test plan of a module.

1. A module to be tested.
2. A set of specifications for the module's output on particular inputs..
3. The number of branching decisions in the source code.
4. The number and types of loops in the source code.
5. The number of function calls in the source code.
6. The number of non-local gotos in the source code.
7. Recursion requires extra attention to make sure the module terminates.

A source code branch point occurs when a decision is made. This can be in the form of a simple "if," or an "if-then-else" structure. A branch point also occurs for each option in a multiple decision statement such as a "switch" statement in C or a "case" statement in Pascal.

Nearly all white-box testing guidelines require that each branch of a decision statement be tested. The guidelines [CSC91] are typical. In fact, these guidelines only require testing each branch of a decision.

We note also that the code of Example 6.1 contains recursion. The recursion must itself be tested for a proper connection between recursive function calls and to make sure that the recursion terminates properly. In our example, but not in general, these cases would also be tested if the module had used iteration instead of recursion.

We now turn to the discussion of white-box testing of the code for which the specifications were given in Example 6.2. The source code to be considered is given in Example 6.3 and is based on source code originally designed by Pleszkoch, Linger, and Hevner [PLES92] to illustrate some issues in code restructuring. Note that the code was not intended as an illustration of production quality code.

```
i = 1;                                    // f1
done = false;
new_one = true;
while (!done)
  {
    if (new_one)
      {
      if (i <= N)                         // p1
        {
        j = 1;                            // f2
        new_one = false;
        rest = false;
      else
        done = true;
      } //end if
    else
      {
      if (rest)
        {
        j = j + 1;                        // f3
        rest := false;
        }
      else
        {
        W(i) = j;                         // f4
        if A(i,j) > 0                     // p2
          {
          T(i) = 1;                       // f5
          new_one = true;
          }
        else
          {
          if (A(i.j) < 0 )                // p3
            T(i) = -1;                    // f6
            new_one = true;
```

```
        else
          rest = true;
      }   // end if
    }   // end if
  } // end if
  if new_one
  i = i + 1;                        // f7
    }         // end if
    }         //end if
  }           // end main loop
```

Example 6.3 Source code for the sample function that was specified previously in Example 6.2.

We can draw a graph that describes the logical flow of control by having each statement of the program correspond to a node on the graph with arrows linking each program statement to all program statements that can follow it logically. Most program statements will be linked to the program statements that follow them directly. Others will also be linked to statements that begin or terminate loops, or to branches of selection statements. The program graph for the code of Example 6.3 is given in Figure 6.1.

Note that straight lines without branches do not contribute to branching. We can simplify the branching using the "reduced program graph" which is shown in Figure 6.2. A reduced program graph is obtained from a program graph by collapsing all nodes that have only one arrow emanating from them.

We can see from the reduced program graph in Figure 6.2 that there are four logical branches in the code and that each of them must be tested. Even the simple error state due to the input of a negative integer must be tested. A very common programming error is to simply print the error message and not set the function's return value to communicate the error to a calling function or routine.

It is important to distinguish between branches of decision statements and the number of execution paths in a program. A program will always have a finite number of branches, but the number of potential execution paths can be much larger. The number can be infinite, as illustrated by the simple example

```
i=0;
while (i>0)
    {
    i = i +1
    do_something();
    }
```

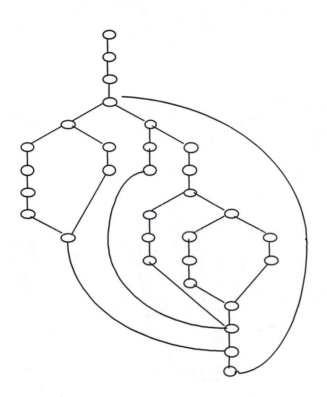

Figure 6.1 The program graph for the code in Example 6.3.

Clearly, we are not going to test an infinite number of program execution paths. We need some way to determine a set of test cases for programs with loops. One common approach to white-box testing of programs with loops is given in Table 6.4.

Table 6.4
The number of test cases for programs with loops.

1. Test the program with 0, 1, or some arbitrary number of executions of the body of the loop.
2. Test that the loop always terminates (assuming that termination is expected.)
3. For nested loops, test both the outermost and innermost loops. If three or more loops are nested, test the individual inside loops at least once.

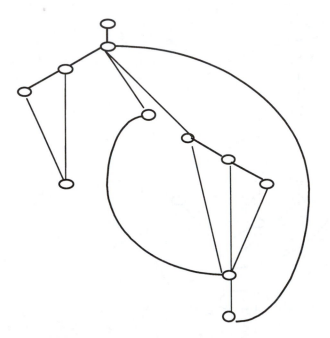

Figure 6.2. The reduced program graph for the code in Example 6.1.

You are probably thinking that this process will generate too many test cases in many practical situations. For nested loops, we have suggested at least nine test cases. Even more test cases have been suggested for loops with more nesting levels. If the bodies of the loops contain branching statements, the number of test cases goes up astronomically. Clearly, we must place some sort of limit on the number of test cases for white-box testing, just as we did for black-box testing. Certainly, the number of test cases can be reduced by careful application of pre-condition, post-condition reasoning and including this with the source code. We will discuss this matter in section 6.5.

6.4 Reducing the Number of Test Cases by Effective Test Strategies

Both testing methods described so far in this chapter, black-box and white-box testing for procedures and functions, as well as most techniques for testing objects, have suffered from the problem of yielding far too many potential test cases. Let's see just how much of a problem this is for realistic software.

We will consider a software system of approximately 100,000 lines of code. We will assume that there are 1000 functions or procedures, each containing 100 lines of code. Let's suppose that the source code for each function contains a doubly nested loop in which the body of the innermost loop contains an if-else statement, a nested loop with a three-way branch in the loop body, and a stand-alone, three-way branch statement. Suppose that the function has three arguments: a boolean, a float, and a pointer to a structured type with two fields, each of which is a floating point number. Pseudocode is given in Example 6.4.

```
float f(int bool, float x, struct f_type *p)
{
  int i,j count;
  float temp;

  count = 0;
  for (i = 0; i < 10; i = i + 1)
    {
    if (bool == 0)   / * false */
       do_something (bool);
    else
       count = do_something_else (bool, x);
    }

  for(i = 0; i < 10; i = i +1)
      for(j = 0; j < 20; j = j+ 1)
        {
        switch (i +j)
            {
            case 0 :
              do_something (bool);
              break;
            case 1:
              do_something_else(bool, x);
              break;
            default:
              do_something_different (p);
            }   /* end switch */
        } /* end for loop */

-----------------other code here------------
```

```
switch (count)
  {
  case-1:
      printf ("error\n");
      exit (1);
  case 0:
      printf ("Count = 0\n");
      return (0);
  default:
      temp = x*x;
      return temp;
  }  /* end switch */
} /* end function */
```

Example 6.4 A sample function that is difficult to test completely.

How many test cases do these functions have? Exhaustive testing is clearly not feasible because of the presence of the floating point and structured arguments. Even using the suggestions given in Table 6.2, we would have two test cases required for the boolean argument, five test cases for the floating point argument, and eleven for the pointer to the structured type. The number eleven is obtained by using the value of five for each of the two fields of structured type, adding these two numbers, and then adding one because of the indirect access by pointers. Thus, black-box testing would require a total of 2*5*11, or 110, test cases if we use the reduced number given in Table 6.2.

Computing the number of white-box test cases is only slightly more difficult, using a count of the number of branches and the guidelines given in Table 6.4 for programs with loops. We have two test cases for the body of the initial for-loop because of the if-else statement. The loop itself is to be tested at least three times, giving six cases for the first loop.

The body of the innermost of the nested loops contains a branching statement with three possible choices. The innermost loop is to be tested at least three times, with a similar number for the outer loop. This yields 3*3*3, or 27, test cases suggested for this doubly nested loop that contains a branching statement.

The final branching statement requires three additional test cases, making a total of 6+27+3, or 36, test cases for white-box testing. Thus, white-box testing yields a smaller number of test cases for this sample function than does black-box testing for our hypothetical example.

How long will testing take? There are 1000 functions, with 36 white-box test cases per function. Each function contains 100 lines of code. Let's estimate that each line of code corresponds to ten assembly-language instructions. This estimate allows for the assignment statements and the need to increment the loop control variables. It greatly under counts the assembly language equivalent of the function calls and, thus, gives a conservative estimate of the time needed to test each function:

1000 calls of functions

    *

36 test cases/function

    *

100 lines of code/test case

    *

10 instructions/line of code

    *

2 (Number of comparison of results with actuals)

= 72,000,000 instructions

(For black-box testing, the conservative total estimate is 220,000,000 instructions to be executed.) For a computer rated at a speed of 100,000,000 million instructions per second, or 100 MIPS, this is, at most, a few seconds.

However, we have ignored the time to develop and perform the test comparisons. If we add the time to assign values to each of the test arguments, the time increases considerably. Since the test input data and the data results would certainly have to be written to one or more files, and file operations are an order of magnitude slower than computer memory instructions, the time can get quite large. The determination of test cases itself can be quite time consuming, as we have seen. To make matters worse, this is merely one function. Clearly, this testing process is too inefficient.

The solution of course is to have a rational test strategy. Such a strategy should reflect the amount of effort the software producing organization wishes to spend on software testing.

We will now briefly describe some simple software testing strategies used by various companies. The purpose of the discussion is to show how the formal approach to software testing is combined with a realistic assessment of the impossibility of complete testing and the desire to make software testing more efficient by uncovering the largest number of software defects in the shortest amount of time.

As part of a contract with NASA, Computer Sciences Corporation developed a System Software Development Methodology (SSDM) in which the approach to software testing is specified [CSC91]. The primary method used is white-box testing. For module testing, each decision branch of each module must be tested in a separate test case and a document describing the results of the test must be approved by a manager. No attempt is made to test loops by a separate test team. It is assumed that the developers will have tested loops within their own source code before releasing it to the test team.

Bellcore had a similar process in which it demanded that any subcontracting organization produce a testing plan and test cases before starting the testing process. The plan had to consider the following as a minimum:

- Computer hardware
- Related hardware
- Testing tools
- Test drivers and stubs
- Other special software developed to aid in the testing process
- Testing reviews and code inspections

Other organizations have similar testing processes, with testing of safety-critical applications being the most complex.

6.5 Testing Objects for Encapsulation and Completeness

Software developed using the object-oriented paradigm should be tested differently from software developed in procedural languages. Object-oriented programs generally consist of separate objects that communicate by sending messages to one another. The first emphasis of object-oriented testing is to ensure the completeness and correctness of objects. Because of the potential for reuse of objects, testing for completeness is an essential part of testing object-oriented software. Objects can be used in situations other than the ones for which they were originally created. We illustrate this point by an example.

Because C++ is descended from C, even simple input and output causes some problems for testing of C++ programs that use both C and C++ I/O functions. The primary difficulty at this point occurs in operator overloading.

We present two simple checklists of items to be considered when testing C++ programs. For simplicity, we will concentrate on those object-oriented features specific to C++.

The first checklist describes the steps necessary for testing programs that use an overloaded operator. This checklist is given in Table 6.5.

Table 6.5
Checklist for testing overloaded operators.

1. Make a list of all overloaded operators. (The operators we discuss in this section will already be defined for some of the standard types.)
2. For each overloaded operator, make a list of each type of operand that can be used with that operator. Be sure to include all predefined types that the operator can be applied to.
3. For a unary operator, test the operator on the new object type.
4. For a binary operator, list all possible combinations of types of the operands.
5. Test each possible combination of allowable operands.

For example, an operator such as + is already overloaded for the `int`, `float`, and `double` data types. If we have some new type for which the operator is redefined, then we must test the + operator for the following combinations of arguments:

```
int new_type
new_type int
float new_type
new_type float
new_type new_type
double new_type
new_type double
```

We need not test the cases that can be assumed to have been previously tested such as:

```
int int
float float
int float
float int
float double
double float
```

The second checklist describes the steps necessary for testing C++ programs that use the standard `I/O` functions of the C language instead of those available in C++. This checklist is given in Table 6.6.

These checklists can help avoid some of the more common errors that beginning C++ programmers make. Consider the object-oriented program shown in Example 6.5.

Table 6.6
Testing of I/O Functions

1. Replace all `printf()`, `putc()`, `putchar()` and `puts()` function calls with the operator `<<` and either `cout` or `cerr`, as appropriate.
2. Replace all `scanf()`, `getc()`, `getchar()`, and `gets()` function calls by the operator `>>` and `cin`.
3. Include the header file `iostream.h`.
4. Rerun the program and compare the results on some standard inputs with those obtained previously.
5. If there are differences, apply manipulators to the I/O stream in order to obtain correct results. Be sure to use the include file `iomanip.h` if you use any I/O manipulators.

```
#include <iostream.h>

class Complex
{
public:
    double real;
    double imag;

    Complex(){double real = 0.0; double imag = 0.0;}

    double realpart (Complex z) { return z.real; }
    double imagpart (Complex z) { return z.imag; }
    void print(Complex z) {cout << z.real<<
" + " << z.imag <<"i" << endl;}
};




Complex operator + (Complex a, Complex b)
{
    Complex C;

    C.real = a.real + b.real;
    C.imag = a.imag + b.imag;
    return C;
}
```

```
ostream &operator << (ostream & stream, Complex a)
{
  cout << a.real << " + " << a.imag << "i" << endl;
  return stream;
}

main()
{
  Complex z1, z2;
  float x1, x2,y1,y2;

  cout << "Enter the real and imaginary parts of "
       << "the first complex number" << endl;
  cin >> x1 >> y1;
  cout << "Enter the real and imaginary parts of "
       << "the second complex number" << endl;
  cin >> x2 >> y2;
  z1.real = x1;
  z1.imag = y1;
  z2.real = x2;
  z2.imag = y2;
  z1.print();
  z2.print();
  cout << z1 << endl;
  cout << z2 << endl;
  z2 = z1 + z2;
  cout << z2;
}
```

Example 6.5 An example of testing object-oriented programs.

Note that we have three overloaded operators in this program: +, >>, and =. The first two have been explicitly declared as functions that can access all of the data in the class Complex. (Nothing in the class Complex has been declared as being private.) We have used the default overloading of the assignment operator =.

Three functions are presented for testing purposes. The member function print() is included to make sure that different functions work correctly. It is much more difficult to find errors if the I/O functions do not work properly unless a debugger is available. The output function call corresponding to this function's definition would have been

```
z2.print(z2);
```

The functions `realpart()` and `imagpart()` were also used for testing the program. Some testing was done using the default conversions of predefined arithmetic arguments in C++.

6.6 Testing Objects with Inheritance

The availability of inheritance causes new testing problems for programs in C++ or other languages that support inheritance. One issue is what needs to be tested in a derived class (assuming that the base class was sufficiently tested). Clearly, testing a derived class requires complete knowledge of the base class from which it was derived.

We will assume that the logic of the member functions has been tested (at least by hand) and that the major concerns are the interfaces between objects.

In order to test a derived class, we should first test all possible member functions not derived from the base class to make sure that there is no interface problem. This is the easiest situation to test, since there is no possible ambiguity between member functions of the same name.

After we have tested the new member functions of the derived class, it is time to test the member functions that have been inherited. These should be tested by making sure that the correct information (base class or derived class) is being used.

Additional problems arise when testing multiple inheritance. Certainly, every test that was applied with single inheritance should also be applied here. In addition, each case of possible ambiguity should be tested carefully.

The following passage from the *Annotated C++ Reference Manual* [ELLI90, page 204] by Margaret Ellis and Bjarne Stroustrup illustrates some of the difficulty due to inheritance. The passage addresses some questions concerning the scope of operators and variables:

> When virtual base classes are used, a single function, object, type, or enumerator may be reached through more than one path through the directed acyclic graph of base classes. This is not an ambiguity. The identical use with nonvirtual base classes is an ambiguity; in that case more than one sub-object is involved...
>
> When virtual base classes are used, more than one function, object, or enumerator may be reached through paths through the directed acyclic graph of base classes. This is an ambiguity unless one of the base classes dominates the others. The identical use with nonvirtual base classes is an ambiguity; in that case more than one sub-object is involved.

The problem is with the complexity of the C++ programming language, not the Ellis and Stroustrup exposition. The complexity indicated in this passage suggests that certain constructions should be avoided for C++ classes in order to make resulting C++ programs easier to maintain.

Recall that C++ allows the use of "friend functions." In C++, friend functions are not members of a class, although they have access to the private and protected member of the class in which they are declared. The use of friend functions can cause a breakdown in the modularity of an object-oriented program. Any testing of friend functions should include code reading to make sure that no private or protected data is used as an lvalue (on the left-hand side of an assignment statement). Other testing should make sure that the program using the object and the friend function avoids hiding one function by another. We note that Java does not allow either friend functions or any important non-object-oriented constructs.

Note that there is a potential "combinatorial explosion" in the number of possible test cases for classes with many member functions or many levels of inheritance. If the testing seems excessive, begin with reading the code and determining if good coding practices were used. Follow this by careful testing of those objects that you believe are the most complex (because of their internal structure, or their most likely use within C++ programs).

6.7 General Testing Issues for Object-Oriented Software

As we have seen, testing of non-object-oriented programs can be done using either "white box" or "black box" methods. The distinction is made between these two approaches depending on whether the selection of appropriate test cases is based on the internal structure of the code. Of course, hybrid testing methods are possible.

Software testing occurs at several stages in the life of a system; these stages are frequently called the module level, unit level, and system level. The corresponding stages for testing object-oriented programs are: method-level testing (which considers individual transformation on a class), class-level testing, module-level testing, and system-level testing. (The term "module" is loosely defined as a collection of related classes and a few related functions.)

The class is the most important unit in object-oriented programming. Unfortunately, the member functions of a class (the so-called "methods," that are used for a class can be combined in arbitrary ways. As such, the possibilities for testing a class are enormous, especially if the class is relatively complete in the sense that it contains many member functions, perhaps with polymorphism and operator overloading.

One view of the test process for a class is that it is a search process for the order of methods with various collections of arguments that give errors [LORENZ89].   A common strategy for testing of objects includes [SMITH89]:

- Encapsulation
- Minimalization
- Exhaustion of a depth
- Inheritance
- Interactive

The "encapsulation strategy" for testing objects makes use of the abstraction used in defining an object. Any set of abstract methods that can be legitimately applied to the abstract object correspond to a set of legal combinations of transformations on the class.

The "minimalization strategy" is to develop the smallest number of test cases for the class being tested where the errors that occur can be overridden by any child class of the tested class.

The "exhaustion of a depth strategy" is to consider all legal combinations of methods allowed for an object, with the number of methods in any chain of methods being less than or equal to the previously determined value of the depth.

The "inheritance strategy" is used for subclasses that are inherited from a parent class. A list of methods to be tested is kept and tests are performed on the class depending on the test results for the parent class.

The "interactive strategy" requires the tester to determine which methods to test based on an assessment of the relative complexity of the internal data structures in the class. The method can be summed up as "use your intelligence guided by your experience."

Note that the "exhaustion of a depth strategy" can be implemented mechanically with relatively little difficulty. Note also that the "inheritance test strategy" has potential for automation, but that the other test strategies do not. In general, automatic testing tools for object-oriented programs are either nonexistent or are very primitive (at least compared to the automated testing and analysis tools available for procedural programs in good software development environments).

Several features of object-oriented programming that encourage efficient program development cause some difficulties in testing. We will describe some of these in the next few paragraphs.

Multiple inheritance implies that a portion of a class may be inherited along different inheritance paths. Many compilation systems handle this potential ambiguity by using a precedence scheme to select proper values. The testing difficulty is due to the potential that a slight change in one of the inheritance paths can lead to an entirely new derived class.

Polymorphism also causes problems. We must determine that when an object receives a message, the object is in the correct form to receive it, and will react in the intended manner.

There are also potential problems in concurrent systems, since the creation or destruction of a particular form of an object may not occur instantaneously and, hence, there may be timing problems. These types of timing problems are notoriously hard to detect by testing.

Note that these issues are not caused by the classes themselves but in the way that they may be combined.

The lack of an implied order in which the methods used for a class are applied appears to make it difficult to use "test data." It is also difficult to use the control flow or data flow techniques commonly used in procedural programming.

For systems of reasonable complexity, there is a tradeoff between using many previously tested classes either directly or by inheritance, and using more complex objects that require extensive testing. Because testing complex objects is difficult, it appears that the better approach is to use more, but simpler, objects, including those in a class library of data structures. There is little hard data available as yet to support this view, but it is the growing consensus of a large group of project managers and software engineering researchers.

6.8 Test Plans

A test plan is more than a collection of test cases. It is a strategy for systematically examining the software to detect faults. There are several elements that affect a test plan:

- There should be a precise list of the requirements that must be tested. Without this list, there is no way to tell if the requirements have been met.

- The test plan must be consistent with the goals of the organization. If the most important goal of the organization is to have a minimal test of the software's essential features as determined by the marketing department, the test plan should test only those features as a first priority. (These essential features may be tested within twenty-four hours in many organizations.)

- After all the requirements in the most essential set of requirements have been tested, the next set of test cases should consider the cases that most users are likely to want.

- The remaining set of test cases should be the ones that would exercise those features of the software that are very unlikely to be encountered in practice. The basic idea is to only test these other features if time permits.

- The test plan should specify the operational environment. Given the huge range of hardware in the personal computer world, this probably means testing the performance of the software in a minimal configuration, the maximum configuration of the hardware, and the most common configuration. (Here the term "configuration" refers to a combination of memory, hard disk space available, monitor, video memory card, and sound card.)

- The plan must allocate a sufficient amount of time to be used for testing (at each phase).

- The set of personnel available for testing must be known and part of the plan.

- The plan must ensure that there are adequate hardware resources available for testing.

- The plan must make sure that there are adequate software resources available for testing, usually in the form of test drivers and testing tools.

- There must be a sufficient amount of available free computing cycles resources that are to be used for testing.

- The plan must address the available tools that can be used for testing data analysis.

- The plan must take into account any existing standards and practices manual.

- The plan must consider the type of software (object oriented, procedural, mixed).

By now, you should be convinced that exhaustive testing is impossible for any realistic software. Thus, there are some tradeoffs that must always be made. These factors must be part of a test plan.

What does a test plan look like? It might be as simple as: test each branch at each decision point or, test that each function is called with the correct arguments.

The important thing is that a realistic plan must be developed and followed during the software's testing. The plan may be influenced by the organization's typical software practices.

6.9 Software Integration

Suppose that we have tested each of the software modules individually for a program written in a procedural language such as C or Pascal. Alternatively, suppose that we have tested each of the classes that are to be used in an object-oriented program. The same issue occurs if the program contains multiple classes. We have to have some assurance that the entire program works correctly as a unit.

In addition, we have to make sure that our program functions correctly as a system. That is, we have to make certain that our program works properly with any software package that we intend to use with our program. Recall that this property, which is known as interoperability, was one of the goals of software engineering that we discussed in Chapter 1.

The process of ensuring that programs that are created from individual program modules that work together as a unit is called "software integration."

Of course, many software systems, including the one we are developing as part of our major software engineering example, consist of both object-oriented and procedural portions. Hence, it may be necessary to employ both procedurally and object-based software integration techniques. The beginning software engineer may be surprised at the formality in which many organizations approach the issue of software integration. Software integration is much more than simply getting the individual modules to compile and link together into a complete system. The final software system must meet the requirements that were set for it initially.

Software integration is not always a smooth process, particularly in modern development environments in which efficiency requires reuse of existing software modules or even existing COTS packages. A major problem can occur if one or more modules are extremely difficult to integrate with others. If the project's management has determined that the reason is the lack of adherence to standards or the low quality of the module in the sense of a large number of software defects, then the original coding team, design team, or requirements team may be called on to help with the problem.

There are three common approaches to software integration:

- Big bang
- Bottom-up
- Top-down

Each of these approaches has considerable advantages and disadvantages and, therefore, each has its proponents and detractors. We describe each of these approaches in turn.

The "big bang" approach to software integration is so named because it attempts to integrate the previously tested software modules and existing COTS products into a complete system without any preliminary software integration activities. The basic idea is to see if the system works as an entirety without any changes to individual modules or configuration. Ideally, the newly created system will work perfectly. The big-bang approach is illustrated in Figure 6.3. In Figure 6.3, the boxes represent individual software modules, subsystems, or COTS products. The lines connecting the boxes in the figure indicate a linkage between the modules, subsystems, or COTS products, but do not represent any type of control flow or data interface. The diagram indicates no special order, which is appropriate because the big-bang approach does not distinguish between modules in terms of relative importance or their relation to the control flow or data flow of the intended system when integrating them.

More commonly, many changes are necessary for the complete system to work properly. The system integration team is then tasked with the problem of determining which modules are causing the integration difficulty and fixing the problems.

We note that in most actual software systems, as opposed to the type of software projects generally done by beginning students, getting the compiler to link the component source code modules is the easiest part of the problem. This is true, regardless of the integration method used. We thus consider only the difficulties caused by logical errors in software modules, incorrect module interface standards, or errors that are due to faulty design or requirements.

The major advantage of the big-bang approach is the potential for reduction of system integration costs if the system design was sufficiently modular and the individual software components adhere to appropriate interface and performance standards.

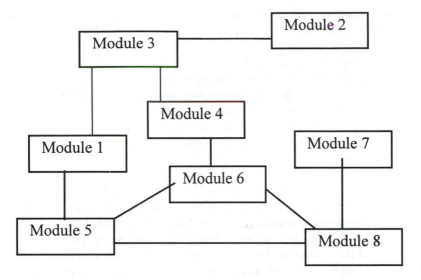

Figure 6.3. The "big bang" approach to software integration

The disadvantage of the big-bang approach for many organizations is the length of time and the amount of resources needed to determine which modules actually caused the problems in integration. The techniques used include the use of debuggers and other software tools to determine the exact place where difficulties occur. This can be a very time-consuming task.

Since one of the goals of proper software project management is to minimize risk, the big bang approach to software integration is probably not appropriate unless the organization has experience with the amount of effort needed to interface individual modules. This would be the case if the application domain was well understood and relatively static, and the organization had considerable positive experience with the team that was responsible for creating the modules to be integrated. (Note that many organizations contract out all or part of their software development. In addition, many organizations produce software components at geographically diverse locations and the quality requirements of a particular location that produces safety-critical software may be much higher than a location that does not.)

We now consider two software integration approaches that can reduce risk, but will be more costly than the optimal case of the big-bang approach because they require additional software to be written in order to perform the integration.

The "bottom up" approach is based on the assumption that a software system is made up of a collection of simple, lower-level software modules and that these simpler modules should be put together to form a system.

The bottom-up integration process is iterative and goes something like the following. Note the continued reliance on the system architecture.

1. The lowest-level modules in the system are determined, preferably from an examination of the system architecture. If the system architecture is not sufficiently detailed, then these modules can be located by examination of the system's call graph either by using a tool such as the standard UNIX `cflow` utility or examining the software by hand.

2. Drivers are written for each of the lowest-level modules. A "driver" is a function that passes arguments to other functions or procedures and determines the return values (in the case of functions). We will give an example of a driver function in Section 6.14, when we discuss integration of our major software engineering example system.

3. The lower-level modules are now tested, together with the new driver functions. After the lower-level modules are tested in this way, they are deemed to be correct and the next step of the software integration process starts.

4. The driver functions are replaced one by one by the next higher level modules in the software architecture. After the driver modules are replaced by the actual modules at the next higher level, new driver functions are written in order to control the actions of all modules below the driver in the system architecture.

5. Steps 3 and 4 are iterated until the top-level module replaces the last artificially created driver.

Note that at each iteration, the system will consist of a set of tested, integrated modules, with small driver functions at the top. The lower-level routines will be correct and, thus, the intermediate steps in the software integration process will always result in a system with correct outputs from lower-level routines such as device drivers. The ability to have actual outputs is a major advantage of the bottom-up method of software integration.

Unfortunately, the user interface of the eventual system will not be tested, or even fully functional until the entire integration process is nearly complete. Thus, a manager or customer will not be able to see the "look and feel" of the system until it is complete. This, together with the cost of writing multiple drivers, many of which can be quite complex, are the primary disadvantages of the bottom-up process of software integration.

The bottom-up approach is illustrated in a series of diagrams illustrated in Figures 64 through 6.7. The four diagrams are intended to show what was not obvious from Figure 6.3: that there are lower level modules in the system and these will be the first ones integrated into a larger system. Modules 2 and 7 are the lowest levels of this system.

Figure 6.4. Illustration of the first step in the bottom-up approach to software integration - determination of bottom-level modules and linking each of them to an artificial driver module.

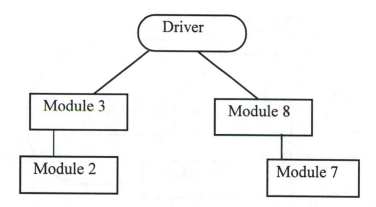

Figure 6.5. Illustration of the second step in the bottom-up approach to software integration – integration of modules that are just above the bottom level with artificial driver modules.

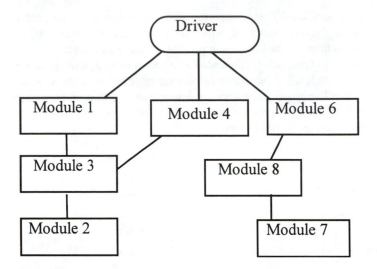

Figure 6.6. Illustration of the third step in the "bottom-up" approach to software integration - integration of the next level of modules with artificial driver modules.

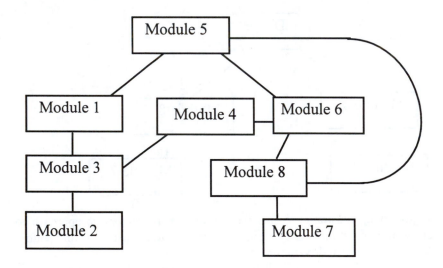

Figure 6.7. Illustration of the final step in the bottom-up approach to software integration – integration of the top-level module into the system with all artificial driver modules replaced by actual modules.

The "top down" integration process is also iterative and goes something like the following:

1. The highest-level module in the system is determined, preferably from an examination of the system architecture. If the system architecture is not sufficiently detailed, then this module can be located by examination of the system's call graph either by using a tool such as the standard UNIX `cflow` utility or examining the software by hand.

2. Function stubs are written for each of the second-level modules connected to the top-level module. A "function stub" is a function that receives arguments passed to it from other functions or procedures and produces the return values (in the case of functions). We will give an example of a function stub in Section 6.14, when we discuss integration of our major software engineering example system.

3. The top-level module is now tested, together with the new function stubs. After the top-level module is tested in this way, the tested version of the system is deemed to be correct and the next step of the software integration process starts.

4. The function subs are replaced one by one by the next lowest-level modules in the software architecture. After the function stubs are replaced by the actual modules at the next lower level, new function stubs are written in order to control the actions of all modules below the currently tested portion of the software in the system architecture.

5. Steps 3 and 4 are iterated until each bottom-level module replaces the bottom-level, artificially created function stub.

Note the continued reliance on the system architecture. You should also compare the steps to those of the bottom-up approach.

Note that at each iteration, the system will consist of a set of tested, integrated modules, with the actual user interface at the top. Unlike the case with a bottom-up approach to software integration, a manager or customer will be able to see the "look and feel" of the system until it is complete. This can be very reassuring to management.

Unfortunately, the interface to lower-level routines will be never be a completely accurate description of the program's computation until the integration process is complete. Because lower-level routines are only stubbed in, none of the intermediate steps in the software integration process can possibly result in a system with correct outputs from lower-level routines such as device drivers. The inability to have actual outputs is a major disadvantage of the top-down method of software integration. This, together with the cost of writing multiple function stubs, are the primary disadvantages of the bottom-up process of software integration.

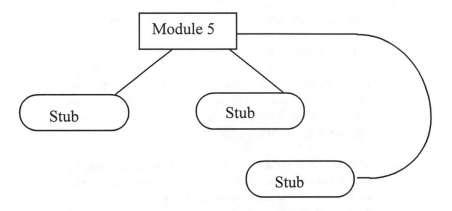

Figure 6.8. Illustration of the first step in the top-down approach to software integration – integration of all software modules below the top-level module with artificial stub modules.

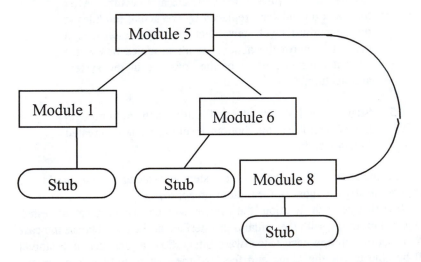

Figure 6.9. Illustration of the next step in the top-down approach to software integration – integration of all software modules at the next level below the top-level module with artificial stub modules.

The top-down approach is illustrated in Figures 6.8 through 6.10. Recall that for this example, module 5 was the highest-level module.

You should note that Figure 6.10 does not use a stub for module 7. Since module 7 was at the lowest level in the sense that it called no other modules, its integration into the system is complete at this stage. The other low-level modules will be integrated later in the process.

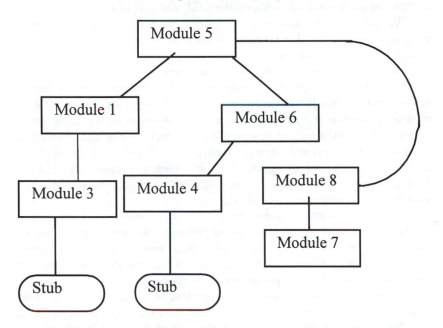

Figure 6.10. Illustration of the next step in the top-down approach to software integration - integration of all software modules at the next level down with artificial stub modules.

There is no need to represent the final step of the top-down integration process – it is the same as the diagram given in Figure 6.7 because it represents the end result of the software integration process.

You should note that the bottom-up and top-down approaches can be employed in the same hybrid integration process. The goal is to reduce the amount of extra drivers and stubs needed when using one of the other integration methods alone.

It is worthwhile to consider each of these integration approaches in the context of software reuse. The big-bang approach can lead to serious problems if large scale software components have not been certified as to having high quality and standard interfaces.

The bottom-up approach is best suited to reuse of software components that are fairly fine grained in the sense that they have a clearly defined, but narrowly limited, functionality. The likelihood of having a large number of such functions to characterize, catalog, maintain, and access is small if there is not a large reuse library of such components.

The top-down approach is best suited to a situation in which there are a few, higher-level components. This can avoid the overhead of maintenance of a reuse library. Reusing large, high-level components has the potential to reduce system costs. However, finding a match of an existing high-level component to an actual set of requirements is relatively rare.

We now turn to a discussion of integration issues for object-oriented programs. It is clear that complete testing of all possible interactions of objects is essentially impossible.

The source code we used for some simple arithmetic with complex numbers that was given in Example 6.5 illustrates this effective impossibility. Consider the possibilities: each of a complex, real, double, or integer operand must be paired with a second operand of the same set of types. This is a minimum of 16 possible cases, each of which must be tested to have even one example of each type tested. There are 64 cases if we allow multiple types of the results of the arithmetic operations, with one test case for each pair of possible argument types and four basic arithmetic operations. This is entirely too much.

Of course, integration issues are even more complex for software that has both procedural and object-oriented portions. We advocate striving for even a higher degree of modularity than normal in this situation. Considering the portions separately as much as possible seems to be the best approach, but there is little research to guide the practitioner.

In some circumstances, another integration technique, known as "plug and play," may be used. It is easiest to explain the technique by an example.

Some software systems, such as those used for aircraft control, can never be taken off-line. For such systems, new modules that add functionality, or modules that are replacements for faulty ones, must be integrated during regular operation. This requires a very careful integration process that we will not discuss here. Of course, new web pages are added to the World Wide Web constantly without affecting essential service, but this is essentially updating the data because of the HTML standard.

As a final note on the technique of software integration, we mention that the coding standards for file organization and naming that we discussed in Chapter 5 can be very helpful in the integration process.

6.10 Managing Change in the Integration Process

We will now consider some issues that occur in software integration, regardless of the approach taken. When a particular software module is changed because of a problem that occurs during system integration, it is necessary to make sure that no new defects were introduced into the system at the same time that another modules was fixed. The interactions between software modules are often quite complex and changes frequently occur. A basic problem that we must address is how to incorporate change into the software integration process.

The change problem can be classified as falling into one of two categories. If the problem occurred because a particular software module was changed, we need to only consider those modules that may be affected by the change. The bottom-up and top-down approaches to software system integration limit the effect of changes to modules that have already been integrated. Thus, only modules at a lower level than the faulty module must be changed in a bottom-up approach. On the other hand, only modules at a higher level than the faulty module must be changed in a top-down approach. Of course, there is no limitation on changes that occur when the big-bang approach is used, which is another objection to the big-bang approach to software integration.

You should note that a configuration management system, such as we discussed in Chapter 5, is essential to control change during integration.

It is clear that we must perform exactly the same tests as before in order to ensure that no new errors are introduced. The test log and test results must be used to compare the results before and after the change. This step is called "regression testing." It should be noted that this use of the term "regression" has only a tenuous connection to a term of the same name that is common in statistics.

There is another issue in software integration, which might be considered as "software change in the large." In this situation, major subsystems or even entire COTS products are changed during the integration process. Perhaps a new version of an operating system or a database software package has been released and the software under integration has to interface with them. This is a relatively common situation in modern competitive software development environments. In this situation, some sort of configuration management is necessary.

At most colleges and universities, computer science students typically compile their programs frequently, making changes to code in response to logical errors that were detected. There are even more compilations during the code entry process, when many students use the compiler to detect typographical or syntax errors.

Most professional software engineers work differently. They may spend much less of their time recompiling and fixing source code and much more time reading it and trying to get the logic correct the first time. The time spent waiting for programs to compile is better spent in more productive activities, at least in the view of most practicing software professionals.

Indeed, many software systems are so large that compilation occurs infrequently. The compilation and linking process may take so long that it only takes place once a day. It would be useless to have each of one hundred programmers spending precious CPU cycles on compilation, when each one might change a single source code file and therefore none of the programmers knows the correct state of the software at any time. In many organizations, the term "build" is used to describe a compiled version of an entire system.

A complex software system may have many builds before it is released. For example, the source code for Microsoft Windows NT, Version 3.51, indicates that this release is build number 1381. Since Microsoft builds its software daily, this indicates the total time that elapsed between the first clean compile of the first version (which was probably a version intended for Microsoft internal use only) and this particular release of the operating system. Restricting compilation of the entire system to once a day is due to the size of the software system. The complete source code and documentation for this release of Windows NT requires four compact disks.

6.11 Performance and Stress Testing

Let's suppose that all relevant software modules and objects have passed their unit tests and been integrated into a complete system. Let's also suppose that the software has passed all integration tests. Before the software is released, it often must go through what is known as "performance testing."

A performance test is just that – it is a means of checking that the software will perform at appropriate levels. There are often requirements specifications that state how fast certain operations will be performed.

A typical performance specification might be something such as:

"The system will process 500 transactions per second."

or

"The system will produce an output of 50 KB per second."

Clearly, these kinds of requirements are common in real-time systems. They are tested by using typical inputs which may be simulations of actual ones expected in operation.

If the software fails a performance test, the performance must be improved. The typical way to do this is to use a "profiler." A profiler is a software tool that allows a software engineer to examine where a software system is spending most of its time during program execution.

Profilers typically "instrument" object code by inserting statements at each function entry point or invocation of an object. These inserted statements control timing information, so that the number of times each function is called and the amount of time spent executing each function can be computed and displayed as necessary. Many profilers also compute the amount of time spent executing specified loops within functions.

Profilers often can be run by setting options on compilers, such as

```
gcc -p file.c
```

on the Free Software Foundation's gcc compiler. This inserts the timing mechanisms in the object code.

On the UNIX system, running the executable (here we have used the default name)

```
a.out
```

followed by the command to produce the output

```
gprof
```

produces something like the following output:

Function	No. Calls	Time	Cumulative
main()	1	1:00:00	100.0 %
slow()	5,000	30:00	50.0 %
slower()	10,000	27:30	45.8 %
slowest()	100,000	2:30	4.2 %

This output indicates that the software is spending most of its time in the functions slow() and slower(), but that only a tiny portion of the execution time is spent in the function slowest(). A person wishing to improve the performance would only look at the modules slow() and slower() rather than the remaining one which accounts for only 4.2 % of the execution time, with only a tiny amount of time for each of the 100,000 calls to it.

A related type of testing is "stress testing." In this type of testing. the intention is to see what happens when the software system is pushed beyond its limits.

Here is a typical scenario. Suppose that the software meets the requirement of processing 500 transactions per second. What happens if the load doubles to 1000 transactions arriving per second? We expect delays. However, we don't want transactions to never get processed by the system because they never get written to a buffer. We don't want the software to crash under excess load, instead it should respond gracefully.

You should note that many systems get overwhelmed by heavy loads. Even the most casual user of the Internet has experienced long delays due to servers being overloaded and unable to process requests efficiently under heavy load.

We note that many techniques for improving software fault tolerance are used to improve operation under stress. Techniques such as exceptions in Java, C++, and Ada, rollback techniques such as those of Randell [RAND75], and denial of service in networks are common approaches to preserve system integrity under stress.

6.12 Quality Assurance

Ask the basic question about the software you are developing: How can I (or my organization) be sure that the software is of sufficient quality to be released? Of course, there must be a systematic process for making sure that everything works as it should. This systematic process of improving quality is called "quality assurance," or "QA."

Quality assurance can be performed by the development and testing teams. Often, it is done by a separate team given just the responsibility of guaranteeing quality.

The QA team may examine the data on the development process to determine if there are many errors that are showing up during the testing and integration phases. The number of software faults detected before release, often referred to as "internal faults," should be decreasing to indicate that many of the faults already have been found and removed. If there is much volatility in the number of faults found in the software, there is reason to suspect the quality of the software. We will discuss this point more systematically in the next section, when we describe software reliability.

The QA team will apply a considerable number of sophisticated statistical tests and techniques with the goal of measuring the quality of the system and comparing it to acceptable standards.

6.13 Software Reliability

Electrical and mechanical equipment is known to follow a "bathtub" curve during its useful life. That is, the equipment is most likely to fail at the beginning of its placement into service because of poor installation, faulty design, or one bad component. After the equipment has been "burned in," it typically works well for some interval of time and then begins to have more and more need for repair, because different components wear out.

Eventually, the cost to repair the equipment becomes too high and it is taken out of service. The situation is shown in Figure 6.11.

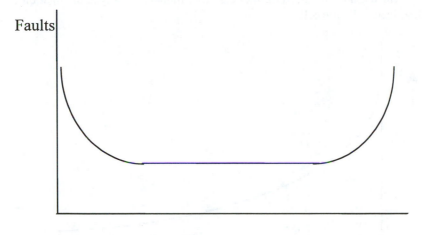

Faults

Time

Figure 6.11. The typical "bathtub curve" for malfunctions of electrical and mechanical equipment.

The term "software reliability" appears confusing at first glance. Software doesn't wear out (although the medium on which the software resides may). Thus, software reliability doesn't seem to be measurable. However, software errors and the lengths of intervals of correct operation *are* measurable quantities.

Software reliability models are based on statistical estimates of the failures remaining in software after each checkpoint in the development life cycle. In this context, the term "checkpoint" can refer to the correction of an error in the software at some phase of the testing process, in some release of the software, or at the time of some external event.

Software reliability models such as those of Musa [MUSA87] or [MUSA93] are the basis for the estimates, which are frequently measured as the mean time between failures, or MTBF.

The basic premise of software reliability is that faults that can cause failures will remain in the software regardless of the efforts used to detect and correct them. Reliability theory estimates the remaining failures, the so-called "residual faults," by using existing fault data collected at the checkpoints to develop a probability model of the distribution of the software's errors.

It is important to note that the data used in the reliability model is collected before the software is released. The data collected is placed into an appropriate probability distribution model that is then used to predict the behavior of the software after delivery.

The organization used for the reliability model in this type of situation is described in Figure 6.12.

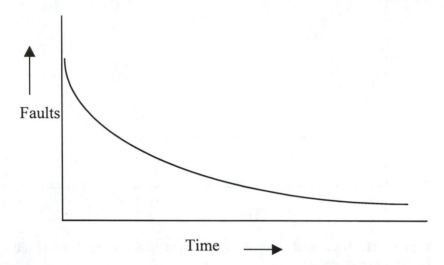

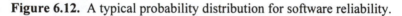

Figure 6.12. A typical probability distribution for software reliability.

The reason for application of a software reliability model to a software system is to determine the probability distribution of software faults over time. The key variable is the time between distinct software faults, the so-called inter-failure time.

This means that the number and timing of faults occurring at each checkpoint in the development process is obtained and the data is then analyzed. The checkpoints can be continually examined during the testing process, at regular time intervals, or at milestones in the development of the source code. A commonly used milestone is the completion of an internal release for the software. Ideally, the information is collected on a per-system or, better yet, on a per-module basis. For simplicity of discussion, we will restrict our attention to a single reliability test of an entire system.

The method of data collection is interesting. The objective is to count the number of failures at each checkpoint in a way that is consistent with the way that the software will actually behave when it is placed into service. In practice, this means that an operational profile must be obtained.

An operational profile is a set of inputs to the software, based on an assessment of how the software will be used in practice. This involves setting likely usage percentages, with sequences of appropriate user inputs also selected. The set of selected inputs is written to a file, which is used as a script to drive the operation of the software that is to be tested for its reliability. Any necessary external data files would also be included. The performance of the software on all the scripts is evaluated for software faults. The scripts should be considered as a stream of inputs to the software.

Clearly, the selection of items in the input stream used for the operational profile is guided by how the software is actually used. Often a profiler is used to determine precisely which functions in the software are exercised in "typical" uses. Many of the choices of inputs are randomly generated. For more details on this process, see [MUSA87] and [FENT96].

Once the data is collected, it must be analyzed. The idea is to fit a probability distribution to the data, so that errors that will occur in the future can be predicted. The most commonly used probability distributions are the Poisson and exponential distributions. See [BOX78], [MONT91] or any good book on applied probability and statistics for more information about estimating probability distributions.

Organizations that collect reliability data should do so using any internal data about errors, as well as modification requests to fix errors after release of the system. The data should be entered into a database and the error prone modules should be checked. This data will help in flagging modules that are likely to cause problems in a reuse situation It will often help in flagging modules and systems that are so complex and difficult to modify and test that they should not be modified unless the change provides extremely large benefits for the organization producing or using the software.

There are several issues to be addressed in reliability modeling. For example, we must be certain that the data is accurate and pertinent. Using only fault data forms in which all information is filled out is not accurate because it may give a biased sample. Test data is not relevant if it attempts to predict failure under operational loads that are different from testing loads.

The recommended practice for reliability is [IEEE88]:

1. Estimate size of source code.

2. Estimate fault density (faults per KLOC). This is best done by reusing the fault density from projects that are similar in their requirements, their development methodology, and their programming environment. If no estimate is available, then a number in the range of 10 (for routine programs) to 1 (in a disciplined environment, with programmers experienced in the application domain) should be assumed.

3. These two numbers are multiplied to give the expected number of faults at the beginning of formal testing.

4. Select a model for the reliability data's probability distribution, generally the Musa Basic Model or the Jelinski-Moranda Model. Several other models, including the Keiller-Littlewood model, could also be used.

5. Determine the key values:

- Initial number of faults

- Probability of executing a specific fault during a single execution (the *fault exposure ratio*). A good default value is $5 * 10^{-7}$. This allows us to model the expected time interval between successive software faults.

- Time for which prediction is to be valid

- Failure probability per fault and unit time

- Initial failure rate

The most important uses of reliability measures are a general assessment about the system's quality and an indication of when to stop testing (when the expected number of errors remaining meets the objective error rate).

This information can indicate where the testing process should be stopped, depending on the ultimate reliability goal of the number of defects remaining per 1000 lines of code.

A typical situation is shown in Figure 6.13. The curved line in this figure represents the probability that a particular number of faults (as measured on the vertical axis) remains in the code at the time indicated by the horizontal axis.

Software fault information is almost always available for software developed in-house. The fault ratio (number of software faults per KLOC) is probably well known and readily available. If not, it can be deduced easily from known size information and testing data. Clearly, any potentially reusable software artifact should be subjected to a severe test of its fault ratio. (Note that detailed reliability information is not likely to be readily available for software that is not developed in-house. It may not even be available for locally developed software if the organization's software development standards to not require the keeping of reliability data.)

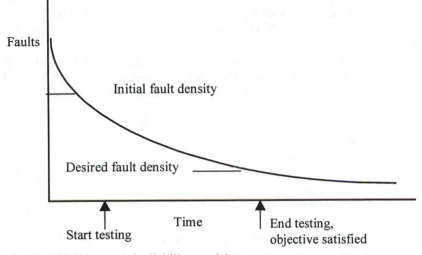

Figure 6.13 The use of reliability models.

In the absence of any information about reliability of the software, it is probably appropriate to assume that it is of the same quality as most other software used for a project. That is, you should assume that its fault ratio is the average for your other systems for similar applications. Be careful of comparing fault ratios between different application domains. There is considerable variation.

6.14 A Manager's Viewpoint on Testing and Integration

Even more than in the early stages of the life cycle, a software manager does not want any unpleasant surprises in the testing and integration phase. The testing process should proceed in an organized, systematic way. A manager will want to review the test plans and some of the test data before testing starts. He or she will also want to make sure that the requirements traceability matrix is checked, perhaps leaving the responsibility for such testing to the QA team. The manager will also insist on regression testing; this is especially critical when an iterative software development process is followed.

Metrics data should be kept and used during testing; the manager will usually arrange to have troublesome modules identified at this stage, with reallocation of resources if necessary.

The integration process must also proceed in a systematic way. Since modules are likely to be changed during integration, the prudent manager will insist on regression testing during integration, also. As was true during testing, the manager will arrange for metrics data to be collected and used during integration. This will also help to identify modules that are troublesome at this stage.

Of course, a manager will also want the process to be efficient, with testing proceeding on schedule. The testing arena is one of the few areas of software engineering where there is agreement about what is desired from a minimal set of tools:

- Test drivers
- Stub generators
- Test harnesses (to execute functions and objects without creating wrapper code)
- Test data management tool
- Regression tester
- Path analyzer (to determine all decision points)
- Static analyzer (to determine anomalies in the source code's organization)

For many software systems, especially those in safety-critical environments, a fault inspection tool will also be used. Such software tools deliberately place faults within code to determine if faults in subsystems can be isolated, or if the effects of the faults propagate throughout the entire software.

6.15 Testing the Major Software Project

We will now apply the techniques of software testing to the large running example that we have been considering throughout this book. Since our system consists of both object-oriented and procedural portions, we will need to employ both types of testing techniques. In addition, we should consider both white-box and black-box methods.

Before we start the testing process, it is a good idea to review the requirements traceability matrix for this project. The goal is to make sure that at least the specific system requirements are tested before system integration begins. We will show the completed requirements traceability matrix in the next section after the system is integrated.

It makes sense to consider the system as being comprised of the subsystems designed in Chapter 5. Thus, the subsystems can naturally be grouped into those that require procedurally based testing using black-box or white-box methods and the interface to the spreadsheet which will use an object-oriented approach to testing. We note also that some requirements are easy to check, such as the ones that require a specific hardware platform and operating system environment in which the software will run.

Let's recall our basic design strategy. We wanted to view the entire software system as being comprised of a set of modules, many of which were obtained from other sources. Clearly our testing strategy should be influenced by the reuse-based strategy that we used to design and implement the system.

What are the natural consequences of this approach? The first thing that comes to mind is that the software utilities we used should be considered as black boxes, with only the interfaces needing to be checked. This is also the approach that we should take when testing the "glueware" used to combine these utilities. It is clear that black-box testing is a natural choice for most of our system.

What about white-box testing? This method appears to be especially appropriate where there are many execution paths and complex internal logic. This seems to characterize the software intended to provide an interface to the operating system for the linking of the names of input files to later routines in the program. Recall that this was to be done by means of command-line arguments. The requirement to allow wild cards in the input file names and to treat multi-level directories properly suggests a complexity that makes checking each path especially important.

Of course some object-oriented methods must be applied to the back end of the system. It seems as if the main questions to be answered about this subsystem's correctness are the completeness of the member functions of the appropriate classes and the proper assignment of default values to member functions.

6.16 Integrating the Major Software Project

We will now apply the techniques of software integration to the large running software example that we have been considering throughout this book. The assumption is that all the modules have been tested individually and that all have passed their tests.

In order to avoid writing a large number of artificial drivers or stubs, we will follow an integration approach that is a hybrid of top-down and bottom-up techniques.

We will start with a top-down approach. The interface will be checked to see if the file names are handled properly. Each input source code file will be checked to see if the first subsystem recognizes the files and the appropriate directories. This is little removed from the testing techniques that we would apply to this subsystem if we tested it by itself.

Once we have tested the initial subsystem properly and linked to the operating system by means of command-line arguments, we will then begin linking the analysis subsystem modules in groups. Naturally, we will consider each of the analysis tools as a single entity for the purpose of software integration.

There is one point to be discussed before we begin. MS/DOS has a facility to connect the output of one executable file to the input of another using pipes, in much the same way that UNIX allows the pipe method of interprocess communication. Commands such as

```
type file.txt |more
```

allow multiple actions to take place with simple commands. It is conceivable that we could link file analysis tools by using a command such as

```
dir | analysis1 | analysis2 > outfile.xls
```

where `outfile.xls` is a spreadsheet input file. We choose not to do this because the system is very fragile in the sense that the entire process will terminate if there is an unexpected error in one of the component processes. We will develop the code incrementally using more program-oriented linking to make an entirety.

The integrated system grows incrementally. The first modules we link in to our desired system are those in the subsystem to analyze C source code files. We develop the "glueware" to bridge any gaps between what is produced by the subsystem we developed to interface to the operating system and the analysis tool we use for C programs. This is tested in the most rudimentary way, using a set of test files that was used for unit testing and checking that the software runs to completion and produces the same output. Our primary concern is the appearance of two different functions named `main()`, one in the initial subsystem and the other in the software tool for analyzing C programs. The easiest thing to do is to rename the `main()` function in the downloaded utility software system. A name such as `C_main()` might be appropriate as the new name.

Precisely the same steps must be followed in order to integrate the other software utilities into an entire package. This again is a top-down approach to software integration.

The integration of the object-oriented portion of the software into the entire system will be done from the other direction. The bottom-up approach will be followed, linking the output to a spreadsheet.

Table 6.7
Completed requirements traceability matrix for the major continuing
software engineering project.

# Requirement	Design	Code	Test
1. Intel-based	Y	Y	Y
2. Windows 95	Y	Y	Y
3. Windows 95 UI	Y	Y	Y
4. Consistent With Excel 4.0	Y	Y	Y
5. System One Size Only	Y	Y	Y
6. One MB System	*	*	*
7. One MB Disk Space	*	*	*
8. One 1.44 MB Floppy Disk	*	*	*
9. Includes Installation	Y	Y	Y
10. No Decompression Utility	Y	Y	Y
11. One input file at a time	Y	Y	Y
12. Size of each function	Y	Y	Y
13. Size of each file	Y	Y	Y
14. Size of system	Y	Y	Y
15. Compute totals	Y	Y	Y
16. Develop std for C, C++, Ada	Y	Y	Y
17. Batch-oriented system	Y	Y	Y
18. Precisely define LOC	Y	Y	Y
19. Measure separately	Y	Y	Y
20. No error checking of input	Y	Y	Y
21. Front end in C or C++	Y	Y	Y
22. Batch processing	Y	Y	Y
23. File names limited to 8.3	Y	Y	Y
24. Wild cards can be used	Y	Y	Y
25. Dead code ignored			
26. No special compilers needed	Y	Y	Y
27. Microsoft Excel 4.0 needed	Y	Y	Y

Finally, the two collections of software modules connect, mesh together
and we have a complete system.

The completed requirements traceability matrix is given in Table 6.7.
Note that we can now measure the size of our system to see if it fits on a
floppy disk and the executable file satisfies the one-megabyte limitation. (Of
course, it didn't – we eliminated this requirement when our customer asked
for a graphical, web-based user interface.)

From a project management perspective, we should also do a status
check. Are we ahead of schedule (unlikely), behind schedule (likely), or

approximately on target? Have there been any unpleasant surprises, any portions of the system that were more difficult than we expected? Does any portion of the system require extra attention, perhaps additional resources? Have technology or market pressures rendered any portion of the system obsolete? (Recall that we did this status check earlier.)

Further Reading

There are many excellent general books on testing software, including two editions of Beizer's ([BEIZ83], [BEIZ90]), Howden [HOWD87], Myers [MYER79], DeMillo et al. [DEMI87], and Marick [MARI97]. Miller and Howden have a tutorial book on software testing that includes many of the earlier research papers in the field [MILL78]. Most of these references concentrate on procedural programs and include little information about testing object-oriented programs.

There is a URL for software testing tools:

```
http://www.stlabs.com/marick/faqs/tools.htm
```

This web site is managed by Brian Marick, who is a well-known researcher in the area of software testing. See also the URL from Reliable Software Technology Corporation

```
http://www.rstcorp.com
```

There are several other URLs for information on software testing. The STORM software testing home page at Middle Tennessee State University contains links to other webs sites for software testing and provides a directory of researchers in the field of software testing. The URL is

```
http://www.mtsu.edu/storm
```

The link

```
www.gimpel.com
```

points to a testing tool, PC-lint, for C and C++. This is a great aid in providing the information so helpful to users of the UNIX utility lint in terms of lack of consistency between program modules.

A web site that provides a test bed of common source code files to be used to validate theories and conjectures about software testing is maintained by several researchers at Howard University. The URL for this project, known as WASTE (Web site for Archiving Software Testing Examples) is

`http://angelou.imappl.org/Waste`

Unfortunately, there are few readily available sources of information on software integration.

Summary

Testing strategies for classes are different from those for testing ordinary procedurally developed programs. Some common techniques for testing object-oriented programs and classes are encapsulation, minimalization, exhaustion of a depth, inheritance, and interactive methods.

Software testing can be white box or black box, depending on whether the details of the source code are used to determine the test cases or just the module interfaces.

Software integration is the process of combining modules, objects, subsystems, and/or COTS products to make complete systems. Integration can proceed top down, in which case lower-level modules must be stubbed in.

On the other hand, bottom-up software integration requires creation of higher-level drivers. Hybrid approaches to software integration are also possible.

Regression testing is the process of ensuring that changes made to fix one software fault do not incur other faults. It is essential during software integration.

Software reliability is a statistically based technique used to determine when testing is sufficient to release the software.

Software that is changed during integration can benefit by being controlled by configuration management

Exercises

1. List all the black-box test cases for the source code given in Example 6.3. Which test cases do you think are the most important? Why?

2. List all white-box test cases for the source code given in Example 6.3. Which test cases do you think are the most important? Why?

3. Examine a common software application. Determine a set of test cases that you would use if you were in charge of testing this software.

4. Devise a new class to describe floating point numbers. The precision of the floating point numbers will be part of the class. The three precisions to be considered are `float`, `double`, and `long double`.

5. Assume that you have created the class described in problem 4. Assume also that functions have been written to perform all arithmetic operations on this class and that these functions overload the +, -, *, and / operators. What combinations of arguments must be tested for the overloaded + operator for this class?

6. List the special cases that should be tested for correct treatment of overloading of the + operator in Example 6.5. Also list the special cases needed for testing of the << and assignment operators.

7. List all test cases that you believe are necessary to test the objects defined in Example 6.5.

8. List all test cases that you believe are necessary to test the objects defined in example 3.2. Compare your answer to the set of test cases that you determined for example 3.1. Which new test cases are due to the presence of inheritance?

9. List all test cases that you believe are necessary to test the objects defined in example 3.4. Compare your answer to the set of test cases that you determined for examples 3.1 and 3.2. What changes are caused by the presence of multiple inheritance?

10. Apply the techniques of software testing described in this chapter to the large running software example that we have been considering in this book.

11. Apply the techniques of software integration described in this chapter to the large running software example that we have been considering in this book.

Chapter 7

Delivery, Installation, and Documentation

7.1 Delivery

Even the best software is of no use until it is made available to potential users. Let's suppose that the software system has been designed, developed, and tested according to the system requirements. It is now time to make the software available to its users.

The software is usually delivered according to one of the following three scenarios, depending on the nature of the relationship between the customer and the software development organization:

1. If there is a single user, or a very limited number of users, then the software is usually delivered on magnetic tape, diskettes, or CD, with the delivery format determined by the project's requirements. The software delivery team is responsible for making certain that the software can be given to the single user and that the software can be installed correctly on the user's machine.

2. If there are many potential users of the software and the software is to be sold in stores or by other retail mechanisms, the software is usually delivered on diskettes or CD, with the format determined by the marketplace. The software delivery team is responsible for making certain that the software can be duplicated properly so that it can be distributed. An installation script or installer is provided by the delivery team. The responsibility for installation rests with the user.

3. If there are many potential users of the software and the software is to be delivered electronically, using ftp or similar transfer programs, there is no need for multiple copies of the software to be created. In this case, the responsibility of the software's delivery team is to make certain that the software can be obtained properly. An installation script or installer is provided by the delivery team. The responsibility for installation rests with the user.

We will now discuss each of these delivery scenarios in turn:

The first delivery scenario describes a software system that is intended for a single customer. The customer is likely to have personnel trained in the use of this software. If the software is not delivered to the customer according to the specifications in the contract's requirements, the customer will not make the final payments. Thus, the customer will inform the software development organization that delivery was not successful.

The typical problems with installation in this scenario are:

- Failure of the physical medium on which the software resides.
- Incorrect placement of the software into directories, resulting in incorrect directory names.
- Incorrect use of names of subdirectories, making subsystems inaccessible.
- Incorrect access permissions, making files inaccessible.
- Incorrect formatting of the software, such as using incorrect conversion tools for compressing or uncompressing files.
- Incorrect documentation of the delivery instructions.

Each potential problem should be considered in a pre-delivery run-through during which the installation steps are tested carefully.

The second delivery scenario is especially appropriate for shrink-wrapped software that is sold in stores or by mail. Each of the points raised earlier in this section clearly also applies in this scenario. In addition, the software producing organization must take into account the lack of a direct developer-customer relationship in this situation. Therefore, the developer cannot have detailed knowledge of each potential customer's hardware environment, or the software that has already been installed on the customer's computer.

The lack of control of the user's environment can create serious problems. Users may have great difficulty installing the software because their environment is different from the one in which the software was developed.

Users may also vary greatly in their computer expertise. (Most of the readers of this book behave heard of the person who called a personal computer vendor's hot line because the "cup holder" was broken. Of course, the "cup holder" was the CD drive!)

In the second delivery scenario, the most important additional step for the organization developing the software is to do multiple dry runs during the pre-delivery process, using a variety of environments and users.

The third delivery scenario best describes software that is to be made available to potential users electronically over a medium such as the Internet. As was the case in the second scenario, all the problems described previously in this section apply. There are similar problems also due to the variation in operating system and application environments.

There are two new problems that can occur in the third delivery scenario: collection of payment for the software and protection of the host computer used as a remote server for the software. A discussion of electronic payment for the software is best left to experts on Internet commerce. In any event, anything you read in a book is likely to be out of date soon, given the explosive growth of the Internet.

The server that contains the software will have some form of remote access, using anonymous ftp or some other method of file transfer. As such, the server is at least slightly vulnerable to intrusions. Thus, a decision must be made as to the relationship between the risk of having intruders trash an entire system and providing no access. The use of such security devices as firewalls is highly recommended. See the book on computer security by Charles Pfleeger [PFLE96] for more information on this topic.

Determining which delivery scenario applies is usually easy. After we have addressed the points raised earlier, we must decide upon proper file formats and compression/decompression utilities. It is often necessary to reduce the size of files to be able to put them on fewer floppy disks, special drives (such as Jaz or ZIP), magnetic tapes, or CDs. Reducing the amount of traffic over the Internet is also a good idea.

We will be content to list a few utilities that might be used when selecting a format in which to deliver software. A brief list of formats for source code and other text files is given in Table 7.1. We have not considered special formats and standards such as JPEG, MPEG, TIF, or GIF for storing graphical or other non-textual material.

Table 7.1

Some utilities used for compressing, decompressing, or storing software files.

Utility	Operating system
tar	UNIX
bar	UNIX
cpio	UNIX
Gzip	Many
Gunzip	Many
Pkzip	Microsoft Windows, MS-DOS
Binhex	Macintosh

We will now give an example of how such compression, delivery, and decompression might be used. My colleague Will Craven at Howard University has developed a set of UNIX shell scripts for file transfer which provide a smooth interface to some standard UNIX utilities that have complex interfaces and are not "user friendly." The scripts use the Bourne shell.

The first script is given the name "stow." The script will allow a user to place all files in a directory in a single archive file that is in the UNIX cpio format. This format is compressed and thus reduces the amount of disk space needed for storage and the amount of traffic on a network.

Before using stow utility, the user must create a directory with all necessary files. The user then changes the working directory to the parent directory. The stow utility is used with the syntax

```
stow  directory_name  archive_name
```

The source code for stow is

```
#! /bin/sh
# 2-7-88 (wdc) Put all files under specified
# directory into archive
#
case $# in
 2) if [ -d $1 ]; then
   if [`du -s $1|cut -f1` -lt `ulimit`];then
      find $1 -print -depth | cpio -oac > $2
   else
      echo " $1 is too large to stow"
   fi
   else
    echo " $1 is not a directory"
   fi;;
 *) echo 'Usage:stow source destination';;
esac
# 11-16-88 (wdc) -- insert `ulimit`
# 10-19-89 (wdc) -- -a option on cpio
# 9-26-94(wdc)--depth option on find
# no -v on cpio
# 10-4-96 (wdc) -- force /bin/sh
```

Let's examine the shell script that makes up the stow utility. The comments (lines beginning with the # sign) help explain the software's operation. The script was created in 1988 by Will Craven. The exclamation point immediately following the # symbol on the first line indicates that the Bourne shell is to be used, rather than the C, bash, Korn, or POSIX shells. This change was added in October 1996. Note that this statement has the effect of constraining the environment of a user to one that is controlled by the software designer.

The `case` statement suggests that we are looking to match the shell variable $#, which represents the number of arguments to the shell script other than its name, with the value 2. If there are precisely two arguments to `stow`, the first argument, $1, is tested to see if it is the name of a directory. If the second argument is the name of a directory, then control passes to the nested `if` statement.

The nested `if` statement is complex, testing for disk usage with `du` and cutting off recursive directory search if the number of disk blocks for the directory specified in $1 exceeds the system limit on file sizes, `ulimit`. The `find` command as given here prints the names of all files and passes them to the `cpio` archive which is stored in the file whose name was given in the argument $2.

Note that the `stow` utility was modified several times. This is an example of software maintenance.

While the shell programming in the `stow` utility is complicated, it is simpler to remember and more intuitive than a call to the single shell command

```
cat directory_name|cpio -oac > archive_name
```

The meaning of the o, a, and c options to the `cpio` command are difficult to remember for the non-expert UNIX user.

The second script described in this section is given the name "huput." The script will allow a user to move an archive file that is in UNIX `cpio` format to the special `rje` directory of someone else (usually an instructor). The purpose of an `rje` directory is to allow individuals to place files in a different user's directory. The name `rje` is a vestige of the early time-sharing multiprocessing period in operating systems design; the name stands for "remote job entry."

The `huput` utility will change permissions of each of the component files in the archive to those of the person to whom the archive is submitted. This utility is used with the syntax

```
huput archive_name source_name
```

The source code for huput is

```
#! /bin/sh
# 10-6-88(wdc)send file(s) to rje directory
#
case $# in
  0|1) echo " usage: $0 file[file ...] user" ;;
  *)   list=$*
    shift `expr $# - 1`
```

```
    login=$1
    if pw=`grep " ^${login}:"  /etc/passwd`
      then  rje=`echo $pw | cut -d: -f6`/rje
    if [ -d $rje -a -w $rje ]
      then  set $list
        while [ $# -gt 1 ]
          do file=${rje}/`basename $1`
            if cp $1 $rje
              then  chown $login $file
                    echo $file
            fi
          shift
        done
    else
      echo " Can't write to rje of login\07"
    fi
    else echo `No such login!\07'
    fi;;
esac
#
# 10-4-96 (wdc) -- force /bin/sh
```

The huput utility is also a UNIX shell script. It has a series of nested if statements within the major case statement. The first shift statement uses the value of an arithmetic expression (included in backquotes) as an argument. This is a tricky construction. See Chapter 2 of the author's book *Advanced Topics in UNIX* for more information [LEAC94].

The value of the login argument is checked against entries in the password file /etc/passwd using the UNIX pattern matching utility named grep. If there is a match, then the files are sent to the rje directory of the person whose directory is the target. The chown utility is used to change ownership of the archive file to the recipient.

The final script described in this section is given the name "unstow." The script will expand a single archive that is in the UNIX cpio format into a directory that contains the files in the archive. The unstow utility is used with the syntax

```
unstow archive_name
```

The source code for unstow is
```
#! /bin/sh
# 2-7-88 (wdc) get all files out of archive
#
case $# in
```

```
 1)      cpio -icdmv <$1;;
 *)      echo 'Usage:  unstow source';;
esac
#
# 10-4-96 (wdc) -- force /bin/sh
```

Fortunately, this script is simpler than the previous two. As before, the first statement in this script forces the use of the Bourne shell. It also constrains the user's environment, at least temporarily. The case statement is used for control of execution flow and the script is well documented.

Obviously, different delivery scripts are needed for different environments. The scripts presented here are highly UNIX-oriented and may not apply directly to any other environment. However, the principles are the same for many delivery situations:

- It is always necessary to give the user or installer access to the files so that any permissions can be changed.
- The user's environment is temporarily constrained for ease of programming.
- It is necessary to provide wrappers to hide users from arcane operating system utilities, especially those with many options.
- It is easier to create an archive and transfer it, rather than ask the user to transfer multiple files.

As a final note, the use of archives and compressed formats can reduce network traffic and is, therefore, considerate of other users.

7.2 Installation

Installation of software can often be quite time consuming. For example, installation of an operating system is often a sequential process of "bootstrapping." That is, a portion of the operating system (a so-called "mini-kernel") software frequently must be loaded first. After this, the first portion is used to install a second portion (the entire kernel and the "root file system"). The second portion is then used to install additional portions (such as the complete /usr file system), and so on.

Because of the issues raised previously in this chapter concerning potential failures during delivery, successful software installation often depends on having precise knowledge of the software that has already been installed on the system. Inconsistencies must be noted, particularly with major upgrades of software. The best installation software utilities often include an installation log to aid in troubleshooting.

We note explicitly that the same ideas, if not the same specific details, apply to such utilities as the "Setup" installer for Microsoft Windows 95, 98, and NT, and the VISE installer for the Macintosh. These utilities are often invoked with formatted text files.

As an example of the use of the Setup utility, the input file for the OSA analyzer developed by Aaron Rogers, Sean Armstrong, and Melvin Henry discussed earlier is given below. Note that the file indicates the name of the executable file, path names where library files can be found, links to dynamically linked libraries (DLLs), and a check of the Windows Registry to determine if the most recent versions of library files are present or need to be updated.

```
[Bootstrap]
SetupTitle=Install
SetupText=Copying Files, please stand by.
CabFile=Omega Source Analyzer.CAB
Spawn=Setup1.exe
Uninstal=st6unst.exe
TmpDir=msftqws.pdw
Cabs=1


[Bootstrap Files]
File1=@VB6STKIT.DLL,$(WinSysPathSysFile),,,6/18/98
1:00:00 AM,102912,6.0.81.69
File2=@COMCAT.DLL,$(WinSysPathSysFile),$(DLLSelfReg
ister),,5/31/98 1:00:00 AM,22288,4.71.1460.1
File3=@MSVCRT40.DLL,$(WinSysPathSysFile),,,5/31/98
1:00:00 AM,326656,4.21.0.0
File4=@STDOLE2.TLB,$(WinSysPathSysFile),$(TLBRegist
er),,10/15/98 1:04:00 PM,17920,2.30.4265.1
File5=@ASYCFILT.DLL,$(WinSysPathSysFile),,,10/15/98
1:04:00 PM,147728,2.30.4265.1
File6=@OLEPRO32.DLL,$(WinSysPathSysFile),$(DLLSelfR
egister),,10/15/98 1:04:00 PM,164112,5.0.4265.1
File7=@OLEAUT32.DLL,$(WinSysPathSysFile),$(DLLSelfR
egister),,10/15/98 1:04:00 PM,598288,2.30.4265.1
File8=@MSVBVM60.DLL,$(WinSysPathSysFile),$(DLLSelfR
egister),,10/15/98 1:04:00 PM,1409024,6.0.82.44
[IconGroups]
Group0=Omega Source Analyzer v1.0
PrivateGroup0=True
Parent0=$(Programs)


[Omega Source Analyzer v1.0]
```

```
Icon1=""Omega Source Analyzer.exe""
Title1=Omega Source Analyzer v1.0
StartIn1=$(AppPath)

[Setup]
Title=Omega Source Analyzer v1.0
DefaultDir=$(ProgramFiles)\osaproj
AppExe=Omega Source Analyzer.exe
AppToUninstall=Omega Source Analyzer.exe

[Setup1 Files]
File1=@MDAC_TYP.EXE,$(AppPath),,,6/26/98      1:00:00
AM,8124720,4.71.1015.0
File2=@RDOCURS.DLL,$(WinSysPath),,$(Shared),6/18/98
1:00:00 AM,151552,5.0.81.69
File3=@MSRDO20.DLL,$(WinSysPath),$(DLLSelfRegister)
,$(Shared),6/18/98 1:00:00 AM,393216,6.0.81.69
File4=@DATAFORM.OCX,$(WinSysPath),$(DLLSelfRegister
),$(Shared),6/24/98 1:00:00 AM,541728,6.0.0.8169
File5=@CHARTWIZ.OCX,$(WinSysPath),$(DLLSelfRegister
),$(Shared),6/24/98 1:00:00 AM,147456,6.0.0.8177
File6=@MSCHRT20.OCX,$(WinSysPath),$(DLLSelfRegister
),$(Shared),6/26/98 1:00:00 AM,1008432,6.0.81.77
File7=@VB5DB.DLL,$(WinSysPath),,$(Shared),6/18/98
1:00:00 AM,89360,6.0.81.69
File8=@MSREPL35.DLL,$(WinSysPathSysFile),,,4/24/98
1:00:00 AM,407312,3.51.623.0
File9=@MSRD2X35.DLL,$(WinSysPathSysFile),$(DLLSelfR
egister),,4/24/98 1:00:00 AM,252176,3.51.623.0
File10=@EXPSRV.DLL,$(WinSysPathSysFile),,,6/18/98
1:00:00 AM,378128,6.0.0.8167
File11=@VBAJET32.DLL,$(WinSysPathSysFile),,,6/18/98
1:00:00 AM,30992,6.0.1.8167
File12=@MSJINT35.DLL,$(WinSysPathSysFile),,,4/24/98
1:00:00 AM,123664,3.51.623.0
File13=@MSJTER35.DLL,$(WinSysPathSysFile),,,4/24/98
1:00:00 AM,24848,3.51.623.0
File14=@MSJET35.DLL,$(WinSysPathSysFile),$(DLLSelfR
egister),,4/24/98 1:00:00 AM,1045776,3.51.623.4
File15=@DAO350.DLL,$(MSDAOPath),$(DLLSelfRegister),
$(Shared),4/27/98 1:00:00 AM,570128,3.51.1608.0
File16=@DBGRID32.OCX,$(WinSysPath),$(DLLSelfRegister
),$(Shared),6/26/98 1:00:00 AM,525352,5.1.81.4
```

```
File17=@DBLIST32.OCX,$(WinSysPath),$(DLLSelfRegister
),$(Shared),6/24/98 1:00:00 AM,200496,6.0.81.69
File18=@COMCTL32.OCX,$(WinSysPath),$(DLLSelfRegister
),$(Shared),6/24/98 1:00:00 AM,609584,6.0.80.22
File19=@RICHED32.DLL,$(WinSysPathSysFile),,,5/7/98
1:00:00 AM,174352,4.0.993.4
File20=@RICHTX32.OCX,$(WinSysPath),$(DLLSelfRegister
),$(Shared),6/24/98 1:00:00 AM,203576,6.0.81.69
File21=@TABCTL32.OCX,$(WinSysPath),$(DLLSelfRegister
),$(Shared),6/24/98 1:00:00 AM,209192,6.0.81.69
File22=@COMDLG32.OCX,$(WinSysPath),$(DLLSelfRegister
),$(Shared),6/24/98 1:00:00 AM,140096,6.0.81.69
File23=@Omega                                  Source
Analyzer.exe,$(AppPath),,,4/21/99            4:45:40
PM,806912,1.0.0.0


; The following lines may be deleted in order to
obtain extra
; space for customizing this file on a full
installation diskette.
;
;
XXXXXXXXXXXXXXXXXXXXXXXXXXXXXXXXXXXXXXXXXXXXXXXXXXXX
XXXXXXXXXXXXXXXXXXXXXXXXXXXXXXXXXXXXXXXXXXXXXXXXXXXX
```

In the remainder of this section, we will provide a sample installation log from the d_malloc software system. This software is available from the Internet from the site

```
ftp.letters.com/src.dmalloc
```

using anonymous ftp. This software is a CASE tool that improves on the C malloc() function. The developer of d_malloc requests a license fee of $35 for use of this system. Notice that this is a simple solution to the problem of obtaining payment.

The d_malloc software is intended primarily to be used on UNIX systems with the GNU C compiler available from the Free Software Foundation. Notice the high degree of information provided to the installer as the installation script is executed. Note also that the installation log provides some instructions to the software installer about the next step in the installation process, which is using the UNIX make utility.

```
loading cache ./config.cache
Configuring for the dmalloc library
```

Please see the PERMISSIONS file if this is being
used in a commercial setting.

checking for build utilities:
checking for gcc... (cached) gcc
checking whether we are using GNU C... (cached) yes
checking whether gcc accepts -g... (cached) yes
checking for compiler flags to enable ANSI
characteristics:
checking whether cross-compiling... (cached) no
checking BSD compatible install...(cached)
./install-sh -c
checking for ranlib... (cached) ranlib
checking for working const... (cached) yes
checking how to run the C preprocessor... (cached)
gcc -E
checking for ANSI C header files... (cached) yes
checking for size_t... (cached) yes

checking for important functionality:
checking for sbrk... (cached) yes
checking for heap ordering...
checking for basic-block size...
checking for getpagesize... (cached) no
checking for data-alignment size...

checking for abort() not calling free...
checking for abort... (cached) yes

checking functions:
checking for atexit... (cached) yes
checking for on_exit... (cached) no
checking for fork... (cached) yes
checking for getpid... (cached) yes
checking for time... (cached) yes
checking for bcmp... (cached) yes
checking for bcopy... (cached) yes
checking for memset... (cached) yes
checking for strchr... (cached) yes
checking for strrchr... (cached) yes
checking for strcat... (cached) yes
checking for strlen... (cached) yes
checking for strcmp... (cached) yes

```
checking for strcpy... (cached) yes
checking for strtok... (cached) yes

checking various functions for argv files:
checking for strncmp... (cached) yes
checking for strncpy... (cached) yes

checking various functions for argument checking:
checking for bzero... (cached) yes
checking for memcpy... (cached) yes
checking for memccpy... (cached) yes
checking for memchr... (cached) yes
checking for memcmp... (cached) yes
checking for index... (cached) yes
checking for rindex... (cached) yes
checking for strcasecmp... (cached) yes
checking for strncasecmp... (cached) yes
checking for strdup... (cached) yes
checking for strspn... (cached) yes
checking for strcspn... (cached) yes
checking for strncat... (cached) yes
checking for strpbrk... (cached) yes
checking for strstr... (cached) yes


updating cache ./config.cache
creating ./config.status
creating Makefile
creating conf.h
conf.h is unchanged
creating dmalloc.h.2
creating settings.h from settings.dist

Done!!

Please check-out Makefile and conf.h to make sure
that sane configuration values were a result.
You may want to change values in settings.h before
running 'make'.
```

The last two statements in the installation log illustrate the implicit assumptions made by the author of the d_malloc software about he level of knowledge and experience of the software installer. The term "sane configuration values" can only be meaningful to an installer who is sufficiently familiar with UNIX to determine if the configuration values are "sane." The same statement applies to anyone considering making changes to the file `settings.h` or to any other header file.

Compare this installation process to the installation process associated with most software for personal computers. A software package (known appropriately as an "installer") can either be a multi-purpose package available for general use or one designed specifically for this application. The installer software usually prompts the user for a choice of installation directories and performs the rest automatically.

This type of installation process is much simpler, at least when it works. The difficulty is the potential conflict with other software already residing on the system. Removal of such conflicts can be very difficult without both installation logs and knowledge of where critical files are stored.

The type of installation process chosen largely depends on the intended user. The three scenarios described for software delivery reflect the likely users and, as such, the degree of automation of the installation process.

There is one last point to make about installation procedures, especially for the personal computer system. While they do require some detailed system knowledge, utilities such as the "Setup" installer for Microsoft Windows 95, 98, and NT do not require any special licensing arrangement in order to use them.

7.3 Documentation

Even the best software with the most intuitive user interface needs some form of documentation. The documentation can be in any of the following forms:

- Internal documentation (embedded in the source code files).
- External documentation in the form of requirements and design documents.
- Additional documentation explaining why design decisions were made, as in a design rationale.
- Manuals, such as user, operations, or installation manuals.
- On-line help that is part of the software itself.

Each of these forms of documentation has its own place within the software development process. Since these forms are so different, we will discuss each of them in a separate section.

There is one issue that applies to more than one type of documentation. Many long-lived systems have multiple releases. There is often a problem for documenters as to how to organize their materials in such cases. The choices are between having a single basis document, with many release notes indicating changes in the most recent version, and having entirely new documentation for each release. The first approach is less costly in terms of printing, but can be a problem in terms of understanding. The second choice makes the documentation easier to understand, but can easily fill up all available bookshelves in an office. Both approaches are used in practice. (Advice to beginning software engineers: avoid sharing an office with a person who has no room in bookcases or filing cabinets because of large stacks of paper documents. There won't be any room for the things you need for your work.)

We note that the Internet can make some forms of documentation easier to disseminate and store. For example, the problem of multiple versions of documentation for different releases can be reduced by the use of some form of configuration management.

7.4 Internal Documentation

The term "internal documentation" refers to documentation that is included within the source code itself. Internal documentation may be limited to comments that are embedded within individual source code files. More commonly, it is also provided in readme files. Usually each source code directory and the parent directory of the entire system contain their own readme files.

Naturally, the coding standards of an organization take precedence over any general statement concerning internal documentation made in this book. You should keep in mind the discussion of coding standards that was given in Chapter 5. Nevertheless, we can make some general statements about internal documentation issues:

1. Most organizations, especially if they are designing software that is to be reused or maintained, require extensive amounts of documentation.
2. It is neither practical nor desirable to document every program statement with a comment.
3. Good coding practices, such as naming conventions for files and subsystem directories, can aid in documentation.

The first point can cause some confusion for beginning software engineers. Many software standards require prologs or file headers for each source code file. The purpose is to indicate the basic functionality of the functions or procedures that are included in the file. This is followed by a detailed information header for each function or procedure included in the source code file. Certainly each major block of source code or each major branch of control will require additional commenting.

The second point to be made about documentation is that not every line needs to be commented. In general, meaningless documentation is not helpful. As an example, notice that nothing is added by the two comments below:

```
i = i + 1;  /* add one to the variable i */
temp = x;    /* assign value of x to temp */
x = y;       /* assign value of y to x */
y = temp;    /* assign value of temp to y */
```

A far better way to comment these lines is:

```
i = i + 1;
/* swap x and y */
temp = x;
x = y;
y = temp;
```

Our third point is the effect of good naming conventions for files and subsystems on documentation. Organization of a source code directory into three subdirectories named database, GUI, and processing, makes it easy to determine the first step when trying to fix a problem with the graphical user interface. Even a cursory examination of directory and file names is often sufficient to eliminate several potential sources of problems.

There is a last, informal rule of thumb that has been passed from programmer to programmer: "If the documentation and source code do not agree, they are both wrong."   Keep this in mind as you are documenting source code. We view documentation as an integral part of software development activity. Attempting to document the code by "commenting" it at the last minute appears to be the greatest cause of this inconsistency problem. Besides, documenting the code as you develop it can make your development more efficient because you can tell what you last worked on.

7.5 External Documentation

External documentation includes requirements and design documents, which are generally not given to potential users of a system, and training guides, which generally are.

The complete requirements and design documents should be produced and made available to the managers and technical monitors of software development projects. The documents may be in both written and electronic form. If electronic form is used, the documents may be stored in the format of the word processing program that produced them, or in a display-oriented format such as PostScript or Portable Document Format (PDF).

Often these external documents are signed off by a group known as the technical publications office, which is commonly known as "tech pubs." Tech pubs is responsible for creating and formatting external documentation that may have been started by others, proofreading the documentation and checking it for technical consistency.

The most important members of a technical publications team are technical writers. They have experience in organizing documents and putting them into concise, standard English. It is important to have technical writers begin working on a software product's documentation well ahead of the deadline for release of a product, so that any major reorganization of documentation can be done if necessary.

External documentation of a software system is, by its nature, separated from the source code associated with the same system. Thus, there is a major problem with consistency between the different forms of documentation. One potential advantage of CASE tools is the ability to have common views of software and its documentation.

7.6 Design Rationales

Many large software systems have design rationales which attempt to explain the thinking behind several decisions that were made in the system's design. These are sometimes helpful in clarifying ambiguities that arise after a system has been put into use.

Perhaps the most widely available design rationale is *Rationale for the Design of the Ada Programming Language* [ICHB86] by Ichbiah, Barnes, Firth, and Woodger. This book is essential for an understanding of the principles used in the creation of the Ada programming language.

While not technically a design rationale, the book *Annotated C++ Reference Manual* by Margaret Ellis and Bjarne Stroustrup provides some related information for the C++ language [ELLI90].

Apart from their historical interest to researchers in the area of programming language evolution, these rationales can explain how to answer many questions about proper program design and library usage that cannot be answered by other language reference manuals.

On a personal note, I was recently involved with an effort at NASA to rehost a software system that was used for acquiring image data from a particular spacecraft, checking and organizing this data, and making the data available to widely scattered scientific researchers in a variety of formats. The original software system was developed in the 1970s. The software was to be rehosted from a collection of mixed FORTRAN and assembly language code on an obsolete mainframe to modern workstations. All paper copies of original requirements and design documents were lost. Only the source code, executable code, and operations manuals were still in existence. Reengineering the system to a modern environment would have been much easier if the other documentation had been available.

Our first task was to develop a rationale for certain previously made design and operational decisions so that it would be easy to determine which portions of the new software could be ported from the existing mainframe and which should be rewritten or discarded due to advances in technology which made porting them inappropriate. The rest of this work was more straightforward once the design rationale was developed. A cost savings of nearly 20% was obtained simply by making the initial effort to understand the naming conventions used in the design, thereby removing duplicates [LEAC98].

7.7 Installation, User, Training, and Operations Manuals

The purpose of an installation manual should be clear from the discussion earlier in this chapter. Any system configuration information should be included there.

A user manual is intended for normal system use. Generally, such manuals are short and describe a few simple commands that can be used to provide most of the functionality of the system. Additional functionality may be documented in a second, longer manual. Many software systems come with a simple "getting started" manual and a more detailed manual for day-to-day operations.

When the software is sufficiently complex or controls mission-critical or safety-critical systems, separate manuals for training and software operation frequently will be necessary. Needless to say, training and operations manuals must be tested on actual people, preferably with the likely users themselves. Typically, a technical contract monitor will be responsible for ensuring that the manuals are adequate.

It should be noted that a large industry has evolved just to handle technical training issues for software packages.

7.8 On-Line Documentation

The term "on-line documentation" refers to assistance that is provided for users as part of the software itself. As such, the decision about including on-line documentation should have been made long before the software system is getting its final documentation.

The creator of an on-line facility must choose between developing an application-specific help system and using a general-purpose one with the information specific to the particular application inserted as necessary. We note that the ability to use a general-purpose, on-line help system provides an enormous competitive advantage to makers of "suites" of related office software such as the Microsoft Office, Claris Works, or Lotus Smart Suite collections of word processors, spreadsheets, database systems, and electronic mail programs.

On-line help for software can be one of two forms:

- A set of pages of documents (often linked in a hypertext format) can appear either from a menu that is always visible or from the use of a particular key.
- An "intelligent agent" or "wizard" that interacts with the user can be invoked automatically whenever certain combinations of actions have occurred.

In the first case, the main difficulty is ensuring that the state of the user's computation or document is the same after selecting help. When the help menu is accessed, the user's work must be interrupted, saved (at least to a temporary location), and resumed when the use of the help menu is completed.

A similar situation holds for the case of an "intelligent agent." Here there is an additional complication: the agent is monitoring the user's progress, in addition to providing help. This greatly complicates program complexity and design. See [TECU98] and [KEEL98] for more information.

In both cases, the most important part of the help mechanism is that it tells the user what he or she wants or needs to know.

7.9 Reading Levels

How can you tell if the documentation is adequate? The most important thing is to test the documentation on people who are not already familiar with it. The idea is to have the tester of the software's documentation give feedback based on what he or she sees or reads, not on what he or she knows about the design of the system. Recall that we discussed different levels of user expertise in Chapter 4.

The reading level is a good metric to use for documentation. Generally speaking, lower reading levels are better, especially if the documentation is to be read by non-developers. A higher reading level is probably sufficient for documentation of a system's user interface.

Note, however, that there may be additional demands on even the most sophisticated user. For example, detailed knowledge of the application domain is generally required to understand more technical details of a potentially reusable system if it is to be reused elsewhere.

The Kincaid and other reading level tests are useful in this context. They are available from many sources and are included in the wwb (writer's workbench) package commonly available on AT&T System V UNIX and other UNIX variants. The wwb tool does what every modern, complete word processing system does: indicates incorrectly spelled words, double words, missing punctuation, and other ungrammatical constructions.

In addition, this software has many features not commonly available in commercial word processing systems. The metrics computed by the wwb tool generally include the reading level and an assessment of the values relative to some documents that are believed to be examples of clear writing. The wwb tool indicates unusual sentence complexity, such as too many compound-complex sentences, or the other extreme, too many simple declarative sentences, which make the document seem choppy. The wwb tool also flags documents with too much use of the passive voice.

A recent project on reading levels was carried out by the Harris Corporation for the U.S. Department of Defense. The project was directed towards reducing the gap between the average reading level of the recruits and the average reading level of the technical manuals. Their solution to this problem was two-fold: to improve the reading level of the recruits by specialized training and to decrease the reading level of the manuals by using certain linguistic approaches to lower the reading level.

You should be careful about using a single measure of reading level as the determining factor in document readability. There are many readability issues, including familiarity of the reader with the general subject matter; technical vocabulary; average length of words; number of simple, compound, or compound-complex sentences; and adjective-adverb ratio.

7.10 A Manager's View of Delivery, Installation, and Documentation

In many ways, a typical manager's perspective on delivery and installation is similar to his or her perspective on most software life cycle activities: avoid risk. However, there is an additional factor that can occur at these stages: embarrassment.

The only surprises that can occur at this point are very unpleasant ones. Certainly the manager expects the entire delivery and installation process to have been checked in detail to detect any problems.

We note that many software development organizations use non-technical personnel when testing installation materials. The purpose is to ensure that no unwarranted assumptions have been made by software developers who were intimately familiar with the software.

7.11 Delivery, Installation, and Documentation of the Major Software Project

The first step for our major software project at this point is to deliver the software. As always, we must use the software requirements to determine what delivery format will be used.

How do we determine the proper delivery format? The answer is simple – read the system requirements. The requirements traceability matrix has several entries that are relevant to delivery. We include only the relevant items.

It appears that the requirements were slightly vague on the matter of delivery. We believe, however, that the system is to be delivered on a single 1.44 MB floppy disk and that no compression utility was to have been used. Since there is no mention of a compiler, it is the responsibility of the developer to determine the environment and compilers that the customer expects to use. Not consulting the customer on this point can only lead to disaster.

As we did at each of the other milestones, we should also do a status check from a project management perspective. Were we ahead of schedule (unlikely), behind schedule (likely), or approximately on target? Were any unpleasant surprises, any portions of the system that were more difficult than we expected? Did any portion of the system require extra attention, perhaps additional resources? Had technology or market pressures rendered any portion of the system obsolete?

In fact, we should do more. Delivery of a project is an excellent opportunity for a serious retrospective analysis. The lessons learned in this project should be shared with other project managers, as well as higher-level managers. If there is any hope of improving the way the organization does process development, data about the project's cost, schedule, and quality should be entered into a database for further analysis.

Table 7.2
A portion of the requirements traceability matrix for the major software project

#	Requirement	Design	Code	Test
1.	Intel-based			
2.	Windows 95			
3.	Windows 95 UI			
4.	Consistent With Excel 4.0			
5.	System One Size Only			
6.	One MB System			
7.	One MB Disk Space			
8.	One 1.44 MB Floppy Disk			
9.	Includes Installation			
10.	No Decompression Utility			

Summary

Software is useless unless it is delivered to the customer and can be installed on his or her computer. Delivery is different, depending on whether the software is to be delivered to a single customer, to multiple customers using multiple media, or over a distribution medium such as the Internet.

Regardless of the medium used for delivery, the following should be addressed in a pre-delivery review:

- Failure of the physical medium on which the software resides.
- Incorrect placement of the software into directories, resulting in incorrect directory names.
- Incorrect use of names of subdirectories, making subsystems inaccessible.
- Incorrect access permissions, making files inaccessible.
- Incorrect formatting of the software, such as using incorrect conversion tools for compressing or uncompressing files.
- Incorrect documentation of the delivery instructions.

Once the software has been delivered, it must be installed. Installation usually follows an installation script that is included with the software.

Software documentation can be in any one of several forms:

- Internal documentation (embedded in the source code files).
- External documentation in the form of requirements and design documents.

- Additional documentation explaining why design decisions were made, as in a design rationale.
- Manuals, such as user or installation manuals.
- On-line help that is part of the software itself.

Regardless of the form of software documentation used, the documentation should be tested for accuracy and usability by persons not intimately familiar with the internal design of the software. Ideally, the persons testing the software's documentation will be chosen from a wide range of potential users, including both experienced and novice users.

Further Reading

There are few books on software documentation; the ones by Horton [HORT94] and Barker and Dragga [BARK97] are among the most accessible. The rationale for the Ada programming language can be found in the book by Ichbiah, Barnes, Firth, and Woodger, [ICHB86]. An annotated language reference manual for C++ can be found in the book by Ellis and Stroustrup [ELLI90].

Exercises

1. Select some software product that you have used recently. Describe how the software was delivered.

2. Install a software product on a computer system. Analyze the installation process, writing down each choice you made in response to prompts given during the installation. If it were your software, what changes would you make to the installation process?

3. Talk to a system administrator for the system or network that you use most often. Examine the log that he or she uses whenever new software is installed. What major decisions were made during the last software installation? What about the last software upgrade?

4. Develop delivery guidelines for the major software project that we have been considering throughout this book.

5. Develop installation guidelines for the major software project that we have been considering throughout this book.

6. Examine a commercially available software package with which you are familiar. Which types of documentation were made available with the software? Evaluate the readability of the documentation.

7. Examine the source code for the large software project that we have been considering throughout this book. The only documentation provided is internal documentation, since it is restricted to the source code. Evaluate the readability of the documentation.

8. Write external documentation for the large software project that we have been considering throughout this book.

9. Write both user and operations manuals for the large software project that we have been considering throughout this book.

10. Write a design rationale for the large software project that we have been considering throughout this book.

Chapter 8

Maintenance

In this chapter, we will consider the part of the software engineering process that takes place after the software is delivered. You may be surprised to learn that for many long-lived systems, maintenance accounts for more than 75% of the total cost of the software during its lifetime.

8.1 Introduction

At first glance, it seems strange to apply the term "maintenance" to software. After all, software doesn't wear out the way that a computer's on-off switch or other hardware might. The medium on which software is stored may change over time, with magnetic particles worn off the surface of a disk or tape, or even having a compact disk bent. Careful system administrators will keep backup copies of all essential software (and user files), ideally in physically separated locations, in order to avoid problems with fire and flood.

Note also that software cannot rust or fail because dirt gets in the middle of an electrical connection. Major changes to the power supplied to computers (110 volt, 60 cycle alternating current in the United States, 220 volts in the United Kingdom, etc.) are not likely. Of course, power spikes or voltage reduction due to overtaxed electrical production facilities may have an effect, but these problems are well known. Prudent computer system administrators use a combination of surge suppressors, conditioned power sources, and uninterruptable power supplies to ensure the proper level of service. These problems are clearly hardware related and pose no particular problem for software engineers.

The reliability of hardware systems generally follows a pattern such as the one illustrated in Figure 8.1. The relatively high number of failures early in the lifetime of the hardware is due primarily to three factors: faulty components, mistakes in the installation of these components, and improper usage by an inexperienced operator. The increased number of failures at the right hand side of the graph represents failures that occur near the end of the hardware's useful lifetime and are due to actual component failures.

Hardware maintenance is different from hardware testing. For example, you should expect that a new car you recently purchased was assembled by experts using high-quality parts and had certain subsystems (such as those for electrical, steering, and braking operations) tested for safety. The car should also have received other basic checks when it was driven off the assembly line to a waiting cargo carrier and when it was driven from the cargo carrier to the dealer's showroom. These are all considered testing activities. If a new car needed to have its brakes or steering fixed during the warranty period, you would probably regard the car as being of poor quality and would certainly not recommend that a friend purchase a similar car.

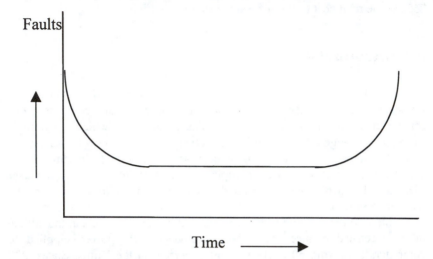

Figure 8.1 The typical "bathtub curve" for malfunctions of electrical and mechanical equipment.

You might also be very concerned if the plastic on your dash split or the car rattled when going over bumps. On the other hand, if you had the same (non-safety-related) problems occur after 100,000 miles of operation, then you would probably consider fixing these problems as normal maintenance. You might choose to not fix these problems, because you might feel that the remaining life of the car was so short that the maintenance expense was not worth it.

A personal note is appropriate here. With the average cost of a new car in the U.S. being over $20,000, the average monthly payment for a five-year term would be in the neighborhood of $400 per month, assuming little or no down payment and a very low interest rate. My decision is based on an estimate of the value of the repairs and the utility of the car. If repairs mean that a car will be able to run safely for an additional two months, then I expect the repairs to cost no more than $800. Beyond that point, I have to ask if the car is worth it. Thus, I apply an informal cost/benefit analysis to determine if the car should be maintained or if the car should be donated to a high school automotive repair program (to take a deduction on my income tax), traded to a dealer, or junked.

Proper maintenance of hardware involves keeping it clean, paying particular attention to moving parts, replacing faulty components, and generally planning to replace components that are old, obsolete, faulty, or at risk for imminent failure. A cost/benefit analysis should also be performed in order to determine if the maintenance effort is cost efficient, given the goals of the organization. Surprisingly, this approach is also a good way to view software maintenance.

Software maintenance could be described as the systematic process of changing software that is already in operation in order to prevent system failures and to improve performance. Software maintenance involves keeping software interfaces simple and standard, paying particular attention to troublesome modules, replacing faulty components, and generally planning to replace components that are old, obsolete, faulty, or at risk for imminent failure. The estimated remaining useful lifetime of the software must also be considered to determine if the maintenance effort is worth the added cost.

After this informal introduction to the reasons for software maintenance, we proceed to a more systematic discussion of the subject. There are several factors that require software to be maintained:

1. Hardware platforms change or become obsolete.
2. Operating systems change or become obsolete.
3. Compilers change or become obsolete.
4. Language standards change or become obsolete.
5. Communications standards change or become obsolete.
6. Graphical user interfaces change or become obsolete.
7. Related applications software packages change or become obsolete.
8. Relationships with developers of other applications or systems software have changed.
9. Software may have defects that become evident only after the software has been used by the customer. These defects must be corrected.
10. Customers demand new features.
11. Software needs upgrades to be competitive with new competition.
12. Existing software errors must be prevented from occurring in new releases of the software.

These factors may be classified as belonging to several distinct groups. Factors 1 through 9 may be classified as adaptive maintenance, since they are intended to help the software adapt to new technology. Factors 10 through 11 may be classified as corrective maintenance, since they attempt to make the software more correct, in the sense that it has fewer faults. The term "perfective maintenance" is also used in this case. Factor 12 may be classified as preventive maintenance, since it attempts to reduce the possibility of future software faults.

There is one common thread, however. An essential step in all types of software maintenance is understanding the software system to be maintained. Before a maintainer can change software in order to fix a problem or add a feature, he or she must understand the software as a whole and the particular modules that need to be modified. Many experiments have indicated that program understanding, which includes understanding of software requirements and designs, takes approximately half of all maintenance efforts.

Different approaches to software maintenance will be discussed in the remainder of this chapter. Keep in mind, however, that nothing in life is free and that any software maintenance activity must be budgeted for as part of the organization's software budget.

We will describe a typical approach to the software maintenance process that will consider the two actions of determining where the problem is and then fixing it.

Many software problems can be traced to one or more of the following:

- Lack of adherence to software development standards. These problems include poor interfaces between modules, such as passing the wrong number or types of arguments to a function.
- Logical errors within program modules, such as loops, branches, or inconsistent program states.
- Non-atomic actions.
- Inconsistency between the requirements, design, code, and documentation for a system.

Students are often surprised by the amount of difficulty that they have understanding either commercial or government code. I have used actual source code from many software development organizations in my classes and the response is almost identical; the code is poorly documented and hard to understand. In reality, the students are faced with the problem of examining all or portions of systems that are too large to be understood in their entirety.

8.2 Corrective Software Maintenance

The first step in corrective software maintenance is to determine what needs to be maintained. In corrective software maintenance, all activity begins with the identification of a problem with the existing software. Determining the particular module that is the cause of a problem can be difficult. The basic approach is based on the technique of trial and error, guided by the maintainer's knowledge of the system and his or her basic knowledge of computer science and software engineering.

Once problems have been determined, a decision can be made as to which, how, or when the problem will be fixed.

This usually requires several related actions:

- Observation that a problem exists.
- Documentation of the problem.
- Determination of the importance of the problem.
- Prioritizing the problems in order of importance of repair.
- Determining which problems will not be repaired, due to insufficient resources.
- Solution of the problem.
- Testing the system to see if the fix to this problem can cause any faults in other portions of the software.
- Documenting the solution as part of the source code.
- Documenting the solution in other forms of the documentation if changes have been made to the original system design.
- Updating a database of information about software errors.

This may seem like a lot of work - it is. Software maintenance must, by its nature, require large amounts of paperwork to update documentation. After all, the developers of software systems in industry or government rarely stay on the same project forever. With high turnover of personnel, written documentation that traces any changes made must be left for future maintainers of a system.

Observation of a software problem can occur at several levels. In the most ideal situation, the observer is a person who is completely familiar with the system's requirements. In this case, the documentation of the problem is immediate and the determination of the source of the problem can generally determined easily.

A more common situation is for the persons observing the problem to be completely unfamiliar with the internal structure of the software. Indeed, the person observing the problem may even be unfamiliar with the software's expected operation. This is typical of the type of problem that is first observed by novice users who then call a toll-free number for technical support of their new word processing or similar application. The technically knowledgeable person working in technical report is responsible for guiding the caller through the steps that led up to this presumed problem, to look for problems in the setup and configuration of the software, and, in short, to determine if the problem is due to an error by the user or an actual fault in the software. There are essentially only two possibilities: the user has misunderstood the installation and operating instructions, or the software is in error.

Once the technical support person has determined that the user has misunderstood the documentation of either the system's installation or operation, he or she has two remaining tasks. The user must be led through the correct steps to fix his or her problem. In addition, the technical support person must document the problem so that the documentation and the user interface can be improved. This is often done in a future release of the product. The technical support person should describe the documentation problems fully and turn them over to a person responsible for new releases of the system so that the user community will consider the new releases to be improvements. We note in passing that most computer documentation could be improved by the employment of a technical writer.

In the case of a software fault, the user is not expected to provide detailed documentation of the details of the problem. The typical user does not have the technical ability and, in any event, it is not his or her job. The technical support person is responsible for taking the user's information and organizing it into a format that can be used in the maintenance process.

The goal of the person documenting a software problem is to be able to fill out a form as detailed as the one shown in Figure 8.2. This form is often called a software maintenance request form, or software maintenance report form. Note that the form has places for complete descriptions of the problem and for an assessment of the relative importance of the problem. A sensible software manager generally will prefer to set priorities for the deployment of maintenance personnel based on an assessment of the relative importance of the problems encountered. A realistic estimate of the difficulty of fixing an incorrect module is also useful in assigning priorities.

After the problem has been fixed, another form should be filled out. This second form indicates the response to the software maintenance form and, as such, is often called a software maintenance response form. Figure 8.3 illustrates a typical software maintenance response form. Many organizations combine these request and response form into a single form as shown in Figure 8.4. Note that the response form will always indicate a list of affected modules and the time needed to fix the problem.

Note the importance of the extra documentation on these forms. The ability to attach hard copies of screen dumps is often very helpful to maintainers. If no screen dump facility is available in the software or operating system, a photograph of the screen can suffice. Obviously, a digital image is best.

You may be concerned about the proliferation of paperwork required by these forms. Why have all this extra information? Who needs it? An actual example indicates the need for these activities.

Suppose that you were examining a software system that had to be of highest quality because it was to be used without modification as the core of many other software products in a safety-critical application. Primarily because of its design and adherence to essential interface standards, this software had a much lower defect ratio (faults per KLOC) than did most other software in the organization. However, high quality was not enough. Since this reusable core had to be reused in so many applications, it was important to check to determine where software errors tended to occur.

Maintenance request number_____

System_____   Version _____   Date_____

Related maintenance request numbers_____

Environment
Computer hardware:

Operating system_____Version_____

Related system software: GUI _____

Related application software _____

Description of problem

Severity of problem
Critical_____Urgent_____Important_____Routine_____

Classification: Hardware_____Software_____ Documentation_____
Person making report

Person verifying report

Date problem verified

Organization responsible for fixing problem

Figure 8.2 A typical software maintenance request form

Maintenance repair number_____

In response to maintenance request number_____

Related maintenance request numbers_____

System_____   Version _____ Date_____

Environment

Computer hardware:

Operating system _____Version_____

Related system software: GUI _____

Related application software _____

Severity of problem
Critical_____Urgent_____Important_____Routine_____

Classification: Hardware_____Software_____ Documentation_____
Person making report

Person verifying report_____Date_____

Person fixing problem_____

Resolution of problem

Person verifying solution_____

Modules affected

Time needed to fix problem

Figure 8.3 A typical software maintenance response form

Maintenance request number_____
Related maintenance request numbers_____

System_____   Version _____ Date_____

Environment

Computer hardware:
Operating system _____Version_____

Related system software: GUI _____

Related application software _____

Description of problem

Severity of problem
Critical_____Urgent_____Important_____Routine_____
Classification: Hardware_____Software_____ Documentation_____
Person making report_____

Person verifying report_____
Person fixing problem_____
Person verifying solution_____
Resolution of problem

Modules affected

Time to fix problem

Figure 8.4 A typical combined software maintenance report and request form.

An examination of a database of maintenance requests and responses indicated that 44% of identifiable software faults were traced to a single set of modules used to interface to an old locally developed command language. It was decided to scrap this command language and use a more modern one with a grammar that could be parsed easily using standard grammatical parsing tools such as `lex` and `yacc`. The identification of the command language parsing tools as major sources of software maintenance costs certainly influenced this decision.

Of course, there is no need to have the forms written on paper. The forms themselves can be stored electronically, with automatic entry of data into a database. Ideally, a software package that supports maintenance activities with automatic forms-generation and storage of information into a database would be available to maintainers. In many software environments, the lack of forms generation capability is the most critical problem.

The simplest solution is to enter the maintenance data in text format directly into a spreadsheet or database. We prefer to use the lowest level of technology in this book in order to be able to work in nearly all situations.

8.3 Adaptive Software Maintenance

Adaptive maintenance is the process of changing software to meet new trends in the marketplace. Expected changes in hardware, systems, interoperable application packages, and new features provided by the competition are all important in determining the need for adaptive maintenance of software.

Consider the case of Microsoft Word, which has gone through many versions since its inception. Some of these changes involve the user interface and usability. Other changes provided additional features and common file formats. Frequently, documents opened in one version of later versions of Word either cannot be read or have page formats changed by an earlier version of the same software. (This problem is not unique to Microsoft. The same statement applies to Corel WordPerfect, among others.)

For some users, the advantage of a common file format in which documents can be read on both PCs and Macintoshes is outweighed by having larger file sizes used for documents. For others, the additional features provided by macros may be less important than the additional security requirements to treat macro viruses, which may migrate from PCs to Macintoshes and vice versa.

As with corrective maintenance, considerable testing of software is necessary, especially regression testing.

It is appropriate at this point to indicate some problems that cannot reasonably be expected to be uncovered during even the most exhaustive software testing.

Unfortunately, standard testing procedures generally cannot detect erroneous events such as race conditions, which will occur very infrequently. The term "race condition" refers to a situation where the result of a computation (or even the continuation of system operation) depends upon the order in which distinct concurrently executing processes get access to the CPU.

An example of a race condition is shown in Figure 8.5. The value of the variable X at the end of the asynchronous computation depends on the order in which the concurrently running processes execute.

```
Process 1                              Process 2

X = 1;                                 X = 1;
Y = 7;                                 Y = 7;
X = X + Y;                             X = X - Y;
```

Figure 8.5. A race condition with different results of a computation, depending on the order in which instructions in a process are executed by the CPU.

There is another equally important problem that can cause problems for maintainers of concurrent systems, especially real-time systems. The maintainer of such systems must pay special attention to functions that call operating system calls, but are not themselves atomic. (An "atomic instruction" is one that cannot be interrupted by an external event and, therefore, such instructions will always complete once their execution has started.)

Scheduling of processes on one or more CPUs cannot be predicted and thus, race conditions and non-atomic system calls can be disastrous.

These two problems can occur in software systems that must execute concurrently with other processes. Both non-atomic function calls and race conditions are extremely dangerous for real-time or safety-critical systems because the system cannot be guaranteed to operate successfully and because system run-time performance cannot be predicted. Even worse, testing cannot provide guarantees of the necessary system quality.

In the case of non-atomic functions used to synchronize access to system resources, even the most exhaustive testing of a software system with concurrently executing processes will be inadequate, because the likelihood of a system failure during testing is small. Figure 8.6 illustrates the issue.

```
Process 1                              Process 2
X = 1;                                 X = 1;

Y = 7;                                 y = 7;
IF (X == 1) AND (Y ==7)                X = X - Y
    ACCESS shared resource;            Y = X;
X = X + Y;
Y = 1;
```

```
┌─────────────────────────────┐
│      Shared Resource         │
└─────────────────────────────┘
```

Figure 8.6.   Access to a shared resource controlled by a non-atomic function.

The problem will occur because the synchronization depends on the values of two distinct variables, X and Y, which are tested in two distinct steps. However, if the processes get access to the CPU in such a way that the third instruction of process 2 executes before the third instruction of process 1, the synchronization condition may not hold and access to the sharable resource may be granted (or denied) incorrectly.

Another problem is particularly vexing for software maintainers. Many software engineers, especially those whose primary experience is with computers with large amounts of physical memory, do not think of their systems as having any limitations.

However, memory can be exhausted, especially if there are COTS products whose memory demands are unknown.

An equally difficult problem for maintainers is the use of excessive numbers of other restricted system resources. For example, two different software packages may each write data to the same socket (which may be implemented as a "winsoock" or a "socket descriptor," depending on the operating system) for network communications, and this may cause unexpected conflicts.

In another more complex example, the number of files that can be open at any one time for a user's process can range from 8 in programs using older versions of C to 20 for ANSI standard C to 64 on some UNIX systems (the so-called "soft limit," which can be increased by a system administrator) to the maximum allowable (the so-called "hard limit," often 100 on UNIX systems).

You should be aware that the situation is especially complex if the software to be maintained must interact with many COTS products whose internal structure is not known.

It is clear that a software maintainer may need many skills beyond simple programming experience.

8.4 Preventive Software Maintenance and the Year 2000 Problem

Preventive software maintenance is the prevention of software problems in existing software before the problems occur. This type of maintenance tends to be a low priority for managers because of the other demands on resources and the need to develop new software.

It is probably best to illustrate preventive maintenance by a topical example – the Year 2000 Problem. (At the time this book is being written, the problem is one of preventive maintenance. By the time you read this, it should be one of corrective maintenance.)

The huge amount of software that might be affected by the Y2K problem has caused a maintenance nightmare, especially because of the lack of qualified personnel. Some companies have begun using the so-called "chess master approach" in which four or five very junior programmers are placed in a room and asked to examine source code for occurrences of date problems. An expert is also in the room. The junior programmers have the authority to correct routine problems, but the more complex ones are given to the expert. (The term "chess master" is used to describe this expert because he or she acts as a chess master playing a large number of games simultaneously, keeping track of each of the board positions mentally.)

There are many scenarios that may cause future problems similar to the Y2K problem:

- Exhaustion of nine-digit Social Security numbers by the year 2010
- Exhaustion of telephone area codes in the United States by the year 2020
- Transition from ASCII to an international character set such as Unicode.
- Overflow of the buffer area used for storage of dates in the UNIX operating system in the year 2038. (Dates and times in UNIX are measured in seconds from some arbitrary date in 1970).

Each of these scenarios has an overflow problem that will have to be treated. Since these problems will occur in the future, preventive maintenance is very important. Software that is certified compliant with these inevitable problems will have a competitive advantage when the problems arise.

As with corrective and adaptive maintenance, a considerable amount of testing, especially regression testing, will be necessary.

8.5 How to Read Requirements, Designs, and Source Code

Once a maintenance problem has been given to a maintainer, the source code must be modified. However, many software systems consist of millions of lines of source code. Each line of source code has the potential to be the place where a problem occurs. Of course, not all problems in the user interface, for example, need to be checked. But where do we begin?

A software maintainer will look at all available information: requirements, design, manuals and other documentation and, of course, the source code itself. The goal is to understand the likely effects of any changes in the software before the changes are made. Everyone who has written software is familiar with having a change in one portion of the software affect performance in some other portion. Thus, a systematic approach is necessary.

Keep in mind the old adage: if the source code and any of the requirements, design, or documentation do not agree, they're both wrong. In this case, the source code is the only certain guide, because it reflects the system as it currently works. The available source code is always read as part of the maintenance process.

Let's suppose at this point that we are only considering source code. What do we look for first?

The answer is composed of several parts. We would start by looking at the maintenance reports for related situations to seek out any suggestions on where to look for problems. We would also make use of any available CASE tool to analyze the source code and show the program's structure. After we had obtained enough information to restrict our attention to a limited number of modules, each of them would be inspected at essentially the same level of detail as it would be in the type of code review discussed in Chapter 5.

8.6 A Manager's Perspective on Software Maintenance

Although it may be surprising to students, software maintenance is one of the most costly items in the software life cycle. One thing that managers like is reducing costs. You can often help your manager by suggesting some ways that maintenance costs can be reduced.

A database of maintenance requests and actions can be very helpful. For example, the system described in Section 8.2 had a maintenance database in which a simple query indicated that one particular software module was causing 44% of the traceable software failures. The problems were traced to new dialects of a command language, which were created with every new version of the software. Freezing the command language caused little functionality loss in the opinion of the users, but it reduced maintenance costs by a considerable amount. Managers like this type of information. It makes their jobs easier.

This kind of analysis of maintenance effort is extremely important to managers at all levels. For most commercial organizations, little revenue is brought in during maintenance unless new releases of the software are planned. Thus, maintenance is viewed as a cost to be minimized whenever possible.

Of course, it is always essential to follow your organization's standards-and-practices manual for documentation procedures.

8.7 Maintenance of the Major Software Project

One view of software maintenance would suggest that the system was already under maintenance when the requirements were changed to use the Internet. We will ignore the previous requirements change and instead consider some possible changes after delivery.

The first type of maintenance to consider is corrective. Does the software behave as it should? After we have considered correctness, we must worry about the user interface and the potential for enhancements. Of course, performance issues can always arise if the response time needs to be improved. We will leave these issues to the exercises.

Summary

Much of the effort for software projects occurs after the software is delivered and installed. This is called the maintenance phase.

There are three major types of software maintenance:

- Corrective maintenance
- Adaptive maintenance
- Preventive maintenance

The Y2K problem is an example of preventive maintenance-until the problem occurs. It will then be a corrective maintenance problem.

There is an adage that describes the skepticism a maintainer must have: if the source code and any of the requirements, design, or documentation do not agree, they're both wrong.

Further Reading

Perhaps the best source of information for a beginning software engineer is a company's software development standards and practices manual. Forms such as the ones given in this text are usually available from these documents.

There are some general references on software maintenance available. The book *Software Change Impact Analysis*, edited by Arnold and Bohner [ARNO97], provides an excellent overview of the state of the art in assessing the impact of maintenance decisions. The recent book by Pigoski [PIGO97] is also useful.

There are several important articles on this subject, and you should check some of the conferences that are more practitioner oriented. There is even a journal related to maintenance issues: the *Journal of Software Maintenance*.

Exercises

1. List at least ten software packages that will have to be changed to accommodate an increase in the number of characters used for Social Security numbers.

2. List at least ten software packages that will have to be changed to accommodate changes in the number of digits used for phone numbers.

3. List at least ten software packages that will have to be changed to accommodate changes in the UNIX date and time computation. Be sure to discuss the use of the make utility.

4. Consider a popular application for personal computers. Describe major changes between successive releases. List them in the order of estimated likely costs

5. Examine the dialog we presented in Chapter 4, when we developed the requirements for the large software project that we have discussed throughout this course. Based on that dialog, what changes do you expect to be made to the software during its useful lifetime?

6. Compare the changes made in the software in the major project with the ones you might have predicted in the previous question.

7. Change the major software project to allow the separation of the computational portion from the user interface. Then incorporate a client-server relationship, with the computation done on a server and the user interface on a client machine.

Chapter 9

Research Issues in Software Engineering

The nature of software engineering has changed considerably in recent years. The concept of a "program" is being replaced by the concept of a "system" which is comprised of many different communicating and cooperating components. Different components may be fully or partially distributed, executing on different computers. This approach to software development requires planning; resource allocation; coordinated scheduling; requirements engineering; risk assessment; modular designs; testing; quality assessment; flexible and repeatable development processes; and proper reviews. In short, this approach has all the aspects of an engineered process.

Market pressures force organizations to produce high-quality, well-documented systems with many new features with technically correct performance in a timely manner and with efficient use of resources. Competitive pressures often make it difficult for many smaller companies, especially those without research and development groups, to spend much time improving their processes, particularly since they are often focused on improving their use of current and future technology. Not keeping up with current technology can cause a company to fail. (So can marketing and distribution, but we will not discuss them here.

However, the cost of *not* improving the software engineering process can be equally disastrous, since those companies that produce high-quality software efficiently will often have an enormous technical advantage based on their efficiency.

In this brief chapter, we will describe how the software process can be improved. In Section 9.1 we list some research issues that are considered to be important now and are likely to be in the foreseeable future. In Section 9.2, we provide some guidance on how to interpret the software engineering research literature.

The purpose of this chapter is to enable you to read and interpret the vast, ever-increasing literature in software engineering. Even if you never intend to be a researcher in this area, the information presented will be important when you have to assess what happened during a project post-mortem.

9.1 Some Important Research Problems in Software Engineering

In this section, we present the author's views on some of the most important research areas in software engineering, together with a few important research question in each area.

The fundamental question

1. Buy vs. build vs. reuse: this decision is arguably the most important choice that must be made in a software development project. Devise a series of case studies, comparative studies, and controlled experiments to determine a systematic process for making this decision in some non-trivial application domain. Note that many of the research questions posed later in this section will address portions of this question. (We will discuss the importance of case studies, comparative studies, and controlled experiments in software engineering research in Section 9.2.)

Requirements

2. Requirements representation: devise and implement an experiment to determine which is the most effective method for writing requirements in a given application domain. Such a determination would consider plain text, graphical descriptions, and formal methods.

3. Requirements reviews and inspections: what is the most effective way to hold a requirements review or inspection?

4. Requirements aggregation: how should a set of requirements be aggregated in order to encourage software reuse?

5. Procedurally oriented requirements: what is the most efficient method of determining requirements for a procedurally oriented system in a particular application domain?

6. Object-oriented requirements: what is the most efficient method of determining requirements for an object-oriented system in a particular application domain?

7. Hybrid requirements: what is the most efficient method of determining requirements for a system that will have both procedurally and object-oriented components in a particular application domain?

8. Requirements generation tools: create a tool (or set of tools) to generate detailed requirements from a particular set of high-level requirements.

9. Validation of requirements generation: develop a method to determine the validity of the requirements generation tool (or set of tools) as an improvement to the requirements process.

10. Comparison of requirements generation and high-level languages: devise and carry out an experiment to determine if the requirements

generation tool (or tools) described above is more efficient than a fourth- or fifth-generation language in improving the efficiency of the software development process.

11. Determine the most efficient way to develop requirements in a particular application domain where the entire system will be written in a functional programming language such as LISP.

12. Determine the most efficient way to develop requirements in a particular application domain where the entire system will be written in logic programming languages such as Prolog.

13. Determine the most efficient way to develop requirements in a particular application domain where the system will be written in multiple programming languages, including procedural, object-oriented, functional, logic, or higher-level languages.

Design

14. Design representations for procedurally oriented systems: what is the most effective method for representing designs for a procedurally designed system?

15. Design representations for object-oriented systems: what is the most effective method for representing designs for a object-designed system?

16. Design representations for hybrid systems that have both procedurally and object-oriented components: what is the most effective method for representing designs for a hybrid of procedurally and object-oriented component subsystems?

17. Graphical design representations: are graphical representations more effective than text-based ones?

18. Design reviews and inspections: what is the most effective way to hold a design review or inspection?

Coding

19. Coding standards: devise and implement an experiment to determine which, if any, coding standards improve the efficiency of writing source code.

Testing

20. Efficiency of testing methods: Develop a methodology to determine which testing method is most likely to be more effective in a particular application domain: white-box or black-box testing.

21. White-box testing: develop a method to determine the most efficient way to perform white-box testing in a particular class of application domains.

22. Black-box testing: develop a method to determine the most efficient way to perform black-box testing in a particular class of application domains.

23. Object-oriented testing: develop a method to determine the most efficient way to perform object-oriented testing in a particular class of application domains.

24. Performance testing: develop a method of software performance testing that provides early feedback about performance issues that may delay software deployment.

25. Stress testing: develop a method of software system stress testing that provides early feedback about system limitation issues that may delay software deployment.

26. Fault seeding and testing: determine a methodology for determining the effectiveness of fault seeding as a way to measure the efficiency of defect removal during testing.

27. Intelligent agents: develop a method for testing intelligent, autonomous agents that may move around the nodes of a network.

28. Testing of functional systems: develop a method for systematically testing software that is written in a functional programming language such as LISP.

29. Testing of logic systems: develop a method for systematically testing software that is written in a logic programming language such as Prolog.

30. Testing of artificial neural networks: develop a method for systematically testing software that is written in the form of an artificial neural network. (This testing is presumed to follow the normal training of an artificial neural network.)

Integration

31. Top-down integration: devise and implement an experiment to determine the efficiency of top-down integration in a realistic application domain with proper integration tools.

32. Bottom-up integration: devise and implement an experiment to determine the efficiency of bottom-up integration in a realistic application domain with proper integration tools.

33. Plug and play integration: devise and implement an experiment to determine the efficiency of plug-and-play integration in a realistic application domain with proper integration tools. (Plug-and-play integration involves the insertion of components into a running system.)

34. Big-bang integration: devise and implement an experiment to determine the efficiency of big-bang integration in a realistic application domain with proper integration tools.

Maintenance

35. Coding standards: devise and implement an experiment to determine which, if any, coding standards improve the efficiency of maintaining source code.

36. COTS maintenance: develop a process for maintaining interfaces to COTS products during the lifetime of the project that includes the COTS product. Make sure that the process includes a mechanism for treating the case where there are multiple releases of the COTS product.

Cost estimation

37. Cost estimation and the Internet: create both a process and a model for estimating the cost of software projects that make extensive use of the Internet. Devise and implement a series of experiments to validate your model and process.

38. Cost estimation, COTS, and reuse: create both a process and a model for estimating the cost of software projects that make extensive use of COTS and reuse. Devise and implement a series of experiments to validate your model and process.

Software reuse

39. Management: what is the most efficient organizational or management structure from the perspective of encouraging enterprise-wide systematic software reuse in such a way as to greatly reduce the organization's total software development and maintenance costs?

40. Domain engineering: what is the most effective method of organizing and classifying the software artifacts within a domain so as to support systematic software reuse?

41. Reuse library search: what is the most effective method for determining the software artifact (or artifacts) within a reuse library that are closest to the desired artifact?

42. Library organization: what is the most efficient method of reuse library organization in order to allow artifacts at many different levels of the software life cycle to be stored in such a way that we can retrieve them according to their functionality, the interface standards the artifacts meet, or the CASE tool that created them?

43. FAST in a single application domain: the FAST (Family-Oriented Abstraction, Specification, and Translation) approach involves concurrent analysis of both the reusable components within a domain and the development of applications using these reusable components. For which domains can the FAST process work efficiently? The FAST process was developed at Lucent Technologies by Weiss, Lai et. Al.

44. FAST deployment: how can the FAST approach be used efficiently within different application domains?

45. Generative reuse: generative reuse is software reuse using highly configurable frameworks and application generators. Develop a method to determine the applicability of generative reuse for particular application domains and the likelihood of this approach being successful.

46. Component reuse: component reuse is software reuse using existing software components. Develop a method to determine the applicability of component reuse for particular application domains and the likelihood of this approach being successful.

47. Generative and component reuse: develop a methodology for predicting which of generative reuse and component reuse is more likely to be successful in a given application domain.

48. Reuse cost accounting: determine an efficient method of cost estimation and accounting for systematic reuse programs that extend across multiple organizations.

49. Reuse and design representations: there are many design representations (Buhr diagrams, Booch diagrams, Rumbaugh diagrams, UML, etc.). Which is the most effective in promoting software reuse?

50. Determine the most efficient way to implement a systematic practice of software reuse where all components are written in a functional programming language such as LISP.

51. Determine the most efficient way to implement a systematic practice of software reuse where all components are written in a logic programming language such as Prolog.

Fault tolerance

52. Recovery blocks and fault tolerance: determine the class of applications for which rollback of a system to a recovery block is an effective technique of improving software fault tolerance.

53. Recovery blocks, fault tolerance and system correctness: develop a method to develop recovery blocks that are error free and, thus, whose incorporation into a program improves, rather than degrades, system fault-tolerance.

54. Exceptions and fault tolerance: develop a formal method to prove the correctness of programs that use exceptions to control program execution after abnormal situations are detected.

55. Assertions and fault tolerance: develop a formal method to prove the correctness of programs that use assertions to control program execution after abnormal situations are detected.

56. Fault tolerance and replication (N-version, or multi-version, programming): determine the class of applications for which a combination of replication of major components of a system and a " voter controller" to determine system correctness by majority rule is an effective technique of improving software fault tolerance.

57. Intelligent agents and fault tolerance: devise and implement an experiment to determine the effectiveness of intelligent agents to detect, and perhaps correct, run-time faults that occur in a system.

Metrics

58. Process metrics: the general problem is to determine which metrics describe the state of a software development process with sufficient accuracy to be able to detect inefficiencies.

59. Descriptive process metrics: determine a set of metrics that can be used to determine if a project is late or over budget at a specified milestone in the development.

60. Predictive process metrics: determine a set of metrics that can be used to predict if a project will be late or over budget.

61. Product metrics: the general problem is to determine which metrics describe the quality of a software product with sufficient accuracy to be able to detect inefficiencies.

62. Metrics for procedurally oriented system requirements: determine which metrics reflect the complexity of the requirements of procedurally oriented programs.

63. Metrics for procedurally oriented system designs: determine which metrics reflect the complexity of the designs of procedurally oriented systems.

64. Metrics for procedurally oriented systems: determine which metrics reflect the complexity of procedurally oriented requirements.

65. Metrics for object-oriented system requirements: determine which metrics reflect the complexity of the requirements of object-oriented programs.

66. Metrics for object-oriented system designs: determine which metrics reflect the complexity of the designs of object-oriented systems.

67. Metrics for object-oriented systems: determine which metrics reflect the complexity of object-oriented systems.

68. Metrics for hybrid system requirements: determine which metrics reflect the complexity of the requirements of systems that are hybrids of procedurally and object-oriented subsystems.

69. Metrics for hybrid system designs: determine which metrics reflect the complexity of the designs of systems that are hybrids of procedurally and object-oriented subsystems.

70. Metrics for hybrid systems: determine which metrics reflect the complexity of systems that are hybrids of procedurally and object-oriented subsystems.

Languages and efficiency

71. Java efficiency: determine the best techniques for grouping of Java language software components into "jars" in such a way as to improve program efficiency.

72. C efficiency: determine the best techniques for grouping of C language software components into files and directories in such a way as to improve program efficiency.

73. C++ efficiency: determine the best techniques for grouping of C++ language software components into files and directories in such a way as to improve program efficiency.

74. Ada efficiency: determine the best techniques for grouping of Ada language software components into packages in such a way as to improve program efficiency.

75. Smalltalk efficiency: determine the best techniques for grouping of Smalltalk language software components into files and directories in such a way as to improve program efficiency.

76. Functional languages efficiency: determine the best techniques for grouping of software components written in functional languages such as LISP into files and directories in such a way as to improve program efficiency.

77. Logic languages efficiency: determine the best techniques for grouping of software components written in logic languages such as Prolog into files and directories in such a way as to improve program efficiency.

78. Interfaces between languages: determine the best way to interface between language components written in multiple languages. Write an experiment comparing Interface Definition Language (IDL), CORBA, COM, Java, and HTML in a particular application domain.

Language generators

79. Lexical analyzers: devise and implement an experiment to determine the relative efficiency of lexical analyzers written using an analysis tool such as `lex`.

80. Devise a method for testing the code produced by a lexical analyzer such as `lex` at high level *before* the source code is generated.

81. Parser generators: devise and implement an experiment to determine the relative efficiency of parsers written using tools such as `yacc`

82. Devise a method for testing the code produced by a parser generator such as `yacc` at high level *before* the source code is generated.

83. Application generators: devise and implement an experiment to determine the relative efficiency of software written using domain-specific parser generators.

84. Devise a method for testing the code produced by a parser generator at high level *before* the source code is generated.

Inspections and reviews

85. General question: what is the most efficient method of running inspections and reviews?

86. Inspections by groups: how should inspection groups be organized and inspections be carried out to discover errors efficiently?

87. False positives and inspections by groups: how should inspection groups be organized and inspections be carried out to reduce the number of false positives but still discover errors efficiently?

88. Inspections by individuals: how should inspections be carried out to discover errors efficiently?

89. False positives and inspections by individuals: how should inspections be carried out to reduce the number of false positives but still discover errors efficiently?

90. The open-source software approach, such as the one used for coding and maintenance of the Linux operating system, depends on detailed inspections of code by multiple reviewers using the Internet [McCO99]. How efficient is this process in terms of reducing software faults per unit of programmer time?

91. This question also concerns the open-source approach [McCO99]. For which types of projects is the open-source approach suited?

Distributed systems

92. Client-server systems: what is the best way to partition a software system into a server and a client?

93. Remote procedures: devise and implement an experiment to compare remote procedure call and Java RMI.

Software project management

94. Software project management: determine the most effective way to manage a project.

95. Self-organizing teams: devise and implement an experiment to determine if allowing a team to organize itself without much direction from a manager is efficient for small projects.

Formal methods

96. Appropriate application domains for formal methods: determine a class of application domains in which formal methods work efficiently.

97. Verifying a verifier: develop a formal method of verifying the theorem provers used to prove the correctness of certain formally defined systems. (Theoretical note – it is impossible to completely verify a "universal" theorem prover.)

Processes

98. General problem: determine the efficiency of several different software development processes.

99. Return on investment of attaining different SEI levels: devise and implement an experiment to determine the return on investment on the efficiency resulting from attaining SEI levels 2, 3, 4, or 5.

100. Return on investment of attaining different ISO levels: devise and implement an experiment to determine the return on investment on the efficiency resulting from attaining ISO 9000 or 9001.

101. Return on investment of attaining DOD 2167A compliance: devise and implement an experiment to determine the return on investment on the efficiency resulting from following DOD 2167A. (The same can be done for other standards.)

Risk management

102. General problem: develop a precise way to determine the risk of any new technology.

103. Risk assessment in the life cycle: incorporate risk assessment into the classical waterfall and rapid prototyping software development models.

Quality assurance

104. Efficient teams: devise and implement an experiment to determine the efficient allocation of personnel to quality assurance teams.

105. Return on investment in quality assurance: determine the return on investment in a quality assurance team.

Configuration management

106. Configuration management for distributed development: develop a flexible process to be used in configuration management for very large software systems that have software developers working in several geographically separate places, perhaps even different time zones.

107. Configuration management throughout the life cycle: develop a flexible process that allows configuration management to be applied to artifacts created at various stages of the life cycle.

Crystal ball

108. Determine the software engineering tool, approach, process, or environment that will be most important in ten years. Keep in mind that doing this ten years ago would have required you to discern the importance of object-oriented programming, Java, and the Internet.

9.2 How to Read the Software Engineering Research Literature

Many research papers in software engineering either describe a theory, a tool, a process, or a software system. Others describe an attempt to show that something works particularly well by means of some sort of numerical evaluation of the performance of the tool, process, or software system. In this section we will consider only the second type. Of course, there will be a considerable difference in the amount of technical detail, especially proprietary detail, between something written for use internally within an organization and something intended for the general literature. (We will ignore anything written by the sales or marketing departments of an organization.)

Generally speaking, any report describing research that attempts to quantify the utility of a tool, a process, or software system can be classified as falling into one of three categories:

1. A case study
2. A comparative study
3. An experiment

Understanding the proper use of these three categories of research can help you to understand the applicability to your particular environment and avoid problems by misusing the research results in a application environment for which the research is not appropriate. We will describe each of these types of research in what follows.

A "case study" describes a particular situation in considerable detail. A good paper presenting a case study will include a description of the environment in which the tool, process, or software system was created. It will describe how the work was done and what conclusions were drawn, such as the following:

"This tool reduced logical software faults by 20%."

"Going directly from requirements to code without creating a system design increased costs by 30%."

"Demanding rigorous inspections reduced testing time by 10% and reduced testing costs by 25%."

"Use of the proprietary cost estimation software made us underestimate cost by 50%."

As a reader of the case-study type of research, you should look for information that suggests that similar results will hold for your organization. This means that you must determine if you have a similar environment and application domain and if you are able do the same thing that was described in the case study. This, in turn, implies that the paper presents the development environment and infrastructure in enough detail for you to compare it to your own environment and infrastructure.

If the detail in the paper is not sufficient, you should look for some additional detail before you try to implement the tool, process, or software system in your organization. If you can't get the additional information you need, you shouldn't attempt to do the same thing without being willing to risk complete failure for the recommended tool, process, or software system.

Even if you have sufficient detailed information to determine if the environment, infrastructure, and application are similar to your situation, you must still be careful. Unfortunately, the problem is due to the very nature of the case study approach.

The primary problem with even the most detailed case study is the lack of controls. There may be factors other than those reported in the case study that may have made major contributions to the results obtained. On the other hand, case studies often describe large systems.

Another type of research approach is the "comparative study." A comparative study also provides an assessment of two or more instances of a tool, process, or software system. It has an advantage over a case study in that there is a framework for comparison. A good comparative study often describes the environment and application domain, but there is frequently much less detail than in a case study because of space limitations. Comparative studies often describe realistic situations.

A case study will often have statements such as the following:

> "System A had 20% fewer logical software faults than system B."

> "Tool A was used by fewer than 50% of the developers, while tool B was used by more than 85%"

> "System A was three months behind schedule. System B was cancelled after missing its deadline by two years.."

> "There was no discernible difference between the two systems in terms of quality or speed of execution. However, system B cost 10% less than system A."

As with a case study, there are few controls in a comparative study and results can only be suggested, not proved. There many be many factors in addition to those presented in the paper that account for the results reported.

When reading a case study, watch that the systems compared in the paper are described in sufficient detail and convince yourself that the comparison is fair. The most common problem with comparative studies is that the comparison is done along lines that may not be fair in the sense that one of the tools, processes, or software systems being compared is used in a way that was not intended.

The last form of software engineering research that we describe is the "controlled experiment." Controlled experiments offer great promise in the sense that well-designed and implemented ones can indicate clearly that a particular tool, process, or software system is effective in some instance. A good experiment will have a clear design and the design will be reported in detail in the research report.

Unfortunately, controlled experiments are usually done in academic institutions, where the students are relative novices. In many experiments with large numbers of subjects, the subjects are usually chosen from beginning programming classes. As such, you should be suspicious that the results will scale up to large development efforts with experienced personnel.

Which of case study, comparative study, or controlled experiment should you believe most? The answer is all three, but you should only believe them a little until there is a body of supporting evidence.

The approach of the Software Engineering Laboratory (SEL) at NASA/ Goddard Space Flight Center is typical. Under the direction of Victor Basili and Marvin Zelkowitz of the University of Maryland and several colleagues from Goddard, a large body of knowledge is being created to support or refute several commonly held expert opinions and industry practices in software engineering. The knowledge base includes all three forms: case study, comparative study, and controlled experiment, and each builds upon knowledge for the others.

For example, case studies suggest comparative studies, which lead to experiments. Analyses of experimental results suggest new case studies. Comparative studies suggest new case studies, and so on.

References

Reading the following papers is a must for the software engineering researcher wishing to study empirical research in the discipline: Fenton and Pfleeger [FENT96], Tichy [TICH95], Kitchenham and Pfleeger [KITC97]. Nearly every issue of *IEEE Software, IEEE Computer, Communications of the ACM, ACM Transactions on Software Engineering and Methodology, IEEE Transactions on Software Engineering, Journal of Systems and Software, Software: Practice and Experience,* and *Experimental Computer Science* contains important and thought-provoking articles on software engineering. You should try to attend a meeting of the International Conference on Software Engineering. There is also a conference devoted to empirical work: the annual Empirical Assessment in Software Engineering Conference (EASE).

Exercises

1. (For those of you who are practicing software engineers.) Choose one of the first 107 research problems listed in this chapter and determine how the issue affects your organization.

2. (For those of you who are considering graduate school.) Choose one of the first 107 research problems listed in this chapter and start working on a Ph.D. in Computer Science.

3. Read a recent issue of one of the journals: *IEEE Software, IEEE Computer, Communications of the ACM, ACM Transactions on Software Engineering and Methodology, IEEE Transactions on Software Engineering, Journal of Systems and Software, Software: Practice and Experience, Experimental Computer Science,* or a recent *EASE* conference proceedings. How many of the articles describe case studies? How many describe comparative studies? How many describe controlled experiments?

4. Read a company internal report that describes a project. How would you classify this report: case study, comparative study, or controlled experiment? Write a critique of this report, using the ideas given in this chapter.

Appendix 1 Command-Line Arguments

The function main() in a C or C++ program can interact with its own environment – the operating system of the computer. The communication between the program and the operating system can go in two directions. If the program has an error such as division by 0, then the program communicates with the operating system and the program is halted. Communication in the other direction is done by means of command-line arguments.

In example A.1, we present an example of a program that has command-line arguments. Notice the form of the arguments to main(). These arguments are character strings that are put into the program by an interface between the command shell, which is part of the operating system, and the running program.

```
#include <stdio.h>

main(int argc, char *argv[] )
{
  int i;
  puts("The arguments to this function are:");
  for (i = 0; i < argc; i++)
    printf("%s\n",argv[i]);
  printf("\n");
}
```

Example A.1

Type in this program and run it. If your executable program was named a.out (which is the default name for executable files under the UNIX operating system), then your output would be the character string

```
a.out
```

on a line by itself. (The corresponding output in computers running under MS/DOS would be the character string

```
progname
```

assuming that the executable file was named progname.) For the input
    a.out Fred Marie Harry Computer Science types

397

the output would be

```
a.out
Fred
Marie
Harry
Computer
Science
types
```

with each string of characters printed on a line by itself. The command-line arguments in the first run of the program were

```
a.out
```

In the second run of the program, there were the seven command-line arguments listed previously. The value of argc was 1 in the first run and 7 in the second run. The value of argc is always at least 1 since the name of the executable file (a.out in this example) is always counted as a command-line argument. The other command-line arguments are stored in argv[]. (On systems running under MS/DOS, the output would be identical except for the name of the executable file.)

This example shows that the command line, which included the name of the executable file and other character strings, was processed by the operating system and the information was given to the program. This is useful when we wish to pass arguments to a C program.

The next example shows how we can read in a command-line argument as a string of characters (the only way to get commands from the operating system) and change it into an integer.

```c
#include <stdio.h>
main(int argc,char *argv[])
{
  int i,lim;
  lim = atoi(argv[1]);
  for(i=1;i <= lim;i++)
    printf("%d\n",i);
}
```

Example A.2

Type in this program and test it with several different arguments. It gives the correct answer if you type in a command line such as

```
a.out 2
a.out 23
```

It also gives a correct output (nothing) if the command line is

```
a.out c
```

where c can be any character. However, there is a serious error if you simply type the command line

```
a.out
```

The program terminates ungracefully with a core dump. The program is not well written from the standpoint of defensive programming since it can fail unpleasantly when presented with only minor errors in input. The example illustrates an extremely important principle of programming (especially C programming): be sure that possible errors in interfaces do not cause the program to crash. This warning applies both to interfaces to a human user entering data and to regular processing in the program.

The best way to write this program is to insert some defensive code immediately after the type declarations. Since the variable argc keeps track of the number of command-line arguments, we can use the argument count to exit if there are not enough arguments. This allows the program to terminate gracefully rather than dump the in-core memory into a file.

The defensive code is

```
if (argc == 1)
    {
    printf("Error - not enough arguments\n");
    exit(1);
    }
```

This code allows the termination of the program by using the exit() function, which is called with an argument of 0 to indicate that no abnormal action should be taken by the operating system. A call to exit() always terminates the program.

REFERENCES

[ADA83] Ada, *Reference Manual for the Ada Programming Language*, ANSI-MIL-STD-1815A, 1983.

[ADA95] Ada, *Reference Manual for the Ada Programming Language*, ANSI-MIL-STD-1815B, 1995.

[ALBR79] Albrecht, A. J., Measuring application development productivity, Proceedings of the IBM Applications Development Joint SHARE/GUIDE Symposium, Monterey, California, 83-92, 1979.

[ALBR83] Albrecht, A. J. and Gaffney, Jr., J. E., Source lines of code, and development effort prediction: a software science validation, *IEEE Transactions on Software Engineering*, SE-9, 639-648, 1983.

[ANSI91] *Standard glossary of software engineering terminology*, American National Standards Institute, ANSI/IEEE Standard 729-1991.

[ANSI92] *Recommended practice for software reliability*, American National Standards Institute, ANSI Standard R-012-1992.

[ARNO92] Arnold, R. S.,ed., *Software Reengineering*, IEEE Press, Los Alamitos, California, 1992.

[ARNO94] Arnold, T. R. and Fuson, W. A., Testing in a perfect world, *Commun. ACM* , Vol. 37, No. 9, 78-86, September 1994.

[ARNO96] Arnold, R. S. and Bohner, S., *Software Impact Change Analysis*, IEEE Press, Los Alamitos, California, 1997.

[ATKI91] Atkinson, C., *Object-Oriented Reuse, Concurrency, and Distribution*, ACM Press, New York, 1991.

[BAKE79] Baker, A. L. and Zweben, S. H., The use of software science in evaluating modularity, *IEEE Trans. Softw. Engr.* SE-5, Vol. 5, No. 3, 110-120, 1979.

[BARB94] Barbey, S. and Strohmeier, A., The problematics of testing object-oriented software, *Proceedings of the Second Conference on Software Quality Management (SQM'94)*, Edinburgh, Scotland, Vol. 2, 411-426, July 26-28, 1994.

[BARK97] Barker, T. T. and Dragga, S., *Writing Software Documentation: A Task-Oriented Approach*, Allyn & Bacon, New York, 1997.

[BARN94] Barnard, J. and Price, A., Managing code inspection information, *IEEE Software*, Vol. 11, No. 2, 59-69, March 1994.

[BASI85] Basili, V. R. and Selby, R. W., Comparing the effectiveness of software testing strategies, University of Maryland at College Park, Department of Computer Science, Technical Report Number TR-1501, 1985.

[BASI88] Basili, V. R. and Rombach, H. D., The TAME project: towards improvement-oriented software development, *IEEE Trans. Softw. Engr.* SE-14, Vol. 14, No. 6, 758-773, 1988.

[BASI90] Basili, V. R., Viewing maintenance as reuse-oriented software development, *IEEE Software*, Vol. 7, No. 1, 19-25, January 1990.

[BASI92] Basili, V. R., Caldiera, G., and Cantone, G., A reference architecture for the component factory *ACM Trans. on Software Engineering and Methodology*, Vol. 1, No. 1, 53-80, January 1992.

[BAT92] Batory, D. and O'Malley, S., The design and implementation of hierarchical software systems with reusable components, *ACM Trans. Software Engineering and Methodology,* October, 1992.

[BEHR87] Behrens, C. A., Measuring the productivity of computer systems development activities with function points, *IEEE Trans. Softw. Engr.* SE-13, Vol. 13, No. 1, 311-323, 1987.

[BEIZ83] Beizer, B., *Software Testing Techniques,* Van Nostrand Reinhold, New York, 1983.

[BEIZ90] Beizer, B., *Software Testing Techniques, second edition*, Van Nostrand Reinhold, New York, 1990.

[BERA93] Berard, E. V., *Essays on Object-Oriented Software Engineering, Volume* I, Prentice-Hall, Englewood Cliffs, New Jersey, 1993.

[BETH85] Bethea, R. M., Duran, B. S., and Boullon, T. L., *Statistical Methods for Engineers and Scientists, second edition*, Marcel Dekker, New York, 1985.

[BIEM95] Beiman, J. M. and Zhao, J. X., Reuse through inheritance: a quantitative study of C++ software, *Proceedings of the ACM-SIGSOFT Symposium on Software Reusability*, Seattle, Washington, April 28-30, 1995.

[BIEM95] Beiman, J. M. and Karunanithi, S., Measurement of language-supported reuse in object-oriented and object-based software, *J. Systems Software*, Vol. 30, No. 3, pp.271-293, September 1995.

[BIGG87] Biggerstaff, T. and Richter, C., Reusability framework, assessment, and directions, *IEEE Software*, Vol. 4, No. 2, 41-49, March 1987.

[BIGG89] Biggerstaff, T. and A. Perlis, A., eds., *Software Reusability*, Vol. 1, 2, ACM Press, New York, 1989.

[BIND94] Binder, R. V., Design for testability in object-oriented systems, *Commun. ACM*, Vol. 37, No. 9, 87-101, September 1994.

[BOEH78] Boehm, B., Brown, J. R., MacLeod, G. J., and Merritt, M. J., *Characteristics of Software Quality*, Elsevier, North-Holland, New York, 1978.

[BOEH81] Boehm, B., *Software Engineering Economics*, Prentice Hall, Englewood Cliffs, NJ, 1981.

[BOEH88] Boehm, B., A spiral model of software development and enhancement, *IEEE Computer*, Vol. 21, No. 2, 61-72, February, 1988.

[BOLL90] Bollinger, T. and S. L. Pfleeger, Economics of reuse: issues and alternatives, *Information and Software Technology*, Vol. 32, No. 10, 643-652, December, 1990.

[BOOC91] Booch, G., *Software Engineering with Ada:, third edition*, (with D. Bryan and C. G. Petersen), Benjamin Cummings, Redwood City, California, 1991.

[BOOC94] Booch, G., *Object-Oriented Analysis and Design with Applications*, Benjamin Cummings, Redwood City, California,, 1994.

[BOX78] Box, G. E. P., Hunter, W. J., and Hunter, J. S., *Statistics for Experimenters*, John Wiley & Sons, New York, 1978.

[BUDD94] Budd, T., *Classic Data Structures in C++*, Addison-Wesley, Reading, Massachusetts, 1994.

[BUHR90] Buhr, R., *Practical Visual Techniques in System Design with Applications in Ada*, Prentice-Hall, Englewood Cliffs, New Jersey, 1990.

[BURT87] Burton, B. A., et al., The reusable software library, *IEEE Software*, Vol. 4, No. 4, 25-33, July 1987.

[CARD82] Card, S. K., User perceptual mechanisms in the search of computer command menus, *Proceedings of the Human Factors Conference*, Washington, D. C., 1982

[CARD86] Card, D., Church, V. E., and Agresti, W. W., An empirical study of software design practices, *IEEE Transactions on Software Engineering*, SE-12, Vol. 12, 264-271, 1986.

[CHIK90] Chikofsky, E. and Cross, J., Reverse engineering and design recovery: a taxonomy, *IEEE Software*, Vol. 7, No. 1, January 1990.

[COAD91] Coad, P. and Yourdon, E., *Object-Oriented Analysis, second edition*, Prentice-Hall, Englewood Cliffs, New Jersey, 1991.

[CONT86] Conte, S. D., Dunsmore, H. E., and Shen, V. Y., *Software Engineering Metrics and Models* , Benjamin Cummings Publ., Menlo Park, California, 1986.

[CORB97] CORBA (Common Object-Oriented Request Broker Architecture), Object Management Group, http://www.omg.org

[DATE95] Date, C. J., *An Introduction to Database Systems, Sixth Edition*, Addison-Wesley, Reading, Massachusetts, 1995.

[DAVI90] Davis, A. M., *Software Requirements: Analysis and Specification*, Prentice-Hall, Englewood Cliffs, New Jersey, 1990.

[DAVI95] Davis, M. J., Adaptable, reusable code, *Proceedings of the Symposium on Software Reusability*, SSR'95, Seattle, Washington, 38-46, April 28-30, 1995.

[DEIT94] Deitel, H. M. and Deitel, P.J., *C++ How to Program,* Prentice-Hall, Englewood Cliffs, New Jersey, 1994.

[DEMI87] DeMillo, R. A., McCraken, W. M., Martin, R. J., and Passafiume, J. F., *Software Testing and Evaluation*, Benjamin Cummings, Menlo Park, California, 1987.

[DHAM95] Dhama, H., Quantitative models of cohesion and coupling in software, *J. Systems Software*, Vol. 29, 65-74, 1995.

[DIJK75] Dijkstra, E. W., Guarded commands, nondeterminism, and formal derivation of programs, *Commun. ACM*, Vol. 21, No. 8, 453-457, 1990.

[DISA93] DISA, Domain analysis and design process, Defense Information Systems Agency Center for Information Management (CIM) Software Reuse Office, Document #1222-04-210/30.1, 1993.

[DOUG92] Dougherty, D. *sed & awk*, O'Reilly & Associates, Sebastopol, California, 1992.

[DROM95] Dromey, R. G., A model for software product quality, *IEEE Transactions on Software Engineering*, SE21, Vol. 21, No. 2, pp. 146-162, February 1995.

[ELLI90] Ellis, M. and Stroustrup, B., *The Annotated C++ Reference Manual,* Addison-Wesley, Reading, Massachusetts, 1990

[ELLI95] Ellis, T., COTS integration in software solutions – a cost model, in *Systems Engineering in the Global Marketplace, NCOSE International Symposium*, St. Louis, Missouri, July 24-26, 1995.

[EZRA99] Ezran, M., Morisio, M., and Tully, C., Failure and success patterns in reuse programs: a synthesis of industrial experiences, *Tutorial TTF3, Twenty-first International Conference on Software Engineering,* ICSE'99, Los Angeles, California, May 17-21, 1999.

[FAGA76] Fagan, M., Design and code inspections to reduce errors in program development, *IBM Systems Journal*, Vol. 15, No. 3, 182-211, 1976.

[FARC94] Farchamps, D., Organizational factors and reuse, *IEEE Software*, Vol. 11, No. 5, 31-41, September 1994.

[FENT96] Fenton, N. E. and Pfleeger, S. L., *Software Metrics: a Rigorous Approach, second edition*, International Thomson Press, London, 1996.

[FINE91] Finelli, G. B., NASA software failure characterization experiments, in Littlewood, B. and D. R. Miller, eds., *Software Reliability and Safety*, Elsevier Science Publishers, London, 1991

[FOWL95] Fowler, G. S., Korn, D. G., and K.-P. Vo, Principles for writing reusable libraries, *Proceedings of the Symposium on Software Reusability*, SSR'95, Seattle, Washington, 150-159, April 28-30, 1995.

[FRAK90] Frakes, W. F. and Gandel, P. B., Representing reusable software, *Information and Software Technology*, Vol. 32, No. 10, 653-661, December, 1990.

[FRAK93] Frakes, W. B., ed., *Advances in Software Reuse: Selected papers from the Second International Workshop on Software Reusability*, Luccia, Italy, March 24-26, 1993.

[FRAK94A] Frakes, W. B. and Isoda, S., Success factors for systematic reuse, *IEEE Software*, Vol. 11, No. 5, 14-22, September 1994.

[FRAK94B] Frakes, W. B. and Pole, T. P., An Empirical study of representation methods for reusable software components, *IEEE Trans. Software Engineering.*, Vol SE-20., No. 8, 617-630, August 1994.

[FRAK94] Frakes, W. B.,ed., *Advances in Software Reuse: Selected papers from the Third International Workshop on Software Reusability*, Rio de Janeiro, Brazil, November 1-4, 1994.

[FRAK95A] Frakes, W. B. and Fox, C. J., Modeling reuse across the software life cycle, *J. Systems Software*, Vol. 30, No. 3, 295-301, September 1995.

[FRAK95] Frakes, W. B. and Fox, C. J., Sixteen questions about software reuse, *Commun. ACM*, Vol. 38, No. 6, 75-87, June 1995.

[FREE83] Freeman, P., Reusable software engineering: concepts and research directions, *ITT Proceedings of the Workshop on Reusability in Programming*, 129-137, 1983.

[FREE87] Freeman, P., Reusable software engineering: concepts and research directions. *Tutorial: Software Reusability,* IEEE Computer Society, Los Alamitos, California, 10-23, 1987.

[GAFF91] Gaffney, J. and Cruickshank, R. D., A general economics model for software reuse, Software Productivity Consortium, 1991.

[GAO93] General Accounting Office, Software reuse– major issues need to be resolved before benefits can be achieved, GAO Report Number GAO/IMTEC-93-16. Washington, D.C., 1993.

[GILB87] Gilb, T., *Principles of Software Engineering Management,* Addison-Wesley, Reading, Massachusetts, 1987.

[GOGU86] Goguen, J. A., Reusing and interconnecting software components, *IEEE Computer*, 16-28, February, 1986.

[GOLD90] Goldberg, A. and Rubin, K. S., Taming object-oriented technology, *Computer Language*, Vol. 7, No. 10, 34-35, October 1990.

[GOMA92] Gomaa, H., Methods and tools for domain-specific software architectures, *Proceedings of the Fifth Workshop on Software Reuse*, WISR-5, 1992.

[GOOD93] Goodman, M. A., Goyal, M., and Massoudi, R. A., *Solaris Porting Guide*, SunSoft Press, Mountain View California, 1993.

[GOUL95] Goulde, M., Developing a reuse strategy, *Open Computing*, Vol. 12, No. 8, 29, August 1, 1995.

[GRAD87] Grady, R. B. and Caswell, D.L., *Software Metrics: Estabishing a Company-Wide Policy*, Prentice-Hall, Englewood Cliffs, New Jersey, 1987.

[GRAD94] Grady, R. B., Successfully applying software metrics, *IEEE Computer*, Vol. 27, No. 9, 28-26, September 1994.

[GREE85] Green, M., University of Alberta user interface management system, *Proceedings SIGGRAPH Conference – Computer Graphics (ACM)* vol. 19 No. 3, 205-213, July 1985.

[GRIS92] Griss, M. L. A multi-disciplinary software reuse research program, *Proceedings of the Fifth Workshop on Software Reuse*, WISR-5, 1992.

[GUER94] Guerrieri, E., Case study: Digital's application generator, *IEEE Software*, Vol. 11, No. 5, 95-96, September 1994.

[HALL92] Hall, P. A. V., *Software Reuse and Reverse Engineering in Practice*, Chapman & Hall, London, 1992.

[HALS77] Halstead, M. H., *Elements of Software Science* , Elsevier North-Holland, New York, 1977.

[HARM91] Harms, D. E. and Weide, B. W., Copying and swapping: influence on the design of reusable software components, *IEEE Trans. Softw. Engr.*, SE-17, Vol. 17, No. 5, 424-435, May 1991.

[HARR92] Harrold, M. J., McGregor, J. D., and Fitzpatrick, K. J., Incremental testing of object-oriented class structures, *Proceedings of the 14th International Conference on Software Engineering*, Melbourne, Australia, 68-79, May 11-15, 1992.

[HART89] Hartson, H. R. and Hix, D., Human-computer interface development concepts and systems for its management, *ACM Comput. Surveys*, Vol. 21, No. 1,5-92, March 1989.

[HASH92] Hashemi, R. and Leach, R. J., Issues in porting software from C to C++, *Software – Practice & Experience*, Vol. 22, No. 7, 599–602, 1992.

[HENN91] Hennel, M. A., Testing for the achievement of software reliability, in Littlewood, B. and D. R. Miller, eds., *Software Reliability and Safety*, Elsevier Science Publishers, London, 1991

[HENN95A] Henninger, S., Developing domain knowledge through the reuse of project experience, *Proceedings of the Symposium on Software Reusability*, SSR'95, Seattle, Washington, 186-195, April 28-30, 1995.

[HENN95] Henninger, S., Information access tools for software reuse, *J. Systems Software*, Vol. 30, 231-247, 1995.

[HENR81] Henry, S. and Kafura, D., Software metrics based on information Flow, *IEEE Trans. Softw .Engr*, Vol. SE-7, No. 5, 510-518, September 1981.

[HENR96] Henricson, M. and Nyquist, E., *Industrial Strength C++: Rules and Recommendations* (Prentice Hall Series in Innovative Technology), Prentice-Hall, Englewood Cliffs, New Jersey, 1996.

[HOAR85] Hoare, C. A. R., *Communicating Sequential Processes*, Prentice-Hall, Englewood Cliffs, New Jersey, 1985.

[HOLL91] Hollingsworth, J. E., Weide, B. W., and Zweben, S. H., Confessions of some used-program clients, *Proceedings of the 4th Annual Workshop on Software Reuse*, Herndon, VA, November 1991.

[HOOP91] Hooper, J. W. and R. Chester, R., *Software Reuse: Guidelines and Methods*, Plenum Press, New York, 1991.

[HORT94] Horton, W. K., *Designing and Writing Online Documentation for Self-Supporting Products*, John Wiley & Sons, New York, 1994.

[HOWD87] Howden, W. E., *Functional Program Testing And Analysis*, McGraw-Hill, New York, 1987.

[HUMP89] Humphrey, W., *Managing the Software Process*, Addison-Wesley, Reading, Massachusetts, 1989.

[HUMP95] Humphrey, W., *A Discipline for Software Engineering*, Addison-Wesley, Reading, Massachusetts, 1995.

[ICHB86] Ichbiah, J.D., Barnes, J. G. P., Firth, R. J., and Woodger, M., *Rationale for the design of the Ada programming language*, ALSYS, France, 1986.

[IEEE88] IEEE, *IEEE Standard Dictionary of Measures to Produce Reliable Software*, IEEE STD 982.1-1988.

[IEEE92A] IEEE, *Standards for Software Productivity Metrics*, IEEE Standard 1045-1992.

[IEEE92] IEEE, *Standard for a Software Engineering Methodology*, IEEE STD 1061-1992.

[ISO87A] International Organization for Standardization, Quality Systems-Model for Quality Assurance in Design/Development, Production, Installation, and Servicing, ISO 9001, 1987.

[ISO87B] International Organization for Standardization, Quality Systems-Model for Quality Assurance in Production and Installation, ISO 9002, 1987.

[ISO87C] International Organization for Standardization, Quality Systems-Model for Quality Assurance in Final Inspection and Test, ISO 9003, 1987.

[ISO87] International Organization for Standardization, Quality Management and Quality Assurance Standards-Guidelines for Selection and Use, ISO 9000, 1987.

[ISO91A] International Standards Organization, ISO/IEC IS 10040: 1991, Information Technology – Open Systems Interconnection – Systems Management Overview.

[ISO91B] International Standards Organization, ISO/IEC IS 10164: 1991, Information Technology – Open Systems Interconnection – Systems Management Details.

[ISO91C] International Standards Organization, ISO/IEC IS 10165-1: 1991, Information Technology – Open Systems Interconnection – Structure of Management Information – Part 1: Management Information Model.

[ISO91D] International Standards Organization, ISO/IEC IS 10165-4: 1991, Information Technology – Open Systems Interconnection – Part 4: Guidelines for the Definition of Managed Objects.

[JELI72] Jelinski, F. and Moranda, P. B., Software reliability research, in *Statistical Computer Performance Evaluation*, W. Freiberger, Ed., Academic Press, New York, pp. 465-484, 1972.

[JENG95] Jeng, J-J. and Chen, B. H. C., Specification matching for software reuse: a foundation, *Proceedings of the ACM-SIGSOFT Symposium on Software Reusability*, Seattle, Washington, April 28-30, 1995.

[JOHN86] Johnson, L. F. and Cooper, R. H., *File Techniques for Data Nase Organization in COBOL, Second Edition*, Prentice-Hall, Englewood Cliffs, New Jersey, 1986.

[JOHN88] Johnson, R. E. and Foote, B., Designing reusable classes, *Journal of Object-Oriented Programming*, Vol.1, No. 2, 22-35, 1988.

[JOHN92A] Johnson, J. A. , Nardi, B. A., Zarmer, C. L., and Miller, J. R. ACE: an application construction environment, *Proceedings of the Fifth Workshop on Software Reuse*, WISR-5, 1992.

[JOHN92] Johnson, B., Ornburn, S., and Rugaber, S., A quick tools strategy for program analysis and software maintenance, *Proceedings of the Conference on Software Maintenance*, Orlando, Florida, 206-213, November 9-12, 1992.

[JONE84] Jones, T. Capers, Reusability in programming: a survey of the state of the art, *IEEE Transactions on Software Engineering*, Vol. SE-10, No. 5, 488-494, September 1984.

[JONE94] Jones, T. Capers, *Assessment and Control of Software Risks*, Yourdon Press, Prentice-Hall, Englewood Cliffs, New Jersey, 1994.

[JONE98] Jones, T. Capers, Bad days for software, *IEEE Spectrum*, 47-52, September 1998.

[JOOS94] Joos, R., Software Reuse at Motorola, *IEEE Software*, Vol. 11, No. 5, 42-47, September 1994.

[JORG94] Jorgenson, P. C. and Erikson, C., Object-oriented integration testing, *Commun. ACM*, Vol. 37, No. 9, 30-38, September 1994.

[KAFU81] Kafura, D., and Henry, S., Software quality metrics based on interconnectivity, J. *Syst. Software* 2, 121-131, 1981.

[KAIS87] Kaiser, G. E. and Garland, D., Melding software systems from reusable building blocks, *IEEE Software,* Vol. 4, No. 4, 17-24, July 1987.

[KAMA93] Kamath, Y. H., Smilan, R. E., and Smith, J. G., Reaping benefits with object-oriented technology, *AT&T Technical Journal*, Vol. 72, No. 5, 14-24, Sept./Oct. 1993.

[KARL95] Karlsonn, E.-A., *Software Reuse: A Holistic Approach*, John Wiley & Sons, New York, 1995.

[KARO98] Karolak, D., Shifting paradigm in software engineering management, keynote address at International Association of Science and Technology for Development (IASTED) Conference on Software Engineering, ACTA Press, Las Vegas, Nevada, October 28-31, 1998.

[KEIL83] Keiller, P. A., Littlewood, B., Miller, D. R., and Sofer, A., Comparison of software reliability predictions, *Proceedings of the Thirteenth International Symposium on Fault-Tolerant Computing*, IEEE Computer Society Press, 128-134, Washington, D.C., 1983.

[KEIL91] Keiller, P. A. and Miller, D. R., Software reliability growth models, in Littlewood, B. and D. R. Miller, eds. , *Software Reliability and Safety*, Elsevier Science Publishers, London, 1991

[KERN82] Kernighan, B. and Ritchie, D., *The C Programming Language*, Prentice-Hall, Englewood Cliffs, New Jersey, 1982.

[KERN84] Kernighan, B, The UNIX system and software reusability, *IEEE Trans. Softw. Engr.* SE-10, Vol. 10, No. 5, 513-518, September 1984.

[KERN88] Kernighan, B. and Ritchie, D., *The C Programming Language, Second Edition*, Prentice-Hall, Englewood Cliffs, New Jersey, 1988.

[KONT95] Kontio, J., OTSO: a systematic process for reusable software component selection, University of Maryland, College Park Technical Report CS-TR-3478, UMIACS-TR-95-63, December 1995.

[KRIS95] Krishnamurthy, B., *Practical Reusable UNIX Software*, John Wiley & Sons, New York, 1995.

[KRUE92] Krueger, C. W., Software reuse, *ACM Computing Surveys*, Vol. 24, No. 2, 131-183, June, 1992.

[LAMO95] LaMonica, M., Object code is not spurring reuse by IS, *Infoworld*, Vol. 17, Issue 39, 19-20, August 21, 1995.

[LEA92] Lea, D. and de Champeaux, D., Object-oriented software reuse technical opportunities, *Proceedings of the Fifth Workshop on Software Reuse*, WISR-5, 1992.

[LEAC93] Leach, R. J., *Using C in Software Design*, Academic Press Professional, Boston, 1993.

[LEAC94] Leach, R. J., *Advanced Topics in UNIX*, John Wiley & Sons, New York, 1994.

[LEAC95A] Leach, R. J., *Object-Oriented Design and Programming in C++*, Academic Press Professional, Boston, 1995.

[LEAC97] Leach, R. J., *Software Reuse: Methods, Models, Costs*, McGraw-Hill, New York, 1997.

[LEAC98] Leach, R. J., Assessment of COTS products from an operating systems-level perspective, Pacific Northwest Quality Conference, Portland, Oregon, October 1998.

[LEDB85] Ledbetter, L. and Cox, B., Software-ICs: a plan for building reusable software components. *BYTE*, 28-35, June 1985.

[LEVE86] Leveson, N. G., Software safety: what, why and how, *ACM Computing Surveys*, Vol. 18, No. 2, 125-163, 1986.

[LEVI92] Levine, J. R., Mason, T., and Brown, D., *lex & yacc*, second edition, O'Reilly & Associates, Sebastopol, California, 1992.

[LILL93] Lillie, C., Software reuse, *Proceedings of the Second Annual Reuse Education and Training Workshop*, Morgantown, West Virginia, October 1993.

[LIM94] Lim, W. C., Effects of reuse on quality, productivity, and economics, *IEEE Software*, Vol. 11, No. 5, 23-30, September 1994.

[LIM95] Lim, W. C., *Managing Software Reuse*, Prentice-Hall, Englewood Cliffs, New Jersey, 1995.

[LIND94] Lindholm, E., Snap-on code. *Datamation*, Vol. 40, 63, Feb. 1, 1994.

[LITT91] Littlewood, B. and Miller, D. R., eds., *Software Reliability and Safety*, Elsevier Science Publishers, London, 1991. (Also in *Reliability Engineering and System Safety*, Vol. 32., Nos. 1 and 2, 1991.)

[LUGI88] Lugi, and Ketabchi, M., A computer-aided prototyping system, *IEEE Software*, Vol. 5, No. 2, March 1988, pp. 66-72.

[MATS89] Matsumoto, Y., and Y. Ohno, *Japanese Perspectives in Software Engineering*, Prentice-Hall, Englewood Cliffs, New Jersey, 1989.

[McCA76] McCabe, T. J., A complexity measure, *IEEE Trans. Softw. Engr.*, Vol. SE-2, 308-320, December 1976.

[McCA95] McCarthy, J., *Dynamics of Software Development*, Microsoft Press, Redmond, Washington, 1995.

[McCL92] McClure, Carma, *The Three R's of Software Automation: Re-engineering, Repository, Reusability*, Prentice-Hall, Englewood Cliffs, New Jersey, 1992.

[McCO99] McConnell, S. Open source methodology: ready for prime time?, *IEEE Software*, Vol. 16, No. 4, 6-8, July-August 1999.

[McGR94] McGregor, J. D. and Korson, T. D., Integrating object-oriented testing and development processes, *Commun. ACM,*Vol. 37, No. 9, 59-77, September 1994.

[McIL68] McIlroy, M. D., Mass produced software components, in *Software Engineering Concepts and Techniques*, Proceedings of the 1968 NATO Conference on Software Engineering, Petrocelli/Charter, Brussels, Belgium, 88-98, 1968.

[MEYE87] Meyer, B., Reusability: The case for object-oriented design, *IEEE Software*, Vol. 4, 50-63, March 1987.

[MILI93] Mili, H., Mili, F., and Mili, A., Reusing software: issues and research directions, *IEEE Trans Softw. Engr.SE-21*, Vo. 21, No. 6, 528-561, June 1995.

{MILL56] Miller, G., The magic number seven, plus or minus two: some limits on our capacity for processing information, *The Psychological Review*, Vol. 63, 81-97, March, 1956.

[MILL68] Miller, R. B., Response time in man-computer conversational transactions, *AFIPS Conference Proceedings*, Vol 22, 267-277, December 1968.

[MILL78] Miller, E., and W. E. Howden, *Software Testing and Validation Techniques,* IEEE Computer Society, Long Beach, CA, 1978.

[MILL83] Miller, E. and Howden, W. E., *Software Testing and Validation Techniques, second edition,* IEEE Computer Society, Long Beach, CA, 1983.

[MILL87] Mills, H. D., Dyer, M. and Linger, R. C., Cleanroom software engineering, *IEEE Software*, Vol. 4, 19-24, September 1987.

[MILN80] Milner, R., *A Calculus of Communicating Systems*, Springer-Verlag, New York, 1980.

[MONT91] Montgomery, D. C., *Introduction to Statistical Quality Control*, John Wiley & Sons, New York, 1991.

[MOOR91] Moore, J. M. and Bailin, S. C., Domain analysis: framework for reuse, in *Domain Analysis and Software Systems Modeling*, R. Prieto-Diaz and G. Arango, Ed., IEEE Press, Los Alamitos, California, 1991.

[MURP94] Murphy, G. C., Townsend, P., and Wong,, P. S., Experiences with cluster and class testing, *Commun. ACM*, Vol. 37, No. 9, 39-47, September 1994.

[MUSA87] Musa, J. D., Iannino, A., and Okumoto, K., *Software Reliability: Measurement, Prediction, Application*, McGraw-Hill, New York, 1987.

[MUSA93] Musa, J. D., Operational Profiles in software reliability engineering, *IEEE Software*, Vol. 10, No. 2, 14-32, March 1993.

[MUSE92] Musen, M. A., Dimensions of knowledge sharing and reuse, *Computers and Biomedical Research*, Vol. 25, 435-467, 1992.

[MYER76] Myers, G., *Software Reliability: Principles and Practices*, Wiley, New York, 1976.

[MYER79] Myers, J. G., *The Art of Software Testing*, John Wiley & Sons, New York, 1979.

[MYER95] Myers, W., Taligent's Common Point: the promise of objects, IEEE Computer, Vol 28, No. 3, 77-83, March 1995.

[NASA88] NASA, Software reuse issues, *Proceedings of the 1988 Workshop on Software Reuse*, sponsored by NASA Langley Research Center, Melbourne, Florida, November 17-18, 1988.

[NASA92A] Proceedings of the Second NASA Workshop on software Reuse, Research Triangle Park, North Carolina, May 5-6, 1992.

[NASA92] Software engineering program: profile of software within Code 500 at Goddard Space Flight Center, *NASA SEP Report R01-92*, December 1992.

[NAVA92] Navarro, J. J., Organization design for software reuse, *Proceedings of the Fifth Workshop on Software Reuse*, WISR-5, 1992.

[NIEL94] Nielsen, J., *Usability Engineering*, Academic Press, San Diego, 1994.

[NIST92] National Institute for Standards and Technology, *Management Information Catalog*, Issue 1.0, NIST, OIW, and Network Management Forum, Gaithersburg, Maryland, June 1992. (There are subsequent catalogs.)

[NIST95], National Institute for Standards and Technology, (Katz, S., Dabrowski, C., Miles, K. and Law, M., eds.) *Glossary of Software Reuse Terms*, Gaithersburg, Maryland, 1995.

[OLSE86] Olsen, D. R., MIKE: The menu interaction kontrol environment, *ACM Transactions on Graphics*, Vol. 5, No. 4, 318-344, October 1986.

[PARN72] Parnas, D. L., On the criteria for decomposing systems into modules, *Commun. ACM*, Vol. 15, No. 12, 1052-1058, 1972.

[PARN85] Parnas, D. L., The modular structure of complex systems, *IEEE Transactions on Software Engineering*, 259-266, March 1985.

[PERR90] Perry, D., and Kaiser, G., Adequate testing and object-oriented programming, *J. Object-Oriented Programming*, Vol. 3., No. 1, Jan/Feb 1990.

[PFLE91] Pfleeger, S. L., *Software Engineering: The Production of Quality Software* , Macmillan, New York, 1989.

[PFLE91A]   Pfleeger, S. L., Model of software effort and productivity, *Information Software and Technology*, Vol. 33, No. 3, 224-231, April 1991.

[PFLE94A] Pfleeger, S. L., and Bollinger, T. B., Economics of reuse: new approaches to modelling and assessing cost, *Information and Software Technology*, August 1994.

[PFLE94] Pfleeger, S. L., Fenton, N., and Page, S., Evaluating Software engineering standards, *IEEE Computer*, Vol. 27, No. 9, 71-79, September 1994.

[PFLE96] Pfleeger, S. L, Measuring reuse: a cautionary tale, *IEEE Software*, 1996.

[PFLE96] Pfleeger, C., *Security in Computing, second edition*, Prentice-Hall, Englewood Cliffs, New Jersey, 1996.

[PIGO97] Pigoski, T. M., *Practical Software Maintenance*, IEEE Press, Los Alamitos, California, 1997.

[PLAU92] Plauger, P. J., *The Standard C Library*, Prentice Hall, Englewood Cliffs, NJ, 1992.

[PLAU94] Plauger, P. J., *The Draft Standard C++ Library*, Prentice Hall, Englewood Cliffs, NJ, 1994.

[PLES92] Pleszkoch, M. G., Linger, R. C., and Hevner, A. R., Eliminating non-transferable paths from structured programs, *Proceedings of the IEEE Conference on Software Maintenance*, Orlando, Florida, 156-164, November 9-12, 1992.

[POHL89] Pohl, I., *C++ for C Programmers,*Benjamin Cummings, Redwood City, California, 1989.

[POST94] Poston, R. M., Automated testing from object models, *Commun. ACM,* Vol. 37, No. 9, 48-58, September 1994.

[POUL94] Poulin, J. S., Measuring software reusability, *Proceedings of the Third International Workshop on Software Reuse*, Rio de Janeiro, Brazil, November 1-4, 1994.

[POUL95] Poulin, J. S. and Werkman, K. J., Melding structured abstracts and the world wide web for retrieval of reusable components, *Proceedings of the Symposium on Software Reusability*, SSR'95, Seattle, Washington, 160-168, April 28-30, 1995.

[PRES92] Pressman, R., *Software Engineering: A Practioner's Approach, 3rd. edition*, McGraw-Hill, New York, 1992.

[PRIE91A] Prieto-Diaz, R., Implementing faceted classification for software reuse, *Commun. ACM*, Vol. 34, No. 5, 88-97, May 1991.

[PRIE91] Prieto-Diaz, R., and Arango, G., eds., *Domain Analysis and Software Sytems Modeling*, IEEE Press, Los Alamitos, California, 1991.

[PRIE93] Prieto-Diaz, R., Some experiences in domain analysis, *Proceedings of the Sixth Workshop on Software Reuse*, WISR-6, 1993.

[PRIE93A] Prieto-Diaz, R., Status report: software reusability, *IEEE Software*, 61-66, May, 1993.

[PUTN78] Putnam, L. H., A general empirical solution to the macro software size and estimation problem, *IEEE Trans. Softw. Engr.* SE-4, Vol. 4, No. 4, 345-361, 1978.

[RADA95] Rada, R., *Software Reuse*, Ablex, 1995.

[RAMA82] Ramamoorthy, C. V. and Bastiani, F. B., Software reliability-status and perspectives, *IEEE Trans. Softw. Engr.* SE-8, Vol. 8, No. 4, 354-371, July 1982.

[RAMA88] Ramamoorthy, C. V., Garg, V., and Prakash, A., Support for reusability: genesis, *IEEE Trans. Softw. Engr.* SE-14, Vol. 14, No. 8, 1145-1154, 1988.

[RAND75] Randell, B., System structure for software fault tolerance, *IEEE Trans. Softw. Engr.*, Vol. SE-11, No. 2, June 1975.

[RATC90] Ratcliffe, B. and Rollo, A. L., Adapting function point analysis to the Jackson system development, *Soft. Engr. J.*, Vol 5, No. 1, 1990.

[RAY92] Ray, G., Software reuse not a panacea; some firms pursue it as a development goal; others question its viability, *Computerworld*, Vol. 26, 47, December 21, 1992.

[REIF95] Reifer, D. J., *Managing Software Reuse*, John Wiley & Sons, New York, 1995.

[REIF96] Reifer, D. J., Quantifying the debate: Ada vs. C++, *Crosstalk: The Journal of Defense Software Engineering,* Vol. 9, No. 7, 28-30, July 1996.

[RENS88] Renshaw, L., Eliminating GOTOs while preserving program structure, *Journal of the ACM*, Vol. 35, No. 4, October, 1988.

[RITC78] Ritchie, D. M. and Thompson, K., The UNIX time-sharing system, *Bell Sys. Tech. J.*, Vol. 57, No. 6, 1905-1929, 1978.

[RIX92] Rix, M., Case study of a successful firmware reuse program, *Proceedings of the Fifth Workshop on Software Reuse*, WISR-5, 1992.

[ROMB91] Rombach, H. D., Software reuse: a key to the maintenance problem, *Information and Software Technology*, Vol. 33, No. 1, 86-92, January/February, 1991.

[RUBI90] Rubin, H., *The Rubin review*, Vol. III, No. 3, July 1990.

[SAMU94] Samuelson, P., Self-plagiarism or fair use?, *Commun. ACM*, Vol. 37, No. 8, 21-25, August 1994.

[SCHA94] Schaefer, W., Prieto-Diaz, R., and Matsumoto, M., eds., *Software Reusability*, Ellis-Horwood, New York, 1994.

[SCHN80] Schneiderman, B., *Software Psychology: Human Factors in Computer and Information Systems*, Scott, Foresman, New York, 1980.

[SCHN87] Schneidewind, N. F., The state of software maintenance, *IEEE Trans. Softw. Engr.*, SE-13, Vol. 13, No. 3, 303-310, 1987.

[SEAT95] Seaton, B. L., Improving software project estimation within the missions operation and systems development division, *Management project for course CSMN 690* , University of Maryland University College Graduate School, College Park, MD, 1995.

[SEL91] Software Engineering Laboratory, *Proceedings of the Sixteenth Annual NASA/Goddard Software Engineering Workshop: Experiments in Software Engineering*, NASA/Goddard Space Flight Center, Greenbelt, MD, December 1991.

[SEL94]   Software Engineering Laboratory, *Software Measurement Handbook*, NASA/Goddard Space Flight Center, Greenbelt, MD, SEL-94-002, 1994.

[SEL95] Software Engineering Laboratory, *Impact of Ada and Object-Oriented Design in the Flight Dynamics Division at Goddard Space Flight Center*, NASA/Goddard Space Flight Center, Greenbelt, MD, March 1995.

[SHAE94] Shafer, W., Preito-Diaz, R., and Matsumoto, M., eds., *Software Reusability*, Ellis Horwood, Chichester, UK, 1994.

[SHAW96] Shaw, M. and Garlan, D., *Software Architecture: Perspectives on an Emerging Discipline*, IEEE Press, Los Alamitos, California, 1992.

[SHOO83] Shooman, M. L., *Software Engineering,: Design, Reliability, and Management*, McGraw-Hill, New York, 1983.

[SHRI89]   Shriver, B. and Wegner, P., *Research Directions in Object-Oriented Programming*, MIT Press, Cambridge, MA, March 1989.

[SINC94] Sinclair, G. C. and Jeletic, K. F., Profile of software engineering within the National Aeronautics and Space Administration (NASA), *Proceedings of the Nineteenth Annual Software Engineering Workshop*, Greenbelt, Maryland, November 30 - December 1, 1994.

[SITA93] Sitaraman, M., Welch, L. R., and Harms, D. E., On specification of reusable software components, *International Journal of Software Engineering and Knowledge Engineering*, Vol. 3, 207-229, June, 1993.

[SORD78], Sordillo, D. A., *The Programmer's ANSI COBOL Reference Manual*, Prentice-Hall, Englewood Cliffs, New Jersey, 1978.

[SPIV88] Spivey, J. M., *The Z Notation:A Reference Manua*l, Prentice-Hall International, London, 1988.

[STRO82] Stroustrup, B., Classes: an abstract data type faculty for the C language, *ACM SIGPLAN Notices*, Vol. 17, No. 1, January 1982.

[STRO84] Stroustrup, B., Data abstraction in C, *AT&T Bell Laboratories Technical Journal,* Vol. 63, No. 8, October 1984.

[STRO91] Stroustrup, B., *The C++ Programing Language, second edition*, Addison-Wesley, Reading, Massachusetts, 1991.

[STRO94] Stroustrup, B., *The Design and Evolution of C++*, Addison-Wesley, Reading, Massachusetts, 1994.

[TATE91] Tate, G. and Verner, J. M., Approaches to measuring size of application products with CASE tools, *Information and Software Technology*, Vol. 33, No. 9, 622-628, November, 1991.

[THAY97] Thayer, R. H. and Dorfman, M., *Software Requirements Engineering, second edition*, IEEE Press, Los Alamitos, California, 1992.

[TRAC89] Tracz, W., *Confessions of a Used Program Salesman: Institutionalizing Software Reuse*, Addison-Wesley, Reading, Massachusetts, 1995.

[TRAC89] Tracz, W., *Software Reuse: Emerging Technology*, IEEE Press, Washington, D.C., 1989.

[UDEL94] Udell, J., Componentware, *BYTE*, Vol. 19, No. 5, 46-56, May 1994.

[VERN89] Verner, J. M., Tate, G., Jackson, B., and Haywood, R. G., Technology dependence in function point analysis: a case study and critical review, *Proceedings of the Twelfth International Conference on Software Engineering*, 375-382, 1989.

[VOAS95] Voas, J., Payne, J., Mills, J. R., and McManus, J., Software testability: an experiment in measuring simulation reusability, *Proceedings of the ACM-SIGSOFT Symposium on Software Reusability*, Seattle, Washington, April 28-30, 1995.

[VOAS95A] Voas, J.M. and K. W. Miller, K. W., Software Testability: the new verification, *IEEE Software*, Vol. 12, No. 3, 17-28, May, 1995.

[WALT95] Walton, G. H., Poore, J. H., and Trammell, C. J., Statistical testing of a usage model, *Software–Practice and Experience*, Vol. 25, No. 1, 97-108, January 1995.

[WARD89] Ward M., Calliss, F.W., and Munro, M, The maintainer's assistant, *Proceedings of the Conference on Software Maintenance 1989*, Miami, Florida, IEEE Computer Society Press, 307-315, October 1989.

[WAUN95] Waund, C., COTS integration and support model, in *Systems Engineering in the Global Marketplace: NCOSE International Symposium*, St. Louis, Missouri, July 24-26, 1995.

[WENT92] Wentzel, K., Software reuse–it's a business, *Proceedings of the Fifth Workshop on Software Reuse*, WISR-5, 1992.

[WEYU86] Weyuker, E., Axiomatizing software test data adequacy, *IEEE Transactions on Software Engineering*, Vol. 12, No. 12, 1986.

[WEYU88] Weyuker, E., Evaluating software complexity measures, *IEEE Transactions on Software Engineering*, Vol. SE-14, 1357-1365, 1988.

[WILK95] Wilkening, D. E., Loyall, J. P., Pitarys, M. J., and Littlejohn, K., A reuse approach to software reengineering, *J. Systems Software*, Vol. 30, No. 1-2, 117-125, July-August, 1995.

[WOHL94] Wohlin, C. and Runeson, P., Certification of software components, *IEEE Transactions on Software Engineering*, Vol. 20, No. 6, 494-499, June 1994.

{WRIG97] Wright, P., Mosser-Wooley, D., and Wooley, B., Using color in computer interface design, *ACM Crossroads*, Vol. 3, No. 3, 3-6, Spring, 1993.

[YOUR79] Yourdon, E., and Constantine, L., *Structured Design: Fundamentals of a Discipline of Computer Program and System Design*, Prentice-Hall, Englewood Cliffs, New Jersey, 1979.

[YOUR89] Yourdon, E., *Modern Structured Analysis*, Prentice-Hall, Englewood Cliffs, New Jersey, 1989.

[ZARE95] Zaremski, A. M. and Wing, J. M., Signature matching: a tool for using software libraries, *ACM Transactions on Software Engineering and Methodology*, Vol. 4, No. 2, 146-170, April, 1995.

[ZWEB92] Zweben, S. H., and Heyn, W. D., Systematic testing of data abstractions based on software specifications, *Journal of Software Testing, Verification, and Reliability*, Vol. 1, No. 4, 39-55, 1992.

INDEX

&, 205
\0, 191
<<, 203
>>, 203
6, 167
a.out, 398
Ada programming language, 108,
    158, 247, 248, 250, 255, 264,
    265, 287, 288, 358, 365, 391,
    401, 404, 405, 411, 422, 424
agent-based relationship, 188
aggregation, 196
Albrecht, A., 401, 137, 167
Allen, P., 257
ANSI/IEEE Standard 729-1991, 401
Apple computer, 257
application generator, 389
arc, 180
argc, 398
argv, 398
Armstrong, M., 164, 165, 348
Armstrong, S., 164, 165, 348
Arnold, R., 382, 401
artificial intelligence, 180
artificial neural network, 387
assignment operator, 310
Association for Computing
    Machinery, 11, 398, 399, 401,
    402, 403, 404, 406, 408, 409,
    410, 413, 415, 416, 417, 418,
    419, 421, 422, 423, 424, 427
attribute, 187, 190. 199, 244
attribute list, 196
Barnes, C., 359, 365, 411
base class, 187, 245
Basili, V., 79, 398, 402
bathtub curve, 366
Beizer, B., 403
Berry, D., 104, 161, 167, 168
Berry, O., 104, 161, 167, 168
big-bang integration, 387
Biggerstaff, T., 403, 404
black-box testing, 264, 265, 386
Boehm, B., 73, 88, 404

Booch, G., 201, 389, 404
Booch diagrams, 175
bottom-up integration, 387
browser, 83, 244
Buhr, R., 389, 405
Buhr diagrams, 175
BVA metric, 263, 265
C programming language, 108, 110,
    115, 127, 152, 153, 155-163, 246,
    247, 249, 250, 253-256, 257, 264,
    270, 277, 285, 287-290, 345, 352,
    353, 359, 365, 378, 391, 397,
    399, 402-406, 408, 410, 412-416,
    418-422, 424-426
C++ programming language, 108,
    110, 115, 152, 153, 155, 157,
    159, 160-163, 246, 247, 249, 250,
    254, 257, 277, 285, 287-290, 359,
    365, 391, 397, 403, 404, 406,
    410, 415, 420, 421, 422, 425
Capability Maturity Model, 79, 269
Capers Jones, T., 137, 167
CASE, 65, 66, 80, 81, 89, 352, 358,
    380, 388, 425
cerr, 203, 308
Charles, E.,.201
checkpoint, 330
cin, 203, 308
class, 190, 191, 199, 200, 244, 312,
    340
class hierarchy, 187
class level testing, 312
class library, 200, 244
classical waterfall model, 91, 140,
    143, 55, 58
client-server, 188
Coad, P., 405
COBOL, 413, 424
COCOMO, 73, 74, 75, 76, 88, 89
coding standards, 245, 250, 251,
    256-259, 261, 266, 274, 280, 285,
    287-289, 356, 386, 387
combinatorial explosion, 312
command-line arguments, 397

Commercial-off-the-shelf (COTS),
71, 112, 113, 114, 132, 162, 165,
377, 378, 387, 388, 406, 415, 426
Common Object-Oriented Request
Broker Architecture, 405
component reuse, 389
computer aided software engineering,
65, 66, 80, 81, 89. 352, 358, 380,
388, 425
configuration management, 267, 394,
395
constructor function, 180, 191
constructor member function, 192
CORBA, 392, 405
Correctness, 11
coupling metrics, 263
cout, 191, 203, 308
cpio, 343, 344, 345, 347
Craven, W., 344, 345
cyclomatic complexity, 261, 262,
263, 288
data flow design description, 38, 170
data flow diagram, 244
data sink, 38, 170
data source, 38, 170
data structure, 196
data type, 191
database design, 180
decision box, 37, 169
decision table, 124, 127, 128, 168,
170, 171
delivery, 56, 58, 88, 341, 362, 364
DeMarco, 38, 87, 170
Department of Defense standard
MIL-STD 2167A, 394
derived class, 187, 245
design, 54, 55, 57-59, 69, 78, 79, 82,
83, 87, 90, 91, 93, 96, 99, 102,
103, 105, 108, 110, 117, 118-120,
124, 130, 146, 147, 148, 150,
151, 166, 252, 260, 263, 266,
269, 270, 285, 286, 290, 346,
355, 358, 359, 361, 364, 365,
366, 368, 369, 371, 379, 381,
386, 389, 396, 397, 417
design rationale, 355, 358, 359, 365,
366
design representation, 244
design review, 266, 386

destructor, 180
documentation, 57, 65, 69, 84, 85,
89, 91, 143, 149, 150, 251, 252,
258, 261, 279, 280, 342, 355-361,
364-366, 368-371, 379, 380, 381
double, 341
dynamically linked library, 111, 349,
350, 351
Efficiency, 10
Eiffel programming language, 108
elicitation, 93, 152
Ellis, M., 247, 289, 359, 365, 406,
424
Empirical Assessment in Software
Engineering Conference, 398, 399
encapsulation, 340
encapsulation strategy, 313
encryption, 59, 131
entity-relationship, 180
E-R, 180, 193
E-R diagram, 180, 196
ethics, 133
exhaustion of a depth strategy, 313,
340
exit( ), 400
experiment,167, 290, 384-387, 390,
392-394, 395, 397-399
expert systems, 180
failure, 34
Family-Oriented Abstraction,
Specification, and Translation
technique, 388, 389
fault, 34
fault exposure ratio, 333
fault ratio, 333
fault seeding, 386
fault-tolerance, 389, 390
Fenton, N., 288, 398, 407, 420
finite state machine, 124, 125, 126,
194
float, 341
flowchart, 37, 169, 244
Foote, B., 413
formal methods, 384, 393
FORTRAN programming language,
108, 246, 252, 253, 359
framework, 403, 418
friend function, 200, 205
function, virtual, 247

function, 191, 244
function point metric, 137, 138, 139, 167, 168, 170
Gaffney, J., 401, 408
Gates, B., 257
generative reuse, 389
getc(), 308
getchar(), 308
gets(), 308
glueware, 218, 286
goals, questions, metrics paradigm, 79
Goddard Space Flight Center, 84, 250, 298, 419, 423, 424
graphical user interface, 95, 97, 145, 154, 257, 357, 372, 373, 374
groupware, 84
Halstead, M., 288, 409
hard real-time requirement, 74
"has-a" relationship, 187
Hatton, L., 246
Hecht, M., 91
Henry, M., 164, 165, 348, 410, 413
Hevner, A., 421
HIPO charts, 175
Hoare, C. A. R., 410
Howden, W., 411, 417
HP-UX, 70
HTML, 82, 83, 145, 392
Humphrey, W., 87, 135, 411
I/O, 306
I/O manipulator, 308
IBM, 137, 257, 401, 407
Ichbiah, J., 359, 365, 411
IEEE Standard 1045-1992, 411
IEEE STD 1061-1992, 411
IEEE STD 982.1-1988, 411
ignorance hiding, 104, 105, 107, 153, 161, 168, 171
information model, 120, 180, 196
information model diagram, 196
information modeling, 196
inheritance, 340
inheritance strategy, 313

initializer, 180
installation, 56, 59, 91, 96, 98, 138, 146, 259, 341, 342, 348, 351, 352, 354, 355, 359, 362, 364-366, 370
Institute for Electrical and Electronic Engineers, 133, 398, 399, 401, 402, 403, 404, 405, 406, 407, 408, 409, 410, 411, 413, 414, 416, 417, 418, 419, 420, 421, 422, 423, 424, 425, 426
integration, 58, 61, 77, 86, 87, 91, 245, 285, 286, 347
intelligent agent, 360, 361, 390
interactive, 340
interactive strategy, 313
interface, 244
interface model, 193
inter-failure time, 331
International Conference on Software Engineering, 398, 407, 410, 425
International Standards Organization, 394, 411, 412
Internet, 53, 82, 83, 84, 89, 250, 288, 289, 343, 352, 356, 364, 381, 388, 393, 395
Interoperability, 11
iomanip.h, 308
"is-a" relation, 187, 245
Java programming language, 145, 152, 153, 155, 157, 159-161, 163, 248, 271, 274, 280, 281, 285, 289, 391-393, 395
Jelinski, F., 412., 413
Joint Photographic Expert Group, 82
Keiller, P., 414
Kernighan, B., 288, 414
Kincaid, 361
Kincaid reading level test, 361
KLOC, 371
Leach, R., 410, 415
Leveson, N., 416
lex, 375, 392, 416
lexical analyzer, 392

Linger, R., 418, 421
linked list, 191
Linux, 94, 111, 145, 393
logic language, 392
long double, 341
Lorenz, 312
lvalue, 311
MacOS, 94, 111, 145
maintainability, 10, 287
maintenance, 56, 57, 61, 62, 69, 70,
    74, 77, 88, 89, 91, 142, 156, 158,
    162, 257, 269, 345, 365, 366-376,
    378-382, 387, 388, 393, 402, 413,
    420, 421, 423, 426
maintenance report, 371, 374, 380
Mandl, D., 63, 84
manipulator, 308
market-driven software development,
    58
McCabe, T., 261, 262, 288, 416
McCabe cyclomatic complexity, 261
McCarthy, J., 63, 87, 115, 257, 288,
    416
mean time between failures, 330
member function, 191, 192, 200
method level testing, 312
Microsoft, 63, 67, 81, 84, 88, 95,
    115, 145, 162, 163, 165, 248,
    257, 259, 287, 288, 344, 348,
    355, 360, 375, 416
Microsoft Excel, 95, 145, 162, 163,
    165, 167, 286, 287, 363
milestone, 64, 77, 78, 140, 390
milestone chart, 77, 78
Mills, H., 418, 425
minimalization, 340
minimalization strategy, 313
modifiability, 10, 138
modularity, 90, 263
module level, 292, 312
module level testing, 312
Moranda, P., 412
Motion Picture Expert Group, 82
MS-DOS, 94, 111, 258, 344
MTBF, 330
multiple examples test, 187
multiple inheritance, 204
Musa, J., 418
Myers, J. G., 418, 419

NASA, 62, 84, 98, 100, 114, 250,
    257, 359, 398, 407, 419, 423, 424
Nassi-Schneiderman charts, 175
National Institute of Science and
    Technology, 91. 491
node, 37, 169
non-object-oriented program, 312
null byte, 191
N-version programming, 390
object, 190, 200, 244
object model, 99, 193, 269
object-oriented modeling, 190
object-oriented program, 340
object-oriented programming, 312,
    313
object-oriented software, 79, 93, 102,
    104, 108, 248, 265, 269, 384,
    385, 386, 391, 395
object-oriented system, 244
operational profile, 331
ostream, 205
overload, 203
overloaded operator, 307
overloading of operators, 189, 237
parent class, 313
parser generator, 392
passing parameters by constant
    reference, 205
pattern, software, 77, 253, 347, 365
performance testing, 386
Petri net, 128, 129, 130, 168-171
Pfleeger, S., 288, 343, 398, 404, 407,
    420
planning, 58, 64, 78, 86, 151, 367,
    383
Plauger, P., 207
Pleszkoch, M., 421
plug and play integration, 387
polymorphism, 188
Portability, 10
Portable Display Format, 82, 358
PostScript, 82, 358
Pressman, R., 421
printf(), 308
private, 310
procedural programming, 314
procedurally developed program, 340
profiler, 256, 290, 332

project management, 53, 54, 63-65,
    79, 80, 81, 83, 87-151, 286, 363,
    393
prototype, 99, 135, 148, 154, 158,
    159
pseudocode, 174
putc(), 308
putchar(), 308
puts(), 308
quality assurance, 57, 148, 149, 166,
    308, 394
rapid prototyping model, 55, 56, 58,
    78, 89-91, 99, 165, 394
readability, 287, 362, 366
real-time software, 96, 102, 115, 116,
    120, 121, 146, 169, 245, 261, 376
recovery block, 389, 390
reengineering, 58, 107
Reifer, D., 422
reliability, 10
requirements, 54, 55, 57, 58, 61, 64,
    66, 68, 69, 73, 74, 76, 77, 79, 82,
    83, 84, 87, 89 - 119, 124, 130-
    136, 139-158, 160 - 162, 164 -
    171, 245, 248, 252, 258, 260,
    261, 266, 269, 270, 285, 286,
    341, 342, 355, 358, 359, 362,
    363, 364, 368, 370, 375, 379-385,
    390, 391, 396
requirements engineering, 89, 93, 94,
    101, 103, 104, 105, 107, 109,
    110, 117, 146, 166, 167, 383
requirements generation, 110, 112,
    167, 168, 385
requirements review, 89, 140-144,
    148-151, 166, 384
requirements traceability matrix, 100
    - 102, 136, 149, 161, 162, 165,
    166, 260, 270, 285, 363
residual software error, 292
return on investment, 394
Reusability, 10
reuse librarian, 32
reuse library, 388

reuse library, 261
Risk assessment, 383, 394
Ritchie, D., 288, 414, 422
Rogers, A., 164, 165, 384
Rombach, H. D., 79, 402, 423
Rumbaugh, J., 389
safety-critical system, 86, 376
scanf(), 308
SCCS, 267, 268
scheduling, 58, 64, 76, 77, 81, 383
Schneiderman, B., 167, 383
SEI, 394, 398
Selby, R., 402
Setup installer, 348, 349, 355
Shooman, M., 424
SIGCHI, see Special Interest Group
    on Human-Computer Interaction
Smalltalk programming language,
    108, 392
Smith & Robson, 312
soft real-time requirement, 96, 146
software artifact, 32
software component, 273, 283, 389,
    402, 415
software cost estimation, 388
software engineer, 53, 54, 59-66, 69,
    71, 76, 80, 83, 84, 87, 89, 90, 97,
    104, 108, 116, 134, 140-143, 148,
    168, 190, 245, 252, 253, 255,
    256, 260, 261, 266, 286, 356,
    365, 369, 377, 382-384, 395, 397-
    399
software engineering goals, 9
Software Engineering Institute, 79,
    269, 394
Software Engineering Laboratory,
    250, 398, 423, 424
software error, 92, 152, 154, 162,
    368, 369, 371
software failure, 380
software fault, 115, 368, 370, 374,
    389, 390, 393, 396, 397
software life cycle, 58, 92, 109, 150,
    167, 260, 362, 380, 388

software maintenance, adaptive, 368, 375, 379, 381
software maintenance, perfective, 368
software metrics, 57, 66, 88, 135, 261, 270, 287, 288, 390, 391, 405, 407, 409, 410, 411, 413
software reuse, 32, 61, 103, 109, 112-114, 155, 162, 166, 245, 259, 261, 285, 384, 388, 389, 422
software testing, 292
Solaris, 409
source code, 92, 100, 133, 163, 174, 249, 250, 251, 254, 256, 259, 261, 265, 267, 269, 270, 286, 363, 379, 386, 387, 401, 402, 406, 415, 419
Special Interest Group on Computer-Human Interaction, 116
spiral model, 55, 56, 78, 166
state diagram, 125-128, 168-171. 194
state machine, 194
state table, 194
strcat(), 204
strcmp(), 204
strcpy(), 204
stress testing, 386
String class, 201
string object, 191
string.h, 204
strlen(), 201
Stroustrup, B., 247, 289, 359, 365, 406, 424, 425
subclass, 313
system call, 102, 248, 376
system level, 292, 312
system level testing, 312
terminal concentrator, 176
termination byte, 191
test cases, 56, 141, 265
Testability, 10
testing, 54, 56, 59, 61, 65, 69, 75, 77, 85-91, 112, 115, 135, 141, 147, 148, 156, 162, 166, 261, 263-266, 285, 286, 288, 306, 313, 340, 345, 361-366, 376-379, 383, 386, 387, 392, 396, 399, 402, 411
testing a derived class, 310
testing multiple inheritance, 311
testing object-oriented programs, 312
testing of friend functions, 311
testing of objects, 312
Thayer, R., 167, 425
Thompson, 422
Thompson, K., 422
top-down integration, 387
transformation, 180, 190, 196, 313
unit level, 292, 312
UNIX, 70, 84, 90, 94, 131, 132, 136, 145, 155, 248, 252, 256, 267, 343-347, 352, 354, 361, 378, 379, 382, 397, 414, 415, 422
usability, 10, 116, 118, 119, 167, 365, 375
user interface, 101, 116-121, 123, 154, 157, 161, 164-169, 248, 270, 285, 355, 357, 361, 367, 370, 375, 379-382
uses-a relation, 188
VISE installer, 348
Visual BASIC, 248, 285
Voas, J., 425, 426
Wallace, D., 91
Waund, C., 426
Weiss, D., 389
white-box testing, 386
Windows, 84, 94, 97, 100, 101, 111, 145, 163, 248, 286, 344, 348, 355, 363
Windows Registry, 348
Woolfolk, ., 201
work breakdown structure, 73, 74
writer's workbench, 361
wwb, 361
Y2K, see Year 2000 problem
yacc, 375, 392, 416
Year 2000 Problem, 78, 85, 86, 87, 90, 378, 381
Yourdon, E., 38, 170